JUDIKA

The Element
Encyclopedia
of 1000 Spells

Dedication

Dedication

For Herta and Zoltan Illes, and Rachel and Jordan Nagengast, without whose love, patience, and support, this book could never have been written.

HarperElement
An Imprint of HarperCollins*Publishers*
77–85 Fulham Palace Road,
Hammersmith, London W6 8JB

www.harpercollins.co.uk

HarperElement is a trademark of HarperCollins*Publishers* Ltd

The material in this book is taken from *The Element Encyclopedia of 5000 Spells*, first published by HarperElement in 2004

1 3 5 7 9 10 8 6 4 2

© Judika Illes 2004

Judika Illes asserts the moral right to be identified as the author of this work

A catalogue record of this book is available from the British Library

ISBN-13   978-0-00-729905-8
ISBN-10   0-00-729905-2

Printed and bound in China

Contents

WARNING!

The Element Encyclopedia of 1000 Spells contains an overview of magical spells and practices from a multitude of eras, traditions, and places. It is intended as an inclusive encyclopedia and reference book. Many of the spells contained within these pages are not to be used and should not be reproduced. Some involve dangerous, potentially harmful, and deadly poisonous botanicals. The author and the publisher strongly advise against using any spells containing noxious substances or poisonous botanicals, or spells containing blood (the use of which could result in the transmission of blood-borne diseases which may be fatal). These spells are only reproduced here to provide a historical context.

Any reader uses the spells entirely at their own risk and the author and publisher accept no liability if the spells do not have the desired effect or if adverse affects are caused.

THIS BOOK IS NOT SUITABLE FOR CHILDREN.

Preface

The image is so familiar as to qualify as an archetype. It appears in countless movies, television shows, and theatrical productions. If you're of a literary bent, you'll find it in countless novels, too. Although there may be variations on the theme, the core image remains consistent: someone, usually but not always a witch or wizard, faced with a serious dilemma, reaches for a massive book of magic spells.

The contents of this book are rarely displayed. (An exception occurs on the television series, *Sabrina the Teenage Witch*. As befitting a twenty-first-century witch, Sabrina's edition is interactive.) Oversized, well-worn, and clearly *used*, this book is obviously no coffee-table book but a familiar companion—in every sense of the word "familiar." Sabrina's book makes almost as many appearances as her black cat, and consistently proves more reliable.

The book's very presence transmits subliminal messages. If there were previously any doubts regarding someone's identity, then the act of reaching for the book, mere possession of this book in fact, is usually sufficient to establish occult credentials. Consider depictions of Merlin or Morgan le Fay: their big books of spells are as much a part and parcel of their magical trappings as any animal familiar, crystal ball, or wizard's robes. Millions of kitschy statues feature an elderly gray-bearded man clutching a massive book. He may or may not be wearing his peaked wizard's hat but his identity is clear. How do we know he's a wizard? By the book that he holds.

This book thus signals that its reader is a metaphysician or is striving to be one. If the reader handles the book with comfort and ease, the implication is that he or she is a person of power. The book, however, can also compensate for the reader's very lack of experience and knowledge. One frequent variation on the theme depicts a complete novice discovering sophisticated magical solutions within the book's pages. Typically the novice is in way over his head in disaster. The very appearance of the book signals that salvation is at hand: the secrets of salvation are contained within the book's pages, if only the novice will follow its directions. (Conversely, Mickey Mouse's inability to use such a book for anything other than a flotation device in *The Sorcerer's Apprentice* only underscores his magical ineptitude and general incompetence.)

This spell book thus possesses transformative powers. It can transform anyone (well, Mickey excepted) into a magical adept. Its aged, well-worn appearance also indicates that this book is timeless: it never outlives its usefulness.

This archetypal book is based on both fact and fantasy.

Collections of spells rank among Earth's earliest written documents. Not only are magical texts among the oldest surviving pieces of literature, but many scholars and anthropologists suggest that it was the need to record spells and divination results that stimulated the very birth of writing. Magic, as we will see, is the true mother of invention. In ancient Egypt, the lunar god Thoth is credited as the inventor of both magic and writing. He is the patron of scribes and magicians. It was rumored that in addition to inventing the systems of spelling and writing, Thoth created the very first book, authoring no less than a sacred revelation of Earth's most powerful secret spells and rituals. The legendary *Book of Thoth* was believed to hold the key to all the secrets of the universe. To possess a copy of the book enabled one to command and control destiny itself.

The ancient Egyptians loved stories featuring books of power. Several of their legends remain to us, including the original version of Walt Disney's *The Sorcerer's Apprentice*. Egypt, at the time, was a theocracy: religion and government were one. The reigning pharaoh was simultaneously the child of the god, the living embodiment of the god, and the god's foremost high priest, and vast temple complexes, financed by the state, contained literary annexes known as *Houses of Life*.

These combination scriptoria/emergency clinics housed wizard priests, on the government payroll. For a fee, these professional magicians would consult their extensive library of magic texts to provide their clientele with enchanted solutions to life's many dilemmas. Perhaps, legend had it, the *Book of Thoth* was hidden in the depths of one of these magic libraries. Perhaps it was stashed in some priest or pharaoh's tomb. Or perhaps it was eventually deemed so dangerous that, too powerful to destroy, the book had been locked into a chained, weighted iron box and thrown into the depths of the sea.

Access to occult knowledge bestowed power and prestige. The magical texts were hoarded and kept secret. Many were written in code, to prevent profane eyes from understanding what was read.

A few centuries before the dawning of the Common Era, the independent Egyptian nation was defeated, first by the Persians, then by the Greeks and Romans. Indigenous Egyptian religion and political structure degenerated. The *Houses of Life* were abandoned; the lucrative, respected profession of government-employed wizard-priest no longer existed. It was the last time in history that working with magic was a secure, respectable profession.

Although the profession ceased to exist, the big spell books survived, at least in fragments. It's difficult for modern readers, so accustomed to printed, standardized texts, to recall that until the invention of the printing press, every book was hand-written and frequently unbound. Copies of copies of copies were made, each perhaps slightly different than the next. In the chaos that ensued as Egypt was successively conquered, individual pages were either smuggled out of the now unguarded temple libraries as personal treasures or auctioned off, page-by-page, papyrus-by-papyrus for personal profit. When Alexandria's famed library, which boasted a copy of every book then in existence (the city stole them from arriving ships), was burned to the ground, the value of the few surviving manuscripts increased.

With the rise of Christianity, magic, together with its texts and professionals, was vilified. Spell books were burned en masse. Yet some were saved, if not whole books, then individual pages and pieces. We know this to be true, because some still remain, their spells reproduced in many books including this one, preserved at great personal risk throughout the ages, during eras when possession of magical texts warranted the death penalty.

These treasured pages survived, secretly passed between adepts and initiates, as did legends of mysterious books of power just waiting to be recovered. The *Book of Thoth* is one but there were others: *The Book of Raziel* is a rival with Thoth's book for the title of first book ever. Another book of spells and rituals, *The Book of Raziel* was allegedly written by a sympathetic angel and given to Adam to compensate for his exile from Eden. Rumors regarding the existence of magical manuscripts attributed to Israel's wizard king, Solomon, were first recorded, at least as far as we know, during the time of Josephus, the first-century chronicler of the Roman conquest of Judea. Fragments of Solomon's pages were allegedly discovered and exist today. Treasure hunters searched desperately for these manuscripts, just like Sidney Greenstreet looking for the Maltese falcon.

In the fourteenth century, a large group of nomadic people arrived in Europe from parts unknown. Although the Romany people derive originally from India, another land steeped in magical and spiritual legend, they may or may not also have spent considerable time in Egypt. (According to some Romany legends, their ancestor was the sole survivor of Pharaoh's army, drowned in the Red Sea.) The association with Egypt was powerful enough and appealing enough that Europeans called the Romany *Egyptians*, the name eventually being corrupted into *Gypsies*.

At the same time as the arrival of the Romany, a deck of mysterious cards began to circulate through Europe. Rumors spread that these tarot cards were what was left of the *Book of Thoth*. Readers scoured them searching for spiritual secrets and clues for obtaining personal power.

With the advent of the printing press came publication and standardization of spell books. Enough were published to warrant their own literary category, the *grimoire*. The word, "grimoire," defined as a book of spells, is related to grammar. The grimoire is basically another type of grammar book, just teaching different spelling skills. The classic grimoires were published in the midst of anti-magic, anti-witchcraft persecutions and, like alchemists' texts, they are often heavily coded to protect authors, compilers, and publishers, and also to maintain secrecy and control over their precious information, reserving true comprehension for a private club of initiated adepts.

On the whole, grimoires are not books of practical magic. The novice cannot pick one up and instantly begin casting life-saving spells. Instead they are largely oriented toward an educated male reader so devoted to his spiritual path that he has largely withdrawn from everyday life, like Dr. Faust, and can thus spend weeks in complex, tortuous preparation for summoning angels and demons.

Other books of magic circulated through Europe. These were still hand-written rather than printed editions. Books of Shadows meticulously recorded an individual witch's personal spells and knowledge. These books were intended to be passed from person to person, and were a means of saving persecuted traditions from complete eradication. Few of these books remain. When a witch was caught, convicted, and killed, her Book of Shadows was inevitably destroyed with her. Modern Wicca has, however, revived the tradition of beautiful, lovingly preserved personal spell and ritual books.

Neither the Books of Shadows, nor the classic grimoires fulfill the Hollywood fantasy of that large, accessible book packed with every spell you might possibly need. One mustn't mock that vision: we long for magical solutions to insoluble situations. We crave the inherent promise of the hidden *Book of Thoth*. We long to discover that one word of power strong enough to stop the sun in its tracks if we utter it, potent enough to vanquish our enemies, fill our bank accounts, and deliver our true love.

Perhaps somewhere, someday, in some archeological dig, that *Book of Thoth* will be found.

Until then, here is *The Element Encyclopedia of 1000 Spells*. There's practical magic, high ritual magic, spells requiring virtually no preparation, and spells that should perhaps never be performed. No secret code has been applied; instead there are explanations so that you understand how and why the spells should work.

Be forewarned: in these pages you will discover methods of communicating with the dead, taming an errant lover, summoning spirits, handcrafting magic tools, and tips for creating magic mirrors and rings—including the one that allegedly gave Helen of Troy her seductive power. I will tell you up-front, however, this book does *not* contain that sole word of power, guaranteed to stop the sun and fulfill your every desire.

Perhaps one day you will find the volume that contains that one word, although the ancient Egyptians warned that in order to attain it you might have to break into a pyramid and wager with its guardian mummy, or else make the sea roll back in order to find the manuscript locked in the iron box and guarded by an army of many-headed venomous sea snakes. In the meantime, enjoy *The Element Encyclopedia of 1000 Spells*.

Introduction

One thousand spells. Are any of them *real*?

What is magic anyway?

What a question. Rational people know how to define magic—magic is illusion, sleight of hand, at best the fine art of tricks, at worst fraudulence—or so goes the definition usually taught to schoolchildren. Another interpretation dismisses magic as supernatural fantasy and wishful thinking—the stuff of fairy tales, Mother Goose, and mythology; tales for children and hence of little value; its only purpose entertainment; its only possible truth metaphoric. A third interpretation is more malevolent, with occult masters—the proverbial evil wizards and wicked sorceresses—attempting to maintain control over gullible and innocent plain folk, their tools fear and superstition, not *true* magic, which, of course, rationalists argue, doesn't exist anyway. Yet another explanation suggests that magic works solely by psychological means, a sort of self-hypnosis. According to this theory, usually offered by old-school anthropologists and psychologists, the poor benighted native's very belief in something, such as a death curse or a traditional healing, is what causes it to come true. Magic happens because you believe in the system not because the system works or even exists, although explanations for why, if their powers of belief are so all-powerful, the natives remain poor and benighted, and forced to tolerate outside observers, are rarely offered.

"Occult" is a word commonly misinterpreted. It doesn't mean evil or satanic. It has no moral connotations whatsoever. Occult really means *"secret"* or *"hidden."* Secrets may be kept hidden for a host of valid reasons. In many cultures and at many times, the definition of real true working magic wasn't a hidden secret, subject to false interpretation, but a normal fact of life. In other cultures and at different times, however, real true working magical practitioners have been subject to torture, persecution, and oppression. Magic's very survival has often depended upon secrecy and a willingness to tolerate patronizing, false definitions.

True magical practitioners, of whom there remain many, would reject the definitions of magic given above, although there are vestiges of truths in all of them. Real magical practitioners consider themselves guardians, preservers, and (sometimes) revivers of Earth's forgotten, besieged, and suppressed occult truths and traditions.

Magic, at its most basic, is the science of Earth's hidden powers. For the true practitioner, there's nothing *supernatural* about magic. *Natural* is just a lot more complex than conventional modern wisdom allows.

Although there are many ways to practice magic, many schools, philosophies, methods, and traditions, the bottom-line definition of what actually constitutes real magic, and why and how it works, is amazingly consistent throughout the world.

According to general worldwide metaphysical wisdom, common to all magical understanding and tradition, there is an inherent energy radiating from Earth and all living things. Analytical traditions and cultures have studied this energy in depth; others simply accept its existence and work with it. Many languages have specific names for this energy. English does not. This increases the confusion when discussing magic—an already vast and confusing topic. In the same manner that English, a language so rich in descriptive adjectives, has but one word for *snow*, while Inuit has many, one word for *love*, while Sanskrit has many, so English has but one word, *magic*, to define its various aspects. Harry Houdini, Harry Potter, Helena

Blavatsky, Aleister Crowley, and countless anonymous village wise-women are all lumped together as masters of magic, as if it were a monolithic art.

English also lacks a specific word to name that power that radiates from all life.

The ancient Egyptians called it *heka*; on the other side of Africa, the Yoruba, parent culture of myriad spiritual and magical traditions, call it *ashé*. The most familiar word may be the Polynesian *mana*. In Morocco, this radiant energy is known as *baraka*. For lack of a better word, let's just call it *magic power*.

This magic power, this capacity for magic, radiates from all living beings to a greater or lesser extent. In fact, it is the existence of this power that defines what, in magical terms, is considered "*alive*," a very different criterion than that required by a coroner's report. (In magical terms, death is not the absence of life. Absence of power equals absence of life. A corpse, although no one denies the person is dead in the conventional sense, is still very much alive, as is the pine box and, most especially, the iron coffin nails. The average plastic bottle, however, lacks life. Confused? More about this crucial concept later.)

This magical life-power is formless: you can't see it, hear it or touch it. So how do you know it exists? How is it quantified and measured? By its effects upon you.

Baraka, the Moroccan term for this power, contains significant implications. The root word can be recognized in another Semitic language, Hebrew, where it translates as "*blessing*." To be in the presence of this power is to receive blessings. Although people have learned to manipulate magic powers for malevolent purposes and ill intent, it is intrinsically a positive, benevolent, and sacred energy. According to an Egyptian legend, having contemplated creation, the Creator foresaw that all would *not* be good and felt pangs of remorse. He therefore imbued Earth with *heka* as a gift to people, so that they might use it to ward off the harsh blows of fate. Magic is the system that attempts to harness this energy.

The closest comparison one might make is to radioactive energy. That, too, is formless, cannot be seen, touched, or smelled. Yet its impact is profound and cannot be denied. Because nuclear radiation has had such a devastating impact on our world, it's difficult to recall how recent a discovery it truly is. Marie and Pierre Curie, and the other early scholars of radioactive energy, were visionaries. They recognized the existence of something that others did not. Not everyone *believed* in their theories, including many very educated people, in much the same way that people say they don't *believe* in magic. Many thought the Curies deluded, crazy or just incorrect, at least until the power they sought had been unleashed with too much force to ever be denied.

If one tells the story of Marie Curie's quest in simple terms, it resembles a modern-day fairy tale. Marie, laboring obsessively in her laboratory/shack resembles the quintessential alchemist feverishly attempting to extract and develop the philosopher's stone, that legendary substance reputed to bestow eternal youth, health, and life.

In a sense, Marie Curie extracted the *anti*-philosopher's stone. Modern fairy tales are sanitized for children; today's adults are uncomfortable transmitting the truths contained in them. Real fairy tales—the original versions—don't always have happy endings, just like the tale of Marie Curie doesn't. Marie's quest ultimately led her to death; many of her surviving books, materials, and tools are so packed with the deadly power into which she tapped that even today they remain too radioactive to handle.

The goal of magic is to tap into a different energy, an energy so powerful and benevolent that all aspects of life improve. The most potent magical books, tools, and materials (just like those books and papers of Marie Curie) hold, retain, and radiate their power and energy infinitely.

How do you measure exposure to nuclear radiation? While scientific tools of measurement have been developed, ultimate, undeniable proof comes in its effects on the body. Similar scientific tools to quantify, measure, and identify magic power have not been invented, yet (to the magical practitioner) its effect upon the individual is equally clear. The term, *a person of power*, is meant literally. People who possess magical power in substantial quantities, who live in close proximity to it, are magnetic and charismatic personalities. They radiate personal power. Other people find merely being in their presence invigorating and empowering. Although into every life some rain must fall, for the person with strong reserves of magic power, the world exists as a place of possibility. If, on the other hand, you feel consistently drained or frustrated, if your libido and life-force are chronically diminished, if you foresee nothing ahead of you but monotony or gloom, if life lacks joy, if your goals seem so out of reach that it's pointless to try, and it's hard to muster enthusiasm for anything, then it's very likely that you suffer from a serious deficiency of this life-power. Most of us fall somewhere in the middle, although these power reserves are continually shifting. Like a gas tank, magical life-power needs to be replenished as you use it, and acquired if you lack it.

This power is contagious. It can be transferred, transmitted, increased, decreased, or lost. These power-exchanges occur continuously, with or without human participation. The power is contained within a botanical plant or crystal, for instance, whether or not a human taps into it. You can ignore this power and these energy transactions, although their effects upon you continue and remain, for good or ill. You can also attempt to harness this power for your own benefit and the benefit of your loved ones.

Perhaps magic may best be understood by considering one of its branches: the school of magical arrangement, *feng shui*. Once obscure outside China, the art of feng shui is now discussed and debated worldwide; it has even grown sufficiently commonplace to merit, for a time, a newspaper column in the *Sunday Los Angeles Times'* real estate section! (Although apparently there were enough complaints about the intrusion of magic into real life for the column to eventually disappear.)

Feng shui's literal translation, *"wind and water,"* implies that this is a natural art, not a manufactured one. According to feng shui, objects are manipulated to create good fortune, minimize hardship, and (hopefully) eliminate disaster. Likewise, one must pay attention to natural earth formations (mountains, valleys, waterways) in order to harmonize one's own energies and desires with them for your maximum benefit. This conscious manipulation and harmonizing of energies and forces is the basis of all magic. By manipulating various magical powers, goals are achieved, success attained, and misfortune prevented. For instance, the presence of lavender theoretically empowers any other spell or materials. Powdered vinca, the sorcerer's violet, transforms any bouquet of flowers into a tool of seduction, although some flowers (roses, orchids, tuberoses) are powerful enough not to require any assistance.

Of course, rationalists refute all of this as nonsense. It can't be proven scientifically—therefore it doesn't exist. Magical practitioners are either gullible idiots or outright charlatans.

The magical practitioners' response to this criticism is that rationalists have invented and are clinging to a very limited notion of a world that really doesn't exist. Practitioners would say that scientific method, as well as so-called logic, are unrealistic, artificial human-created constructs designed to deny and place limits on Earth's true mystery and grandeur. According to magical theory, some sacred mysteries cannot be explained, defined, or controlled, although one can attempt to use them for one's benefit. Ultimately, one could say, magic is another way of looking at and understanding the world. If you are not yet initiated into this magical world, then be prepared: once you've learned some real magic and successfully cast some spells, you will see the world in a different way than you did before. Will you trust your own experiences and insights? Or will you be among the many who say, *"I can't believe what just happened to me?"*

Although modern science is the child of the magical arts, most especially alchemy, its world vision and goals are diametrically opposed to its parents'. To enter into the magical world is to be a willing, conscious participant in a dream landscape. One accesses power by surrendering control over boundaries. The magical world is a huge, unruly, fluid, dream-like place filled with invisible powers, psychic debris, positive *and* negative forces, guardian spirits, and radiant beings existing on all sorts of planes of energy that defy human definition, domination, and control. Everything pulsates with vibrant, potentially powerful life, including you.

Magic is a partnership between powers, human and otherwise. The question of whether magic is used for good or ill depends upon the practitioner's intentions, not the inherent nature of the system. Every interaction is an energy transaction of some kind, although, obviously, some are more significant than others.

Scientific method demands consistent, predictable replication of results. Magic revels in the unique, the unusual, the individual, and the exception. Magic refutes the entire concept of coincidence. Anything that appears coincidental possesses some magical significance; the more unusual and freakish the coincidence, the more worthy of attention and analysis. Anything too easily replicated is either a very basic natural law (stick your finger into fire and it will hurt) or else lacks power and is thus magically worthless (that lifeless plastic bottle).

Confusion derives from a limited word pool, as we have seen. Identical words are used to indicate different meanings. Magic defies boundaries: life doesn't terminate with death. Death is not the end, nor is it the opposite of life; it's merely another mysterious stop on the spectrum of existence. *Dead* as in "Uncle Joe is dead," may be meant literally, but *life*, *living*, or *alive* usually refer to something very different in magic-speak. *Life* in magical parlance is a quality, a capacity for power: someone or something has it, in varying quantities, or they don't. If something is unique, not entirely predictable or reproducible, and also possesses potential for power, it's *alive*.

Everything that exists naturally on Earth or is constructed from naturally occurring parts possesses the capacity for power, including you. This magic power, this *baraka*, is what ultimately fuels Earth. Fans of Philip Pullman's *His Dark Materials* trilogy may recognize parallels to those novels' controversial power, *dust*. Without it, existence is drained, *lifeless*, frustrating, joyless, and bereft.

This holistic power expresses itself on all planes simultaneously: physical, spiritual, mental, sexual, and emotional. This power is not generic. Every plant, every stone, every species of living creature radiates a specific type of power, although the most powerful are incredibly versatile. Roses seduce, but they also heal, comfort, and summon benevolent spirits. Individual members of a species radiate these powers to varying degrees, depending upon circumstances and personal power.

That's a lot of powers to remember. Luckily practitioners have been contributing to the magical repertoire of materials, the *materia magica*, since that old, proverbial time immemorial and continue to

- ★ By magical definition, anything occurring naturally on Earth, whether plant, animal, element, stone, or metal, is alive
- ★ Anything radiating any degree of magical power whatsoever is perceived to be alive, although the manner in which different beings are alive is not identical. A stone may be alive but even the most hard-core practitioner won't look for a pulse
- ★ If something can be recreated so that there are identical, indistinguishable specimens, and if that something is completely predictable and controllable, it lacks life. Lacking life, it contains no power, no innate magic, and is of little value to the magical practitioner

do so. It's not necessary to re-invent the wheel, although experimentation can be fun. A font of established information exists for you to draw upon. *The Element Encyclopedia of 1000 Spells* merely scratches the surface of world magic.

What is Magic?

Magic is an individual action, undertaken because the cosmos is not believed to be benevolent by nature, or, at least, not benevolent enough to that person.
Maya Deren, *Divine Horsemen: The Living Gods of Haiti*,
London, 1953

Magic spells stem from the observation and consideration of an Earthly paradox.

Earth is beautiful, full of power and promise. Yet despite all that potential for fulfillment and happiness, individual existence is too often harsh, hungry, painful, limited, bitter, dangerous, and just plain miserable. Yes, life holds promise, but will *your* promise be fulfilled? Can you depend upon benevolent forces of the universe to provide your needs and desires for you, or is further action required? It is significant that Adam didn't need a book of magic spells until he was forced to leave the paradise of Eden.

Magic is a realistic art, not an idealistic one, although it is a game for optimists. The *one* thing magic requires is a belief that things *could* get better.

Not every promise is fulfilled, not every power is realized. Life is not fair. Some are born with looks, brains, talent, vibrant health, all their limbs, and a loving family, while others are not. Some have a head start toward success that others lack, even within the realm of metaphysics. Some come from families immersed in magic traditions, eager to transmit secrets and techniques. Others do not.

Occult knowledge, however, is egalitarian. All you have to do is acquire it. In theory it's not even necessary to understand it in order to tailor your destiny more to your liking, fulfill your dreams and aspirations and, perhaps most crucially, ward off life's harsh blows, just like the ancient Egyptians said you could.

Magic levels the playing field.

Magic encourages creativity and inventiveness. It rewards persistence and curiosity. People have discovered thousands of ways to exploit Earth's natural magic power. There is basically no technique, no material, providing it possesses some life (and, once upon a time, prior to mass industry, there was virtually nothing on Earth that didn't possess life), that can't be used for a magical purpose. Magic accesses a huge repository—rock, paper, scissors, you name it, somewhere it has been used in a spell.

Wealth and status are not necessary for acquiring magical power; the crucial requirements are desire, will, curiosity, awareness, knowledge, and education. That is the secret message hidden within the Celtic tale of Taliesin. A poor, beaten, oppressed orphan child is forced to labor endlessly for the great witch-goddess Cerridwen, stirring the fuming, boiling cauldron where she brews a potion capable of transmitting all Earth's wisdom. By accident the child tastes the brew intended for Cerridwen's own son. Those mere few drops of wisdom immediately transform a miserable, ignorant child into a shape-shifting master shaman, a pre-eminent wizard, and his ultimate

★ Magic is the manipulation of Earth's naturally occurring powers in an attempt to provide the spell-caster with the success and happiness she or he desires

★ Magic spells are deliberate, specific attempts to harness and manipulate this energy, following some sort of formula or direction

★ Magic power is inherent on Earth; people didn't create it, imagine it or make it up. By various means, they learned how to use it: magic spells are the result

★ Every magic spell was created by at least one person and probably refined and improved by thousands more

rebirth as a true child of the goddess, a child Cerridwen cannot deny. Who cares about transforming pumpkins into coaches or pulling rabbits from hats? Real magic holds the key to self-transformation.

Although rare, precious materials, gemstones, and fragrant tree resins are packed with power, there's also tremendous magic in blades of grass, handfuls of dirt, moonbeams, and ocean water. Plenty of the most powerful magic is free, available and abundant for all.

Is Magic Evil? A (Very Abridged) Secret History of Magic

Another issue must be addressed, as it is the rationale most frequently offered for centuries of concerted efforts to eliminate magic and persecute practitioners, and because it is an issue that prevents some from accessing their personal power. You think you'd like to cast a spell, but you're afraid. Is practicing magic evil?

According to general worldwide metaphysical wisdom, magic is a source of power. Power may be used benevolently or selfishly, with varying degrees of mal intent. Thus it isn't the abstract practice of magic that is either good or bad; it's what each practitioner chooses to do with it. Responsibility for one's actions and the consequences that stem from them rest securely on the individual practitioner's shoulders. Have evil people ever abused magic power? Sure. Just take a look at some of the hexes in this book. Is magic the only power capable of being abused? Of course not. How about financial power, political power, brute strength, nuclear power, and so on and so forth? In the sweep of history, abuse of magic power is far less responsible for the accumulated sufferings of the world than many other forms of abuse.

There is a general rule, accepted across the board, that magicians reap what they sow. Cast an evil spell—ultimately receive evil back. Negative efforts attract negative returns, at a return rate of three-, seven-, or nine-fold. The standard rule of witchcraft is do what thou will, but harm none. Many modern witches are absolutely terrified of transgressing that rule.

So then, why magic's bad reputation?

Yes, there are legends of wicked sorcerers using their skills to hold others in thrall. However, if one examines those legends closely, it's usually revealed that the magical aspect is but a smoke screen for more reliable, conventional methods of coercion, like brute force and access to greater wealth, although I suppose one could argue that magical prowess enabled their acquisition. Suffice it to say that any position of power, in any profession, is vulnerable to corruption and temptation. Let's talk about the average working magical practitioner.

Magic is concerned with the immediate needs and desires of the practitioner in the here and now, or at least in the immediately fore-seeable future. It is not about "pie in the sky." The average magician doesn't want to wait for the possible rewards of the sweet hereafter. Magic is not for the passive; if you're willing to passively accede to your fate, the destiny others decide for you, whatever it is, why waste time, effort, or money casting a spell?

Magic recognizes that Earth is full of gifts and the practitioner wants his or her share *now*. Magic is not the same as religion, although many religions have historically incorporated magic into their prac-tice, and still do. To put it mildly, magic is not an inherently reverential system. Magic demands that *my* will be done, not necessarily *thine*, or at least, let's find a compromise. It is not a humble art. Magic possesses an intensely powerful independent, egalitarian streak.

An infinite quantity of magic power exists in the world, enough for everyone. It's not like a scarce commodity, where if I have it, you don't. Magic power is constantly being generated, although various modern practices, especially those that affect the natural environment, have diminished present quantities drastically. Similar to Pullman's *His Dark Materials'* dust, the energy that each individual generates enters the universe where it affects and may be drawn upon by others. It is to everyone's benefit (except perhaps for that elite few already achieving their heaven on Earth at the expense of others) that every individual, creature, or thing, maximizes its potential for power.

Furthermore, not all powers on Earth are positive: intense extended misery, suffering, and oppression generate a negative energy that ultimately affects everyone badly, diminishes *baraka*, obstructs magic power, and limits everyone's access to it. In addition, the extinction of Earth's life forms—the loss of plant and animal species—eliminates every practitioner's potential access to their unique powers. Thus general oppression and certain policies affecting the environment, beyond any ethical considerations of right or wrong, hamper the magician's ability to maximize personal power and the power of their spells.

There is an inherent tension between the individual practitioner seeking power, and authority of all kinds, most especially religious authority, which seeks to maintain its authority by retaining and controlling access to the divine, as well as to tools, theology, and ritual. Religion frequently seeks to establish rules and boundaries about who has direct access to the divine, and who bestows that access and the proper channels. Correct methods of worship and spiritual communication are prescribed, including what is permitted and what is not.

If something has power, magicians usually want to try it out, regardless of whose tradition or faith it comes from, regardless of whether some authority says its use is forbidden. Although magic is a conservative force in ways, harking back to humanity's most primal arts, it also evolves endlessly, adapting new materials, new traditions and new methods as they appear. It is fluid and defiant and resists control.

Fundamentalists of all kinds are inevitably opposed to magic, but this tension exists even among liberal faiths that prize their magical traditions—so-called magical religions. Here, inevitably, religious tradition stipulates a right way to practice magic. Knowledge may be reserved for the few, with methods reserved for those going through the proper, authorized channels. Tension will exist between the officially initiated and independent practitioners.

That tension between authority and magical practitioner is, I suspect, the real reason why secular rulers and religious authorities (frequently in conjunction with each other) attempt to brand magic and its practitioners as evil influences, a cancer among the submissive. Lack of obedience rather than lack of morality is what really draws down the wrath of authority.

It is no accident that the Bible records that Israel's diviners, shamans and necromancers were *"put away"* during the reign of its very first king, Saul. When the prophet Samuel warned the children of Israel that choosing a king would mean losing sons, daughters, land, and livestock, he neglected to mention that they would also lose their previous access to professional magical advice. Or perhaps he didn't bother to mention it because he was aware, as apparently was the king, that those magical services are so crucial that they are never entirely suppressed. In fact, King Saul himself is very soon shown, in his hour of need, searching out one of those prescribed, forbidden bone-conjurers for a private consultation.

Because the Bible has so often been used as an excuse to persecute and exterminate witches, it's significant to note how the Bible depicts the Witch of Endor actually accomplishing her task. She's not painted as a stranger with strange talents, or as a foreigner, but as a member of the community. Neither is she shown to be a fraud; she capably fulfills her royal client's request. Nor is she depicted as malevolent or evil, but as a good-hearted woman: having accomplished the unhappy task that every fortune-teller dreads, of delivering *really* bad news, she comforts and feeds the distraught king, providing his last meal on Earth, at personal sacrifice (she kills a calf to feed him) considering that he is responsible for her loss of profession and, presumably, income.

Fortune-tellers, readers, and diviners hold an especially tense relationship with political authority. Historically, rulers, particularly the all-powerful, very much like to have the future revealed. They also typically wish to retain exclusive control over this information. Because others may use a diviner's skill to plot rebellion, historically diviners have been imprisoned, or one is imprisoned for the ruler's private's use, while others are killed. To make matters worse, rulers usually desire to hear only the future as they envision it; a diviner can only read what entrails, shoulder blades, or other tools reveal. You see the need sometimes to keep your power secret. Although it frustrates us today, there's a very good reason Nostradamus recorded his prophesies in code.

Wherever efforts have been made either to subjugate or convert another country or people, among the first acts traditionally taken is the attempted subversion or elimination of native shamans and traditional magical practices and practitioners. This is inevitably perceived as necessary for the pacification of the masses. This is not purely paranoia on the part of those seeking to assert and retain authority.

Traditional shamans and magical practitioners are consistently in the forefront of resistance to oppressive authority. (Because winners write history, the conventional historical explanation for this phenomenon is that shamans attempt to impede the *"path of progress."*) In the British West Indies, historical records show that Obeah men and women (the local shamans) led slave revolts or attempted to do so. The Haitian revolution, which ended slavery in that French colony and established the first independent black republic in the Western Hemisphere, was inaugurated at a Vodoun ceremony dedicated to the Spirit of Iron, the material, with the sole exception of menstrual blood, singularly most charged with magical power—although as soon as native dictators proceeded to seize and consolidate power, not surprisingly, they too attempted to restrict or eliminate Vodoun.

This, not evil, power-hungry sorcerers, is the hidden history of magic. In the United States, the prominent Voodooists Marie Laveau and Mary Ellen Pleasant rescued and redeemed slaves, with Pleasant providing funding for John Brown's raid on Harper's Ferry. (Their male counterpart, Dr. John Montanet, was himself a freed slave, as was Pleasant.) Lest you think that this association between magic and social justice is limited to African influence, Native American shamans were (and remain) in the forefront of resistance to white encroachment, and traditional practitioners led desperate resistance to Christian domination of Europe. Who knows what attempts to defy limitations on women's magical and spiritual traditions were destroyed in the flames of the craze of medieval witch-burning? Virtually all the records that remain are filtered through the eyes of the torturers.

Although men suffer too, societies that suppress the magical arts will, as a rule, also limit women's voices and power, often with terrible brutality. Significantly King Saul, in need of a necromancer, requested that his minions find him a conjuring *woman*. Although it's since taken many twists and turns, magic ultimately derives from women's mysteries and the mysteries of creation, and the history of magic's suppression cannot be separated from the history of women's oppression.

Is magic evil? Well, if your perception is that sex is inherently evil, Creation inherently tainted with sin, and that women constitute Earth's weakest link, then I guess you'd better lump magic in there with the rest of these moral dilemmas.

If magic cannot be entirely divorced from religion, even less can it be separated from herbalism, the root of all traditional medicinal systems, systems that for millennia have investigated botanical impact on health and (above all) on reproduction. Magic is the primordial human art and science. It stems from awe inspired by all Earthly creation, but especially the mysteries of human creation. Every new human life is the ultimate act of magic. Conscious attempts at conception probably constitute the first magic spells, especially if you consider that our remote ancestors didn't understand pregnancy in the detached, technical manner that we do today. Primordial religions venerated the divine in the form of human genitalia with joy, awe, and respect, not prurience, recognizing their capacity for sacred generation and creation.

Although these symbols still survive in isolated pockets of official religion, magic remains suffused with sexual imagery, in ways that may surprise us today, in efforts to maximize the blessings inherent in the powers of anatomy, both male and female. However, magic stems from fascination, on the part of both women and men, with women's mysteries: the capacity to produce life where it didn't exist before, magic blood that flows on schedule from no wound and then is mysteriously retained, the links between that blood, fertility, women, the moon, and the sea. These were and remain conduits to the sacred for primordial magic and spirituality alike.

Where Do Magic Spells Come From?

According to the author, folklorist, and scholar of magic, Zora Neale Hurston, *"magic is older than writing. So nobody knows how it started."* Very true, but what we do know is that magic comes from all over the globe. There is neither a people nor a culture on Earth that did not at one time possess a magical tradition, whether they recall it today, or whether or not they still use it. Some cultures and religions revel in their magical traditions. Others are ashamed of them or deny that the traditions ever existed. Some ethnic groups like to point the finger and suggest that magic comes from other people, not them, oh no, never—any practices of their own are only isolated bad habits picked up from disreputable magical wanderers or neighbors.

When a large cache of papyri from Alexandria in Egypt was found to be largely devoted to magic spells, anthropologists, Egyptologists, and other scholars exulted. Not because they were necessarily so interested in magic, although some were, but because magic spells reveal a tremendous amount about a culture and its circumstances. Read between the lines of a spell and you will discover important details about people's expectations of life and death, their daily problems, the materials that they cherish, their spiritual outlook. For example, recently published books intended for the urban magical practitioner attempt to minimize or even eliminate the need for botanicals. Beyond their value to their intended audience, these books also transmit a crucial message to all of us regarding the state of our environment. As another example, only cultures that possess a belief in the possibility of legal justice, however remote, produce court case spells. Love spells reveal cultural sexual dynamics. So you see, magic spells have tremendous value as history, anthropology, and sociology way beyond their practical value to the spell-caster.

Translations of these Alexandrian papyri, now known as the Magical Papyri, were eagerly awaited. Stemming mainly from the second century BCE to the fifth century CE, they span a crucial, fascinating period of history: the times of Cleopatra, Jesus, the rise of Rome, the fall of Jerusalem, and the emergence of Christianity as a cohesive faith and world power.

Alexandria, although it became Egypt's capital, is not an ancient pharaonic city. It was founded by the Macedonian conqueror, Alexander the Great, one of several cities he named in his own honor. Its orientation is the Mediterranean, not the Nile, like other older Egyptian cities. At various periods, indigenous Egyptians were not even permitted to live within Alexandria's boundaries. It was a Greek outpost in Egypt, with Greeks as the elite citizenry. Cleopatra, descendant of one of Alexander the Great's generals and the last of her dynasty, was the only one of her lineage who troubled to learn the Egyptian language.

The city achieved a reputation as a world capital of magic. Alexandria supported a sizeable population of magic practitioners of all kinds—diviners, dream interpreters, professional spell-casters—all presumably serving the needs of their specific communities rather than Alexandria as a whole, because Alexandria was a rigidly divided city. Although Alexandria, like many cities of its time, was divided into quarters, true divisions, like many a modern city, were cast along ethnic lines. Two of Alexandria's quarters were Greek, one was Egyptian (the only area in which they were permitted to reside), and the fourth housed a sizeable Jewish community.

Divisions between the quarters were distinct, reflecting hostility between these communities, which periodically bubbled over into rioting and violence. It was a turbulent, volatile city, demonstrating ethnic tensions only too familiar today. This may be ancient history but it's a familiar landscape to many contemporary urban dwellers or anyone who reads a current newspaper. It was precisely the city's divisions, its multi-ethnic population, and varied religious and spiritual traditions (Alexandria was also the birthplace of Gnosticism) that so excited the archeologists and scholars—it provided the potential for something like historical "control groups."

Expectation was that the orientation of the papyri would be largely Greek. In Athens, there was a tendency to associate magic with out-of-towners—Thracians or Thessalians. Would this practice continue? Would there be completely Greek magic, or would the Alexandrians transfer the outsider role to the native Egyptians? Would the Greeks, traditionally impressed by Egyptian mysticism (Pythagoras studied in Egypt) adopt some of their host country's practices? Would it be possible to clearly trace the emergence of Gnosticism as well as Pagan reactions to Christianity? Answers to these crucial questions were anticipated with bated breath as translation of the papyri progressed.

What was uncovered is a mess. The spells, on the whole, are neither clearly nor even mostly Greek, or Egyptian, or that third ethnic group, Judaic, but a scrambled jumble of all three, with a healthy dose of Pagan *and* Christian Gnosticism, together with a sprinkling of influences from other parts of the Greek and Roman empires. Any individual spell may incorporate the God of Israel, assorted angels, Egyptian gods, Mesopotamian gods, Greek gods, Nubian gods, Jesus Christ and Christian spirituality, botanical magic, divination, names of mysterious things we have no way of presently identifying, some or all of the above, and definitely not necessarily in that order.

What was a poor scholar to do? How to interpret and sort this material, determine who wrote it, and to whom it truly belongs and applies?

None of the information in the papyri is mundane everyday material that you might say any individual on the street was bound to know. The spells and incantations are the height of occult knowledge. The Magical Papyri are the descendants of highly guarded spiritual secrets, the ancestors of high ritual magic. Alexandria was an intensely urban community. These spells don't reflect the knowledge common to any village wise-woman or cunning man but are highly detailed and specialized, occult in every sense, the stuff of initiates and adepts. Who wrote them? The information contained in them defies all attempts to pigeonhole these spells.

They derive from over centuries and so can't be attributed to one person, not even the legendary Hermes Trismegistus. Nothing in Alexandria's history indicates a mingling of cultures that would provide a general intercultural exchange like this—quite the opposite. Furthermore, although Greek was Alexandria's *lingua franca* and many Jews, for instance, spoke that language rather than their own, spiritual secrets were still recorded in each community's distinct tongue. Sacred, secret, spiritual texts in each possible tradition were maintained in the most obscure version possible specifically so that profane eyes could not access them. Egyptian, Greek, and Hebrew aren't even written with the same alphabets. Who had access to all this vast information? How was it transmitted?

Intense debate ensued regarding who compiled these spells and who actually cast them. Were they Greeks, as had originally been anticipated, or were they Egyptians? Were they Greeks gone native? Controlled attempts had been made to combine aspects of Greek and Egyptian religion, culminating in the cult of Serapis. But then, why the Jewish references? Were they Egyptians striving to Hellenize? But then, why the Christian references? Maybe the spells were compiled by unemployed wizard-priests trying to find a new professional niche market, but then why don't they hew more faithfully to centuries of conservative Egyptian tradition? They couldn't be Jews, because, of course, Jews are monotheistic and don't participate in this kind of thing, but then, if not, how did the spell-casters learn all those obscure Hebrew names of power, names extremely difficult to access even within the Jewish community? But if they were Jews, what were they doing invoking Hecate, Hathor, and Hermes? They couldn't be Christians because Christians forbade magic in general, because Alexandria was home to a particularly militant branch of Christianity and because the rift between Christians and Pagans was especially violent and bitter in Alexandria. But if they were not Christians, why all the references to Jesus Christ? These mysteries were not the ones that scholars had so eagerly anticipated investigating and debating.

Translation of the Magical Papyri occurred only recently. Perhaps more information will be uncovered. Volume one of *The Greek Magical Papyri in Translation Including the Demotic Spells* was first published in 1986. Egyptologists, anthropologists, historians, linguists, and other scholars continue to discuss their origin and broad scope. The only experts, I suspect, who have not been consulted are contemporary urban magical practitioners, for whom the entangled ethnic and spiritual roots of the Magical Papyri's spells would come as no surprise.

When historians counted Alexandria's four quarters, they neglected a fifth community, who quite obviously rejected, transcended, and ignored those boundaries: Alexandria's vast community of magical practitioners, a quarter unto themselves. Where other residents of Alexandria found divisions, these magical practitioners discovered a crossroads. Magic thrives where roads meet. What the Magical Papyri manifest is the birth of modern magic.

If you were an up-and-coming metaphysical seeker or magical practitioner back then, Alexandria was the place to go. Why? Not just to make money; you'd retain more of a monopoly by staying home as a big fish in a small pond. No, you'd go to Alexandria to meet other practitioners, learn what they had to teach and share some secrets of your own. The spells of the Magical Papyri demonstrate what happens at those crossroads.

Where others obeyed the rules and kept to their own kind, magical practitioners went wandering, with magic as the *lingua franca*, the common tongue, exploring each other's secrets, deconstructing them and putting them back together in whole new confabulations. This mixing is not necessarily about improvement; spells that hew faithfully to one tradition work just as powerfully as blended spells. Instead it's about experimentation and the desire (common to all practitioners), to adapt something of power to one's own needs. (This process is not always a happy one. One person's *sharing* is another person's *appropriation*. The Egyptians, for example, were appalled when they learned that Greeks had discovered aphrodisiac properties in their sacred temple incense, *kyphi*.)

Alexandria presaged the modern city, filled with immigrants from Earth's different corners. Previously, opportunities to meet other practitioners were limited. Nearby practitioners probably came from your own family; everyone shared the same knowledge and repertoire of tools and materials. Sure, there was the occasional wandering stranger, but nothing like the vast landscape of Alexandria, where practitioners from so many traditions could sit and share secrets. Magic, back then as it does today, transcends and defies boundaries of language, ethnicity, race, gender, or religion to form its own community.

When I first read the Magical Papyri my immediate reaction was recognition: all those mixed-up, boundary-jumping spells resembled, in nature if not in specific detail, the culturally diverse magic that I learned in my own hometown, that crossroads of the modern world, New York City. New York, like Alexandria, has had its moments of tense ethnic division, but you wouldn't know it from the metaphysical community. Fearing the law, fearing ridicule, people may hold themselves aloof, at least until genuine magical credentials, knowledge, respect, and curiosity are demonstrated, but then the walls come down.

One thing magical practitioners have in common all around the world is curiosity, the quest for knowledge. We are the original enquiring minds who wish to know. Obstacles to knowledge are bitterly resented and are persistently undermined. Magicians always wish to expand their power, and increase their knowledge and repertoire. There is a reason that so many of the earliest books printed were grimoires, or books of magic—the same reason that Lord Thoth is patron both of scribes and magicians. Providing that a society is at all literate, magical practitioners, on the whole, are great readers, from ancient Egypt's *Houses of Life* to the Voodoo queens of New Orleans.

There is only one thing better than learning from a book and that's learning from each other. Magical practitioners are, in general, an open-minded bunch. Put a few in a room together and fairly quickly tools will be compared, secrets shared, and demands for knowledge made.

Spells are constantly evolving to suit changing needs. This is particularly true where cultures live closely alongside each other. Nothing crosses borders faster than a magic spell. For instance it can be almost impossible to separate totally the intermingled strands of various European magical traditions. Because certain methods, materials, and styles are more popular and prevalent in one area than another doesn't necessarily mean that they originated there or, at least, not in isolation. Even the most sedentary, isolated communities received periodic magical cross-pollination from Jews, Romany, tinkers, and assorted wanderers.

These entwined traditions become even more complex in the magical and spiritual traditions of America and the Western Hemisphere.

During the height of the African slave trade, people were kidnapped from all over Africa. What were originally distinct cultures, each with specific spiritual and magical traditions, found themselves thrown together in dire circumstances, the type of circumstances in which many reach for magic. In Haiti, the traditions of the Fon people of Dahomey were dominant and evolved into Vodoun, although not in isolation. These traditions evolved, adding components of indigenous Taino magic, diverse other African traditions, French, and Spanish magic, thus also transmitting Basque, Jewish, Moorish, and Romany influences and, last but not least, Freemasonry. You think this is beginning to make Alexandria look simple? Just wait.

Following later political turbulence, many Haitian refugees fled to New Orleans, where Vodoun evolved once more, retaining its frame but picking up new influences, this time from the local black population, whose own magic derived from Congolese sources rather than Fon, and also British, Italian, and Native American magical traditions. New Orleans, the Crescent City, became known as the capital of American magic. Its traditions would soon be incorporated into what might be called mainstream magic, that magic most accessible to the population at large. This magic would eventually be transmitted to Europe where, who knows? Maybe it's now been picked up by African emigrants to evolve and transform once more.

After extended contact, New Orleans Voodoo can be hard to distinguish from Hoodoo. Hoodoo's basic framework also derives from Africa, mainly from Congolese traditions, but again not in isolation. Deprived of the botanicals with which they had been familiar in Africa, their *materia magica*, enslaved African magical practitioners consulted with Native Americans and acquired a whole new botanical tradition, sharing magical and spiritual secrets as well. These Hoodoo doctors typify the proverbial questing, intellectually curious magician. In addition to Native American, West and Central African roots, their tradition soon incorporated European folk magic, the Egyptian mysteries, Freemasonry, and Kabbalah. The great grimoires became available to all. Transmission was cross-cultural. With the exception of a very few isolated mountain pockets, American magic in general demonstrates tremendous African influence.

Further north, Pow-Wow is the magic of German immigrants to Pennsylvania, the Pennsylvania Dutch (a corruption of *Deutsch*). The basic framework is, of course, the German magic the migrants carried with them, both high ritual and folk magic, which incorporated a healthy dose of Jewish and Romany influences as well as those of neighboring European people. In America, strong further influence (and the tradition's name) came from Native Americans, especially the Iroquois, and from the Chikkeners, the so-called *Black Dutch*: Romany (Zigeuners) forcibly deported from Europe who, separated from clan and family, found discreet safety among the Pow-Wow artists.

In 1819 or 1820, dates vary, Pow-Wow artist and *hexenmeister* John George Hohman compiled a canon of Pow-Wow wisdom and published it under the title *The Book of Pow-Wows: The Long Lost Friend*. This book, still in print, traveled to the cities of the South, carried largely by Jewish merchants, who sold it to Voodoo and Hoodoo practitioners, who incorporated it into their already multi-cultural blend of magic and, no doubt, sent some equally valuable information up North with the returning merchants, who were learning from everybody and spreading the news.

There is an important exception to this magic melting pot, of course. Very isolated areas, places where people have historically had little or no contact with others, maintain extremely pristine, ancient magical traditions. Like the unique creatures of the Galapagos Islands, their traditions developed in isolation and thus may have very unique, easily identifiable characteristics. It's much easier to clearly identify a spell from Papua New Guinea, for instance, than it is to distinguish between French, German, or Swiss spells. Because these traditions are so unique and because one *can* identify the spell's origins, it's very tempting to constantly point out which spell came from which isolated culture. The danger is that this creates a lopsided effect, akin to those old-school anthropologists who were so quick to note the curious habits of the "Natives" while failing to remark on similar practices, parallels, and traditions back home.

I can't emphasize more that every distinct people, every culture, every nation, every religion and spiritual tradition has, at one time or another, incorporated, developed, and created magic spells. Each one of us has a magical history somewhere along the line. Loss and abandonment of these traditions tends to accompany loss of cultural or religious autonomy. These spells, therefore, are our shared human heritage, not isolated odd things engaged in only by strange *other* people, very different from us.

In some cases, in this book, I have pointed out where spells come from and which traditions they represent, especially if there's some interesting factoid associated with it or if that knowledge may help you cast the spell, or sometimes just to give credit where credit is due for a particularly beautiful spell. However, I have not done so in every case. Sometimes I did not wish to keep emphasizing one culture, as if they were Earth's only magical ones, especially those cultures whose vast magical repertoire has stimulated others to vilify, stereotype, and persecute them. In other cases, the roots were too tangled to identify their origins honestly.

Although many of the spells in this book are meant for use, others are included purely for historic value and perspective, so that we may remember and learn from them.

Magic Today

These are both the best and the worst of times for magic.

On one hand, there is currently less persecution of magical practitioners in more parts of the world than at any time since the rise of Christianity. This very book that you hold in your hands would once upon a time have earned reader, writer, publisher, and bookseller alike a slow and painful death.

Materials, once rare, craved, hoarded, and often forbidden are available and affordable to more people than ever before. Think about that the next time you sip some mugwort tea, an herb that might have branded you a witch just a few centuries ago. Frankincense and myrrh, once the most precious expensive commodities on Earth, may now be purchased in any well-stocked health food store. Salt, packed with magic power, once extracted from Earth and sea with terrible human effort, once very expensive and precious, is now so cheap and common that every fast-food vendor gives away free packets by the handful.

Although fewer people have private gardens, there is greater access than ever before to the botanical material that constitutes the foundation of magic. Some spells in this book refer to what may seem to be very obscure items and plants: virtually nothing is unattainable, however. Once upon a time, a practitioner was limited to local botanicals. Now you can import living as well as dried plants from virtually anywhere on the globe for your private use. Do you want to access the power of Peruvian shamanic plants? Go on the Internet; you'll be able to buy some. Where botanical material isn't practical, modern essential oils and flower essence remedies reproduce alchemical methods to bring you the power of even more flowers, available in a simple, easy-to-store, user-friendly, inexpensive form.

Practitioners are unafraid to teach and to share information. I remember when booksellers didn't generally stock spell-books. Now you can buy them everywhere. Classes are advertised in newspapers. You don't have to be a member of an inner circle to discover metaphysical companions. There's little need to hide in back rooms, fearing arrest or worse, as in previous days. In industrialized nations there is new-found appreciation for magical wisdom and traditions.

Yet it's also the worst of times in other areas—ironically, in those isolated communities where magical knowledge was preserved in such purity for so long. Many of Earth's surviving magical traditions are vanishing as quickly as the rainforest, coral reefs, or any other endangered species.

While some re-embrace a magical heritage rejected for so long, traditional practitioners who've maintained those spiritual traditions for millennia lack similar privileges and protection. Like those vulnerable creatures of the Galapagos, having never before met attempts at suppression, they may never have developed the skills of subterfuge developed over generations among other more frequently oppressed people.

As rainforests are cut down, as ancestral lands are annexed, traditional practitioners and shamans have less access to the botanicals they depend upon than ever before. Instead of open-minded, questing fellow magical practitioners, eager to learn and share knowledge, the only outsiders these traditional practitioners are likely to meet are those who undermine their magical traditions, and pressure them to abandon their own faiths and convert to others.

Every day, somewhere on Earth, a traditional practitioner is pressured to abandon shamanism, divination, or some variant of the magical arts. Sometimes suppression is violent. Tools are destroyed, modes of transmission suppressed. Shamans and leaders of magic are isolated from their communities, or as the Bible so eloquently says, *"put away."* The stimulus to reject old magical traditions may also come from within, from a culture's desire for modernity, to appear *civilized* and *rational*. In other cases magic and traditional knowledge are victims of war and political unrest.

It is ironic to observe precisely which information appears to be vanishing versus what appears to be preserved for posterity. Once upon a time, very recently, Western magical adepts and elite scholars of magic alike favored the remote "pure" traditions of the Himalaya and Indonesia. Scholars and adepts journeyed with tremendous personal effort to the far corners of the Earth to meet with Ascended Masters while simultaneously scorning magical traditions found closer to home as superstitious nonsense.

Today it is those previously respected traditions that are rapidly being eroded and are vanishing for a host of religious, political, and environmental reasons. Closer to home, Celtic traditions, once reviled as foolishness, have been revived and energized by a massive number of new practitioners. The Romany people, terribly persecuted for centuries, scorned sometimes precisely because of their magical traditions, have recently re-asserted control over those traditions and how they are to be perceived. Hoodoo, once beheld by both academicians and elite occultists with particular scorn, largely for race-based reasons, appears to have its survival assured, thanks to the dedicated efforts of its own scholars, Zora Neale Hurston, Harry Middleton Hyatt, and Catherine Yronwode.

Silver Raven Wolf, modern chronicler of Pow-Wow, once dismissed as ignorant folk-practices that were unworthy of scholarly interest, writes of scouring Pennsylvanian nursing homes, looking for old people with snippets of information that she may then preserve and share. Perhaps others will fulfill this role for other genres of magic in other parts of the world. It takes only one generation for information to be lost forever. How many traditions, how much hard-won human experience and accumulated wisdom from every inhabited continent, have already been lost? This big book that you hold in your hand is but a tiny portion of Earth's magical wisdom. In keeping with the inquiring, questing spirit of magical practitioners throughout the ages, don't be too respectful with the spells in this book. If you find something that suits you or intrigues you, use it. If something isn't quite right, play with it. Tap into your own magic powers and continue the evolution of our magic repertoire.

Elements of Magic Spells

How do you cast a magic spell? *Do you shout abracadabra, turn around three times on one foot and shoot sparks from your wand? Or do you stand within a circle of lit candles, magic sword at the ready, attempting to read unknown, unpronounceable words from a dusty grimoire? Will you tuck one single crumb of bread, one single grain of salt, and some burned-out charcoal into a scrap of red fabric, and then make knots in the cloth as if your very life depended upon it? Perhaps you will stand at the crossroads and just … stand?*

Magic spells come in virtually unlimited form, some dramatic, some shocking, and some perhaps surprisingly mundane. Definitions of exactly what constitutes a magic spell depend a lot upon one's personal history and experience, the stories you were or weren't told as a child, and cultural expectations. What separates a magic spell from just any random series of actions is you, your intent, goals, and desires.

A magic spell is a conscious formalized attempt to manipulate magic power and energy (heka) *in order to achieve your own personal goal.*

There are many styles of spells, featuring all sorts of ingredients. If one style of spell doesn't suit you, there are others. Afraid of fire? Cast your spell by creating enchanted baths. Don't have a tub? Brew potions or tie magical knots. If one ingredient is unobtainable, there are substitutes. If you can't afford precious gems and resins, there are plenty of powerful magical

materials masquerading as common kitchen ingredients. Magical energy is irrepressible; magic spells are the controlled conduit for directing this magical energy. There is only one component of every magic spell that you cast that cannot be replaced and that is YOU. Yours is the unique binding energy that provides the spark of life which transforms actions, words, and thoughts into magic spells.

Everyone's secret desire, of course, is to possess enchanted words or objects that achieve our goals for us without even our slightest effort. Just say "hocus pocus!" and poof! Your boring date is instantly transformed into Mr. Right. There is a grain of truth in this fantasy: the most magically charged objects will perform a lot of the work for us, although magic spells are never completely effortless. Some naturally occurring items inherently possess this type of magic power (iron, menstrual blood, salt, certain botanical plants); in other cases, some extremely intensive spell-casting is required in order to craft a tool of requisite intense magical power (a magic wand, sword, or mirror).

Magic spells take many forms, avail themselves of many powers, and depend upon various elements, tools, and components. Some of these elements, tools, and components occur naturally on Earth, while others are crafted by people. Sometimes these elements and components can be put neatly into categories and sometimes, magic being the unruly, disobedient force that it is, they overlap and merge in a surreal dream-like manner.

Some spells are object-driven; others are dependent upon the power of words. Some require dozens of unusual plants and minerals, while other spells, which rank among the most difficult to cast because you must do all the energy transformation independently, require nothing more than the force of your personal will. Some spells walk a razor's edge between religion and magic on the one hand, and traditional healing and magic on the other. Partly this is because of magic's tendency to appropriate any object, system, or method that demonstrates potential for power, and partly this is because, once upon a time, distinctions between various arts and sciences weren't drawn as rigidly as they are today. Awareness of magic power and the desire to use it for one's own benefit is the primordial human art and science. Religion, traditional medicine, astrology, alchemy, aromatherapy, perfumery, music, dance, visual art, and more are all rooted in magic and shamanism.

Before any spell is cast, the initial requirement is that you have a personal goal. What do you want to achieve? What do you wish to prevent? What are your secret desires, your deepest fears? Magic spells are always cast for a purpose, even if it's a generic one like "personal happiness," the proverbial "peace on Earth," or obtaining vague "good fortune." The more specific your desire, the more clearly articulated your vision, the deeper your passion, the more likely it is that your spell will work. There is not one type of spell that is inherently more powerful than another; there are only spells and styles of spell-casting that are more effective for a specific individual. Part of the fun and challenge of spell-casting is finding the spells that best suit you.

In this section we will examine various styles of spell-casting, the various elements of magic, and the tools and ingredients required to cast spells.

Spell-casting

Spell-casting Using the Power of Animals

Spells are cast using the power of animal allies and familiars. Animal allies, familiars, and the magic power inherent in specific animal species can help you achieve your spell's goals.

Notice that the above sentence reads *"power of animals"* not *"parts of animals."* If this book included spells utilizing anatomical parts of animals, it could easily have been called *The Element Encyclopedia of 10,000 Spells.* It's not necessary to point any fingers; more cultures than not have engaged in this practice. It's not necessary to discuss whether those spells ever worked or not, either. If they did

work, would that make them acceptable today? That discussion veers dangerously close to the opinion frequently expressed about how tragic it is that tigers may soon be extinct in the wild because poachers kill them for medicines and aphrodisiacs that don't work. If the medicines *did* work, would the situation be any less tragic? Whether those old spells ever worked or not, we now live in an era where the balance of nature is terribly tipped. Those spells are no longer viable. Because spells that rely on any part of an animal, physical or otherwise, are ultimately dependent upon the good-will of its presiding Animal Spirit, those old anatomy-dependent spells will no longer work for us and may even backfire on the spell-caster. Magic is a living, evolutionary art, not a static situation; what worked once must be adapted to present needs.

Whether those old practices (rabbits' feet for money spells, badgers' feet for childbirth spells) were ever as prevalent as some would have us believe is subject to debate. The most sensational, lurid aspects of magic are inevitably emphasized by outsiders and story-tellers. The only thing many know about the vast, sophisticated magical system Hoodoo, for instance, is the infamous black cat bone. Spells using parts of animals are also taken out of context. Once upon a time, people were responsible for killing their own food. Nothing was wasted. What wasn't eaten was utilized for other purposes, including magic. Out of context, a spell can sound terribly cruel. Thus, a Romany amulet called *"eyes of the crayfish"* implies that only the eyes are used, having been plucked out of the poor creature. In reality, *"eyes of the crayfish"* refers to scrapings from inside the shell, the crayfish itself having been served for dinner.

If you perceive power in this type of spell, however, they can be modernized, adapted, and improved. Candles, charms, and images, for instance, allow us to access the inherent energy of a specific animal species in a manner that retains magic power and is safe for both animal and practitioner. For example, hummingbirds are a frequent component of Central American love spells; a copper or gemstone hummingbird charm allows you to synchronize the inherent animal energy with a compatible material for enhanced spell-casting. For maximum effect, consecrate the charm to the animal spirit, which you would be unable to do if you were using actual body parts obtained through the animal's suffering.

This should not be considered mere New Age fluffy-bunny adaptation. Since ancient days animal image magic has been among the most powerful. What-was the Biblical golden calf after all but a magic image? A living calf would have been far less trouble. It was the specific juncture of animal magical symbolism with metal's inherent magical energy, guided by human fear and desire, that accurately and potently manipulated and directed magic power.

Animal sacrifice has no place in magic; it is religious ritual entirely and completely, without overlap. All religious traditions at one time or another conducted animal sacrifice, some just further back than others. Some continue these traditions while others do not. What is certain is that *no* religious tradition permits laypeople to conduct these sacrifices. Permission is granted only after strict training and initiation. Where magic approaches the border of religion, symbols are used rather than actual animals. Burn a dove-shaped candle to petition Aphrodite during a love spell or offer her the gift of a figurine, rather than killing her sacred bird. Again, this is not fluffy-bunny magic but ancient tradition. How can you reconcile the idea of a deity who accepts sacrificial offerings of a beloved, sacred creature in one context, but who angrily punishes anyone who harms a hair on the head of that creature in another? Over two thousand years ago, Hecate accepted sacrifices of dogs in her *official* temples, killed only by *official* priestesses in the context of very specific ritual. Even back then, individuals who preferred to make independent, private offerings, or who could not afford to pay the temple the cost of a dog, successfully offered tiny stone dog fetishes to Hecate instead.

There are magic spells contained in this book that require the participation of animals. It's assumed that they'll be treated with the respect one would pay human or spirit partners. It is also assumed that at the conclusion of the spell, the animal will be in as good a condition, if not better, as it was at the spell's beginning.

Several spells require cuts of meat similar to those you might eat for dinner, assuming you are not a vegetarian. Meat for these spells should be purchased in the same manner that you would normally obtain meat for a meal. There are many spells that require eggs, honey, and milk. Vegans may choose not to perform these ones, and there are many more spells in the book that do not use animal products. Magic spells are not divorced from real life. If something offends you in any another context, then it's likely to be inappropriate for you magically as well.

Manipulation of fragrance is an extremely important component of magic spells. As most fragrances derive from botanicals, the topic will be discussed in greater detail in that section. However, certain very famous fragrances have traditionally derived from animal sources, most notably civet, musk, ambergris, and castoreum. Castoreum, derived from beavers, is today only available in synthetic versions. *One* spell featuring *one* drop of civet is included in this book (it is the only ingredient in this sex-magic spell) because, in theory at least, the fragrance may be obtained without unduly harming the animal, and arguments have been made that this may be the only way to guarantee the seriously endangered civet's survival. I can't honestly say that I'm entirely convinced. You, too, may wish to engage in further research.

Frankly, it's unlikely that you'll be able to purchase anything other than synthetic versions of these fragrances, the authentic article being rare and prohibitively expensive. Because they have *always* been rare and prohibitively expensive—and synthetics are a recent invention—historic botanical substitutes have always existed, and those substitutes are used within the spells of this book:

★ For **Musk**, *extracted from the musk deer:* **Ambrette** (Abelmoschus moschatus), *a shrub native to India, also known as musk mallow and treasured for its scented seed*

★ For **Ambergris**, *derived from sperm whales:* **Labdanum**, *a resin excreted from the leaves of the rock-rose* (Cistus creticus, Cistus ladanifer). *Allegedly labdanum from Crete has the closest resemblance to ambergris, although it is also obtained from French, Moroccan, and Spanish sources*

Whether the tendency to utilize animal body parts was ever as prevalent as some believe is debatable. Certainly, grimoires are filled with spells specifically requesting assorted species' feet and hearts and eyes. Many classic grimoires are based largely on various fragments of ancient spell-books that were in circulation throughout Europe, Arabia, and North Africa before the development of modern printing. Many of these spells derive from turn-of-the-Common-Era Alexandria. Professional magicians of that time, attempting to keep spells secret yet needing to write them down so that they themselves would remember complex formulas, created an elaborate code, so elaborate that someone had to write it down in order to use it. That list was discovered and translated amid the Magical Papyri.

★ *Does a spell call for the* heart of a hawk? *No need to catch that bird, so sacred to indigenous Egyptian religion—what the spell is really asking for is heart of wormwood*

★ *Do you hesitate to cast a spell requiring* lion's tongue? *No need, all that that spell really requires is a* "tongue" *of turnip*

★ *Wondering how in the world you'll ever extract* Hercules' semen? *Not a problem; just go out to the garden and pick some arugula*

Not every animal reference encoded in the Magical Papyri is a botanical, although (as with magic in general) plants do predominate. The spell that demands a *physician's bone* neither commands you to commit murder nor to dig around in the cemetery: a piece of sandstone is what's really being requested.

Many, if not all, of these animal references may originally have referred to botanicals and minerals. Of course, by the time the descendant of a single fragment of papyrus reached Europe, hundreds of years later, copied and re-copied over and over by hand, lacking the accompanying code, and some magician desperate to access the forbidden secret magic of Egypt got his hands on a spell…

The spells recorded in the Magical Papyri are fairly mean-spirited in general, full of commanding and compelling. Were the magicians irresponsible, not caring if others misinterpreted their instructions, or was this just an example of professional secret code, full of in-jokes and personal references, similar to the secret languages (*sim*) still employed by some modern Egyptian entertainers? Across oceans, continents and time, some modern Amazonian shamans also share a secret shamans' language—a professional language only understood by other professionals—in order to protect their information from those who don't know how to use it properly.

Is this what those old Alexandrian magicians intended? We may never know. The moral of the story, however, is never cast spells that aren't comfortable for you. It is neither uncommon for botanical and other materials to be named for animals, nor is the practice relegated to ancient history. Many spells in this book, for instance, call for deer's tongue. I assure you, no deer need be harmed. *Deer's tongue* is a type of grass, reputed to provide eloquence: the name is a pun on the plant's appearance and its ability.

Swallow's blood is a red powder that allegedly transmits the magical power of that long-migrating bird; no blood of any kind is required. *Dragon's blood*, an extremely potent magical material, surely ranks among the Top 20 most popular spell-casting ingredients. No need to emulate Saint George, dragon's blood is the resin from *Dracaena draco*, an Indonesian tree. Unlike most resins it's red, hence the name. If you burn it, it does indeed bear a resemblance to blood. (There is also *another* dragon's blood, used in Peruvian magic. This one, too, is a botanical substance, although completely distinct from the Indonesian resin.)

Spell-casting Using the Power of Botanicals

Botanical just means *plant*, however because of the vast variety of forms used (some no longer remotely *"plant-like"*) any type of plant-derived power, in its original form or otherwise, is categorized as a botanical. Botanicals, as a category, are probably the most common ingredients in spell-casting. Many people will never cast a candle spell, never work with crystals or wands or magic mirrors, but it's virtually impossible to engage in magic without relying on botanical power to a greater or lesser extent. Plants are ubiquitous in magic. Their power is accessed via many forms, which lend themselves to various styles of spell-casting, so that botanicals are incorporated into virtually every style of spell.

Casting Magic Spells in Partnership with Your Living Plant Allies

Fairy-tale witches reside in huts, cottages, or castles surrounded by magically empowered gardens. When Prince Charming seeks Sleeping Beauty in her enchanted castle, the surrounding garden, full of thickets and thorns, actively reaches out to prevent him. Although one must never rely on one's Protection Spell Garden to play the role of armed-response guard, there is a metaphoric truth hidden in this story.

Gardens can be both products of enchantment and independent producers of enchantment; they are a living, on-going magic spell. Gardens may be arranged in any variety of ways—color-coordinated, whatever was on sale at the nursery, even completely haphazardly. If you select, coordinate, and arrange plants according to the magic powers they radiate, then planting a garden becomes one style of casting a spell. Thus your desire to draw wealth, protection, or fertility to one's home is manifested by carefully arranging the appropriate plants, and vigilantly removing those possessing opposing, contradictory powers.

This obviously is a long-term extended magic spell, rather than the type of quick-fix luck spell you might choose for a spontaneous trip to a casino. How will you benefit from this type of garden spell?

★ *The actual spell-casting, and then time spent among the botanicals and their radiant energy creates the desired adjustment on your own energy*

★ *The radiant energy of the coordinated garden draws and/or repels the targeted goal to you and to your home in a more powerful manner than one botanical or amulet could achieve alone*

★ *This spell is a symbiotic, reciprocal process, which ultimately strengthens all living participants for their mutual benefit. The garden will additionally attract complementary animal and spirit allies who will also contribute to the success of your spell*

This type of magic spell is not limited to those with access to personal property or sunny weather. Magic spell gardens may be created indoors in pots. Furthermore, an entire garden need not be created; one or two individual plants may be grown as part of a magic spell or to further other magic spells.

There are several very good reasons to maintain living plants:

★ If you are pursuing a spiritual or magical alliance with a specific plant, this is best accomplished with a living plant, redolent with power and consciousness, rather than processed, dried plants that retain power but lack conscious intelligence

★ You can grow plants necessary for magic spells and/or physical healing. As you nurture the plant, communicate with it: share your fears and desires, let the plant know what you want from it. These plants will potentially provide more power for you than any others. They become your partners in healing and magic. It is a symbiotic relationship: they care for you as you care for them

★ In many cases if you want to work with a plant, you'll have to grow it. That's the only way it is guaranteed to be available. The plant realm is as ecologically devastated, if not more so, than the animal kingdom. Many plants are extinct or seriously endangered. The only way to work with some magical plants (Solomon's Seal or Low John the Conqueror, for instance), the only way to incorporate them into any spell, is to grow and nurture them. It is the only way their power will be available to you

Because there have always been economic, space, and climatic reasons why working with living plants is impractical, and because different parts of a plant (roots, leaves, flowers) manifest different magic power and energy, and thus are used independently in different spells, various methods of processing plants have evolved over millennia. These include: dried botanicals including incense, flower essence remedies, hydrosols and oils, including fixed, essential, and fragrance oils.

Harvesting Botanicals

In order to maximize botanicals' magic potential, magic rituals and spells are incorporated into their harvesting.

Because plants are alive, removing them from Earth is a risky operation. One has the option of increasing and enhancing their inherent power, or of offending Earth and the presiding Plant Spirits. Once upon a time, all harvesting, for magical or other purposes, was accompanied by spells, rituals, and propitiation of various Earthly and Spirit forces. Unless you purchase your botanicals from magically oriented vendors, one can safely assume that modern harvesting is accompanied by no such rituals or spells.

If you practice extensive botanical spell-casting you may wish to incorporate similar gestures in other ways, to enhance your spells and to provide spiritual protection for yourself. If however, you grow and harvest your own botanicals, ancient spells and rituals may be borrowed or adapted.

Because they're alive, have power, and must be treated with respect, it's not appropriate to just go out and grab a handful of plant. Botanical materials are safely harvested through magic ritual. Essentially you cast a spell in order to gain materials to cast more spells. The plant (or its presiding spirit or Earth herself, however you best understand this) must be addressed. The purpose for gathering should be explained. Because of the principle of reciprocity, gifts are exchanged. Libations of water are always appropriate, however different traditions favor different gifts. Native Americans offered pinches of tobacco; Anglo-Saxons once offered oatmeal. The ancient Romans offered bread and wine. Honey, wine, and menstrual blood are popular offerings. Fragrant incense may be burned in the vicinity as a gift.

Magic spells are always as simple or as complex as the practitioner wishes. An involved, formal harvesting spell follows; follow it precisely, if it suits you, or consider how best to adapt for your own personal needs.

Sometimes distinct plants demand distinct rituals. Two spells follow, one from Wales, the other from ancient Greece, one for an extremely popular magic plant, the other for a more obscure one. Consider these spells, follow them precisely if you like or consider how best to adapt them for your own harvesting needs.

Virtually any list of Top 10 magical plants will include vervain. Legend says vervain sprang from Isis' tears; the herb is believed to have a special fondness for humans and thus works extra hard to provide happiness and success for us. It is believed to have been one of the crucial ingredients of Cerridwen's Cauldron. The Druids insisted that vervain be harvested with an iron knife. An ancient Welsh formula stipulates how vervain must be gathered in order to guarantee its maximum magic power:

WARNING!

Many people exhibit a dangerous tendency to assume that if a plant is used for magical reasons, particularly benevolent ones, it does not also create a physical impact. This is not true, and this assumption can lead to disaster.

Botanicals are an holistic power: they affect us simultaneously on spiritual, emotional, magical, and physical levels. It is possible to cast word charms, image magic or play with candles and crystals without profound physical effect. This is not so with plants. Plants are the basis of medical knowledge, and even magical plants have a physical effect.

Because something has power doesn't mean it is always the right power for you. For instance, many magic spell sites on the Internet offer directions for protective spell baths featuring the herb rue with nary a health warning, despite the fact that it has abortifacient properties and the British master herbalist Nicholas Culpeper said that he couldn't recommend that a pregnant woman even walk through a room containing rue, let alone handle or bathe with it.

Be careful. If you have anything that could be perceived as a physical vulnerability, it is your responsibility to verify whether any botanical may aggravate your condition. If you are pregnant, attempting to become pregnant or nursing a child, the potential safety of all botanicals must be determined. This is not obscure information. Many excellent literary sources on herbs and botanicals exist. Knowledgeable, professional herbalists, physicians, and medical providers can give you information as well. This does not only apply to traditional modes of internal application such as consuming botanicals, but also inhaling fumes or topical application such as bathing, or even perhaps intensive, concentrated handling, depending on the potency of the plant.

Magic is always intended to improve one's life; injuring one's health in the process of casting a spell defeats that purpose. Incorporate your personal needs into choosing the best spells for you.

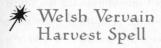
Welsh Vervain Harvest Spell

1. The plant must be harvested during the rising of Sirius, the Dog Star, at an hour when both sun and moon are beneath the horizon.

2. Before uprooting the plant, offer a libation of honey.

3. You may only use your left hand during the entire operation, whether you are left or right handed: pull up the plant and wave it aloft.
4. Separate leaves, flowers, and roots, and dry them separately in the shade. (Each has its own magical uses.)

Ancient Greek Black Hellebore Harvest Spell

Although poisonous, black hellebore, the Christmas rose, is perceived to have magically protective powers.

1. Cast a magic circle around the intended plant, using a magic wand or knife. If you do not work with those ritual tools, consider a respectful way to demarcate the harvest space.
2. Request permission to gather the plant from Apollo and his son Asklepios, the plant's presiding spirits.
3. Burn incense and make offerings to the spirits.
4. Offer a libation to the plant, and then gather it.

Casting Spells Using Dried Botanicals

The most prevalent ingredients of magic spells are processed botanicals, especially dried plants and oils. Drying plants preserves them for extended use, allowing you to work with plants out of season and those that cannot be grown in your personal region. Dried botanicals from all over the world, representing many magical traditions, may be purchased from herbal suppliers.

Dried botanicals are frequently sold already chopped up, cut or powdered. As this frequently needs to be done before spell-casting, purchasing botanicals in this form can be a real time and effort saver—with one caveat. Leaves and blossoms, even chopped, often remain easily distinguishable. Peppermint doesn't smell like vervain or hibiscus, for instance. Roots, on the other hand, often the most magically potent part of a plant, once chopped or powdered, are fairly indistinguishable from each other. It is not uncommon for unethical or ignorant vendors to substitute one root for another. If you are looking for a distinct root, say High John the Conqueror, for which this is a common problem, buy the whole root and grind and powder it yourself, even though this can be difficult. It is the only way to guarantee that you are receiving what you want, the only way to maintain control over what may be a pivotal ingredient. Familiarize yourself with botanicals. Know what they *should* look like and what they *should* smell like, and you will be less likely to be fooled.

If you grow plants or have access to fresh plants, it's extremely easy—virtually child's play—to dry them yourself.

Drying Botanicals

Hang botanicals upside down in small bunches, so that they are not too crowded. Professional herb dryers, resembling horizontal ladders, can be used, or attach bunches to a wire hanger. Allow botanicals to hang in a well-ventilated area away from direct sunlight until dry.

Casting Spells by Burning Botanicals

Magic spells are cast by burning botanicals (incense), thus releasing their magic power into the atmosphere (fumigation).

One of the most ancient methods of casting spells is consciously, carefully, and deliberately burning botanicals. This method incorporates all four primal elements into one spell. By applying the power of fire, botanical power (which has been nourished by Earth and by water) is transformed into smoke (air) and dispersed into the atmosphere to provide magical solutions and fulfill magical desires. If you burn incense on a metal pan or burner, then you incorporate what many consider to be the fifth element, metal, into your spell as well.

Modern incense frequently takes the form of sticks and cones, which require a little technical know-how. However, incense is an ancient, ancient art. If cave people had the technology to create fine, viable incense, of course you do, too. The original incense was loose dried botanical material, ground and powdered. Most magic spells assume incense will be in this form.

Mortars and pestles are ancient magical, medical, and culinary tools. They may be used to break down and blend botanical material. Once upon a time, incense was created by repeated grinding with a mortar and pestle, and then sifting with a sieve (also an ancient magic tool). However, if you desire the fine powder that many spells specify, a coffee or spice grinder, particularly an old-fashioned manual one, can make life easier.

If you prefer stick incense, blanks may be purchased and doctored to your taste.

To Form an Incense Cone

1. Dissolve gum arabica in water, approximately one part powder to two parts water.
2. Allow the material to soak for approximately three hours.
3. In the meantime, pulverize the herbal material to be used until it is finely powdered (using mortar and pestle or other grinding tool).
4. Mix this powder into the liquid until it can be shaped into small cones.
5. Allow to dry completely in a warm area.

Botanical Infusions

An infusion is the process by which one medium (or power) is encouraged to permeate another. The most common are botanicals infused in water or oil. The most famous infusion in the world is a cup of tea. If you make tea with loose leaves rather than a tea bag, you already know a lot about infusions. Infusions allow you to insert specific botanical power into potions, baths, floorwashes, and magical oils, among many other things.

WARNING!

Botanical power comes in many forms. These powers are not interchangeable. When a spell requests a dried herb, substituting an essential oil may not be appropriate or even safe.

Water-based Infusions

The standard formula for a water infusion is one teaspoon of dried herb, or one-and-a-half teaspoons of fresh herb for every cup of boiling water. Unless otherwise advised, maintain these proportions even when using multiple herbs, adjusting the proportions of the individual ingredients rather than the whole.

1. Place the botanicals into a non-reactive pot or container (glass rather than plastic, for instance).
2. Pour the water over the botanical material.
3. Allow it to brew, usually for between five and fifteen minutes.
4. The plant material may be strained from the liquid or allowed to remain, depending upon the purpose of the spell. For a floorwash, you'd want to remove the botanical; for a particularly potent magical bath, it may be more powerful to retain the botanicals, even though this may leave a mess to clean up.

Sometimes a stronger, more concentrated infusion is desired for a bath or floorwash, but *not* for drinking.

1. Place a more substantial quantity of botanical material into a non-reactive pot or container.
2. Pour only enough boiling water over the botanical material to cover it.
3. Allow it to brew for as long as it takes the water to return to room temperature.
4. Strain the botanicals from the liquid or retain, as desired.

Oil-based Infusions

The process of creating infused oils is slightly more complex, however it is still easily accomplished in the home kitchen. The standard proportion suggested is that for every cup of oil, one ounce of fresh herb or one half-ounce of dried herb is required. Unless otherwise advised, do not exceed these proportions.

1. Place the botanical material in a stainless steel bowl.
2. Cover with the oil.
3. Gently heat over simmering water, either in a true double boiler or in an improvised water bath—a saucepan one-quarter filled with water. The bowl with the herbs must not sit on the bottom of the pan but float in the water. As it is very easy for oil

to scorch and burn, this process needs constant supervision for safety. Keep the oil covered.

4. Stir once in a while. Simmer gently for thirty minutes. The oil should not be allowed to get too hot because if it smokes, bubbles, or burns, an acrid fragrance will develop, spoiling the infusion.
5. Allow the oil to cool. Then all the botanical material must be strained out through multiple layers of cheesecloth or a fine non-metal strainer. Strain twice, if necessary, or more. If the plant material is not removed, the oil may turn rancid.
6. If an infusion spell includes essential oils or flower remedies for enhancement, add them now, once the oil is strained and cooled.
7. Store the infused oil in an airtight container.

You can substitute a crock-pot for the water bath. Maintain the same proportions. Leave the pot on a low heat for approximately two hours, then strain as above.

Solar-charged Infusions

If you can depend upon consistent warm, sunny weather, extremely powerful infusions may be created via solar power. These infusions contain the power of the sun as well as that of botanicals.

1. Place the botanicals inside a jar with a tight-fitting lid.
2. Pour oil over them (make sure the botanicals are completely covered).
3. Add one tablespoon of apple cider vinegar.
4. Leave the jar to sit exposed to warm sun all day and in a warm cupboard (or exposed to moonbeams, if it's warm) all night, for two weeks. Strain as above.

Flower Oil Infusion

There is also another method of infusing oil that does not require heat. This method is usually used to capture the power-transmitting fragrance of delicate flower petals.

1. Separate the petals.
2. Place substantial quantities of clean, dry petals into an airtight jar and cover with oil. (An oil with minimal fragrance of its own is usually preferred to allow the

flower's scent to transmit most powerfully.)

3. Let the petals steep in the oil for three days, shaking the jar occasionally, keeping the jar in the sun in the daytime and in a warm cupboard at night.

4. Strain out and discard the petals, ideally using some cheesecloth or other non-metal sieve, but retain the oil.

5. Fill the jar with a substantial quantity of fresh, clean, dry flower petals and cover them with the reserved oil.

6. Again allow the petals to steep, repeating all the previous stages. The oil will retain the fragrance; repeat until the desired intensity of fragrance is achieved (usually three repetitions is needed), then carefully strain out all the solid botanical material and reserve the oil.

If you are creating large quantities of infused oils that will not be used up quickly, it's best and safest to add a natural preservative. One quarter teaspoon of simple tincture of benzoin, available from many pharmacies, may be added per cup of infused oil. Benzoin is derived from styrax gum, believed to have sacred properties and to create a cleansing, protective action. (Make sure you have simple tincture, not compound tincture, which is also known as Friar's Balsam.)

Vitamin E may also be used as a preservative. However, be aware that much of what is readily available is synthetic. Pierce one Vitamin E capsule and add the contents per every cup of infused oil. Jojoba oil is not a true oil but a plant lipid with antioxidant properties. Blend it with other oils to discourage them from turning rancid. (Maintain the basic proportions of oil to botanicals, however, even when using multiple oils.)

Casting Spells Using Oils

Oils have always been prized components of magic spells. However, not all oils are truly oils, and not all oils are even truly botanical.

Essential Oils

Essential oils are not true oils, despite their name. They are volatile liquids extracted by various methods (usually, but not always, by steam distillation) from aromatic botanicals. Modern aromatherapy is the manipulation of these essential oils for therapeutic, cosmetic, magical, and spiritual purposes. The roots of aromatherapy stretch back to ancient China, Egypt, Mesopotamia, and the Middle East. If you would like to access the power of a botanical, essential oils are the most concentrated form and as such have many magical uses. Once upon a time, essential oils were also referred to as chemical oils, especially in older grimoires. This relates not to their chemical constituents, which we are only now beginning to understand, but to their previous use in alchemy, the term being a corruption of alchemical oils.

Their potential physical impact upon you is as concentrated as their magical power:

★ Never *take essential oils internally without expert supervision*

★ *Even when taken externally, they are used sparingly, drop by drop. Each drop packs a lot of power. More is rarely better*

★ *Because their power is volatile and fleeting, when creating magical baths, potions, or oils, essential oils are usually the last ingredients added so as to maximize the intensity of their power and fragrance*

★ *In general, essential oils are not appropriate for use during pregnancy, especially early pregnancy*

★ *Because essential oils are so concentrated (and because some are profound skin irritants) they are usually diluted in true oils (usually referred to as "carrier oils") before using*

Fragrance is an extremely important component of magic, particularly in romantic spells and spirit-summoning spells. Each spirit has a characteristic aroma, which calls them and by which they may be identified. In ancient Egypt, this was one way that true spiritual visitation was determined: the deities signaled their presence through the sudden appearance of their characteristic fragrance. Vestiges of this belief survive in folkloric Christianity, where the devil is described as appearing amid the smell of brimstone. (Signature fragrance isn't limited to the spirit realm alone. In the 1944 Ray Milland movie, *The Uninvited*, the ghost signals her presence via the scent of mimosa.) Fragrance, especially as transmitted by true botanicals, is the primary and most effective magical device for communicating between realms.

The human sense of smell remains the most mysterious of our senses. The olfactory system (the part of our brain that processes scent) is near what is known as the *reptilian brain*, the most ancient and least-understood part of the human brain. Scent is our primal sense, the one shared most closely with the animal and spirit realms. Magic is a primordial art; to truly master it, one must access these inherent primordial talents. The sense of smell may be the most concrete, accurate way we have of identifying and accessing *heka*, magic power. Essential oils are frequently the most concentrated, potent, and accessible way of accessing an individual plant's *heka*, even though this very power means they must be handled with care.

True Oils

True oils, also known as fixed, carrier, or base oils (because they carry essential oils' energies and serve as their base) have always been perceived as precious and sacred. The ancient Egyptians had an astonishing repertoire of true oils, far greater than our own. Although true oils are used as carriers for the magic powers inherent in dried botanicals or essential oils, they also have their own magic power, and spells can be cast using true oils alone. Castor oil has protective, commanding magic properties, while sweet almond oil is a component of many romantic and erotic spells, for instance. Mineral oil (baby oil) is not a botanical, but a petroleum product: its magical uses are restricted mainly to hexes—malevolent spells.

There are several ways to distinguish essential oils from true oils. Essential oils, also known as *volatile* oils from the Latin *volare*, "to fly away," evaporate completely into air, without leaving a trace. Although they may deteriorate and their power fade, they do not grow rancid. In contrast, true oils will leave a ring or residue and will not evaporate— as anyone who's had to clean out a greasy pan can attest. True oils will also grow rancid over time, although some become rancid more quickly than others.

True oils are, in general, extracted from the seeds or fruits of plants. Cold-pressed oils (which will almost always be labeled as such) are preferable, when possible. (Grapeseed oil, for instance, can only be extracted via the use of solvents.)

Fragrance Oils

Because real essential oils are extracted via expensive, labor-intensive, time-consuming processes, synthetics are often substituted. If an essential oil is too reasonably priced, be cautious. Often we do get what we pay for. Labeling is not always clear and manufacturer's terms may be meant very loosely.

Essential oils cannot be obtained from every botanical. There is no such thing as cherry or cucumber or apple essential oil. Furthermore, essential oils must be derived, by definition, from botanical material. There is no such product as essential oil of rain, although products exist that reproduce the fragrance of a rainy day. Invariably, these products are crafted from synthetic materials, known as fragrance oils, the staples of the perfume industry. Some are real dead ringers for the genuine material and can fool many an expert.

However, because no plant material is actually contained, fragrance oils lack true, complete magical power. That said, sometimes, especially for candle magic, fragrance alone may be sufficient to spark *your* magic, to evoke a response from your brain. In general, fragrance oils are fine for dressing candles, but not for the body.

Hydrosols

Hydrosols, also called hydrolats, are the other product of the aromatherapy industry. When essential oils are produced by steam distillation, water is passed through the botanical material and then eventually separated out; that water has also been magically transformed by the distillation process: it is no longer plain water but contains plant molecules. Although other flower waters are sold (usually rose or orange blossom water) these are frequently only flower-scented or flower-infused waters. Hydrosols actually carry the power of their respective botanicals. Hydrosol production is an old alchemical process, although it lay dormant, forgotten, and unappreciated for centuries. Now fresh attention is paid to hydrosols; new ones become available every day. They are an increasingly important component of magic spells.

Flower Essence Remedies

Alchemists, witches, and herbalists have always painstakingly gathered morning dew from individual plants to access its magic powers. Infused with the specific power of the particular plant, these tiny liquid dewdroplets also contain the perfect balance of the four primal elements: the power of water, the earth radiating through the plant, the surrounding air and fire from the sun.

Once upon a time, if you wanted to access this power, you were limited to the plants growing on your lawn. This is no longer the case. Modern flower essence remedies bring the power of flowers from all over Earth—from the Amazon rainforest to the Australian outback—right to your door.

The pioneer and founding father of modern flower essence remedies was Dr. Edward Bach, a Harley Street physician and homeopath. Dr. Bach eventually came to the realization that true, complete healing was not possible when approached solely from the physical plane. Emotional and spiritual imbalances are the root causes of dysfunction of all kinds. True healing and transformation must be accessed through the soul and emotions. Dr. Bach devoted the rest of his life, at great personal sacrifice, to developing the original Bach flower essence remedies, which provide the vehicle for this healing and transformation. According to Dr. Bach, the flowers communicated to him directly, sharing their secrets and potential for healing with him. Since then, many other flower essence practitioners have followed in Dr. Bach's footsteps to bring us greater access to a wider variety of botanical material than ever before.

It's easy to be confused between flower essence remedies and essential oils: they have extremely similar names and are even packaged in a similar manner (in tiny glass vials). Although they complement each other's powers and work very well together, they are extremely different and *cannot* be substituted for one another.

Essential oils are true plant extracts, with extremely potent and sometimes scientifically documented physical effects. When I taught therapeutic aromatherapy, many of my students were nurses learning to incorporate essential oils into conventional hospital practice. All essential oils are, to a degree, antiseptic; many have potent anti-bacterial and anti-viral effects in addition to whatever magical power they also hold.

No one completely understands how flower essence remedies work, although they do—profoundly. General consensus is that it is a form of vibrational healing. Flower essences are pure water, infused and charged with the plant's energy and vibration. There's no need to kill the plant to access this energy; typically only a few carefully chosen leaves are used. By definition, the remedy won't work if the plant used is not a powerful, healthy specimen. These essences provide a healing bridge between the soul of the botanical and your own. While essential oils may be understood as the lifeblood of a plant, flower essence remedies capture the plant's aura.

Flower essence remedies are the exception to the rule regarding botanicals' impact on the physical plane—there is no direct physical effect. All the effects are felt on the emotional, spiritual, and magical planes. They are safe for everyone's use: children, animals, crystals, and other plants.

When using flower essence remedies the most common mode of administration is internal. Manufacturers will supply directions, however the standard dose for most is four drops four times a day. Topical administration is also extremely effective: massage the flower essence remedy into the body, particularly into the soles of feet and the thin skin stretched between thumb and forefinger.

Every manufacturer of flower essence remedies has a specific repertoire of botanicals. When flower essence remedies are cited in the text, the name of their manufacturer follows in parenthesis. For example: Mugwort (FES).

Spell-casting Using the Powers of the Elements

In Western magic and philosophy, Earth's power is traditionally broken down into four components, known as the elements: Air, Earth, Fire, and Water. Air and Fire are traditionally considered male or yang energies, while Earth and Water are most typically perceived as female, or yin. Life springs from earth and water but air and fire are necessary to spark the process. Healthy magic power derives from the harmonious balance of these elements.

From a magical standpoint, the power of each element is unique, specific, and alive. Depending upon the purpose of your spell, one element may be invoked or emphasized over the others. Power also derives from the interplay between the elements. Power is enhanced when the elements intermingle and form a threshold. Steam emerges from the marriage of water and fire, for instance, and is a potent force for spiritual cleansing and protection.

Individuals are influenced by these elements, too. One or more elements will predominate in every individual's natal astrological chart and will thus influence not only their character but also the type of magic spell that usually appeals most to that individual and is most accessible. I have listed the elemental affiliations of the astrological signs below, however an accurate gauge can only be received from a complete birth chart. Someone who is a Taurus, an earth sign, but who has five other planets in a water sign is a very watery person, despite their sun sign.

The elements are easily understood if one considers their qualities.

Air

Air serves as a transmitter and a messenger. Because magic (and some schools of higher physics) asserts that nothing that exists truly disappears, to say that something "vanishes into thin air" is meant very literally when discussing magic spells. Candles that access the power of fire also summon the power of air: what is burned disappears into the air.

Air is associated with astral travel; witches fly through the air even if the journey is accomplished with dreams or visions.

Air is considered a masculine, yang energy.

Fragrance is the language of air. Word charms also draw upon air power.

Air signs: Gemini, Libra, Aquarius.

Earth

Earth is our battery and generator, providing capacity for growth and solidity. Earth is a particularly important element for those journeying into magical realms because earth provides stability, reality, and gravity. Magicians should spend time in the garden, even if not gardening, and barefoot whenever possible. If this isn't appealing, play with real clay (not synthetic), or make mud pies like a child. Go to the spa and take a mud bath.

Earth is considered a feminine, yin power.

Earth's magical power is accessed through the botanicals that are rooted in Earth, figures formed from clay, and dirt itself, as in graveyard dirt or crossroads dirt.

Earth signs: Taurus, Virgo, Capricorn.

Fire

Fire is the most independent of elements, defying all illusions of human control. Fire heals, energizes, cleanses, and purifies. Fire is transformative and must always be treated with respect. Although you can get into trouble with any element (think floods, mudslides, tornadoes) fire is commonly the most dangerous. I cannot emphasize enough: *never assume that because you're engaged in magical or spiritual acts that common-sense fire safety does not also apply*. Fire is *never* completely safe. Be vigilant.

Fire is a masculine, yang energy.

Candles are the most popular form of fire magic. Magical bonfires and lamps are also lit. Magic mirrors are sometimes used to access fire's transformative (and potentially destructive) powers.

Fire signs: Aries, Leo, Sagittarius.

Water

Water is the element most affiliated with magic. Water is where life originates, not just as an abstract concept or in Darwinian theory, but literally for each of us as we emerge from our mother's amniotic sacs. Water is the element of psychic power and intuitive knowledge.

Water is a feminine, yin energy.

Water spells are conducted in the bathtub and at the seashore. Water spells include those incorporating lunar charged waters, magically charged waters, and captured rainwater.

Water signs: Cancer, Scorpio, Pisces.

Fire and Water, extreme yang and yin, are a matched pair, leaving Earth and Air paired with each other. Like yin/yang forces in general, the elements don't exist in mutual exclusivity. Magic may be performed with only one element (an Air-magic word charm) but is most frequently a combination of two or more forces. For instance, incense combines botanical power (Earth) with Fire, to produce fragrant smoke (Air). A complex spell that involves dressing a candle with botanical oil, and then burning it while you're bathing in a magical infusion combines all four elements simultaneously.

This grouping of the four elements of Air, Earth, Fire, and Water is the traditional Western system and is the one most commonly shared by magical traditions. However, it is not the only system:

★ *Chinese magic traditionally counts five elements. Although metal is important in most other traditions, too, Chinese philosophy emphasizes this importance by counting Metal as one of the elements, alongside and equal to the Western four*
★ *Jewish magic traditionally counts three elements. Air (or ether) is considered so ubiquitous that it doesn't need to be counted as an element. Therefore only Water, Earth, and Fire are recognized as elements*

Casting Spells Incorporating the Power of Metal

Although magic in its modern form stems from the discovery of metal and smithcraft, metal today is an under-utilized modern magical material. Perhaps this reflects ancient taboos on the material and the role of the blacksmith.

Each metal, like each stone or botanical, projects a specific magical energy, although as there are fewer metals than the vast quantities of botanicals or crystals, it's easier to sum up these powers.

★ *Brass: protection, love*
★ *Copper: love, healing*
★ *Gold: wealth, vitality*
★ *Lead: domination, binding (the most frequent material for curse tablets)*
★ *Silver: protection, fertility*
★ *Tin: wealth, luck, divination*

The most powerful magical metal, however, and among the most magically charged of all materials on Earth, is iron.

Iron

The metal most associated with magic, worldwide, is iron. Because iron is not found in its pure state except as a meteorite, it was known as the Metal of Heaven and perceived as a gift from sacred powers. Meteors were carved into representations of deities: the original cult statue housed inside the Temple of

Artemis at Ephesus, one of the ancient world's Seven Wonders, was carved from a meteorite. The most sacred representation of the goddess Kybele was an uncut meteor, believed by many to remain buried under the foundations of Saint Peter's Basilica, which was built over her Roman temple.

Iron provides power and protection. Magically speaking, iron is reputed to restore health, provide vitality, both physical and psychic, and cure impotence. Malevolent spirits are invariably frightened of iron: it repels them and chases them away. Iron boxes protect magical tools the way a lead blanket protects a person during the x-ray process. Because iron is the metal of truth, traditionally in areas of Africa, and perhaps in some areas still, people would swear on iron in the way that others swear on the Bible or Koran. One of the simplest protective spells involves placing an iron knife or tool under one's pillow, not to serve as a ready weapon but to offer spiritual protection while you sleep.

With the exception of menstrual blood, no single item is more associated with magic than iron. In fact the two powers, menstrual blood and iron, are intrinsically linked. While other metals, like stones, may be perceived as Earth's bones, iron ore is regarded as Earth's menstrual blood.

Despite or because of its great power, iron is a dangerous, volatile element. Iron is used for healing, in magical ritual, and also through surgery, dentistry, acupuncture, and any field of medicine that requires metal tools. It is also an instrument of death: knives and guns wound and kill.

Earth's Original Professional Magician: the Smith, Master of Fire

Magic in its modern state arrived with the advent of the Iron Age. The smith's art, the original alchemy, was kept secret for centuries: those who knew it were able to forge weapons that could completely dominate their neighbors. By virtue of their contact with this magic material, and because they alone were privy to its secrets, smiths were more than just artisans: they were the original magicians, the Masters of Fire. Smiths became the first professional magicians (as opposed to shamans), called in to perform spell-casting on behalf of others.

Smiths were simultaneously respected and needed, feared and persecuted:

★ *Because the smith is in close contact with the ultimate power substance and, in fact, bends it to his will, he is perceived as possessing more magic power than the average person. He is protected and his personal magical energy continually replenished and reinvigorated by iron*

★ *However, because iron ore may be perceived as Earth's menstrual blood, a substance typically restricted or taboo, the ironworker who handles it openly and constantly may also be perceived as tainted. On the one hand, the smith is powerful enough to break taboos and thrive, but on the other, this contact makes conservative elements of society uncomfortable. The smith is able to go where others cannot, perform rituals that others cannot: whatever spiritual cleansing or protective rituals the smith requires for his own spiritual survival and protection are unknown to everyone outside the ironworking clan, and thus are suspect*

★ *Another perception derives from Central Asia's Turkish tribes. They believed that raw metals in general came from Earth's bowels. The raw materials were Earth's waste products, which would ultimately develop into finished metal, by itself, over long periods of time, if they were left undisturbed and buried. The smith's oven is, thus, a substitute for Earth's womb. This artificial womb gives birth to metal. The Master of Fire is thus believed to assert power over Time as he accelerates the process. Because of this he has healing powers and can read the future, but he is also always on the verge of spiritual disaster: digging ore out of the Earth, rooting around in Earth, any kind of digging is akin to rape. Only the ironworker knows if and how he can be purified*

The ironworker became a much-needed member of society. Beyond smith craft, he was typically also a healer, herbal practitioner, dentist, surgeon, body artist, and often the sole person permitted to perform circumcision and thus in charge of spiritual initiation. He carves amulets, devises rituals, and confers with the Spirits on behalf of others, a combination artisan-shaman. Secrets of metalworking were carefully guarded. Smiths evolved into clans, their techniques into family secrets.

The concept that one can pay someone else to cast a spell for you enters magic as well. A professional class of magical practitioners was born. The smith's wife, the woman who has sex with the Master of Fire, bears his children, and may be his professional assistant, becomes transformed into a person of power in her own right, typically performing the role of herbalist, midwife and women's healer, henna artist (henna also being a substance associated with menstrual blood), and, especially, fortune teller. In some traditional African areas, a wedding may be delayed until the smith's wife can arrive to dress the bride's hair, provide her henna or otherwise bless and attend her.

Societal ambivalence toward the smith cannot be emphasized enough; it will eventually be projected onto magic itself. The history of ironworking to a great extent parallels the history of magic working. Although the smith is required by society, he and his family also remain apart and distinct. People need them, their services are necessary, yet people are afraid to get close to them, or allow them to live as fully integrated members of society. Their very power and skill sets them apart. The Bible associates ironworkers with the Kenites, descendants of Cain, a Jewish tribe that isn't one of the Twelve Tribes of Israel. The most famous Kenite, the otherwise unarmed woman Jael, kills the fleeing enemy general Sisera with a hammer, one of the smith's primary tools.

Ironworkers developed into nomads, traveling from town to town, village to village, staying as long as there was work, and then moving on. This is still true in parts of Africa and Western Asia. There are still Bedouin tribes who await the arrival of the smith to perform circumcisions.

Complicating the picture even further is that the smiths providing services to the majority culture are frequently members of minority groups. It is a complex relationship with tremendous potential for tension: the ironworker performs ritual functions and serves as a repository of spiritual knowledge for traditions that he may or may not share.

In Europe, smithcraft is associated with Tinkers, Travelers, and, most especially, the Romany, who traveled with the Tatar and Mongol armies, performing metalwork. Romany culture, as first witnessed by Europeans, is very typical of ironworking clans: the men were metal smiths while the women told fortunes. In rural Africa and Western Asia, smiths are frequently of Jewish origin, although their personal traditions may have veered far from conventional Judaism. Persecution of the Ethiopian Jewish community, the *Beta Israel*, derives both from their religion *and* from their traditional occupation as ironworkers. The *Ineden*, smiths associated with the at least nominally Muslim Tuareg, are also believed to be of Jewish origin. Distinct clans, they perform the role of general handymen for the majority group: blacksmith, jeweler, armourer, woodworker, healer, herbalist, poet, musician, singer, and general consultant on spiritual and traditional matters. Essential to traditional Tuareg culture, they are simultaneously of low status.

With the coming of Christianity, European ironworkers would be vilified and identified with the devil, who was frequently depicted in the guise of a smith.

Some of their traditional spiritual power remained: in the original Gretna Green weddings, the couple was able to cross the border from England and be married by the smith.

Saint Patrick's Breastplate, a famous Irish prayer attributed to the saint, calls on God for protection against *"incantations of false prophets, against the black laws of paganism, against spells of women, smiths and druids, against all knowledge that is forbidden the human soul."*

Because one can safely assume that any modern metal has not been extracted from Earth using respectful, propitiating spells and rituals, any new metal with which you work should be thoroughly cleansed and charged. That said, silver and iron are both believed to be incorruptible; although they may be used for ill, malevolent vibrations should not cling to them as they will to other metals or materials.

Metal is incorporated into all manner of spells, from the simple to the complex. Metal steadily, constantly and consistently radiates its power: the spell, thus, keeps going even after initial human participation is ended.

Magic rings, for instance, need to be initially crafted, charged, and consecrated but once this has been done, they radiate their own power, drawing toward you whatever they have been programmed to pull, even as your attention turns elsewhere.

Basic household and farm tools are often incorporated into magic spells. What we perceive as mundane was once recognized as exceptionally magically charged. The magic remains, it is human perception that changes. Hammers, knives, and other metal tools are shared by many occupations. The anvil is reserved for the smith and thus is full of power and sacredness.

An anvil converts to an altar and may be used as such even by someone who is not a smith. That person begins the following spell at Step 3 and assumes the role of the smith in Steps 6 and 7.

✳ Anvil Blessing and Magical Activation Spell

1. Before the anvil is made, the smith prays and petitions that it will be reliable, powerful, and will bring luck.

2. When the anvil is complete, it's hidden until its activation ceremony.

3. The owner of the new anvil gives a feast in honor of the anvil.

4. After drinking and dining, the anvil is brought out to receive the crowd's admiration. Placed in the center of the table, it becomes an instant altar.

5. A white candle is placed atop the anvil, with another placed at each side, for a total of three candles.

6. The smith leads prayers that the anvil will bring healing, prosperity, and *baraka*.

7. The smith strikes the anvil for the first time, then the crowd showers it with offerings—small metal coins, libations of brandy—so that good fortune will be shared by all.

Spell-casting Using the Power of Minerals

"*Minerals*" includes rocks, crystals, and gemstones. Many associate crystals with New Age philosophy, but gemstone therapy and the magic of minerals are about as old age as you can possibly get. Modern magic is profoundly influenced by the power of iron, but prior to the Iron Age there was the Stone Age.

You think you've never accessed gem power? Most of us have, even if unwittingly. The diamond ring placed on the finger of an affianced woman serves to ensure sexual fidelity *and* relieve sexual inhibitions. Jeweled earrings, of all kinds, offer protection to a vulnerable threshold of the body. Many anthropologists assert that all jewelry originally derives from amulets. Alongside shells and seeds, the earliest jewelry was stone. Jewelry may be placed on the body carelessly. However, if it is combined with conscious intent, incantation, petition and/or visualization, something as simple as adorning the body becomes a powerful magic spell. Placing a ring, a bracelet or a locket on someone else's body is potentially a discreet but very powerful method of casting a spell upon them.

Crystals are worn, placed upon altars, added to conjure bags, placed under pillows and used in a wide variety of spells. Beyond specific geologic analysis, distinctions between rocks, crystals, and gemstones tend to derive from human perception of value, with the term *"gemstone"* implying greatest value, *"plain rock"* the least. Of course, what's valuable from a financial or aesthetic perspective may not correspond to magical value.

Every specific type of mineral formation, like each specific botanical, has its own hidden powers, attributes, and gifts. Like botanicals, from a magical perspective the mineral kingdom teems with life. The magical quality that characterizes the mineral kingdom (to distinguish it from others) is memory. Stones are believed to retain memories of everything that occurs to them or in their presence. They are Earth's silent witness to history.

Because their nature is so different from our own, even more so than with botanicals, which are clearly born, eat, and die, it can be very difficult to perceive minerals as *alive*. Although anyone can access the magic power of crystals superficially just by tucking a crystal into a mojo hand, in order to work closely with them, it's necessary to acknowledge that unique memory, that minerals can feel emotions of a kind (the spectrum runs from loyalty and benevolence to resentment of bad treatment) and can communicate their knowledge. Stones have no mouths: they can never learn to speak in the exact manner of a human. However, we can learn to hear and listen to them.

Once upon a time, because of great respect for minerals' magic powers and their formidable powers of memory, as much care, if not more, was taken when gathering (harvesting) stones as it was with botanicals.

Many cultures perceived stones and metals, not as distinct products of Earth for human use, but literally as part of Mother Earth's body. Stones are often perceived as her bones or teeth. From that perspective, great care must be taken when extracting and using them. Only certain people were authorized to gather stones, using very specific propitiatory ritual. Profound cleansing rituals were undertaken before and after their harvest. Stones were removed with care and respect. Offerings and libations were given to Earth as reciprocal payment and compensation.

Perhaps you have access to a stone that's been treasured for a very long time, a museum piece, as it were. In that case, appropriate rites and care may have been taken. Otherwise, it is fair to assume that the rocks and crystals available today were not removed from Earth with love and care, but yanked out brutally and disrespectfully. As crystals have grown in popularity, the temptation to exploit this popularity for the purpose of some quick cash frequently outweighs any metaphysical concerns.

Assume therefore that crystals may arrive complete with grouchy, resentful attitudes. Furthermore, minerals are the witnesses of human experience too. Minerals are absorbent, absorbing surrounding emotion. Many minerals, particularly the most expensive—diamonds, emeralds, and rubies—are extracted amidst great human suffering. The stones carry these emotions with them as they travel to your hands.

All is not hopeless, however. Stones may be cleansed. Cleansing can remove memory stores, like wiping a computer's memory, allowing for a fresh start. The depth of memory removal depends upon the stone and the cleansing methods used.

Stones need to be charged for a purpose or to harmonize with your personal energy, to enhance your partnership.

＊ To Program or Charge a Crystal

1. Cleanse the crystal using the most suitable technique.
2. Hold it in your hands.
3. Clear your mind.
4. When you feel that your energy and that of the crystal are synchronized, state your intention, goal, or desire clearly, lucidly, and succinctly.
5. Repeat it until it feels right. Speak out loud if possible.
6. When charging feels complete, put the crystal down and consciously detach your attention from it.

Stones are used in their natural state or polished and cut. A specific stone can also be selected and then engraved with a specific design. This creates a talisman, which is then usually worn or carried on the body. There are healing talismans, love-drawing talismans, and protective talismans, among many others. This practice brings magic into the realm of professionals.

Anyone can find a special stone on the beach; not everyone can engrave a gemstone with accuracy and precision.

The following ritual for cleansing and activating gemstones for healing and magic comes from India, birthplace of extremely sophisticated gemstone therapy.

✴ To Cleanse and Activate a Gemstone

1. The night before you intend to wear your stone, immerse it in a cup of fresh milk.
2. Remove it and place the milky stone on an altar, before a sacred image, in the company of quartz crystals and any other objects you hold sacred.
3. Leave it overnight.
4. Arise at dawn and rinse the stone.
5. Raise it towards the rising sun.
6. Pray and petition that the stone fulfills your desires.
7. Wear, carry, or use it as needed.

Diamonds, emeralds, sapphires, and rubies have profound magical uses as well as their more conventional role in jewelry. Both magical and conventional uses, however, are limited to those who can afford these expensive gems. Luckily, the absolutely most powerful magic stones are easily affordable and, in some cases, free, if you can only find them. The following are some of the most magically powerful stones.

Quartz Crystals

Quartz looks like beautiful sparkling ice. It is believed to be tied to that watery trinity of lunar/oceanic/female energy. Clear quartz crystals are used as scrying tools: they are able to enhance the psychic ability and magic power of those who handle them consistently or who are in their presence. Likewise, quartz crystals are used to activate and empower other stones or tools. Quartz crystals may be attached to magic wands. Pack quartz crystals in with tarot cards, runes, or any other magical tools to enhance their power. Quartz crystals are used for cleansing purposes. Larger specimens left in a room have a vacuum cleaner effect on negative energy, helping to maintain a fresh atmosphere. (Remember to cleanse the crystal periodically, as if the vacuum bag was full.) It is a protective, empowering stone.

Hag, Witch, Holed, or Holey Stones

These names all refer to the same type of stone. Holed stones are exactly as their name describes: small pebbles or stones with naturally occurring perforations, they are gifts from the Earth Mother. They cannot be manufactured. Sometimes you'll just find one: a common pebble with a hole. Pick it up. It is a priceless magical gift. Holed stones provide enhanced magic power, protection against malevolent spirits, humans, and the Evil Eye. They are also used to regenerate and protect physical vitality. Wear it around your neck or hang it over your bed so that you can absorb its power while you sleep.

Lodestones

Also known as magnetite, lodestones are magnetic iron ore. They are the magical bridge between the realms of stone and iron. They possess transcendentally powerful magic energy. Lodestones attract and draw good fortune: money, success, and love. They're also used in healing rituals: lodestones can draw pain from the body in the same manner that they can draw a lover or money towards you.

Lodestones may be used individually or in matched pairs. They are perceived to have gender; depending on purpose, you may require a male or female lodestone or a pair. It's easier to determine the gender of a lodestone than that of a parakeet. Female lodestones are rounded; phallic-looking lodestones announce their manhood.

Wherever people have been in contact with lodestones, they have used them magically. Alexander the Great distributed lodestones to his troops to protect them from djinn. Chinese magic favors lodestones as wedding rings, to ensure the happy survival of a marriage. In ancient Rome, statues of Venus and Mars were carved from lodestone so as to be magnetically attracted, demonstrating the powerful sexual magnetism between the two forces.

The origins of lodestones are shrouded in mystery. Their use goes back to ancient times. Magnetite, their more scientific name, derives from the ancient city of Magnesia, from whence they were once mined. Lodestones are a positive, benevolent force, always used to draw good fortune. Lodestones, like the root charm High John the Conqueror, are thus not tools for hexing. The worst thing you can do with a lodestone is fail to avail yourself of its power.

Christian legend has it that the stone upon which Christ's body rested for three days following his crucifixion was a lodestone. Its miraculous properties were revealed to Godfrey of Bouillon when he led the First Crusade to Jerusalem. While praying in Christ's Sepulcher a voice whispered to him that his victory was assured if he'd only carry away a bit of the stone. He listened to the voice's advice, which proved true. However, according to this legend, the kings who succeeded him paid no attention to the stone and therefore the Holy Land was lost to them.

In addition to memory, lodestones are acknowledged to possess consciousness, intelligence, even wit, and especially a soul. Although any rock or crystal is alive, lodestones are *really* alive! Because of this perception, lodestones must be replenished consistently by "*feeding*" (though all crystals need to be recharged periodically). Now you can't just give a lodestone a little bit of your own dinner, the way you'd give a treat to a dog. Lodestones have their own preferred nutritional supplement: fine iron shot, also known as iron filings, iron dust or, in Hoodoo parlance, *magnetic sand*. Magnetic sand is also perceived as possessing a "*drawing*" power all of its own, and is a component of many magic spells, with and without lodestones.

Feeding Lodestones
There are various techniques for feeding lodestones, depending upon different traditions.

 A Mexican Method

Just like people, lodestones have a working week, but then need some time off for rest and relaxation.

1. On Friday evening, place lodestones in a glass of wine, water, or aguardiente (strong liquor), and leave it there overnight.
2. Remove it from the liquid on Saturday and sprinkle it with magnetic sand.
3. Let the lodestone rest until Sunday evening or Monday morning, then send it back to work in a conjure bag, pocket charm, or whatever normally does for you.

✴ Hoodoo Method

1. Dress the lodestone with your choice of condition oils. Coordinate the oil to suit your desired results. Thus if you want the lodestone to draw a new romance to you, choose a love-drawing oil, like **Come to Me, Lover**. Substitute essential oils, true oils, or sprinkle the lodestone with a few drops of whiskey or similar beverage.
2. Sprinkle with magnetic sand.

Sometimes, after extensive spell-work or when used to make **Magnet Oil**, a lodestone can become excessively drained.

The following formulas are intended to feed a drastically depleted lodestone:

✴ Overtired Lodestone Spell (1)

1. Anoint the lodestone with olive oil.
2. Place it in a pouch filled with dirt for three days. (Crossroads dirt is best, if possible.)

✴ Overtired Lodestone Spell (2)

1. Place the lodestone in a glass, stone, or metal bowl.
2. Cover it with dirt. (Again crossroads dirt, if possible, but any dirt will work.)
3. Keep the bowl inside a closed cabinet for three days.

Gem Elixirs

The power of minerals may also be accessed in liquid form. This ancient method has been revived by manufacturers of flower essence remedies. Modern gem-stone elixirs are sold with flower essence remedies and used in the same manner. Commercial preparations are, as of the time of writing, of consistently high quality and provide access to a greater number of gems at accessible prices than most people will ever have access to, in a controlled, safe, easy-to-use manner.

However, this is an ancient technique. Gem elixirs may also be crafted for oneself.

An Ancient Egyptian Method of Creating Gem Elixirs

1. Place crystals on the grass and leave them outside overnight.
2. Collect the dew in the morning.

Modern Methods for Crafting Gem Elixirs

★ Fill cut-crystal bottles with spring water. Let them charge in the sun and/or moonlight. This water may then be consumed or added to the bath

★ Place the crystal in pure spring water in a glass bowl. Energize and activate in the sunlight. The water absorbs the crystal's power and vibrations. Bottle and use as required

Spell-casting Using the Power of People

Yes, yes, of course, this sounds so obvious. Every magic spell is the product of a person. Without the person's intent and direction, magic energy just radiates and isn't channeled into a spell. However, some magic spells draw upon more than the energy, desire, and creative properties of one individual.

Not every spell is cast alone. Some spells require partners and

participants. In particular, healing and cleansing spells must often be done *for* the person intended to benefit from the spell. Always choose your spell partners wisely. Their individual magical energy radiates through your spell as powerfully as that of any botanical, mineral, or element. It's also crucial that those who might undermine the success of your spell, whether willfully or unintentionally, are not chosen as partners. Choose those whose goals are in harmony with your own, those who desire your success as much as you do.

An entire, living, breathing person isn't always required. Various parts of the human anatomy are believed to radiate with magic power, and just as they perform different anatomical functions, so different parts of the body perform different magic spell functions. Typically, the power of the body part is represented symbolically through an image of the particular part: the power of images is an important component of magic spells, and the milagro is a metal charm depicting a specific part of the anatomy. The most commonly depicted parts of the human body include the eyes, genitals, hands, and hearts. These are especially incorporated into healing and protective spells.

Sometimes, however, actual parts are required by spells, although "*part*" may be the wrong word. No pain is inflicted obtaining these parts although they may be obtained for the purpose of inflicting pain. Certain materials generated by the body are perceived as exceptionally magically charged. These materials, which the body sheds, still retain the essence of the body and a connection to the person they come from. By working on these materials, one may profoundly affect that other person. These materials are the *intimate items* deriving from a person's body. Hoodoo refers to them as *personal concerns*.

Because they render the other person vulnerable to magic, in theory, all these intimate items may be used for hexes. However, that is not their only or even their most frequent purpose.

Hair
Most frequently used in love and binding spells, hair is both an object of tremendous power and vulnerability.

Menstrual Blood

Menstrual blood is the ultimate magic power item. If you were forced to reduce magic to its most primal elements, you would be left with menstrual blood and iron (which may be perceived as Earth's menstrual blood).

Menstrual blood is the ultimate controlling mechanism. It provides spiritual protection, allegedly repels demons, and puts out fires. One drop is said to cause others to fall madly in love with you.

Many consider that oppression and discrimination against women stems from perceptions of menstruation as "unclean." An alternative view is that oppression and discrimination stem from the fear of women's power. Menstrual blood is considered the strongest magical substance on Earth. Menstruating women were isolated because of fear of their power. Until recently, for instance, in parts of Thailand, women were discouraged from riding on the top level of double-decker buses because that would place their genitals above men's heads, potentially destroying their power as well as that of their amulets. There are some who feel that all magic stems from menstrual and lunar mysteries. Judy Grahn's book *Blood, Bread and Roses* postulates that all human civilization stems from responses to perceptions of menstruation.

Menstruation may be referred to as a woman's *moon-time*, indicating that menstrual cycles, pregnancy, and tides all reflect the phases of the moon. It's also sometimes called *dragon-time*, the dragon being a metaphor for menstruation (which opens up new paths to ponder when considering tales of dragon-slaying heroes, especially those attempting to save virginal princesses).

You don't have any? You used to be able to buy menstrual blood. In ancient Italy, spiritual goods merchants sold used menstrual rags to those who couldn't provide their own.

Nail Clippings

These are used in a similar way to hair, however with slightly less impact. Frequently they are used together, each to reinforce the power of the other.

Saliva

Saliva has profound controlling and protective magical capacities.

Like menstrual blood, saliva is believed capable of repelling malevolent spirits and magic spells, hence the custom of spitting in the face of perceived danger. Saliva is also used magically to transmit desire.

Sexual Fluids

Male and female sexual fluids are considered intimate items of extreme power and vulnerability. Although these sexual fluids leave you vulnerable to the most notorious of love spells, they also have other uses. Semen is often invoked in healing spells (topical application allegedly cures headaches), while women's sexual juices provide access to the life-force: it was not an uncommon ingredient in ancient Chinese alchemists' potions. Women's vaginal secretions, both sexual juices and menstrual blood, were frequently the preferred food for vampires seeking increased sexual vitality and/or life-force.

Sweat

Sweat is most frequently used in love and sex spells. It is the closest natural substance men possess that compares to the magical power of menstrual blood.

Urine

While hair and nail clippings used in spells most frequently derive from another person, urine is almost inevitably your own. Many spells will instruct you to urinate on something. This is not intended as desecration, more in the fashion of a dog marking territory. Urine is believed to create a dominating effect.

There are plenty of spells involving fecal material, too. However, you won't find them in this book. Every author has her limits. The ancient Egyptians cultivated a science that distinguished between the powers inherent in the fecal material of various species—crocodiles, donkeys, humans, cats, all sorts of animals.

Casting Spells Using Names

The magical perspective does not always correspond with the modern scientific view as to what constitutes the human body, or where it begins and ends. Most magical systems acknowledge the existence of a subtle body, the aura, a radiant presence that surrounds the human body, so far undetectable by science. A person's name or names may also be considered magically as part of an individual's intrinsic identity and thus a source of great power and vulnerability.

Knowing someone's true name renders him or her vulnerable to your power. Think about Rumpelstiltskin. Once upon a time (and it still happens in some places), people were given various names, one for public use, one for ritual use, and another to be kept secret. Mothers would whisper names into their babies' ears, never to be repeated, so that one name would *always* be kept secret. In ancient Egypt, to describe someone possessing

exceptional magic power it was said that even their mother didn't know their name.

That connection between name and mother is crucial magically. As the ancient world became increasingly male-oriented, patriarchal cultures identified people by their own name and their father's name, so that someone might be called, for instance, Dana, child of Bill. The mother is rarely mentioned. There's one important exception: magic spells and magical documents. There, it's the mother's name that counts. Many consider that this reflects some sardonic humor; for the magical spell to be effective, the name has to be *right*. Because a mother is never suspect but may however harbor unsuspected secrets, the only way to guarantee true identity was to use the mother's name instead of the father's. This tradition is maintained in the directions in this book; follow it if you choose. Unless otherwise advised, the magical formula to write or call someone's name is: "[Name], child of [their mother's name]."

Names of Power

Angels, demons, and spirits of all kinds are summoned by calling their true name. Supposedly they can't resist the call. Much summoning magic depends upon this premise.

Of course, there is a caveat; this information was once transmitted orally: to be effective the names are supposed to be pronounced correctly. One has only to observe the conflict between historians, magical practitioners, and scholars of all kinds over how the names of relatively famous Greek and Egyptian deities are pronounced to appreciate the inherent problem.

There is a style of spell-casting that incorporates reeling off series of magical names. The Magical Papyri have some of these spells: there's nothing to

indicate that the practitioners of their time recognized these names any more than we do. They don't figure in surviving mythology; these names completely lack context.

Call me cautious, but I'm not comfortable summoning someone to enter my home (and life) if I'm not personally familiar with them, or at least have a little background information. Something about not talking to strangers. I wouldn't recommend it to you either. Where the original version of a spell veers off on a tangent of reciting a long list of Names of Power, I've indicated this but omitted the names. My recommendation is to insert your own Names of Power—those Spirits whom you trust, ancestral spirits, even perhaps living people whose assistance would be appreciated and whom you feel you can trust.

Spell-casting Using the Power of Planets

Because they're old systems that pre-date modern astronomy, in magical and astrological parlance, the luminaries, the sun and the moon, are considered planets just like other heavenly bodies, although this does not concur with modern scientific classifications. Modern astrologers *know* that technically the sun and moon are not planets, however both astrology and magic are *geocentric* systems, meaning that everything is perceived as revolving around Earth, even when this is not literally the case.

Some spell-casters rely heavily on astrological wisdom. Every day, every hour, every topic, every category has a planetary correspondence. The same applies to Chinese and Hindu magic, although their respective astrological systems differ from the Western system, which is based on the Babylonian astrology that so influenced Egyptian and Greek versions.

If you would like to synchronize your magic with the planets to this degree, information is easily obtainable from astrological sources and from many traditional grimoires.

Every planet possesses an astrological and magical influence (ancient Greek and Roman curse tablets were under the dominion of Saturn, for instance), however the planets most strongly identified with magic are our own, Earth, and its satellite, the Moon.

Earth

While the moon represents psychic ability, then Earth is our general vitality. Both are required for optimal magic power. According to many worldwide traditions with little else in common, Earth is the material from which humans are created. Earth is our mother: we are born from her body, and are then returned to her to await rebirth while the corporal body decays and becomes part of Earth once more, in a never-ending cycle. Without actual extended consistent physical contact with Earth our vitality, and hence our magic power, suffers and diminishes.

Earth is also very literally the dirt under our feet. Dirt may be used to empower us and empower our spells. There are various traditions that pursue actual physical healing by packing the patient into heated sand. Moor mud is used to detoxify the body. The dirt at shrines and saints' tombs is perceived as exceptionally charged with power. Bits of dirt are carried as talismans; they may also be sprinkled over items to empower and revitalize them.

Not all dirt is equal. Currently perhaps the most famous dirt in the world comes from the Roman Catholic shrine at Chimayo, New Mexico, although the dirt's miraculous reputation precedes Catholicism in the area. Every year thousands converge on Chimayo for the healing dirt. A testimonial room bears witness to miracles received. This dirt heals more than body and soul. When a good friend's computer crashed, at her wit's end, she placed a canister filled with Chimayo dirt on the computer and it miraculously started working again.

Certain magical traditions rely on the power of dirt more than others. In the twenty-first century, the Afro-Caribbean tradition of Palo Monte probably utilizes more types of dirt than any other. Palo spells may request four handfuls of dirt from a police station, two from a courthouse, three from a hospital, and so on. This magical tradition dates back at least to ancient Mesopotamia.

Although not every tradition pays such detailed attention to Earth, most utilize certain specific types of magical dirt, including:

★ *Crossroads dirt*
★ *Footprint dirt*
★ *Graveyard dirt*

Inherent energy is transmitted through contact with the dirt itself. Each will be discussed in greater detail elsewhere in this book.

The Moon

The moon is considered the ruler of all magical arts, and magic is timed to the phases of the moon:

★ *Spells intended to increase something (like money), or intended to initiate something new (a fresh romance) are coordinated with the waxing moon. Begin these spells on or just after the New Moon*
★ *Spells intended to decrease something (like debt), or cast for the purpose of banishing (an enemy) are coordinated with the waning moon. Begin these spells on or just after the Full Moon*

★ *The Dark of the Moon, those few days where the moon is not visible, just prior to the rebirth of the New Moon, is controversial. Some traditions will not cast spells during this period. Others, particularly those devoted to Dark Moon spirits like Hecate or Lilith, consider this a period of profound magical power which may be exploited as needed*

In Arabic folk custom, it's recommended that you keep an eye on moon phases. Whatever you find yourself doing at the moment when you first catch a glimpse of the brand new moon is the right thing for you to do.

Although it doesn't eliminate the need to charge items with personal energy, exposing virtually all magical tools, charms, and preparations to the beams of the Full Moon provides enhanced magical empowerment.

In general, although not always, magic worked with the moon herself (rather than just by timing via the phases) is women's magic. There is a trinity between the moon, women, the ocean and, by implication, all water. The moon is recognized as having a profound effect upon menstrual cycles and the tides. It is a reciprocal arrangement: since women have a natural affinity for the moon, they may more readily draw on its power.

In many cases lunar deities are female, with Artemis, Diana, Hecate, Selene, Lady Chang'o, and Ix Chel only a few of many examples. In other cases, particularly in ancient Egypt, the moon was perceived as male, but this perception was precisely because of the moon's perceived influence on women. The moon was seen as playing a male role. To the Egyptians, the moon was male because it was demonstrated to have profound control over women's fertility. It was believed that pregnancy could occur from exposure to moonbeams, and who else gets a woman pregnant but a man?

Drawing Down the Moon

This term is most familiar today as the title of Margot Adler's influential book, and refers to specific Wiccan spiritual rites by which the Goddess is requested to enter the body of her priestess and speak through her. (Some traditions also possess a parallel Drawing Down the Sun ritual, which invokes the male energy of the god.) However, this is a very ancient term that predates modern Wicca and may refer to various other rites or practices, depending upon magical tradition, and most especially the process of creating moon-infused waters.

Moon-infused Waters

The ancient Greeks called this technique "drawing down the moon" or the "Thessalian Trick." The Greeks believed that Thessalian witches held great power and metaphysical knowledge. This was considered one of their most important formulas.

This Chinese technique of drawing down the moon is used to create a magic mirror:

☀ Lunar-charged Magic Mirror

A small round mirror is required, ideally one crafted from precious metals such as gold or silver and ornamented with auspicious symbols of protection and good fortune.

1. On the night of the Full Moon, hold the mirror so that it reflects the moon for a minimum of three hours.

2. When you feel that sufficient lunar energy has been absorbed, wrap the mirror in a protective fabric pouch. This mirror is now off limits to everyone but its owner. Although one person may prepare this mirror for another, once given, the mirror belongs to one person exclusively. The remaining steps of this spell must only be performed by the mirror's owner.

3. For the next consecutive fifteen nights, reflect your face in the mirror over substantial blocks of time, so that the absorbed lunar power merges with your own. This is an interactive process, a sharing of essences: gazing into the mirror, you absorb the lunar gifts of radiance, beauty, psychic ability, and fertility, but the mirror simultaneously is imprinted with your personal power and desires.

4. When the fifteen-night period is complete, the mirror is considered charged and in harmony with the individual who owns it. It is now a profound magical tool for obtaining your wishes and desires.

To use the mirror repeat the initial ritual of drawing down the Full Moon, but now use the mirror as a direct communications device, a sort of personal hot line to the moon, to request gifts of love, marriage, psychic power, creative inspiration, personal fertility, or healing.

Spell-casting in Conjunction with the Power and Assistance of the Spirits

This style of spell-casting is unique. In other methods of spell-casting, the practitioner casts the entire spell from beginning to end. Spirit-oriented spells involve inducing, persuading, or coercing a powerful Spirit, usually a specialist in a field, to perform the magical action for you, on your behalf. Thus your spell is cast in order to persuade the Spirit to cast the crucial spell or create the needed magical energy transaction.

This area of magic veers dangerously close to religion and sometimes cannot be separated. In some cases, magical practices are what remain of what were once formal and sometimes very important religions. It is worthwhile, when considering the *permanence* of modern religions, to recall that organized worship of Isis, for instance, was not limited to Egypt but eventually expanded further south in Africa, throughout Western Asia and into Europe as far as what is now modern London, and spanned a period of several thousand years.

Spirits worshipped in religion as "*gods*" and "*goddesses*" are incorporated into magic spells. There is a crucial distinction between magic and religion though: religion may involve devotion to and worship of these spiritual entities. Magic invariably requests a reciprocal, cooperative relationship, although it may be a relationship characterized by love, respect, and awe. Both spirit and human are perceived as having needs, which, ideally, are mutually fulfilled by a successful magic spell.

Ultimately the most potent, powerful magic derives from spiritual partnership, working with guardian and allied spirits. This is also for many the most challenging, hard to access and *believe* magic, because it doesn't feel *real* to many people. It may be hard to believe or comprehend that a rock has a memory, but at least you can hold the rock in your hand. When you're working with spirits, are you actually working with *anything* or is this all just the stuff of myth, fairy tale, and make-believe?

Discussions about finding the goddess within, although perhaps extremely valuable from a spiritual or therapeutic perspective, present a further magical obstacle. If the goddess (and, by projection, any other magic power) is truly an aspect of oneself, why bother with any of the physical materials at all? Magic spells are, in general, a partnership between inner and outer powers—powers that are part of you, and those that are distinctly independent from you.

Our limited word pool also compounds the problem. Because we approach spirituality *literally*, we also approach religion. Seemingly neutral simple terms like *god* and *goddess* are actually highly charged with personal meaning and resonance. We think that when we use these terms we are all on common ground, but that's not necessarily so. Some use these terms to indicate supreme creators of the world; others use the terms for any type of spiritual entity. So to level the playing field, let's just use the term *spirits*

to name those powerful entities that resist human efforts to define them.

Like magic in general, every people, every culture on Earth, has at one time or another practiced some sort of spiritual interaction. Although it might be suggested today that someone claiming to have personal contact with spirits receive psychiatric counseling, at one time this was a common, if never commonplace, human experience.

Spiritual communications of all kinds, but especially the various methods of requesting spiritual participation in magic spells, exist in very consistent ways all around Earth.

If this seems unreal to you or if, based on religious background, you perceive that contact with spirits is potentially evil, there's good news. Although this is a powerful form of magic, it's easily avoided. Simply skip these spells and find others. Hoodoo, some of the most powerful magic of all, is practical magic devoid of spiritual encounters, as are many other systems. Work with what empowers you and makes you feel comfortable. On the other hand, if you are devoted to a spirit, you may incorporate spiritual petition into virtually every spell.

There is a host of spirits, legions. There are spirits to serve every purpose, and spirits with a vested interest in every topic. In addition to love spirits, protective spirits, healing spirits, etc., there are spirits of the bathroom, beer, and perfume. If something can be conceived, then there is at least one spirit attached to it.

Why do they assist us or even pay attention to us? For a variety of reasons, which ultimately may depend upon the nature of the particular spirit in question. Some are benevolent in general, some may have affection for you specifically; however the basic answer is because it is their job to do so. Dentists take care of teeth, doctors treat the ill, and spirits have their own department of expertise. It is thus important to petition the correct spirit for a specific purpose, although the spirits who work most consistently and powerfully for you are always your personal guardians and allies as well as your ancestral spirits.

One person's guardian angel can be someone else's demon: I Corinthians 10:20 describes Pagan sacrifices as being made to demons. The Pagans would have disagreed with that assessment. Many of the spirits invoked in magic may seem obscure today, however once upon a time they were huge stars of the spiritual firmament. The emergence of Christianity and Islam demoted many once-renowned spirits to the side-lines. This does not diminish their potential power. If you're willing to believe that a spirit has the power to assist you, then that spirit should be treated with respect and consideration. Never underestimate the power of even the lowest-level spiritual entity. Furthermore, other spirits, depending upon spiritual tradition, are more vital and empowered today than ever before.

At best, this human/spirit alliance creates mutually beneficial relationships of great affection, love, and devotion. There is something of a barter relationship involved: we feed the spirits and they care for us, so that we may feed them more and they may care for us more. The key to this relationship, even more than any other kind of magic, is reciprocity. Make an offering when you make a request. Respond with an acknowledgement of thanks when the request is fulfilled, whether by prayer, gesture, or through a gift or offering. Spirits, like people, possess preferences. These practices stem back thousands of years; there's a tremendous quantity of accumulated wisdom. It's not necessary to figure everything out for yourself, although intuition may be divinely inspired.

Spirit Categories

Angels

Angel literally translates as "messenger" in Greek, a direct translation from the Hebrew. Unlike other categories of spirits, angels do not accept "offerings," or at least not officially. They are customarily called through prayer, petition, and fragrance, although High Ritual Magic, based largely on information attributed to King Solomon, compels the presence of angels through sigils and talismans.

Specific angels maintain charge of all matters of life. There is an Angel of Conception, the Angel of Thieves, angels of various specific countries, and individual guardian angels. According to the Talmud, there are eleven thousand guardian angels per person. If you can think of it, it has a custodial agent.

In general, they are dynamic and fierce; creatures of light so blinding you can't help but see them even with your eyes closed. According to Jewish mysticism, angels are beings of light, but when an angel wishes to manifest in physical form, it takes earth, fashions clothing from it, and transforms itself.

Angels are discussed before other spiritual entities because they are somewhat different from others, and because (according to Islamic and Jewish traditions), angels are personally responsible for humanity's ability to cast spells. The Creator may have created magic power but angels taught people how to recognize it and what to do with it. They are our magical teachers.

Christian magic, reflecting theology, demands the existence of angels as creatures of pure goodness (with the exception of the fallen angels, who essentially lost their status as angels during the Fall), in clear opposition to demons, who are plainly *"bad."* This is not the case in Islamic, Jewish, and Pagan perceptions, where angels are just beings of power. There are good angels, "evil angels," and angels who may be persuaded to behave in either direction. Pious descriptions of "good" angels insist that they are asexual and gender-less, although ironically this is in opposition to the Bible, which describes the lust angels feel for human women (Genesis 6:1–4). Because these women conceive children, we can assume these particular angels to have been male with all working parts intact.

Instead of courting these human women with chocolates and roses, the angels bestowed the gift of knowledge—teaching the arts of astrology, magic, witchcraft, and cosmetics (not the triviality it may appear today but an ancient magical art). According to the *Book of Enoch* these teaching angels and their subjects included:

★ *Semjaza: enchantments and root cutting*
★ *Armaros: the resolving of enchantment*
★ *Baraquiel: astrology*
★ *Kokabel: constellations*
★ *Ezequeel: knowledge of the clouds*
★ *Araquiel: earth signs*
★ *Shamsiel: sun signs*
★ *Sariel: the phases of the moon*

Angels are ranked in various manners: Archangels, Throne Angels, Watchers, Seraphim, and Cherubim among others. The archangels command spirit hosts. Various spells request assistance from the archangels, however whether they are personally expected to appear or to delegate another from their host may be subject to interpretation.

There's little agreement among experts or traditions, particularly as regards to the archangels. Are there seven or are there four? And which ones are they?

The standard four archangels are Rafael, Gabriel, Michael, and Auriel, also spelled Uriel or Ariel. That much, at least, is agreed upon in Christian, Islamic, and Jewish traditions, and probably pre-dates all three. But do they serve alone or are there really seven archangels, corresponding to the seven planets visible with the naked eye and to that magic number, seven? If that's the case, who are the other three? Some possibilities include Cassiel/Kafziel, Zadkiel, Samael, Chamuel,

Jophiel, Raziel, Metatron, and Iblis. Even Lucifer makes it onto some lists, although obviously he loses his status after his Fall. (Most angels, but not all, have names ending with "-el," El being the ancient pan-Semitic name for the Creator, literally "*the Lord*.")

Demons

Demons are most frequently understood to be evil spirits. This is a misnomer, a perhaps deliberate misinterpretation of the Greek "daemon," which merely indicates one's personal guardian spirit, who may be benevolent, malevolent, or both, as the case may be. With the emergence of Christianity as a power, any spirit interaction beyond what was authorized by the Church was perceived as evil. Thus the daemon, once a part of one's personality and existence, was transformed into the demonic.

The word "demon" is frequently understood, within the context of the classical grimoires, to indicate a low-level malevolent spiritual entity and it is used in that context within this book. In general these low-level entities are anonymous, jealous, maliciously mischievous, and stupid.

Orisha and Lwa

These very similar spirit beings emanate from West Africa. The orisha derive from Yorubaland, part of modern Nigeria. The lwa derive from Fon traditions in Dahomey/Benin. "Vodou" means "spirit" in the Fon language.

Adored in their homelands for thousands of years, these spirits accompanied their enslaved devotees to the West. Traditional African religions were outlawed under slavery, devotees were persecuted, and the spirits were driven underground, but they were not forgotten. Instead they emerged in great prominence in the latter part of the twentieth century as the foundation of increasingly prominent and influential African-derived spiritual traditions.

The orisha are the presiding spirits of the Santeria religion as well as the Afro-Brazilian cults, such as Candomble, Umbanda, and Quimbanda. The Portuguese spelling is *orixa*; many of the same spirits are prominent among the different cults. Their names may be spelled differently, sometimes the same spirits use different names, their personalities may even manifest slightly differently depending upon location, but underneath their basic nature remains the same. For instance Oya, spirit of storm winds and the Niger River retains that name in Cuba but is known as Iansa in Brazil. Her mythology and basic personality remain the same.

The lwa are the presiding spirits of Haitian Vodou as well as its descendants, New Orleans Voodoo and Dominican Vodo. (*Lwa* is the modern Kreyol spelling; older French texts may use the term *loa*.) Although there is an entirely different pantheon of spirits, a few are common to both traditions and the behavior and manifestations of orisha and lwa are similar.

The influence of a few spirits was particularly well distributed in Africa and thus they are common to virtually all African Diaspora traditions. This refers particularly to the trickster Master of the Crossroads, Eshu-Elegbara, and Ogun, spirit and embodiment of iron. Although their names may vary depending upon location—particularly that of Eshu who, by nature, enjoys tricks, illusion, and confusion—their core essence remains consistent.

Conventional wisdom has it that there are thousands of orisha, but only approximately forty have any interest or dealings with people. These forty, however, are passionately interested and involved with humans.

The official, formal African-derived religions, Santeria and Vodou in particular, continue to expand, attracting new devotees. The orisha and lwa, in addition, are gregarious powers. They're eager to work, eager for attention. Because they are constantly fed, they're full of energy. They will also work with independent practitioners and have been assimilated into some Wiccan, Pagan, and Goddess traditions. However, ritual possession, the spirit's use of a person as a medium, common to a vast number of traditions worldwide, only occurs in the formal, official setting, as it should. These are extremely powerful, potentially dangerous practices that should not be attempted by the novice, the unsupervised, or the unitiated. Ritual possession is a shamanic art, not a magic spell.

There is a formal, lucid, structured way of working with the orisha and lwa, which serves as an excellent model for any spiritual interaction. Vodou and Santeria are monotheistic faiths:

there is a supreme deity who created all of existence. This creator, however, prefers to be an overseer. Olodumare, the Yoruba equivalent of God, created the orisha spirits to supervise creation. Each orisha or lwa is responsible for certain departments of life. Conversely every area of life has its own presiding orisha or lwa. Each individual person also has presiding orisha or lwa, typically a male and a female, the *"masters of your head."* They are your patrons, protectors, and advocates—providing you don't anger them too much.

Each orisha and lwa has a distinct personality. Each has a color, number, special foods, plants, and objects in which they recognize themselves. Attract their attention by manipulating these things: thus spells invoking the power of Oshun, Spirit of Love and Beauty, inevitably draw upon the color yellow, the number five, water, cinnamon, and honey, all of which share Oshun's essence. Petitions to Oya draw upon the color purple and the number nine. The spirits will communicate with you with these colors, numbers, and items as well. In general, when spirits perform a service for you, they want the credit. They will attempt to let you know that they have accomplished the miracle or the magic as the case may be. This system may be used to effectively communicate with spirits of other pantheons as well.

The orisha most involved in human every-day matters are sometimes invoked as a group and known as the Seven African Powers:

1. Elegba
2. Ogun
3. Obatala
4. Oshun
5. Either Oya or Orunmila, depending on individual tradition
6. Chango
7. Yemaya

By petitioning the orisha as a group, you may rest assured that all your bases are covered. The Seven African Powers provide all of Earth's potential blessings and protections. Commercially manufactured Seven African Powers products frequently depict them in their guise as Roman Catholic saints (see Identification/Syncretism, pages 90–3).

The Exus and Exuas (Pomba Giras)

(Singular, exu and exua, pronounced "Eh-shoo" and "Eh-shoo-ah.")

The West African trickster orisha Eshu-Elegbara is traditionally the first spirit petitioned during a ritual or spell. Because he controls all doors and the access to roads, Eshu determines whether your petition will be blocked or will reach the proper ears. Similar to the Greek god Hermes, devotees contact him first, propitiate him, then request that he invite and escort any other desired spirits. Although some traditions encourage everyone to simply contact whom they please directly, others consider this initial communication with a gate guardian to be proper spiritual protocol.

Eshu, more than most, manifests different aspects of himself in different places and to different people. But then, he is a trickster. In his original West African incarnation, he's young and handsome, always ready for sex and romance. In the Western hemisphere, he rarely displays this side of himself, usually appearing as a deceptively frail old man with a cane or as a young, rambunctious, playful child.

In Brazil, Eshu transformed into a completely different type of spirit, into a class all his own, the exus, multiple personalities, distinct from the other orixa (orisha). Powerful, volatile, and dangerous, the exus emphasize the extreme trickster aspects of the spirit. Because an exu is closer in nature to humans than the other orixa, he is the spirit most frequently appealed to for mundane matters, like money and love.

By definition, Afro-Brazilian spiritual paths possess this concept of exu.

Each orixa possesses his or her own exu, who serves as the orixa's personal messenger.

Confused? The confusion only increases.

There are a multiplicity of exus, each with a slightly different nature and slightly different role. There are also female exus, the exuas, except that that term is rarely used. The female aspects of exus are instead known as the Pomba Giras, the whirling doves. Despite the fact that these traditions are grounded strongly in West African spirituality, and despite the fact that exus, in particular, clearly derive from Africa, the Pomba Giras are not completely African. Rather they seem to represent a merging of African traditions with those of the Portuguese Romany, deported en masse to the Brazilian colonies, concurrent with the African slave trade. The preeminent Pomba Gira, Maria Padilha, is a deified former Queen of Spain, also known in European magic spells. The superficial image of the Pomba Gira, at least, has little to do with the historic Maria de Padilla, wife of Pedro the First of Castile and Leon, but derives from what is at best an outsider's romantic fantasy of Gypsy women and, at worst, an embodiment of every clichéd, negative stereotype: a promiscuous, hard-drinking prostitute/fortune-teller with a razor hidden in her cheek, a rose clenched between her teeth.

In addition to their function as messengers and servants of the orixa, exus and Pomba Giras may also be petitioned independently, specifically for more selfish, malevolent forms of magic in which the orixa may refuse to participate.

Exus and Pomba Giras are frequently perceived as dangerous and volatile, although this is somewhat in the eye of the beholder. Those who approach exus and Pomba Giras from a purely African or Pagan perspective will find them no more or less volatile than any other spirit. Maria Padilha Pomba Gira, in particular, can be a being of great power and generosity. Because many devotees are also either devout or lapsed Roman Catholics, there is often inherent ambivalence toward magic. Yes, it's powerful but is it *"good"* in the ethical sense? From this perspective, exus are frequently associated with Satan, the Christian conception of the devil. The qualities that most correspond to this concept are emphasized in the Brazilian concept of the exu: lurking at the crossroads, the smell of brimstone, and assistance that brings ultimate doom.

The Pomba Giras in general are perceived as dangerous, disreputable spirits. Their favorite haunt is a T-crossroad. They prefer working with women but will work with men, if requested. Those who fear them suggest that long-term contact will inspire transvestitism in men and prostitution among both men and women.

The traditional offering for exus are plates of yellow manioc flour cooked in oil or drizzled with oil. Pomba Giras prefer flowers to food. Exus drink wine, rum, and cachaca while Pomba Giras prefer anisette or champagne.

Saints

Whether fairies are spirits or humans may be subject for debate. Many spirits, from orishas, to those of ancient Greece and ancient Hawaii, may or may not be deified humans. The important orisha Chango, for instance, was once a king in Yorubaland. After death, he was deified and took his place among the orisha. That's one version of his sacred story, anyway. The ancient Greeks demonstrated this process when Heracles and Psyche, both originally mortals, were permitted to shed their human energy and enter the Realm of the Divine.

Saints, however, are resolutely human—or at least they were when they were alive. Because the word "saint" has become so strongly associated with Roman Catholicism, it often comes as a surprise to realize that a concept of sainthood, albeit not an identi-cal concept, exists among many other cultures, including the African Diaspora, Buddhist, Jewish, and Muslim traditions.

Roman Catholic saints are required to fulfill certain expectations before sainthood is officially conferred, and it can be a lengthy, bureaucratic process to prove their miraculous deeds. Other traditions use different criteria: sometimes the magic power (*heka*, *baraka*) contained by a person is so potent that it defies death, allowing others to continue to access it, for purposes of healing and magic. For many traditions, power of this magnitude is what confers sainthood. It is usually an informal process. There's no official beatification or canonization: word of miracles simply gets around. Shrines spring up and crowds gather.

The behavior of these saints may or may not be exemplary. Many are described as devout, charitable, generous people, although others demonstrate what might be characterized as *profligate tendencies*. Regardless, a saint's great power, *baraka*, is accessible to those in need.

Marie Laveau, the self-proclaimed Pope of Voodoo born

in 1792, has ascended to this concept of sainthood. Thousands venture to her grave in New Orleans annually to beseech her for favors. In particular, Laveau has earned an excellent reputation for remedying legal issues, as she did during her life. Attempts to contact her are made by knocking three times on the front of her tomb or by drawing three x's in red brick dust or chalk on the stone. Offerings and payments are left, most customarily salt water or seven dimes.

What is euphemistically called *"folk Catholicism"* has been the bane of the Roman Catholic Church for centuries. The desire to work with a saint, as with a spirit, or perhaps the desire of the saint or spirit to work with the person, is too strong to resist: magical practices creep in. Certain official Vatican-approved saints are also frequent participants in magic spells, particularly Saint Anthony, San Cipriano, Saint Martha the Dominator, Saint George, and John the Baptist. A saint's magic powers may have little to do with their official hagiography: Saint Anthony, for instance, is invoked in almost as many love spells as Aphrodite. San Cipriano may or may not

have been a reformed wizard in real life, but as far as magic spells are concerned, he's returned to his old profession with gusto. When they are invoked for magic, these saints are treated like any other spirit: offerings and payment are made for miracles begged and received. Saints, like spirits, have favored numbers, colors, fragrances, and gifts.

Unofficial Saints

The impulse to work with saints can be too powerful to wait for permission—or sometimes even to ask for permission. This isn't a problem with traditions with no "official" concept of sainthood. In a sense, all Jewish saints, for example, are "unofficial." There's no authority or criteria to make them official, although popularity conveys its own kind of official status. It's between saint and person. What happens, however, within a system where these criteria do exist? What happens when, during what usually starts as a local phenomenon, people begin to recognize a saint's capacity for miracles, without official recognition? Will people be patient and wait for the official verdict or will they create their own rituals? For those who are inclined to magic, the choice is obvious.

So-called *"unofficial saints"* are invariably tied to the Roman Catholic tradition, because it is the only tradition that insists on a lengthy organized bureaucratic procedure of conferring saint-hood. There is a vast range of unofficial saints. What they have in common are consistent miracles performed following death. They may be accessed in magic spells in similar fashion to any other spirit.

Identification/Syncretism

Syncretism is the system by which one spirit is identified or fused to varying degrees with another. Although the process is most commonly and consciously associated with modern African-Diaspora faiths, the tradition goes back millennia.

When the ancient Greeks began to travel their world, they encountered other people (Egyptians, Persians) with other pantheons. This frustrated them. Although they didn't insist on one god, they did insist on their own gods. Who were these other spirits? In some cases, spirits from abroad (Dionysus, Hecate) were merged into their own pantheon. In other cases, the Greeks decided, other cultures simply used other names and told other stories about spirits who were the same as the Greek gods. Thus they created a system of identification: Hathor was a beautiful spirit of love, who liked perfume and music. She must be Aphrodite, also a beautiful spirit of love, who liked perfume and music. Although sometimes neat, obvious identifications can be made, sometimes this leads to confusion. The Persian spirit, Anahita, was a beautiful deity interested in human romantic and reproductive matters. Obviously she was identified as Aphrodite (identification means she *was* Aphrodite), but Anahita also had a martial aspect, driving a chariot, leading men to war. Therefore she must be Athena, too.

Identification therefore attempts to identify one spirit within another. Syncretism takes this a step further. One spirit wears the mask of another. When one pantheon is outlawed, the only way to continue devotion to now-banned spirits is to pretend that you're worshipping others

This is precisely what happened to enslaved Africans in the Western hemisphere. Forbidden to practice their own faith, they accommodated it to another. Syncretism permits forbidden spirits to wear acceptable masks. Syncretism also means that acceptable saints are incorporated into magic spells in surprising ways because, in essence, they are fronting for that forbidden someone else. How else can one reconcile the conventional and devout "*official*" Saint Anthony of Padua with the witch-doctor persona he displays so powerfully and benevolently in a multitude of magic spells?

Spirits, like magic in general, are fluid in nature. Shape-shifting isn't hard for them, even without conscious syncretism. Hence India's Durga is an aspect of Parvati. In a moment of terrible stress, Durga unleashed her alter ego, Kali. All three are aspects of one, but all three are distinct beings, too. Confused? Well, you should be, it *is* confusing.

The realm of the spirits is like a journey through a dream landscape. Syncretism only increases the confusion.

Because the syncretism of the African slaves was born of desperation, quick, frequently visual identifications were made. Slaves were forbidden to practice their own religions but were permitted Roman Catholic chromolithographs of saints. They scoured them, looking for coded references to the orisha and lwa. Sometimes these identifications really work: Ogun, spirit of iron, was syncretized with the archangel Michael because in his most famous image Michael wields a sword. Yet they genuinely have much in common: both are tireless workers and warriors on behalf of human safety. Michael even has his own associations with iron. Sometimes syncretism is surreal: Chango, that most virile spirit of fire and lightning, is syncretized to the virgin martyr Saint Barbara, because her chromolithograph depicts a lightning bolt.

The first generation to engage in syncretization is conscious of what they're doing. After that, though, all bets are off. At what point, if any, do these spirits genuinely fuse? Perhaps Saint Peter, syncretized to road-opener Elegba because of his keys, really *is* Elegba or vice-versa. And if you're invoking Saint Peter in a magic spell, are you really invoking the saint or Elegba, hiding within, even if, after three generations, the orisha is no longer remembered?

Santeria earned its name, "religion of the saints," because of syncretism. Those who emphasize Roman Catholic ties prefer to emphasize the saints or perhaps a combination. Those who emphasize African roots prefer to emphasize the orisha or perhaps a combination. Others can no longer separate saint from orisha; true fusion has occurred for them. In Brazil, there have been calls to end syncretism as it is no longer necessary.

Were authorities truly unaware of the slaves' subterfuge? It's hard to say. This system of identifying and syncretizing spirits is present whenever one faith demands that another abandon and deny its spirits. Sometimes religious authorities presented syncretism to a population to make the new religion palatable. Hence, Goddess Aine becomes a Fairy Queen. She remains accessible to old devotees in that role, if not in her old one, which was perceived as dangerous to the new religious authority. Celtic spirit Brigid, the Druid's daughter, becomes identified with Saint Brigid. They merge; where one stops and the other starts becomes very difficult to determine.

Sometimes, however, this process backfires. In the case of Maximon, also known as Brother Simon, missionaries' attempts to assimilate the Guatemalan spirit Maam with Saint Simon backfired. Maximon, spirit of male primal energy, defied boundaries and took on a life of his own. The Church then attempted to syncretize him with Judas Iscariot or even with the devil. This only enhanced Maximon's outlaw image, making his devotees love him even more. Although intended to merge, to syncretize, with an *"official"* saint, Maximon instead has emerged as a powerful *"unofficial"* saint.

Sometimes syncretism occurred so long ago that the original spirit hiding underneath is completely forgotten. The only way to recognize that syncretism *may* have occurred is the observation that the saint behaves in a strangely *un-saint-like* manner. This applies particularly to the Big Three of magical Catholic saints, Saint Anthony, Saint George, and John the Baptist. Although perhaps completely forgotten spirits lurk within, many believe that under their respective masks lie Hermes, Baal, and Adonis.

Spell-casting with Words

Working magical practitioners tend to have a loose definition of what constitutes a magic spell. Once one becomes truly involved with magic and spell-casting, every action of the day can become transformed into a magic spell. Scholars of magic, particularly those who study a topic that fascinates them but in which they don't actually *believe*, may have more rigid definitions. For many, verbal spells are the strictest definition of what constitutes a spell.

Technically, the use of the word "charm" to indicate a *"lucky charm"* is a misnomer. Lucky charms are talismans, amulets or magically empowered items. "Charm" derives from the same source as *"Carmen"* or *"carol,"* as in a Christmas song, and indeed *charm* at its most archaic means a song. To be *en-chanted* literally means to be under the magical influence of a chant. By the strictest, most scholarly defini-

tion of a magic spell, every spell should have a verbal component, preferably sung, and perhaps only a verbal component. Certain magical traditions do emphasize this verbal component, particularly traditional Russian magic and modern Pow-Wow. However, this strict definition can only be used in an abstract, theoretical scholarly setting; it doesn't take into account either the realities of magic or the needs of many spell-casters.

Great, renowned systems of magic, such as those belonging to the Finn and Saami traditions, are under-represented in this book. Their magical systems were traditionally based on each individual practitioner's unique repertoire of songs and thus cannot be reproduced in book form. Legendary practitioners were able to sing magic into fruition; any practitioner worth his or her salt, for instance, allegedly possessed a song that could stop a wound from bleeding.

This desire to insist upon a verbal component to every spell is very Eurocentric. This emphasis on the magic power of words doesn't necessarily exist, or at least not to the same extent, in traditions from Asia and Africa.

That said, the power of words in magic spells is profound. Words convey power and intent, and can be used to create realities where none existed previously, which is, after all, the goal of many magic spells. Words, sounds, and syllables may possess their own inherent power in the same fashion that minerals and botanicals do. Zora Neale Hurston, the author and scholar/practitioner of magic, on considering the origins of magic and magic spells, suggested that God was the original Hoodoo Doctor, having spoken the world into creation with magic words.

Verbal components, like spiritual petition, may be incorporated into any spell. However, words are tricky and subject to individual taste. The classic is *abracadabra*: some perceive it as a word of power, others as an old joke. The verbal component of the spell has to suit the spell-caster's taste, otherwise it can derail the whole spell.

Some tips on spell-casting language:

★ *Repeating the words of a magic spell should never make you feel foolish, stupid, self-conscious, or uncomfortable. Change the words*

to suit your taste and temperament. It will undoubtedly not be the first or last time they are changed

★ *The majority of the spells in this book are traditional. Not every traditional spell has a verbal component, however where traditional verbal components of spells exist they have been retained. Many spells feature archaic language—language as it's no longer spoken and perhaps never was. An attempt to enhance magical ambience often means resorting to pseudo-archaic language. Some enjoy throwing "thees," "thous," and "forsooths" into spells. This author isn't among them. In general, except where archaic language was somehow intrinsic to the spell or to conveying its specific character, I've used modern language, updating and adjusting where necessary, because magic spells, no matter how ancient their roots, are a modern art, not relegated to the dusty past. However if you like all those "thees" and "thous," if you enjoy archaic language, if it enhances your sense of magical ambience, adjust the spells to suit your taste and put them back*

★ *Many associate the verbal component of spells with rhymes. If you enjoy rhymes, that's fine,*

however rhymes are not required.
The advantage of rhymes is that
they're easily remembered, which
can be crucial if it's a spell that
requires you to exactly repeat
incantations at intervals, however
what is being said is almost
invariably more important than
the literary devices used to say it

★ *It is crucial that the verbal*
component of a spell express your
goals and desires accurately,
concisely, and without ambiguity,
because living magical forces
sometimes enjoy playing tricks.
Change and adapt as needed.
Make up your own words, keeping
them simple and to the point, or use
words composed by others that best
express your desires. Psalms are
traditionally used in this way;
poems or the lyrics of your favorite
songs may be able to articulate
your desires and goals more
accurately than any ancient charm

Speaking the Spell

Verbal components of spells are usually spoken aloud, however not all spells are spoken the same way. There are different techniques of speaking and enunciating used in spell-casting. Directions are incorporated into the text of the spells but you must understand these directions in order to put them to best effect.

Murmuring and Muttering

In many cases, the verbal component of the spell is not meant to be easily understood by others. This is not necessarily or only because of secrecy. In these spells, you are actually interjecting the power of your words into something, even if only the atmosphere, but more frequently into an object. A classic and simple spell is to murmur words over a glass of water, transforming it into a potion. By then giving it to another to drink, you are magically transferring and transmitting your magical message and directions.

Announcing and Chanting

Sometimes, however, words are used to express and announce one's intentions and desires to the universe or toward a specific magic power. In that case, words need to be clearly understood. Articulate distinctly, expressively, and at a volume that you deem appropriate.

Key Concepts for Casting Magic Spells

Although one can just start casting spells, learning by trial and error, understanding certain key concepts boosts the chances of a spell-caster's success.

Thresholds

Magic energy radiates from everything and everyone that occurs naturally on Earth to varying degrees, or is derived from naturally occurring parts. Some objects are sources of greater power than others. Frankincense, roses, and wild Syrian rue, for instance, permit greater access to magic power than many other botanicals. Certain *areas* are also sources of greater power than others, with "area" meant both in a literal and a metaphoric way.

Thresholds are border areas where one force, power, or element encounters another. These meeting areas are potentially the most highly magically charged of all. Thresholds exist everywhere: the seashore, that transitional area where ocean meets land; the foot of mountains, where land begins to rise; and caves, the subterranean thresholds between Earth's outer and inner powers.

There are architectural thresholds: doors and windows. There are thresholds in time: twilight and dawn, where an incoming power approaches before the outgoing power has completely dispersed. Life cycles are thresholds: the birth of a new baby, particularly a first child whose birth transforms someone into a parent. Death is a threshold between one existence and the next. Someone who lingers in a half-life is described as having a foot in both worlds, straddling the threshold. Any transformative ritual is defined as a threshold, by virtue of its very capacity to transform. There are thresholds on the body: the mouth is the threshold between thought and speech.

Thresholds are simultaneously the areas of greatest magical potential and also of extreme vulnerability. A vast percentage of protective amulets, rituals, and spells are designed to guard thresholds and the transformative process. In fact, every magic spell can be perceived as a transformative threshold, from a past that has left something to be desired toward the future that the spell hopefully produces.

Most thresholds consist of a simple boundary: with one foot you stand inside the house, with another you stand outside. If your feet are small enough and your balance is good, you can stand poised, neither inside, nor outside.

With one foot you stand in the river or ocean, with the other, you stand on the land. The ancient Egyptians called their country *"the land of the red and the black,"* because there was a distinct division, a visible dividing line between the black fertile land of Nile silt and the stark red land of the desert. You could literally stand with one foot in each color. Each color also typified a different kind of magic and a different spiritual ruler. The black belonged to Osiris, with his arts of orderly civilization; red belonged to his brother Seth, anarchic, chaotic Lord of Magic.

These are simple boundaries: you can hop from one to the other. There are also expanded, exponentially super-magically charged thresholds.

The Crossroads

The crossroads are literally where different roads meet and where they separate, where opportunity emerges to change directions. They are unpredictable; you could take any one of a variety of choices. Magically speaking a crossroads is the place where multiple forces converge, where anything can happen, where transformations may occur. Energy is liberated and expanded at the crossroads. Instead of hopping over boundaries, you can stand in the center and be inundated by power, potential, and choices.

There are four-way crossroads and three-way crossroads—the proverbial fork in the road. A classic movie scene, albeit one that occurs in real-life if you've ever been lost in the country, shows someone arriving at a fork in the road. With no identifying road-sign in sight, our hero or heroine is forced to choose a road. Choose either one and your destiny may be altered forever. Crossroads offer the opportunity for transformation, for a change of direction, a change in destiny.

Crossroads are ubiquitous in magic. Many spells demand to be cast at the crossroads; others require that the remnants of spells—left-over candle stubs, ashes, and the such—be buried at the crossroads, where their energy can safely disperse.

Specific types of spiritual entities, known as *"road-openers"* and inevitably beings of great power, preside over crossroads. These beings can be petitioned for knowledge, information, and for a change in destiny. They control thresholds and roads, and determine who has free access and who finds roads barred, who will choose the right fork in the road and who will wander hopelessly lost forever.

In ancient Greece, Hermes ruled the four-way crossroads, while Hecate presided over three-way crossroads, her epithet *Hecate Trivia* emphasizing this aspect. *Trivia*, from which the English *trivial* derives, literally means *three roads*.

In West Africa, Eshu-Elegbara rules the crossroads, as does his Western hemisphere incarnations Elegba, Papa Legba, and Exu. In Brazil, Exu's female counterpart, Pomba Gira, presides over T-shaped crossroads.

Once upon a time, crossroads were where people met, where nomads rendezvoused, where gallows stood, where the death penalty was enacted and corpses left to hang, where suicides were buried. If magic spells were cast according to direction, then midnight at the crossroads must have frequently been a crowded, busy place, especially on a night like Halloween when the veil that divides the realms of living and dead is at its most permeable, leaving an open road for inter-realm communication.

Christian authorities frequently urged people to avoid the crossroads, particularly at night, as it was the devil's stomping grounds. If you were looking to meet Satan, however, if you had a proposition or a request for him, the crossroads was where you were most likely to find him. When legendary bluesmen Tommy and Robert Johnson journeyed to the crossroads to trade their souls for musical ability, were they looking for this devil or for the sometimes lame, Papa Legba, or could anyone even tell the difference anymore? (*See* Identification/Syncretism.)

Unfortunately, the most accessible modern crossroads are traffic intersections. The magic energy remains, however. Think about a busy intersection: on a good day you fly straight through, making a journey faster and easier. A traffic tie-up, however, is an energy build-up with added potential for accidents and road rage.

Faithfully attempting to follow a spell's directions may leave you playing in the middle of traffic. In Rio de Janeiro, Pomba Gira's devotees take this into account: offerings aren't left where you might expect, at the center of the crossroads, but by the side of the road. No matter how powerful your spell, it will have no opportunity to work if you get hit by a car during the casting. Find an appropriate old-fashioned crossroads, a safe area of a modern crossroads, or read between the lines—figure out what the spell *really* requires (*why* you're being sent to the crossroads, for what purpose) and adapt and substitute as needed.

Not all crossroads are literal intersections of roads. Magic spells also emphasize other, very specific crossroads.

The Cemetery

The cemetery is the threshold between the realms of the living and the dead. It too is a place of transformation. Many spells demand that a spell either be cast in the graveyard or that spell remnants be buried there, as if one were conducting a funeral. These include protection, banishing and love spells, as well as hexes. Significantly, many necromantic spells, spells, for communicating with those who have passed on to the next life, do *not* require a trip to the cemetery.

The cemetery, like the more general crossroads, swirls with energy, albeit of a more specific kind: ghosts, souls of the departed, abstract life and death forces, spiritual entities, protective guardians, and those malevolent beings who are attracted to grief or decay all make their home in the cemetery.

Whether the cemetery is a benevolent or a threatening place depends largely on cultural perceptions of what happens to the soul after death. Cultures that depend on protective ancestral spirits rarely fear the cemetery; cultures that believe that human memory and emotion truly dies, leaving nothing but a hungry, destructive ghost will avoid the graveyard except for purposes of malevolent magic.

The Pros and Cons of the Graveyard

The cemetery is the place where dangerous entities lurk, dangerous people, too! Although a Greek word, the term "necropo-lis," city of the dead, stems from ancient Egypt. Once upon a time, the devastatingly poor made their home among the graves. This situation still exists in many places, to greater or lesser extent. On the other hand, cemeteries are places of great neutral power (think of all that swirling radiant energy!), which is able to be harnessed for good or evil, as the practitioner intends or desires.

Even in the cemetery, bypassing actual grave-sites, certain areas are more packed with power than others. The threshold of the threshold, so to speak, is at the cemetery gates. Older cemeteries traditionally feature iron gates to provide this boundary. Iron, with the exception of menstrual blood, is the single most protective substance on Earth, and will repel and contain malevolent spirits and ghosts. Many spells request that items be left at the cemetery gates: this is not because people were afraid to enter the graveyard itself, but because that threshold is so much more powerful.

Many powerful spirits, such as India's Kali and Shiva, Matron and Patron of Tantra, reside in the cemetery, as do ancient

Egypt's road-openers, Anubis, the jackal-headed inventor of embalming, and Wepwawet, a wolf deity. (Say the name fast and hear that wolf cry.)

Accessing the power of crossroads and cemeteries is common to most magical traditions, to varying extents. Specific other traditions recognize and incorporate still other crossroads.

The Bathhouse

Prior to the advent of private, indoor plumbing, the public bathhouse was a place of great social importance, a crossroads to which everyone eventually came. Its purpose was not only hygienic and social, but spiritual and magical, too.

In the days before privacy, public bathhouses were required for spiritual cleansing rituals as well as physical ones. The bathhouse attendant, now most frequently a lowly janitorial occupation, was once a respected, and perhaps feared, ritual leader who wielded great power. In many cases they might be the only ones privy to occult secrets.

Many traditions still retain the equivalent of a bathhouse: the Jewish mikveh, the Native American sweat lodge, the Aztec temescal. Not all bathhouses feature water, as the sweat lodge demonstrates. Finnish saunas and Turkish steam baths access other methods. In the same way, cleansing spells are as likely to use smoke, sound, or other methods as water. The bathhouse, whether wet or dry, was frequently the scene of many threshold experiences:

★ *Babies were born in bathhouses*
★ *Preparation for brides and sometimes grooms occurs in the bathhouse*
★ *Cultures that isolate menstruating women frequently have rituals held in the bathhouse to signal her return to society at large*
★ *Bodies are prepared for funeral rites in the bathhouse*

The frequency of these experiences in the bathhouse would exponentially increase the potential power contained within.

The bathhouse is the descendant of ancient springs, each the home of resident magic spirits. Many bathhouses were built on the site of springs, and the spirits took up residence in the new bathhouse. Water spirits, like the nature of their element, are frequently volatile, replete with treasure, but also with dangerous currents. These can be tremendously benevolent spirits (water spirits rank among the most powerful love spirits), but you have to know how to handle them. With the coming of Christianity and Islam, rites of devotion and pacification were forbidden and abandoned. Many spirits packed up and left; those remaining, starved of attention, are frequently grouchy. Thus the bathhouse is both a place of power and danger. Enter alone to access the spirits or avoid entering alone so that the spirits cannot access you!

Russian magic, in particular, manifests this ambivalence and will direct many spells to be performed in the bathhouse, usually at midnight.

Ruins

Ruins of buildings and cities, particularly (but not necessarily) those that met their ruin in violence, are perceived as swirling with power. This is the stuff of fairy tale: the European witch convicted purely because she has been gathering herbs amidst the ruins. It's not like there's any other reason to be there, the witch hunters say. Indeed, some of the most powerful magical herbs, mugwort and Syrian rue, thrive best among ruins. Many practitioners believe that these botanicals, already more powerful than most, are at the height of their power when picked there, especially at midnight, twilight or just before dawn.

Stone ruins are most powerful because stone, although silent, is in magical terms hardly inanimate. Stone is believed to retain memories of whatever occurs in its vicinity. Those memories may be accessed by those who know how.

Souls of those who perished in the ruins may linger, as may others drawn to the site. They may be accessed, if you dare. Djinn not found lurking in the desert, behind doorways or at natural springs will be found amidst ruins, the more broken the better. If you want to access them, that's where you'll find them. If you're afraid they'll access you, hurry past without stopping.

Altars

Crossroads and cemeteries are places of power precisely because they allow energy extra space and opportunity to radiate. Sometimes you want the opposite effect, a concentration of energy. The need is to concentrate power and energy in one spot, a focal spot, the very center of the crossroads, if you will. An altar allows you to do this.

Many spells direct that you build an altar.

Although the term is used by many religions to indicate an area dedicated to a deity, this may or may not be the case magically speaking. An altar in its most basic magical definition is a tableau or arrangement of specific articles. Small children are inveterate builders of tableaux, with no conscious conception of religious devotion. They simply pick up power objects and arrange them. For practice, pick any theme, magical or not, and devote a shoebox diorama or a table top to it.

The simplest ancestral altar consists of a white candle and a glass of water. The most complex Vodoun altar is an entire room, with each object carefully chosen and arranged meticulously. Nothing on an altar, whether simple or lavish, is random or arbitrary. If it's there, it's there for a reason.

Altars are generally erected for one or both of the following reasons:

As a communication device to summon a spirit. By adjusting objects, colors, and fragrances, you send out a specific signal requesting attention. Thus the Yoruba deity or orisha, Oshun, recognizes herself in the spectrum of colors from yellow to orange, in certain types of flowers, in honey and cinnamon. Her objects include peacock feathers and mirrors. Her number is five. The concentration of special themed objects catches her attention and invites her presence. Ideally she'll drop by to see what's going on. Because certain objects may be shared between deities (Aphrodite, Juno, Kybele, and Maria Padilha all love roses, although not necessarily the same color or number, and Maria Padilha prefers hers with long stems but no thorns), the more specific and detailed the tableau, the more likely you are to summon the right spirit.

Altars may be erected in tribute, as an offering of thanks for previous favors, or as part of a petition process.

As a means of concentrating energy. An altar can be devoted to a spell, not necessarily to any kind of spiritual entity. Spells that are conducted over an extended period of time, for instance nine-day spells, may benefit from a concentrated area: the spell doesn't blend in to the background but remains distinct, its boundaries and thresholds clear. Thus all objects involved in the spell (and some spells may involve several candles plus assorted dishes and objects) are arranged together in formation.

Altars are most frequently placed atop flat furniture surfaces—dressers, bookshelves, and coffee tables. Old-fashioned televisions built into wooden cabinets were once popular altar areas.

There is a wide variety of altars beyond the tabletop tableau. Candle spells require that an altar be kept in plain sight, and many prefer this method because the constant visual presence of the altar empowers many spells. However, it is not necessary. An altar may also be maintained discreetly,

within a cabinet or closed box: a shadow box altar. Miniature altars can be created within old-fashioned cigar- and match-boxes.

Altars may also be created outside. A garden, window box, or flowerpot can contain a living altar, an Earth altar. The possibilities are endless.

Altars may be intensely private or public: visualize the roadside shrines frequently erected at the site of fatal accidents. French Caribbean altars are created in sheltered places within tree trunks. If a statue is placed within the tree, passers-by can come with offerings of flowers and candles. Spells of petition dedicated to the Brazilian spirit Maria Padilha invariably begin with directions to lay black and red cloths on the ground: you are demarcating the spell's space, effectively setting up an altar. Spells dedicated to deities of the sea often instruct you to dig a shallow pit in the sand, within which to burn candles. That hole in the sand becomes the altar.

Altars can be created from anything and erected anywhere. Water spirits, for instance, frequently prefer the bathroom to other rooms of the house, as the most watery place. A shrine (essentially a more lavish altar) dedicated to mermaids belongs in the bathroom rather than in another room that might be considered more "spiritually appropriate." Spirits dedicated to love prefer altars in the bedroom where they can supervise and stimulate activity. Intellectual spirits like Yoruba's Oya or India's Sarasvati prefer their altars to be placed near books. Access the childlike, creative, playful part of yourself and it's not difficult to build an altar.

Objects may decorate an altar or serve *as* the altar. Watermelons are sacred to the Yoruba spirit, Yemaya. Place a slice on her altar to call her. Hollow out a watermelon, insert some candles and the watermelon has *become* the altar. Wood may be used as altar decoration but also as the altar. This is particularly true of special sacred woods, such as sandalwood or aloes wood. Sometimes the deity *is* the wood. Hera was represented by the oak in Greece, while Diana was represented by that wood throughout Europe. A log segment is given center-stage, dressed with oil and adorned with ornaments, small candles or charms.

Unsurprisingly, the bed serves as the altar for many love spells: sheets are sprinkled with powder; power objects are tucked beneath the mattress and the pillows. Botanicals may hang over the bed or candles burn alongside it.

The body serves as an altar in many spells, particularly those for healing, love, and protection. Oil and powder may be applied to the body in the same manner as to a candle. Henna and other body decoration transforms the body into a living altar. Next time you get dressed, as you apply cosmetics, jewelry, and other ornaments, consider that you are dressing your altar—an altar that serves to communicate with other beings and concentrates your power and energy.

Not every crossroads is a location: a formal magic spell is a crossroads where the inherent magic energies of the spell's components converge. The result of the spell is the symbiotic reaction to that convergence.

★ One might also consider an altar a method of demarcating sacred space

★ A spell may be cast by creating an altar; similar to feng shui, articles and objects are arranged to create a desired energy transformation

★ Although some spells specify creating one, even when it isn't suggested, an altar may always be incorporated

★ Likewise, if you are seriously challenged for space, remember, magic is always about improving your life. The goal of magic is to eliminate difficulties and stress, not produce new ones. If you have no room for a formal altar, delineate space as possible. Plenty of people burn candles in the bathtub; you won't be the first

Balance

Consider the herbalist's scales: things are carefully weighed out to achieve a desired balance. Magic plays with balance, too. Sometimes the desire is for all forces to be equal and harmonious. At other times goals are accomplished by deliberately, consciously tipping the scales to provide the required effect.

Left and Right

Once upon a time, not too long ago, the concept of Dualism associated the direction *right* with God, high, male, and all those good things. Thus children were

forced to use their right hands, *the dexterous hand*, whether that was their naturally dominant hand or not. Children who were naturally left-handed (*the sinister hand*) literally had it beaten out of them until they were dexterous too. Consider various phrases: *in the right, Mr. Right, the left-hand path, a left-handed compliment.*

Connections between genders and these directions, however, predate Dualism *and* Christianity. They exist in completely unrelated cultures, including some that were isolated for a very long time. Hawaiian magic, for instance, associates left with female, right with male as surely as the Chinese and many Asian, African, and European traditions. Frequently offerings to female deities are made with the left hand (by both men and women) while offerings to males are made with the right (by both men and women). Feng shui suggests that it's beneficial for women to sleep on the left side of a common bed, while a man should sleep on the right. (Although spells intended to reverse the power dynamic within a relationship may suggest those sides be switched.)

Sometimes spells direct that an action be performed with either your left or right hand. Either one of two things is being requested.

★ *Because left is yin and yang is right, the left side of everyone's body is yin or affiliated with "female forces" while the right side is yang and affiliated with "male forces." Most frequently a spell's success depends upon accessing one force or emphasizing one quality over the other*

★ *Sometimes the spell's success depends upon not using your dominant hand. Because until recently everyone was forced to be right-handed, many older spell books will specify casting a spell with your left hand, because it's*

assumed that everyone is right-handed. This is, obviously, no longer the case

Where the importance lies in not using your dominant hand, this is specified in spell-directions. Left-handed people will be directed to use their right hands. Where no such direction is given, if the only stipulation is to use your left hand, then this applies to everyone across the board.

Materia Magica

Spells utilize various items and materials. Many items occur naturally on Earth (rocks, metals, flowers); others do not, but are creations of people, crafted from one or more of those original materials (magic wands, candles, magic mirrors, etc.).

There is a vast quantity of materials to choose from. It's unlikely that you will need them all. Some will appeal to you, will resonate for you: those are your best tools. If you don't like them, if they fail to hold your interest, it's not likely that they'll work for you, at least not consistently.

Once upon a time, all magic was made by hand from scratch,

from soup to nuts. If a spell required paper, you would make that paper, perhaps even gathering the material. You'd make the ink, too. Old-fashioned, you say? Yes, but this soup-to-nuts method has very important benefits, notably, control over your materials and your spell. When you do it yourself, you know that things were done correctly, all powers were properly propitiated, all ingredients genuine. That said, magic is intended to make your life easier, not more difficult. If you are challenged for time, purchase as much ready-made as possible. The botanicals you grow with love and care will always have more power for you, but if you don't have a garden or green fingers, buy them from someone who does. If you're not "crafty," you can still cast spells. Plenty of other people are and they'll be happy to sell you their wares, oils, candles, wands, and herbs. However, hold these craftspeople to the same high standard that you'd hold anyone else. Don't be afraid to ask questions and specify your needs.

Preparing For Spell-casting

Cleansing

Cleansing is not meant literally but refers to methods of removing spiritual residues. Not everything requires cleansing because not everything retains this residue. Botanicals and candles do not, for instance. Rocks, crystals, and magic mirrors may require cleansing, particularly the first time you use them, because they retain memory and impressions. You don't necessarily know

Remember: Magic spells take many forms, from spoken word to candle burning, from mixing oils to something as simple as posting a specific image on the wall. Your energy, focus, and intent are what transform simple actions, words, and gestures into magic spells.

everything that's retained within a mirror. (Harry Potter fans: remember Tom Riddle's diary. There was a lot hidden within those seemingly blank pages.) Cleansing gives you the opportunity to wipe the slate clean and start afresh.

Most metals fall in a category between rocks and botanicals and so sometimes need cleansing, with the exception of silver and iron, which are impervious to spiritual tarnish. You can still cleanse them, however, if you prefer.

Two areas are typically cleansed prior to initiating any important spell: the ritual space and you—your body. Cleansing will empower you and your spell, removing impediments and obstacles to success.

(*See also* sections on cleansing, techniques, and spells below.)

Charging the Materials

Magic is latent in everything containing life. How is it accessed? How is it directed toward your purpose? By charging the materials.

Charging the materials is magical parlance for imbuing the physical components of your spells, be they stones or plants or fabric or anything else, with your personal energy and the goal of your spell. It is a crucial magical concept, and is akin to charging a battery—a transfusion of energy.

Exactly how necessary it is to charge a substance depends largely upon specific traditions. Some place greater emphasis on charging than others, although no tradition would tell you *not* to charge an item.

Although every spell does not direct you to charge your materials, it is a given that doing so will increase your chances of success.

Charging techniques *are* spells; they can be used to imbue any object with your magical energy and power, whether these objects will be used in a formal spell or otherwise.

This is the simplest charging technique of all:

1. Hold the object with two hands, clasped together so that the object or a portion of it is sandwiched between them.
2. Close your eyes and take a few slow, deep breaths.

3. Clear your mind so that there are no conscious thoughts. If thoughts arise spontaneously, consider whether this derives from communication of one sort or another with the object. Make a note of the thoughts so that you may return to them later, and clear your mind once again.

4. Just hold the object, focusing on energy flowing out of your hands and into the object. (Depending upon the nature of the object, this may be a one-way or two-way energy flow.)

5. When you feel that the object has absorbed sufficient energy or is now in harmony with your personal vibration, place it down and consciously withdraw your attention from it.

If you would like to charge the object with the purpose of a specific spell, follow the instructions up to Step 3. Instead of clearing your mind, visualize the achievement of the spell's desired goal. Hold this steady in your mind. When you feel that the object is sufficiently charged, remove it from your hands and consciously withdraw your attention.

✳ Expanded Ritual Charging

1. Perform appropriate space and personal cleansings, as needed.
2. Prepare an altar dedicated to charging the materials.
3. Hold a white candle between your palms while you concentrate on what you wish from the article you are charging.
4. When you're ready, place the candle on the altar and light it.
5. Hold the article between your palms, charge it with your energy or goals, using the technique explained above.
6. When you're ready, place it down next to the candle.
7. Allow the object to remain there until the candle burns out completely.

Objects can be charged with specific forces, usually sunlight or moonlight, so that they will contain some of this essence. Objects may also be charged with elemental forces.

Blessings of the Elements

Each element can provide ritual blessings for spell tools and materials. Whatever is blessed is empowered and charged with that element's special energy. Choose what is appropriate or desirable, alone or in combination.

★ *Air: Pass the object through or hold within incense smoke. Smudge with a smudge stick*
★ *Earth: Sprinkle with dirt, particularly specially chosen dirt (crossroads dirt, or dirt gathered from a shrine or holy place)*

★ *Fire: Pass through a flame or hold within the flame for a few moments (obviously this is for materials that won't burn or be damaged)*
★ *Metal: Allow the object to rest overnight atop the specific metal*
★ *Water: Sprinkle with regular water or magically charged formula water (see Formulary). Obviously this is for materials that won't be damaged by this technique*

IMPORTANT CONCEPT: RECIPROCITY

Because magic is an exchange of powers, consistently effective magic isn't all about *me, me, me!* The universe doesn't exist solely to serve you; there is always an exchange of energy, an exchange of gifts. Magic is about *mutually satisfying relationships* between forces and powers, including but not limited to your own. Power and favors must be balanced. You are as much a contributor to the universe as a receiver of its bounties.

When you want something from a power, offer something in return. When you receive a gift or favor, give one in return. This maintains a balance of power in the universe. In some cases, it's necessary. Botanicals work more powerfully for you if you reciprocate, offering libations, when harvesting. Many spirits will not work with you, unless they essentially receive payment of some sort, which may be as simple as devotion or as complex as a specific ritual, depending upon the power.

Ritual Tools and Techniques

Tools, like spells, are creations of people. What may be indispensable to you depends upon your personal traditions and needs. For the practitioner of Wicca, an athame is necessary; in the old Saami tradition it was the drum. If ceremonial "High" magic appeals to you, you may need a lot of "*stuff.*" For others, what's necessary may be as little as what fits into a medicine bag—or even less.

Because so many published works focus on the more ceremonial aspects of magic, there is often an emphasis on tools. These may or may not be necessary to you: poor people's magic, the magic of slaves or nomads who travel light, is no less powerful but may require less *stuff*—or at least different stuff.

There is a tremendous variety of magical tools, demonstrating human ingenuity and creativity at its finest. Some creations serve no other purpose but magic, while others masquerade as common household tools. Get to know your needs, your taste, and your own power, and then gravitate towards tools that call to you, that resonate for you.

Amulets and Talismans

"*Amulet*" and "*talisman*" are used somewhat interchangeably, but basically talismans are the archetypal lucky charms, drawing some specific good fortune towards you, while amulets tend to have protective, preventative, or curative powers. Confusion derives from the tendency in the English language to skate over these topics very quickly. Other languages have specific names for every specific type of talisman or amulet, all very precise. Our word "amulet" is believed to derive from the Latin *amuletum*, meaning "a method of defense" (reminiscent of ammunition).

There are typically two forms of talismans and amulets:

★ *Those that are written*
★ *Independent objects*

Magic spells are frequently required in order to create talismans and amulets.

Bells

Bells are a multi-purpose magical tool of ancient provenance and international use. They are incorporated into a variety of spells:

★ *Fertility spells (a bell won't "work" without the clapper inside it)*
★ *Spirit-summoning spells*
★ *Protective spells*
★ *Space-cleansing spells*
★ *Healing spells*

Church bells derive from magical use, not the other way around.

Bells are crafted from many materials: silver and iron are considered most auspicious, especially for protection, fertility, and healing. In addition, bells intended to do double-service as amulets may be crafted for symbolic use: thus bells are found in the shape of pinecones, cats, and frogs.

In some Asian traditions, having been well used, bells are then melted down and the resulting metal used to create other magic tools, such as ritual cups and plates. The grease from large bells, such as church bells, may also be scraped out and used as a component of banishing and hexing spells. It is a frequent component of **Goofer Dust**.

Books

There was a drastic increase in persecution and prosecutions for witchcraft, sorcery, and paganism in late antiquity. Among the charges, besides astrology, divination, the making of love potions, and the presentation of petitions at pagan shrines, was possession of magic books.

Books serve many purposes in magic beyond serving as a source for spells. The book may itself be a form of a spell, serving as an amulet. Certain books don't have to be read; their very presence in the home provides protection from a host of ills. Besides the Bible and Koran, other books of this ilk include *The Book of Raziel, Book of Pow-Wows: The Long Lost Friend* and the Russian *Dreams of a Virgin.*

Books serve as magical tools. Specific books are often used as sources of divination. These especially include the Bible, the Koran, Homeric verses, and the works of Virgil.

The Book of Psalms possesses an alter ego as a magical book. Psalms are used to cast a host of spells for a variety of reasons. Many assume that this originated with Hoodoo, where recitation of psalms is a common practice, but this is based on the false assumption that the Hoodoo doctors were uneducated and thus must have *"made stuff up."* If fact, it is quite the contrary—incorporation of psalms into magic stems back centuries. The practice was popular enough to stimulate publication of a medieval compilation of the uses to which psalms and their individual verses might be put. *The Magical Use of the Psalms*, a popular work of its time, was frequently reprinted in pocket-sized editions and was translated from Latin into several European languages. It was eventually placed on the *Index Librorum Prohibitorum* of the Roman Catholic Church.

Similarly, spells from the Islamic world may incorporate recitation of appropriate verses from the Koran.

Sacred Texts

The Koran, the Bible, and other books are perceived as having inherent magical power because they are sacred texts. Sacred texts are not restricted to monotheistic faiths. The works of Homer and Virgil, the Indian

Vedas, and the Chinese I-Ching or Book of Changes are all considered sacred texts. The crucial question, in terms of successful spell-casting, is *"are any of those texts sacred for you?"* Sacred texts, by definition, are so inherently charged with *baraka* and *heka* that, like a saint from beyond the grave, anyone may access that power. However, magic is both in the transmitter and the receiver; it is a reciprocal process. The most powerful sacred texts for you are those that *you* perceive as sacred. If your sacred texts are Broadway show tunes or doo-wop songs, then incorporate them into your spells in the same manner that you would any other sacred text.

Methods for the magical use of psalms and sacred texts include:

★ *Whispering texts over a cup of water, which is then given to someone to drink (although the spell-caster may also desire to drink it, depending on the purpose of the spell)*
★ *Writing texts down on paper, then dissolved in liquid and drunk (by the spell-caster or the target of the spell: this derives from ancient Egyptian methods)*

★ *Wearing them as amulets, for empowerment and to transmit constant, consistent magic energy*
★ *Tracing them on an apple with a pin; depending on the nature of the spell the apple is then eaten by the spell-caster or fed to the spell's target*

Books of Shadows

Many practitioners like to keep a record of spells cast and created. Blank books are filled with magic spells. Eventually, especially if you incorporate magical inks and designs into your Book of Shadows, the book itself will be highly charged with magic power.

Books themselves sometimes need protection, and mugwort, wormwood, and Saint John's Wort are believed to physically preserve books. They provide spiritual protection and keep page-nibbling vermin away.

★ *Place leaves of these protecting botanicals between pages*
★ *Maintain living plants in and around libraries*
★ *Kabikaj is the name of the djinn with dominion over insects. Allegedly writing his name in*

books and on manuscripts magically prevents their being eaten by worms and other vermin

Paper

Many spells contain a written component. Something often needs to be written down, if only to be burned. And so, paper is required.

Classical grimoires often suggest that one uses parchment or vellum, especially when creating a talisman. The advantage of these is durability, although they may be difficult to acquire nowadays. Hoodoo often suggests the use of brown paper. Use cut-up paper bags or butcher's paper. The advantage of this is the low cost, easy availability and color—brown is the color of justice. This paper thus enhances any spell that demands that justice be done.

It is also very easy to create your own paper with minimal skill and artistic talent. Children's craft kits contain basic paper-making supplies. A spell rarely requires more than a sheet of paper. The advantage of making your own paper is that one can imbue it with desired botanicals and fragrance.

Paper Can Be *The Spell*

Certain scripts are perceived as inherently powerful, for instance, Arabic, Chinese, and Hebrew. If there was a pagan Greek belief that the world was created and activated via the sound of the vowels, in traditional Judaic teaching life is activated through the Hebrew letters. Ancient Egyptians utilized different scripts for different purposes, mystical and mundane. Northern European runes and Celtic Ogham script are specifically for magical and spiritual use. Many contemporary Wiccans and ceremonial magicians use various magical scripts.

Paper can create lasting amulets. The most readily accessible example is the Jewish mezuzah, attached to doorposts. The use of mezuzahs has been adopted by some Hoodoo practitioners. Similar written amulets exist in Chinese, Japanese, Ethiopian, Muslim, and Tibetan traditions.

Paper as we know it was invented in China in 105 CE, and China remains the primary home of paper magic. Paper charms are traditionally written in red cinnabar ink on yellow or red paper with a peach wood pen, in special magical script known as "*thunder writing*" or "*celestial calligraphy*." Charms are used in various ways: pasted over the door or on the walls, worn in the hair, or carried in a medicine bag.

Some paper spells are created in ordered to be destroyed, via fire or water. Destroying the paper spell releases its energy into the atmosphere so that the spell can work as intended. Sometimes water and fire are combined: some Chinese charms are burned first, and then the ashes are mixed with tea or water and drunk. Rice paper is particularly effective for this as it dissolves easily in water.

★ *A written spell doesn't necessarily require paper: an ancient custom was to inscribe a clay bowl or plate with spells and incantations. It is then shattered to release the energy into the atmosphere. (If you make your own pottery, the traditions can be combined: insert tiny pieces of paper directly into the pottery, inscribed further, so the magic is contained inside and out, then shatter.)*

★ *Not all paper spells require words. Spells can be cast with images.*

Chromolithographs incorporate the power and blessing of a spirit. They may also substitute for a statue. If you can't afford them or locate them, create your own. If you have no artistic ability, a collage of sacred and power images creates an amulet

★ *A traditional alternative is to write the name of the desired divinity in gold ink on red paper and post it on the wall*

Many spells suggest using "magical ink" formulas. Although this is never required, it can empower a spell. Recipes for creating magic inks can be found within the *Formulary*.

Pen and ink are only one form of magic writing. There are many traditions of drawing designs on the ground, particularly to invite, invoke, and honor spirits. Materials used include flowers, flour, cornmeal, and special rangoli powder.

★ *Angelic sigils are written on paper or engraved onto metal. Each angel has a specific sigil that can be used to summon them. The vèvè designs of Haitian Vodou have similar purposes. Each lwa or spirit has a vèvè that expresses its essence and is thus worthy of meditation, but the vèvè may also be used to summon and honor the spirit. Vèvès may be drawn on paper but are most frequently drawn on the ground. Candomble and Romany spirits also possess sigils, as do others*

★ *Rangoli, the women's spiritual art of India, utilizes rice flour with brightly colored flowers and spices to create patterns. As Earth's tiny creatures eat the rice flour, they carry imbedded prayers and petitions to the Earth's womb*

★ *In Brazil, pemba, a kind of chalk which may contain pulverized herbs, is used to create invocational markings on Earth. Originally an African practice, the finest pemba is still thought to come from Africa and may be imported and purchased at great cost to a less-than-wealthy practitioner*

Broomsticks

The fantasy image of the witch riding around on her broomstick is actually based on fact. Broomsticks were common ritual instruments in Western European fertility rites. People rode around fields, women on brooms, men on pitchforks, jumping high in revelry to encourage crops to flourish. The pitchfork, the male tool, would eventually be identified as among the devil's attributes.

Why a broom? It symbolizes the perfect union of male and female energies, with the stick representing the male force plunged into and attached to the female straw. Vestiges of the broom's role in fertility magic survive in the handfasting custom of jumping the broomstick.

In ancient Greece, the broomstick was considered an attribute of Hecate, matron of witches and midwives. It became, for a time, the professional emblem of midwifery, similar to a barbershop pole or pawnbroker's balls.

The use of broomsticks is not restricted to European magic: the symbol arose independently in Mexico as well. The conquistadores, familiar with these images from home, were shocked by images of Tlazolteotl, fierce Aztec spirit of love and witchcraft, riding on a broomstick, naked but for jewelry and a conical bark hat, accompanied by raven and owl familiars.

The broom is used for a variety of purposes:

- ★ *It has evolved into the emblem of witchcraft as surely as it once represented midwives. They may be displayed as a source of pride and as a device to memorialize the Burning Times*
- ★ *Brooms serve as an amulet against malefic magic*
- ★ *Brooms are used in a vast variety of magic spells, especially those for cleansing, banishing, and fertility*
- ★ *The broomstick was the traditional tool used for topical application of witches' flying ointments*

Various types of brooms may be used:

- ★ *Single-use ritual brooms, usually loosely put together from botanical material and taken apart and dispersed immediately following use*
- ★ *Special ritual magical brooms, only to be used in ritual, as beautifully carved and crafted as any magic wand or sword. These are particularly popular among modern pagans and Wiccans*
- ★ *A plain household broom, the same one used to sweep the floor, the staple of Hoodoo banishing spells. Spiritual and mundane household cleansings may be accomplished simultaneously, through the use of ritual floorwashes*

To Sweep or Not to Sweep?

In some traditions, modern paganism or Wicca for instance, a ritual broom may never touch the floor, let alone dust anything. Brooms, whether single-use ones or exquisite hand-crafted tools, are reserved for ritual use. Hoodoo, on the other hand, is practical magic: there's no need for two brooms where one will suffice. A household broom will serve both mundane and magical purposes, often simultaneously, as with the use of ritual floor-washes. Floorwashes accomplish two purposes at the same time: a magic spell is cast *and* the floor is cleaned. Cleaning the floor effectively casts the spell.

This does not really indicate a split between European and African-derived magical systems. Hoodoo's extensive use of the broomstick may in fact derive from its European roots. However, possessing an extensive collection of expensive tools reserved solely for ritual use has certain economic implications. One needs space to keep these items as well as privacy to practice ritual in safety. Instead, mundane activities can camouflage magical ones. Magic spells may be discreetly yet consistently cast, during such everyday activities as sweeping or scrubbing one's front steps.

Whether the fifteenth-century European woman, for instance, who typically resided in a small, crowded house lacking privacy and personal storage space, and who lived in mortal fear of accusations of witchcraft, would have considered it safe and practical to maintain a broomstick reserved for ritual use in addition to a household tool is something we may never know.

★ *The most basic witch's broomstick is constructed from an ash stick, which provides consistent magical protection, bound with birch twigs, meant to entangle low-level malicious spirits*

★ *An alternative choice would be willow twigs, because it is the tree belonging to Hecate, Dark Moon Goddess and supreme teacher of magic (Circe and Medea rank among her finer students)*

★ *Small handcrafted brooms are crafted to be placed and maintained on altars. Embellish the brooms to coincide with their purpose. For instance, decorate a small broom dedicated to sea spirits with sea glass and shells*

Candles

The use of candles as a common ingredient of magic is relatively recent: until recently real candles were very expensive, hence the early popularity of lamp magic. Beeswax was dangerous to obtain; natural plant waxes are very labor intensive. The earliest use of what we would call a candle apparently dates to approximately 3000 BCE.

The first true candles combined a wick with wax, oil, or fat that solidified at room temperature, unlike the more ancient and common oil lamps. Beeswax was a luxury item, as rare in its way as sandalwood and frankincense. The most common candle until the development of paraffin was tallow, animal fat, a household item. The downside to tallow is its strong aroma. Still popular in some Latin American magical traditions, you can often find small tallow candles at spiritual supply stores.

Today candle magic has become one of the most popular forms of spell-casting, because of the prevalence of inexpensive candles. Modern candles are most commonly formed from paraffin, a petroleum wax. There are also beautiful natural waxes: beeswax, bayberry, and candelilla. The material is inherently more powerful and benevolent than paraffin, however they are much more expensive. Those who burn candles extensively may find their cost prohibitive. Also those who prefer figure candles may have a very difficult time finding them formed from the finer waxes.

Basic Candle Magic Instructions

There are four necessary steps before a candle is burned.

1. *Choose the appropriate candle.* Candles come in a variety of shapes, sizes, and colors. Choose what is appropriate for your spell (*see* Table of Color Associations). When in doubt, a white candle will substitute for any other. If a candle must be burned in one sitting, it may be advisable to burn a smaller candle. Likewise, if a candle is to be burned incrementally over seven days, a birthday candle may not be the wisest choice.

2. *Charge the candle.* Follow the basic charging instructions. Hold the candle in your hands and focus on the desired goal of the spell.

3. *Carve the candle.* Carving and dressing the candle personalizes it. Using a carving tool, engrave your name, mother's name, birthday, astrological sigil, and other information into the wax. That's the typical *identifying information*, however a spell may specify exactly what to carve. Visualize that the candle will ultimately disappear into thin air, carrying your magical message to the Spirit World. Whatever you wish transmitted should be carved into the wax. A carving tool is anything with a sharp point. Because it will likely transmit your most secret fears and desires and may retain this as a kind of "inner memory," it's advisable to keep carving tools reserved for personal magical use. A very traditional carving tool is a rose thorn, which may be disposed of with the spell remnants.

4. *Dress the candle.* No need for little clothes. Dressing the candle indicates that it must be anointed with oil, commonly called a "dressing oil." The spell will

specify which type of oil to use. The oiled candle may be dressed more elaborately by rolling it in powdered herbs or color-coordinated glitter.

Common Figure Candles

The following are among the most popular, accessible figure candles and some typical uses for them. These candles are easily purchased in a witch store or spiritual supply store. Candle specialty stores will have a greater variety, although they may not stock candles that are strongly associated with the occult.

Cats

Black: return hexes, negativity, and evil intent
Green: good luck, money
Red: sex and romance

Cross or Crucifix

Although they exist in many colors, white is most commonly used
Altar candles
Uncrossing rituals

Devils

Green: fast cash and to have debts repaid
Red: sex spells
Black: domination spells

Human Figure

Use male and female figure candles to represent either yourself or the targets of your spells. They come in a variety of colors that can be coordinated with either the purpose of your spell or the people they are meant to represent.

The typical figure candle is a single naked male or female. There are also special situation figure candles:

★ A Couple Candle *is a single candle depicting a conjoined man and woman, standing side by side, dressed in wedding clothes. Use for marital, binding, and other love spells*
★ A Loving Couple Candle *is a single candle depicting a naked man and woman, entwined in passionate embrace. Use for romantic and binding spells*
★ A Divorce Candle *is a single candle depicting a conjoined male and female, standing back to back. Use for divorce and other separation spells*

Skulls

White: persuasion, communication, uncrossing

Black: domination, hexing, spell-reversals

Witch

For luck, love, and reversing spells

To have the witch's blessing on your endeavors

Seven Knob

Black: to prevent and eliminate conflicts of personality, banishing spells

Red: romance, emotional issues

Green: employment, luck, finances

Usually one knob is burned per twenty-four hour period, so that it takes seven days to burn the candle entirely.

Types of Candle

Double-Action Candles have two colors, usually red and black or green and black, one column of color atop the other. They are usually burned to increase beneficial forces and dispel harmful influence. *Triple-Action Candles* have three layers of color.

Reverse-Action Candles are red candles coated with a layer of black wax. Similar to Double-Action Candles, although some feel Reverse Actions have a more powerful effect. Use these to reverse negative spells and send them back where they came from.

Seven-Day Candles are designed to burn over approximately a seven-day period. They come in many colors and may be used for virtually any purpose. Typically Seven-Day Candles are encased in a glass sleeve. Once upon a time, the candles slid out of the sleeves for easy dressing. This is rarely the case any longer.

You can still dress a glass-encased Seven-Day Candle: drill holes into the top of the candle to insert your oil. Sprinkle with herbs and glitter dust.

The basic Seven-Day Candle is one solid color and comes in a clear glass sleeve. Manufacturers also market Seven-Day Candles with special sleeves. These will have special designs on the glass. The design may depict a saint or spirit, such as Saint Anthony, Saint Expedite, or the Seven African Powers. The actual candle's color will be chosen to coordinate with the spirit.

The candle may also be intended to coordinate with the goal of a spell: gambling luck candles, for example, will be green and the sleeve may be decorated with images of dice, cards, horseshoes, and other lucky charms. Or, the candle may be manufactured to coordinate with a specific formula oil: an Uncrossing Candle to use with **Uncrossing Oil**, for instance, or an Essence of Bend Over Candle to be used with that oil.

These decorated sleeve candles essentially become a spell unto themselves. Those dedicated to saints and spirits may have suggested prayers or petitions printed on the back of the sleeve. Use these candles to enhance any spell dedicated to a spirit. Many are available, especially those of the Hindu, Roman Catholic, Santeria, Vodou, and Unofficial Saint persuasions. If you can't find one dedicated to the spirit of your choice, or if there is a particular image dear to you, decorate your own sleeve:

1. Obtain a Seven-Day Candle in the color of your choice inside a clear sleeve. (Candle supply stores may sell empty sleeves.)

2. Attach your image or a photocopy of the image to the candle. A craft store will sell special glues that adhere to glass.

3. Decorate with glitter glue or with objects appropriate to the purpose of the candle. Attach shiny imitation coins to a candle dedicated to Lakshmi, for instance.

Using this method you can personalize a candle for any purpose put your ex-lover's image on a Summoning Seven-Day Candle to draw him or her back into your life, for instance.

When a candle has burned down, reserve the glass sleeve. Refill Seven-Day Candles are available. Just carve, dress, and slip into the sleeve.

Keep an eye on the flames for more than fire safety: they provide an oracular response to your spell. Observe whether the candle burns strong with a bright steady flame or whether it's a moody flame, alternately burning high and low. Sometimes a candle burns very fast while other times it's very slow. If you habitually burn standardized figure candles this becomes very apparent: in theory, candles should burn at a similar rate. If your Seven-Day Candle burns out in six, you know you have a speedy candle. Flames may even spontaneously extinguish and then be impossible to relight.

There are many ways to interpret these patterns. However, a bright, steady, healthy flame is invariably considered auspicious. The way the candle burns may advise regarding the likelihood of a spell's success: a candle that burns bright and quick indicates that magic forces are with you. A low, struggling flame doesn't necessarily mean that your spell will fail—it merely indicates that

it is working against tremendous opposition.

The patterns made by melting wax may also be interpreted. Any remains, ashes, or bits of wax, may be significant.

Some common candle wisdom:

★ *If flames shoot high, the spirit you've invoked is now in your presence*
★ *A very low, dim flame, on the other hand, may indicate the presence of ghosts*

Cauldrons

Many older spells assume that you will have ready access to a source of open fire: a hearth, fireplace, wood-stove, or even a bonfire, because before the modern stove this was a necessity of

In most circumstances, unless a spell specifies otherwise, it is considered metaphysical bad manners to blow out ritual candles. Either pinch them out with your fingers, or deprive them of air instead. Beautifully crafted, long-stemmed, mystically themed snuffers exist and may be consecrated to the archangel Michael, the angel in charge of candle magic and fire safety. Alternatively, a fire-proof dish may be placed over the flame until it goes out.

life. In the twenty-first century, however, access to open fire may be limited, especially for urban dwellers.

An iron cauldron of appropriate size can often substitute for a hearth or fireplace. A traditional witch's tool, a good cauldron has many uses, from brewing potions, to burning incense, to cooking a meal.

Charm Bags

A magic spell inside a bag. There are a wide variety of names for this most popular spell style, and I've used them somewhat interchangeably in this book. In addition to charm bag, there's conjure bag, medicine bag, medicine hand, mojo bag, mojo hand, just plain old mojo, gris-gris bag, ouanga bag, dilly bag, amulet bag, magic bag, and, for the scholarly, phylacteries. And those are just the English names! These are single-handedly the most popular method of carrying magically charged items around the world.

The charm bag is a bag filled with one or more power items. Some can be seen as a miniature spell or an altar in a bag. Others are work-in-progress: an ever-evolving collection of power objects.

Medicine bags can be extremely simple. A Moroccan spell recommends that an amulet bag be filled with dirt taken from a three-way crossroads and worn around the neck, to ward off the Evil Eye and/or find and maintain true love.

Medicine bags can also be complex. The Brazilian charm bag, the *patua*, is made from leather or cloth and might contain a danda root shaped into a figa, the fig hand, and be placed between leaves of rue and mucura. Garlic and cloves may be added, then prayers written out with special ink and sewn into the bag.

Some traditions carry a multitude of items in one bag. In Native North American tradition, a medicine bag is initiated via an activating agent, for instance a pinch of tobacco, pollen, corn kernels, sweetgrass, white sage, or a little bit of earth, tied into a piece of red flannel. Other traditions insist on one item per bag; magic is forbidden in orthodox Muslim tradition, the exception being the use of Koranic verses as amulets. A separate pouch is needed for each amulet. African nomads may be covered in leather and metal talisman cases.

The variety of this type of magic is endless. The container itself becomes part of the spell. Materials are carefully chosen. Fine Arabic and Tibetan amulet bags are finely crafted from metal and sometimes bejeweled. Other "bags" may be as simple as a knotted handkerchief. The drawstring bag is most familiar. Hoodoo recommends red flannel, while Romany tradition suggests red silk.

Although the words are now used somewhat synonymously, technically a "hand" is a closed bag, rather than an open one. There's a fine line between a sachet and a hand, largely drawn by the fabric it's crafted from (sachets are muslin, hands flannel) and the items they contain (a sachet contains only botanical material, a hand may contain a variety of materials, including botanicals).

Although modern Hoodoo and Conjure magic almost invariably used red flannel drawstring bags, early African-American mojo hands, immediately post-slavery and continuing onwards, were sewn red squares. With the material sewn inside, they resemble an isolated single quilt square. The traditional British mojo hand is very similar: two pieces of red flannel, cut into a heart shape, stuffed, sewn together, and the outside decorated.

Bags possess the advantage of accessibility, however there are other methods of carrying charms. The bag may be sewn into clothes, or individual items sewn into clothing, Romany style, for privacy and for added contact with the body. Igor Stravinsky wore his sacred medals pinned to his underwear.

In some traditions the mojo hand is charged before use. The following is a typical ritual, common to Hoodoo and Wicca.

✳ Charging the Mojo

Once the bag is complete:

1. Light a match and plunge it into the bag, extinguishing it. (Do *not* set your bag or its contents on fire. Be very careful if the bag contains dried botanicals or volatile essential oils.)
2. Spit in the bag and pull the string tight.

An alternative version of the mojo bag is the charm vial, popular in Central and South America. Instead of fabric, metal or leather, miniature glass bottles are filled with charms and power objects, essentially a mojo hand-crafted from glass. The items are visible, creating a talismanic, protective effect.

Tiny bottles are recycled for magical use: charms are often made from medical ampoules with yarn or cord attached so that they can be worn or hung. They typically include layers of charms, suspended in oil such as seeds, botanicals, minerals, tiny carvings or votive image cards.

Charm bags are carried in the pocket, worn around the neck or waist. They may also be hung up on the wall like an amulet or kept discreetly inside a drawer or cabinet—a small altar in a bag.

Crystal Balls

Crystal balls are used for divination (scrying), and spirit summoning.

The art of scrying transcends the stereotype of the fraudulent crystal ball reader. It is an ancient and well-respected technique. In fact, crystal balls are perhaps the most recent evolution in the ancient art of scrying. Scrying is the art of divination through the use of reflective surfaces. It is among the more difficult divination techniques, although perhaps the most ancient. The modern clear round crystal ball is particularly effective because it evokes the image of the moon.

However, the crystal ball is only one of many scrying tools. Presumably the first scryer gazed into a still lake. Roman images of the primal goddess Kybele depict her holding a flat pan of water for divination. A scrying tool may be as simple as that pan of water or as lavish as a star sapphire or star ruby, both famed divination devices. (Should you be privileged enough to have access to either of these precious gems and wish to try your hand at scrying, gaze at their crossed lines and let your mind wander.) Less expensive gemstones are also used: aquamarine and clear quartz stones, as well as polished balls. Smoky quartz is considered particularly beneficial as a device for communicating with spirits or ghosts.

In India, the water in the pan may be replaced by a pool of ink. Egyptian techniques involved gazing into ink held in the left palm. Technically the only tool required is already in your hands: buff your left thumbnail to a high polish and gaze inside.

Unlike pans but like mirrors and gemstones, crystal balls store visions and memories. Cleanse as needed. A new crystal ball must be cleansed and charged prior to its first use.

★ *Charge crystal balls by exposing them periodically to the light of the Full Moon*
★ *In some traditions, a crystal ball must be fully activated through exposure to the light of thirteen Full Moons before it's ready to use*
★ *If you use your crystal ball for spiritual communication, you may wish to keep it covered with a dark cloth between uses*

Dolls

These are also known as poppets. "Doll" derives from similar sources as the word "idol" while "poppet" is related to "puppet." The stereotypical witch's doll is made from wax and stuffed with pins to inflict pain and suffering. However, magic spell dolls may be crafted from a variety of mate-

rials and serve a variety of spell purposes. Wax dolls have been recovered from ancient Egypt, so they have certainly existed for a long time, but dolls are also formed from fabric, botanicals, wood, clay, and bone.

Dolls may be used in positive magic to:

★ *Heal disease*
★ *Induce love*
★ *Unite the estranged*
★ *Promote and enhance fertility*

On the other hand, dolls have also been used to cause injury, impotence, fatalities, pain, insanity, and a wide assortment of other human miseries.

To some extent, modern candle magic, especially the use of figure candles, is an outgrowth of doll magic.

Fabrics

In many cases, spells must be encased in fabric. The fabric itself becomes incorporated into the spell. Many traditions possess "sacred" fabrics. In many cases, the technique needed to create these fabrics derives from magical or spiritual traditions, such as batik or *ikat*. The most common fabrics used in spell-work are red silk and red flannel.

Spells are cast by embellishing fabric: many traditional needle-work arts are intrinsically connected to spiritual traditions. The exquisite traditional embroidery motifs of Baltic, Hungarian, Romany, and Slav women confer blessings, power, protection, and fertility.

Among the most vital descendants of magic fabrics are flags.

Flags and Banners

Flags are used:

★ *To honor and summon spirits*
★ *As amulets*
★ *As protective devices*

The use of flags and banners in religion and heraldry is rooted in this magical use. The sacred quality attributed to many flags, including those representing nations, derives from this history; the agitation experienced by those who feel that their flag has been "desecrated" also derives from this origin.

Symbols incorporated onto flags are perceived as providing protection—or a threat. Pirate flags weren't limited to the Jolly Roger. The more notorious pirates made sure that a specific flag trumpeted their presence and perhaps provided protection for the pirate himself.

Among the most powerful examples of flags used as a spiritual or magical tool are Haitian sequined flags, so-called Vodoun flags. Sigils, symbols, and images of the lwa or their affiliated saints are reproduced onto fabric using sequins.

Magic Belts

This category of magic tool includes anything that circles the waist or hips, and is crafted with magical intent. The category could also have been called "girdles," a word that has fallen out of fashion but was once considered seductive and magical: Aphrodite and Ishtar both wear romantic, love-inducing belts or girdles, which they have been known to lend to others in need. The belt is typically a woman's magical article, although not always. Even as a woman's article, however, the belt isn't exclusively about love, seduction, and babies. Aphrodite and Ishtar both have martial aspects. Belts are also associated with the powerful female warrior orisha, Oya. Belts also indicate that one's loins are girded: they are used in fierce, protective women's power spells.

Magic belts were once far more popular than they are at present. In Cro-Magnon graves, women were buried wearing cowrie shell belts. They lie across the abdominal area, to indicate fertility. Amulets including mojo bags hang from the belts. Ishtar's magic belt finds its descendants among belly dancers' spangled belts. The most powerful belt of all may be shed snakeskins for enhanced fertility and easier childbirth. (Shed is the key word; it's crucial that the skin not be taken by force. Cooperation of the snake powers is needed: fertility as the gift of the snake.)

There is an erotic component to many magic belts. In traditional Africa, waist beads were perceived as very erotic and seductive and thus private. To some extent, beads move to the neck to offset this aspect.

Magic Boxes

Boxes are used for a variety of purposes.

Cache Boxes

Cache boxes are needed to secure ritual tools and/or small magical items. The size of the box depends upon its purpose: obviously, if you wish to store swords or wands, a full-sized chest may be required.

Among the most powerful boxes are the following, in descending order of power:

★ *Iron boxes radiate protective power and serve as a battery, continually re-charging the box's contents*

★ *Spice boxes, crafted from cinnamon and clove wood as originally made in Indonesia*

★ *Wooden or leather boxes embellished with magic designs drawn with alkanet, indigo, woad, or henna. (Although a temporary stain on skin and hair, henna is a permanent dye on objects.)*

Spell Boxes

Spells are cast by constructing a spell box, which are enclosed altars or tableaux. In general, a spell box is filled with power items necessary to achieve a goal, although you should follow directions given for specific spells. It may be a cumulative spell done in increments: items are gathered one by one and added to enhance the power of the box. Sometimes a special box lends itself to a magical or spiritual goal. The box itself can become an intrinsic part of the spell:

★ *Attach and incorporate the power items to the box itself, such as charms, shells, beads, and feathers*
★ *Decoupage images on the outside or inside of the box to correspond to the spell's goals*
★ *Embellish with sigils or other fortuitous symbols using magic ink, henna, or another natural dye*

Shadow Box Altars

An enclosed altar maintains the advantage of discretion and privacy. Certain spirits, such as dark moon goddesses or some protective spirits may prefer an enclosed altar. Open altars disperse their power through an area; an enclosed altar's power is concentrated within. Each has its advantages; choose which suits you.

What is now called a "shadow box altar" has its roots in medieval Roman Catholic religious cabinets. Shadow boxes range in size from full-size cabinets to miniature altars contained in matchboxes.

Magic Mirrors

Among the most popular and beloved of magical tools, the magic mirror is common to many traditions, being especially beloved in ancient Egyptian, Chinese, Western ceremonial, Aztec, and Italian folk magic. It is most commonly used for:

★ *Scrying*
★ *Spirit summoning*
★ *Protective magic*
★ *Romantic magic*
★ *Lunar magic*

The ancient Egyptian word for *mirror* is a pun for *life*. This is made explicit by the shape of the handle-hand mirror, which echoes the shape of the ankh, the symbol of life held by all the Egyptian deities with the sole exception of Osiris, Lord of the Dead. The visual aspect of the pun remains today, in the *akua'ba*, the fertility-producing and thus life-affirming doll from Ghana, whose shape also recalls the ankh.

Although the mirror is a reflective tool, magically it's also believed to possess powers of absorption. Like a crystal, mirrors absorb and store information. Anything once reflected in a mirror, particularly over an extended period of time, is "stored" and may be accessed for future use. Thus the mirror is a primary tool for drawing down lunar and solar energy. It also bears a reputation as a soul catcher. Whether this use is positive or malefic depends upon the intent of the spell-caster.

The earliest mirrors were not made from glass but from natural materials that could be polished until they showed a reflection.

Ancient Egyptian Mirrors

Although mirrors might be created from other precious metals (gold, silver, electrum), the most typical ancient Egyptian mirror was made from polished copper. Copper is under the dominion of Hathor, among the most primordial of the Egyptian deities. Hathor presides over beauty, cosmetics, love, sex, fertility, and magic. She and copper share the same essence—to hold a copper mirror is to hold Hathor in your hands. Depictions of Hathor typically crafted into the mirror's handle makes this explicit. To gaze into a Hathorian mirror is to absorb her powers of beauty, grace, and love as surely as gazing into a lunar-charged mirror evokes the moon's gifts.

From Egypt, this type of polished hand mirror was exported through the Mediterranean into Europe, where it would meet its finest expression in medieval Italian hand mirrors.

Chinese Magic Mirrors

Chinese occult traditions utilize mirrors more consistently and inventively than any other.

Allegedly one man became Emperor of China through the use of a magic mirror. The favored Chinese magic mirror is a small or moderately sized circular mirror attached to a handle, crafted preferably from gold, although other precious metals may be used. Like the Italian mirror, its power is enhanced by decorating the mirror's back with auspicious power symbols.

Mirrors are traditionally used to capture and focus energy. Although the use of mirrors originally derived from lunar magic, the mirror may also be used to channel the power of the sun.

 Drawing Down the Sun: Creating a Solar Charged Mirror

This is among the easiest spells in this book. It is also potentially among the most dangerous. If done incorrectly, it can have tragic consequences. It must not be attempted by children. Adults: remember the cautionary tale of Icarus, who underestimated the power of the sun.

1. On a bright, sunny day, hold a small mirror in the palm of your hand, tilted to catch direct sunlight.
2. Maintain this position for no more than a few seconds. Nine seconds is the maximum.

IMPORTANT! SAFETY MEASURES WHILE PERFORMING THIS SPELL

★ Do not look into the mirror until the ritual is complete and the mirror is withdrawn from the sun: you must not watch the reflection within the mirror
★ Keep your eyes averted
★ Do not perform this ritual in the vicinity of dried paper, dried leaves or botanicals or anything else that could potentially catch fire
★ Make sure no one is nearby who could be inadvertently blinded or burned

3. That's it: the mirror is charged. The sun is so powerful that nine seconds is all it takes, and half of that is probably more than sufficient.
4. This mirror must be reserved for magical purposes. If it is accidentally used for another purpose, it must be cleansed, reconsecrated, and the ritual repeated.

There are many ways to make and use magic mirrors. Any mirror may be converted into a magic mirror; in a sense every mirror *is* a magic mirror.

Reproductions of ancient Egyptian mirrors may be used, as can traditional Italian or Chinese mirrors. It is also not hard to make your own. Consider what you will do with your mirror. The most popular uses are:

★ *Divination*
★ *Spiritual communication*
★ *Spell-work*
★ *Romantic or protective amulets*
★ *Banishing spells*

If you are using the mirror for casting spells, spiritual communication or as an amulet, you may not wish anyone else to have the opportunity to look into your mirror. Therefore you will need a small, discreet mirror. If used for divination, whether professional or for personal use, a larger mirror may be used and perhaps left out in the open.

Mirrors are sometimes used as negative spiritual entity detectors, something like a metaphysical cross between a smoke detector and a mousetrap. In theory, any large, powerful mirror is capable of detecting spirits. You may wish to use an antique wall mirror for this purpose, although Chinese tradition recommends that a mirror for such purposes should not be used for any other use, but kept covered when its services are not required.

 The Basic Western Ceremonial Magic Mirror

This is a good all-purpose magic mirror. It is expected, however, that you will begin the process from scratch. A round, concave piece of glass is required.

1. Coat the back, the convex side, with matte black paint. Apply it thickly but smoothly and evenly.
2. Allow the paint to dry.

3. Mount the mirror on cardboard or similar.
4. Place in a picture frame and embellish as you will.

Another Western Magic Mirror

This mirror is most appropriate for spell-casting. It has the advantage of starting with a commercially manufactured mirror.

1. Purchase a mirror.
2. Inscribe angelic formulas on the back (you may have to carefully pry off the back of the mirror). Formulas may be obtained from many classical grimoires, such as *The Key of Solomon* or *The Black Pullet*. It is recommended that you use your own blood for ink; dragon's blood ink would be a good substitute.
3. Bury the mirror at a crossroads under the Full Moon, marking the spot so that you can retrieve it later.
4. Dig it up after three days.

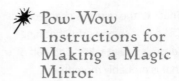

Pow-Wow Instructions for Making a Magic Mirror

Pow-Wow magic mirrors are most frequently used for scrying.

1. Obtain clear glass in whatever size suits you.
2. Construct a special three-sided frame, so that the mirror, once inserted, may be easily slid in and out.
3. Cleanse and consecrate the glass.
4. Make a strong infusion by pouring boiling water over chamomile, dragon's blood, and eyebright.
5. Let the infusion cool; then use it to "paint" one side of the glass. (Use a paint or pastry brush.) Allow this sufficient time to dry.
6. Paint over the same side, once again, this time with black paint, so that now you have one black side and one unpainted side.
7. When the paint is dry, slide it into the frame with the unpainted side facing up.

If at all possible, when scrying, hold this mirror so that it points toward the physical direction of whomever or whatever you wish to see.

In some traditions no one but you should ever look into your magic mirror. In others, someone else should always have the first peek inside the mirror, preferably your animal familiar.

 Consecrating a Mirror

1. Add three spoonfuls of sea salt to a dish of spring water.
2. Stir gently until dissolved.
3. Using a new cloth or a natural sponge, use this solution to cleanse your mirror.
4. Gently wipe it dry with another new cloth.

Milagro

A milagro is a magical object most commonly crafted in the form of an isolated human anatomical part, a heart for instance, or an arm. These objects are today most commonly associated with Latin American magic, however their roots are prehistoric. These objects, known in Latin as ex-votos, have been found in what are today Greece, Italy, and Switzerland. The most ancient are believed to derive from Iberia.

Milagros are a very fluid form of magic: most frequently found in miniature form, life-size milagros are sometimes crafted in Brazil. Typically crafted from inexpensive silver-colored metals, they may also be carved from precious metals and gemstones, as well as created from wax. Milagros are easily obtainable from spiritual goods stores and from many exporters of Latin American arts and handicrafts. They can also be easily cut from a sheet of tin or copper. Milagros are most frequently used in healing spells, spirit-summoning spells, protective spells, and romantic spells.

Mortar and Pestle

At some point it is extremely likely that you will have to grind something or blend some botanicals together. Mortars and pestles are ancient, primal tools. They come in many sizes and materials: glass, brass, marble, volcanic stone. Mortars and pestles are the finest grinding tools for two reasons. First, the tool clearly mimics the sexual act, the act of creation. And what is magic after all but an act of creation, an act of generation? This is made explicit in one of the more obscure Greek myths. Although the more famous story of the discovery of fire involves its theft by Prometheus, in another version, Hermes, the Opener of Ways, first creates fire by vigorously grinding the pestle in the mortar.

Secondly, the very physical act of manual grinding allows you to grind your intentions into the botanicals in a way that pressing the button on a food processor cannot.

If you do not have a mortar and pestle, it is preferable to substitute manual methods rather than a food processor. You can fold a piece of wax paper and place the material that needs to be ground in between the fold. Alternatively, you can smash the material with a hammer, which puts the power of metal in your hand, or roll a rolling pin over it, focusing on your desired results while you work.

The mortar and pestle is also a witch's vehicle: perhaps a hint as to the botanical origins of flying ointments. Baba Yaga, wild Russian forest witch and master herbalist, rides a mortar and pestle through the air, sweeping away her traces with a broom.

Musical Instruments

Did magic adopt the use of specific musical instruments or was the creation of these instruments stimulated by magical need? The earliest magical rituals involved music and dance. Although a spellbook cannot accurately record these rituals, these traditions continue in healing and trance ceremonies throughout the world. Exorcisms and spiritual communication are accomplished through music.

Drums and Other Percussion Instruments

It is probably impossible to separate drums from magic. Drums express the human heartbeat; they are used for a wide variety of magical purposes, including healing, banishing, protective rites, and spirit summoning. One type of drum or another is enjoyed by virtually every culture on Earth. The earliest visual depictions of spiritual rituals include drums. The Egyptian protective spirit Bes is almost never seen without his frame drum. Similarly Kybele, perhaps the most ancient deity still familiar to us today, carries a frame drum. The use of percussion instruments is central to both Bes's and Kybele's mythology. Interestingly, as opposed to the modern perception of percussion as masculine, drums, particularly frame drums and tambourines, were once identified strongly as women's instruments and were a sacred tool in many women's spiritual traditions.

Drumming remains central to African-derived rituals, as each orisha and lwa possesses their own rhythms and songs, which are used to summon and communicate with the spirits. Drums are also traditional shamanic tools, and tools of divination.

Percussion is easily incorporated into ritual. Many inexpensive instruments are available; they are also easily handcrafted.

Flutes

These are also ancient instruments; flutes appear as a component of many myths and fairy tales. Greek Pan and Athena played different forms of the instrument. Fairy tales abound with stories of magic flutes that may be used to summon spirits, allies, animals, or loved ones. The Pied Piper is only the most famous example.

★ *Native American cedar flutes are used for romance and seduction*
★ *Chinese bamboo spirit flutes are used to invoke a specific spirit, whose name may be carved into the bamboo*
★ *European custom suggests that an elder wood flute played at midnight in a remote, isolated location will summon spirits to you*

Any other instrument may also be incorporated into spell-work. Instruments may be played "live;" recordings may also be incorporated into ritual and spells.

Sieves

This seemingly mundane kitchen tool has a long history of magical use. An old-fashioned term for a sieve is a *riddle*, as in riddled with holes.

The term does not refer only to the modern metal strainer, but to any type of sifter, including grain winnows. An example of ancient multi-tasking—frame drums may have tiny perforations, so that they may be used to finely sift henna and herbs, in addition to their musical uses.

Sieves have fallen out of fashion, exiled to the kitchen cabinets, but they were once considered common magical fare. The sieve is sacred to Isis; she collected Osiris' limbs in a sieve. The sieve is also featured on many Gnostic engraved gems. The Roman Catholic Church would later ascribe the symbol to Satan.

Sieves are used in many spells, especially for fertility, influencing the weather, and divination.

Swords

Magic swords have historically played a role in Chinese, Japanese, Jewish, and Persian magic, as well as in modern Wicca. Actual functional swords may be used or ceremonial replicas. Use of the sword invokes primal metal magic, although just as there are metal wands, there are also wooden swords, particularly in classical East Asian magic.

Once upon a time, each sword was made to order, measured to suit the bearer as surely as a magic wand. Crafting was a secret operation. Master swordsmiths hoarded their formulas; rumors circulated periodically that human blood was needed to forge a magic sword. Vestiges of these legends are still found in Japanese mythology.

A fine sword was considered as much an individual as a person; each had a name, its own proclivities, and was believed to possess a personality. A legendary sword of this type may be observed in the movie, *Crouching Tiger, Hidden Dragon.*

In Chinese tradition, the most valued magic sword would be one inherited from a famous and consistently successful warrior, even if one only intended to use it for magical purposes. The next best bet is either a peach wood or iron blade consecrated in the name of the famed sword it's supposed to represent. Willow and mulberry wood are also favored. Similarly in Western magic, swords of famous warriors held magical associations. Weapons once belonging to the Knights Templar, for instance, that elite knightly order disbanded and doomed because of alleged occult practices, are priceless magical tools.

The sword's power may be enhanced through embellishment. The grimoire, *The Key of Solomon*, recommends engraving Kabalistic inscriptions on hilts and blades. Other powerful embellishments include runes, sacred verses, hieroglyphs, and Chinese calligraphy.

Swords are used in various ceremonial rites. They are used for casting circles. They are a protective device and may be used in exorcisms and to repel malevolent spirits. When not in use, swords are kept wrapped in fabric, especially red silk.

Not all magic swords are actual swords. Small Chinese amulet swords are constructed from coins and red silk cord, and embellished with a complex series of knots and tassels. Typically inexpensive, they are readily available through Chinatown markets and feng shui sources. These coin swords serve as a protective device as well as talismans to balance and improve finances.

In addition to full-sized swords, knives and daggers also have magical uses.

The most famous ritual knife is the *athame*, the Wiccan ceremonial knife. It is reserved exclusively for ritual use: in particular, it cannot be used to draw blood. In case of accident or emergency, it must be purified and re-consecrated. You may craft one yourself or find an interesting knife or dagger and consecrate it to the purpose. Among its uses are inscribing the circle for magic, mixing potions and charged waters.

Like swords and wands, the power of knives and daggers may be enhanced through embellishment.

Magic Wands

Because magic wands are such an important component in portrayals of fantasy magic, it's crucial to point out that it is not the wand that *works*; it is the practitioner. The wand is merely a tool with which to direct the user's will or intention. Obviously some wands are superior to others; certain wands suit certain purposes, practitioners, or traditions better than others.

Historically, magic wands are common to magic traditions all over Earth. Today, they are especially significant in Druid, Wiccan, and High Ritual traditions. Wands are used for spiritual and religious ritual purposes as well as a magical tool. Some traditions require use of a wand—it is a mandatory magical tool. Let it be noted, however, that not every practitioner, spellcaster, or witch uses a wand. It is not a requirement for magic.

We enter the realm of very personal magic with wands: some practitioners collect wands, preferring different woods for different magical purposes. Others desire only one wand, with which they can forge an intensive relationship, the wand virtually becoming an extension of the body. There are those for whom an exquisitely, meticulously crafted wand is an absolute necessity. Others prefer to work with an unornamented, uncarved branch, a fallen stick, or a piece of driftwood.

In some cases, particularly where privacy is an issue, substitutions may be made. A folded-up umbrella serves nicely for discreet, outdoor rituals. In that case, treat the umbrella like the ritual tool that it has become, giving it the same care and consideration as a more traditional magic wand.

Although wands are famously wooden, metal wands can be extremely effective too. Master Magus Aleister Crowley, for instance, typically alternated between two wands: a heavy cast-iron wand and a lighter wooden wand, usually almond wood.

Finding Your Wand

★ *Wands may be inherited from another practitioner, a mentor, or coven member*

★ *You may receive a new one as a gift*

★ *You can purchase a pre-crafted one: a skilled artisan can often create an aesthetically more beautiful wand than a layperson, if this is important to you. There are professional wand-crafters who will craft a wand to suit your specific desires and needs*

★ *You can craft your own*

If you inherit or purchase a ready-made wand it is crucial that it be cleansed of previous influences and charged with your own personal energy and vibration.

Of course there is always the rare exception: if you have inherited a wand from a particular powerful and revered practitioner—if you've discovered Merlin's very own wand, for instance—you may not wish to erase previous vibrations but to maintain and build upon them.

1. Hold a quartz crystal between your hands and charge it with your energy and power.
2. When the wand is not in use, wrap the crystal around it with a piece of red silk.
3. Roll the wand, with the attached crystal, into black velvet and let them remain together.
4. Periodically, cleanse and re-charge the crystal.

Crafting a Wand

The traditional length of a magic wand is eighteen inches long, or from your elbow to the tip of your forefinger.

To Cut or Not to Cut?

As usual, much depends upon tradition. In the Romany tradition, branches are not cut. Instead, one looks for the right branch to appear. Magic wands are gifts of the trees and, in fact, wands are used very specifically in tree magic—magic to call upon the power of the trees and their presiding spirits. If you desire a specific kind of wood or crave a wand from a specific tree, one may request that the tree drop a branch, and return periodically to see if the wish has been granted. If it is, even though no cutting is done, a libation is still offered at the spot where one picks up the branch.

Before you cut a branch, remember to ask permission from the tree. The branch will always contain the essence of the tree, and will work more harmoniously and dependably if it is received in a spirit of cooperation.

1. Look for a healthy tree that can afford to give you a branch. Having chosen your tree, should you discover an appropriate branch waiting for you, fallen on the ground, or hanging from the tree, this is an extremely auspicious sign, a true gift of the tree. The wand created from this branch offers you great power.

2. Talk to the tree. Really talk—speak out loud. This enhances the reality of the situation for you. Leave some silence in order to receive answers, as well. Explain why you want a branch and ask permission to take one.

3. Get a response. To receive your answer:
   ★ Use divination: consecrated wooden runes are ideal communication tools, as is the simpler flipping a coin
   ★ Sit quietly by the tree and wait for the answer to become clear to you
   ★ Request a sign: if you see a red bird within the next five minutes, for instance, your request is granted
   ★ Request that the tree or its presiding spirit answer you in your dreams

4. Cut as swiftly and painlessly as possible.

5. Offer a libation: water is a requirement. You may also offer an exchange of gifts: honey, tobacco, wine or spirits, crystals and gemstones are traditional.

6. Take the wood and carve the wand.

7. Embellish, if you like, by carving runes or other magical symbols into the wand. Add a crystal to the tip or enhance with feathers, fabric, and stones. Let your personal magical vision guide you.

Choosing Your Wood

Although specific types of wood are favored in various traditions and for various purposes, realistically these may not exist as an option. Most of us have access to only limited types of wood. Neither should we search out endangered or rare specimens.

No wood will work as well for you as the wood from a tree with which you have forged an alliance:

1. Develop a relationship with the tree: visit it, talk to it, bring it gifts, listen to it.

2. When you're ready, either request a branch or wait until one is given to you.

3. Having obtained your wand, if you continue your relationship with the parent tree, you will continue to enhance the power of your tool. Re-energize your wand by resting it against the roots of its mother tree.

Good all-purpose wands include ash, hawthorn, hazel, and rowan. Lightning-struck wood is considered packed with power. Driftwood makes an excellent wand; it does not have to be cut and combines the powers of Earth and sea.

Some woods are favored for specific purposes and thus some practitioners prefer multiple wands for use with different purposes.

★ *Divination: ash, rowan, willow*
★ *Exorcism: date palm, tamarisk*
★ *Healing magic: hazel*
★ *Love magic: apple, ash tree (a.k.a. Venus of the Woods)*
★ *Necromancy: cypress*
★ *Prosperity magic: ash*
★ *Protective wands to ward off malicious spirits and malevolent magic: blackthorn, olive, rowan*
★ *Spirit work: elder*

Favored Woods for Magical Wands According to Tradition

★ *Ainu: bamboo, with leaves remaining. Top carved into spiral designs*

★ *Berber: oleander*
★ *Celtic: hawthorn, hazel*
★ *China: peach, willow*
★ *Druid (British): hawthorn, rowan, yew*
★ *Druid (Gaul): oak*
★ *Romany: elm*
★ *Russian, Slavic: birch*
★ *Scythian: willow*

Wands are not limited to wood. Metal wands are excellent power conductors. Embellish with crystals, seashells, and charms. Copper is a particularly excellent conductor of energy. An iron wand provides power and protection.

Specialized Wands

★ *A wand for love and seduction: copper topped with rose quartz*
★ *Lunar wand: place a moonstone atop a silver wand, for moon, love, and fertility magic*
★ *A mermaid's wand: driftwood topped with coral, pearls or shells for lunar, love, fertility, and money magic as well as rituals by the sea*
★ *A highly protective ritual wand: wrap copper wire around an iron wand, embellish with hematite and black tourmalines*

- ★ A quartz crystal tip empowers any all-purpose wand
- ★ A rose quartz attached to the wand enhances romantic spells
- ★ Amethysts empower spiritual quests and cleansings
- ★ Black tourmalines, Herkimer diamonds and smoky quartz used to embellish a wand provide added protection during ritual use

Wrap your wand in leather, red silk or other magical fabric when not in use. Store it in a box for safety, if you like, however wrap it in cloth first.

For optimum power, keep your wand beside you as much as possible to absorb your energy and desires and harmonize your vibrational energies. Many sleep with their wands, either beside them in bed or beneath them.

Staff

The distinction between wands and staffs often has to do with size: a staff is thicker and substitutes as a walking stick. In theory, a staff should be long and solid enough to lean on. Historically associated with ancient Egyptian and Semitic magic, staffs are associated with the Bib-lical Moses and his Egyptian opponents.

The modern staff is most associated with Obeah, the African-derived traditions native to the British West Indies. The *Obeah Stick*, also called an *Obi Stick*, is a carved wooden staff, usually featuring a serpent motif. The simpler ones are carved so that a snake-like groove encircles the staff. The more elaborate *Staff of Moses* usually features a snake carved from bottom to top. Staffs may be hollowed out and filled with botanicals.

Divining Rods

Hazel twigs and forks cut on Midsummer's Eve are recommended for divining purposes.

Fans

A folding fan, held closed, may substitute for a magic wand. Fans may also substitute for broomsticks. An enchantress in the *Arabian Nights* reveals herself by riding a fan.

Fans are also used in a variety of magical traditions, not as substitutes but in their own right. Chinese magic favors the sandalwood fan, especially for protective purposes. The fan creates a personal psychic and spiritual shield. Sandalwood possesses sacred, benevolent, protective qualities. These may be enhanced through ornamentation: fans are frequently embellished with magical images and/or words. Strengthen and maintain the fan's power by periodically passing it through sandalwood incense smoke.

As with wands or staffs, fans are not tools to be shared. When not in use, the fan should rest discreetly hidden, wrapped in fabric, and placed in a magic box.

The powerful Yoruba orisha, Oshun, counts peacocks among her sacred birds. Devotees keep peacock feather fans in her honor. They are used in rituals to honor her and when not they are not in use are kept on her altar. Peacock feather fans are also appropriate for use with other spirits, such as the Hindu Lakshmi and the Roman Juno.

Fans crafted from various types of feather or an intact bird's wing complete with feathers are used in Native American and Native American-influenced traditions as a device for wafting incense, especially for cleansing purposes.

Key Magical Techniques

Bathing

Although this may seem like the magical equivalent of instructions for boiling water, many spells are accomplished through baths. Various magical techniques increase the odds of a spell's success.

★ *In general, it is beneficial to submerge completely in the water at least once, although some spells may specify the number of submersions*

★ *When you want to rid yourself of something—a problem, bad debts, your annoying boyfriend—bathe down and out: start at the top, work your way down your body and out the arms and legs*

★ *When you want to draw something toward you—love, cash, or a job— start at the feet and move in toward your heart. Start at the ends of your hands and move inwards*

★ *Allow yourself to air dry. Drying yourself with a towel wipes much of the residue, the aura of the bath, off your skin. Nothing will happen if you use a towel but you will receive consistently stronger, better results if you take the time to air dry*

What may be the most ancient magical techniques of all may be unfamiliar to the modern practitioner—foot track spells and knot magic.

Foot Track Magic

"Leave nothing behind but your footprints"—or so go the instructions for today's eco-tourists. Even footprints, however, have their magical uses. Foot track magic, as its modern name goes, is most closely associated today with Hoodoo traditions. But it is actually a particularly primal, international magical technique. There are oblique references to it in the Talmud. Instructions attributed to Pythagoras forbade people to pierce footprints with nail or knife, although similar spells are contained in this book.

This ancient practice derives from dry lands, where a foot-print lingers. To some extent, men lend themselves more to foot track magic because of their generally heavier, deeper imprints.

There are two varieties of foot track magic: in one, usually used for banishing or hexing, some-thing is done to the actual foot-print in the ground. The other method is to scoop up the dirt from the footprint in its entirety. This will usually be later com-bined with other ingredients for magical purposes, both positive and malevolent.

When gathering up footprints, it is vital to the success of the spell that the entire footprint is gathered. It is also crucial (and not always simple to determine) that one obtains the footprint of the correct person!

Knotting

Knots are so intrinsically and anciently connected with magic that tying knots was once synony-mous with magic in general. The art goes back to the Babylonians and who knows how much fur-ther back in unrecorded history. The Hebrew word for amulet, *kame'a*, has a root meaning *"to*

bind." Knotting is the original binding spell.

Any intension or force can be tied or controlled by the knot. What separates the magical knot from tying a shoelace is the focus and intention of the one making the knot. However, the act of tying a shoelace can be transformed into a magical act: tie a child's sneaker: focus on blessing and protecting as you pull the knot tight.

In a knot charm, it goes without saying that you are focusing and concentrating your energy with every knot. Materials used in knot charms include threads, cord, plant stems, metal wire, animal or human hair.

Knots can be used for positive or malevolent intent. Common uses of knot magic include love, healing, wealth, and weather spells (i.e., controlling the wind and rain).

Knots are used to bind intent, and also to remove spells. They are common Celtic, Chinese, Egyptian, and Scythian motifs. The concept of the "lover's knot" lies in ancient love knot magic. Some believe that the inspiration for the ring arose from knot magic.

The animal patron of knot magic is the spider.

 Basic Knot Spell

1. Focus on your goal and desire, while holding a red cord in your hands.
2. Tie a knot.
3. Wrap it in fabric, place it in a magic box and keep it in a safe, secure location.

A Traditional Knot Incantation

This incantation accompanies the tying of nine knots.

By knot of one, the spell's begun!
By knot of two, my spell comes true
By knot of three, so mote it be
By knot of four, power I store
By knot of five, my magic is alive
By knot of six, this spell I fix
By knot of seven, this spell I leaven
By knot of eight, it is fate
By knot of nine, what's wished is mine!

Animal Spells

Is it time to measure the cat for a magic wand? Perhaps the parrot needs to learn some chants? Maybe there is a set of domination spells so that the dog can force you to walk him on the schedule *he* chooses? No, spells regarding animals are still meant for people to perform, although some benefit from some animal assistance. Many of these spells involve protecting animals from physical and spiritual harm. Others benefit humans, through the power and gifts of animals.

Magical Partners

Animals who participate in your spells and rituals, enhancing them with their own powers, tend to fall into one of two categories:

★ *Familiars*
★ *Allies*

The concept of an animal as a *pet* is a modern one. Those who possessed this concept of interspecies friendship ahead of their time often found themselves condemned for witchcraft on grounds of familiarity with demonic creatures like cats, birds, rabbits, black dogs, reptiles, and amphibians. Sounds like what you'd find for sale in any local pet store? Well, familiar animals are exactly that: *familiar*. The classic witch's cat, rabbit or toad, a familiar is an actual, individual animal with whom one can live and share an intense psychic, personal bond. If this characterizes a relationship you have ever had with an animal, then you have had a familiar, regardless of whether you engaged in magical practices together. A dog who won't sleep unless it's under your bed, the cat who follows you from room to room, the bird who spends the day perched on your shoulder: these all qualify as familiars.

A familiar's presence may be sufficient to spark and enhance your magic, whether there is any conscious active involvement or not. For others, the psychic and magical bonds possible between animal and human create profound power and satisfaction.

In general, familiars are creatures who can realistically live with you: cats, dogs, rabbits, birds, toads, and snakes are most typical. Those living and working closely with other species—those species that usually do not live among people—may discover psychic and magical bonds, as well. Wild animals that remain wild can also qualify as familiars, though invariably they choose you rather

than the other way round. These include those birds or bees that, taking a liking to someone in the family, stop by daily. Scandinavian witches traditionally favored flies as familiars. Wild dolphins occasionally single out an individual human and initiate a relationship. It is not unknown for people living on the edge of woods or in a wilderness place to develop a special relationship with an individual creature.

A familiar is a specific, individual creature with whom you have established a psychic bond. Of course, this limits the creatures with whom you can magically interact. What if your magic requires a rhinoceros or crocodile? What if it requires a dragon or unicorn?

A familiar may be considered an animal ally but *animal allies* transcend the boundaries of familiars. Animal allies are a form of spiritual relationship: because the relationship may occur entirely in the realm of spirit, any animal may be approached. The presiding spirit of the animal may also be approached, rather than any individual creature.

A person may have as many familiars and/or allies as needed.

Animal Images

Among the oldest existing human artifacts are the beautifully detailed prehistoric cave paintings, indicating the profound magical link between humans and animals. Small portable images of specific animals, usually crafted from clay or stone, have also been used since ancient times for assorted magical purposes, especially healing, hunting, and protection, and pursuit of enhanced psychic power.

The Zuni, a Native American people from New Mexico, have turned this tradition into an art form. Zuni stone fetishes, miniature carvings of specific animals, were originally created for ceremonial and hunting purposes. Today most are intricately carved, displaying the creator's artistry and skills. Originally, this was not the case: Earth provided the artistry and the magic. Traditional fetish-carvers searched for stones where the shape of the creature was already apparent. At most, minimal shaping was needed to see the animal within. Because the stone charm is discovered, rather than consciously created, the animal spirit is given the opportunity to choose you rather than the reverse.

1. Search for similar stones. You will recognize one when you see it; like holed-stones these are gifts from Earth.
2. Charge and consecrate your stone fetish by placing it in a magic box together with images, food, and magical botanical activators. Traditionally corn pollen was used to feed and activate the fetish; use whatever seems appropriate and sacred to you.
3. When not in use, keep your fetish protected in its box or container. Feed it on schedule to keep it activated and powerful.

Animal Communication Spell: Eve Oil

Eve Oil may be used to assist and enhance communication with animals.

1. Place apple blossoms, dried pomegranate seeds, and snake root in a bottle.
2. Cover with sweet almond and jojoba oil.
3. Dress candles with this oil to accompany visualization as well as actual physical communication.

✳ Familiar Consecration Spell

To cement and/or formalize the psychic bonds between you and your familiar:

1. Cast a circle large enough to hold you, your familiar and any magical tools that you wish simultaneously to consecrate (these may include leashes, collars or similar pet paraphernalia, as well as spell components or ritual tools).
2. Burn frankincense on the periphery of the circle.
3. Sit within the circle, with your familiar, until you feel that it's time to come out.
4. Repeat as needed.

Live dangerously! If your familiar is a cat, cast your circle with dried catnip, and instead of frankincense, burn diviner's sage to enhance your powers of prophesy. Let the cat play, while you allow yourself sudden bursts of inspiration.

Although you can bring any animal into your home, you cannot force it to be your familiar. This profoundly affectionate relationship, built on love, respect, and personal chemistry, must develop independently. Likewise, animal alliances cannot be forced.

They may, however, be requested. Many believe that we are each born with the alliances we need, whether animal, botanical, or spirit. The key is to discover these alliances and learn how to work with them for maximum power and benefit.

Various methods exist for discovering allies and requesting new relationships. Many card-based divination systems exist. Animal allies also manifest themselves in your dreams. Any animal or species that appears consistently to you, whether in dreams or in waking life, may be an ally, or may potentially become one.

If you desire a specific alliance, request it via a combination of your altar and visualization:

✳ Animal Ally Invitation Spell

1. Choose a focal image for your altar, something that represents your ally for you. Use a toy, a photograph, or an image. It is more crucial that it resonates strongly for you than that it be a literal depiction.

2. Surround it with objects or images that would normally be used to lure this creature. A dish of honey, for instance, summons a bear. Make the invitation as strong as possible.
3. If you can find candles in the shape of your desired ally or its food, add them to the altar.
4. Grind cinnamon and frankincense together and burn them as a spirit-summoning incense.
5. In addition to Step 2, offer literal food (a dish of milk for a snake, for instance). Alternatively, burn images of appropriate food.
6. Relax. Let your eyes go slightly out of focus and await visitations.
7. Try this for up to thirty minutes a day, until you receive results.

Although this spell requests a waking vision, realistically your response may still occur during your dreams: have paper and pen by your bedside to record any significant dreams.

Sometimes familiars and allies are discovered for you.

In traditional Mexico and Central America, many shamans and witches are believed able to transform themselves into animals, known as *nagual*. A coyote observed walking down the road may be a regular coyote or it may be a witch in disguise. In the Mexican state of Oaxaca, however, a different concept exists. The *nahual* (as it is spelled in Oaxaca) is perceived to be a guardian spirit acquired at birth, a sacred gift from parents to their child.

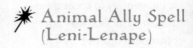

Animal Ally Spell (Leni-Lenape)

Sometimes a more concrete familiar is desired. According to a Leni-Lenape Indian tradition, babies are given a living, tangible animal ally rather than just an abstract protective spirit. Usually a puppy or kitten is chosen, or some other appropriate companion animal. The animal is treated as a pet and encouraged to be the child's companion. These pets are not shared: every child has his or her own. This is a life partnership.

★ *Should the animal die, it is perceived as having been a buffer for the child, essentially having taken the "hit" meant for the child, particularly if the child has been threatened by illness or accident. The animal is buried with ceremonies, releasing the child from the relationship. The child is given another pet immediately*

★ *Should the child die, funeral rituals release the animal from the bond*

Animals may also be dedicated to specific spirits, not just to humans. This creates a profound triangular relationship between human, spirit, and animal. In an indigenous Siberian ritual, the animal dedicated to the deity lives a charmed life:

⁂ Animal Spirit Dedication Ritual

1. A specific animal is chosen to be dedicated to a specific deity.
2. Purify the animal with juniper incense.
3. Sprinkle it with wine.
4. Decorate the animal with ribbons in colors associated with the specific spirit.
5. The animal is returned home or to its flock. It is now never ridden, worked, or eaten, but is instead treated exceptionally well (or at least left alone to enjoy life) as a gesture of sacrificial devotion. This treatment may be extended over the creature's entire natural life or for a specified period of time, although this must be stipulated from the first initiation of the ritual.

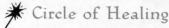

Animal Healing Spells

⁂ Circle of Healing

Cast a circle with blooming thistles: demarcate the entire circle or place one bloom in each of the four cardinal points. Bring the animal within the circle in order to intensify the effects of any healing or cleansing spells.

⁂ Saint Benedict's Healing Spell

In his lifetime, Saint Benedict persecuted pagans and witches. One wonders how he would have reacted had he known that, centuries later, he'd be magically petitioned to assist ailing animals?

Burn a white candle dedicated to Saint Benedict and offer him a glass of brandy or Benedictine. Make your petition of healing; Saint Benedict's animal ally is the crow. Look for the appearance of a crow to indicate a response to your petition.

⁂ Masterwort Strength Spell

Masterwort allegedly imparts greater physical strength and has thus been used to assist beasts of burden. Place masterwort in an amulet bag and attach to the animal as desired.

Lost Animal Spells

Crossroads Lost Animal Spell

A Russian method for calling lost animals home involves journeying to a crossroads, where, magically speaking at least, roads merge and separate and you never know who or what might turn up from any direction at any time.

1. Go to a crossroads.
2. Face west, the direction of the setting sun.
3. Bow from the waist nine times.
4. Do this three times, for a total of twenty-seven bows, calling the animal as you normally would, and also chant prayers and petitions and recite sacred texts.
5. Don't stop calling and/or petitioning until three series of nine bows each are complete, then take ten steps backward without turning around.
6. Turn around and go home.

When an animal goes missing, one common immediate response is to post signs requesting information and assistance from others. This next Russian spell takes that notion a step further: assistance is requested from Earth's various spirit powers, so that they will locate and send your animal back home. As with standard signs, a reward is posted. Should the spell work, be sure to pay it. (The Forest Tsar is chief of all woodland spirits; the Water Tsar is chief of all water spirits, and so on. Adjust the spell if necessary to suit your circumstances.)

Magical Sign Animal Spell

Write messages on three pieces of birch bark (one for each of the nature tsars) as follows:

I'm writing to the Forest Tsar and the Forest Tsarina and their small children.

I'm writing to the Earth Tsar and the Earth Tsarina and their small children.

I'm writing to the Water Tsar and the Water Tsarina and their small children.

I'm writing to inform you that [INSERT YOUR NAME] has lost a [INSERT COLOR, GENDER, DESCRIPTION] [INSERT TYPE OF

ANIMAL INCLUDING AS MUCH DESCRIPTIVE MATERIAL AS YOU FEEL IS NECESSARY TO IDENTIFY AND DISTINGUISH YOUR ANIMAL FROM OTHERS].

If you have him/her please send him/her back without delaying one day, one hour, one minute, one second.

If you don't comply with my wish, I swear to pray and testify against you.

If you comply with my wish, I shall give you [INSERT SPECIFIC PLEDGE].

Fasten one message to a tree in the forest. Bury the second in Earth. Attach a small stone to the third and throw it into some living water.

The animal is expected to find its way home shortly.

Protection Spells for Animals

An animal's collar provides an excellent framework for protection spells; just remember to charge objects before attaching them. You can also incorporate knot magic wherever possible, to make the magic more powerful.

The following may be attached to the collar:

★ *Quartz crystal to enhance the animal's aura and provide protection*

★ *Rose quartz, to bestow the protective properties of your love*

★ *Other crystals, protective amulets, religious medals, and similar may be attached to the pet's collar as desired*

✳ Animal Candle Protection Spell

1. Find or create a candle shaped to resemble your companion animal.
2. Carve the animal's identifying information, protective runes, or other symbols onto it.
3. Anoint the candle with **Protection Oil** and burn.

If the candle is too cute to burn, get two. Maintain one permanently, while burning the second.

✳ Animal Image Protection Spell

Use an actual photograph of your pet or if unavailable, choose something, another image, statue, or candle bearing a strong resemblance for this spell.

1. Paint protective runes, hieroglyphs, or other symbols onto the image.
2. Anoint with **Protection Oil**.
3. Keep the image in a safe, discreet spot, touching up periodically with Protection Oil.

*As an alternative, you could trace invisible runes, sigils, or protective hieroglyphs onto the image with **Protection Oil**.*

Assorted Spells to Protect Domestic Animals From Malevolent Magic

★ *Build your barn near birch trees*
★ *If the barn is already standing, transplant birch trees nearby*
★ *Adorn the birch trees, or other nearby trees, with red and white ribbons*
★ *Surround the barn with lilies and primroses. (Maintain them, replacing as needed.)*
★ *Bury a hatchet, sharp side up, under the barn's threshold, so that the animals must walk over it as they enter and depart*
★ *Horseshoes protect animals as well as humans. Post them over the barn door. The Hungarian method is to draw a horseshoe*

over the barn door using black chalk
★ *Keep a piece of real silver in a dish or bucket of water, out of reach of the animals. This may be a small charm or a real silver coin. Once a week, sprinkle the animals with this water, then replace with fresh water*
★ *Sprinkle the animals with **Rose of Jericho Water** once a week*

Animal Conjure Bag Protection Spell

Create this charm for any companion animal that sheds teeth.

1. Collect the animal's baby teeth and place within a conjure bag.
2. Add a coin minted in the animal's birth year if known, otherwise substitute a lucky medal or charm plus a tag with the animal's name or initials scratched into the metal.
3. Keep the bag in a safe place for protection.

✳ Egg Cleansing Spell

Just like people, animals need periodic ritual protective cleansings. (See Cleansing Spells.) Fumigations and asperging, the most popular methods for people, are equally effective for animals. However this may be easier said than done: try explaining to horses or cats that wafting smoke over them is really in their best interests. The following may be easier to accomplish:

1. Rub the animal with a whole, raw egg in its shell, working from head to tail and down, rather than up, the legs.
2. Flush the egg down the toilet for a house pet; otherwise, dispose of the egg outside the home or barn.

✳ Hair and Wax Protection Spell

1. Collect one hair from the head and one from the tail of every animal you wish protected. (Substitute one feather each from head and tail for each bird.)
2. Melt wax.
3. Add the hairs to the wax.
4. Remove the wax from the heat source and allow it to harden.

5. If possible, now lead all the animals needing protection around the perimeter of their home, in a sunwise direction. A minimum of two people is required for this: the person leading the parade holds the block of wax in one hand and a sacred image in the other. The person bringing up the rear drags an axe on the ground behind.
6. When all animals have safely returned home, bury the wax in a safe, secret place.

Dogs
✳ Child's Dog Hair Medicine Bag

1. Fill a medicine bag with loose dog hair.
2. Add any other lucky charms, as desired.
3. Give to a child to wear or carry for protection.

✳ Greyhound Spirit Protection

A home where a well-cared-for, happy greyhound lives will allegedly never be haunted by malicious spirits.

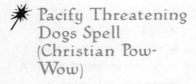

Pacify Threatening Dogs Spell (Christian Pow-Wow)

Pow-Wow strongly incorporates the use of spoken charms. This one is used to soothe a threatening dog and provide protection—excellent for those forced to walk past a snarling, snapping canine.

The charm must be repeated three times before you reach the dog (or the dog reaches you!)

Dog, hold thy nose to the ground!
God has made thee, me, and hound.
In the name of the Father, the Son,
    and the Holy Ghost.

Then form the sign of the cross three times.

This spell as recorded in 1820 by John George Hohman in his definitive Book of Pow-Wows: The Long Lost Friend, *omits the last line of the charm, but includes the crosses.*

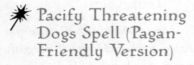

Pacify Threatening Dogs Spell (Pagan-Friendly Version)

Historically, there have always been two movements within the Pow-Wow community: those who emphasize Christian orientation *and those who do not. Rhymes were adapted as needed and continue to evolve. This pagan-friendly version calls upon those Greek divinities that exert great influence over hounds:*

Dog, hold your nose to the ground!
Creator made you, me, and hound
In the name of the triple goddess,
    Selene, Artemis, and Hecate

Repeat three times. The cross, as a pre-Christian symbol of protection, may still be formed. A pentacle, crescent moon, downward-facing triangle, or other shape may also be substituted, as desired.

Stop Dogs Barking Spell

Place leaves of hound's tongue in your shoes, beneath your feet. Alternatively, carry within a charm bag.

Sweet Nature Dog Collar

Sew a piece of flint and a piece of coral inside a dog's collar to protect against illness and ill temper.

Banishing Spells

There's often confusion over the difference between banishing spells and binding spells, however it's crucial that you understand this difference.

★ *Binding spells attach something or, more frequently, someone to you with great intensity, often permanently*

★ *Banishing spells remove something or, more frequently, someone from your presence, often permanently*

It's an important distinction. Although magic spells are typically used to manifest something or someone, quite often the reverse is needed. Something or someone needs to be sent packing quickly.

Banishing spells are traditionally timed to coincide with the waning moon, in the hopes that, just as the moon diminishes, so will the unwanted presence.

Also falling under the category of banishing spells are *Avoidance Spells*—those spells required when you wish to avoid contact, for instance with creditors or debt collectors. Banishing spells are used to prevent any unwelcome returns, too. However, you may wish to consider *Protection Spells* to reinforce, or in some circumstances replace, banishing spells.

Banishing People and Other Pests

✳ Balloon Banishing

1. Write the target of your spell's name onto a slip of paper.
2. Insert this paper into a balloon, either before or after blowing it up, whichever you find simpler.
3. Take the balloon to an appropriate place and release it.

✳ Banish Evil Spell

Sometimes it's not clear what or who needs to be banished. There's just a prevailing sense of evil that needs to be expelled. This spell is most effective during the Dark Moon. An iron hammer is required, as is a flat rock, and either a coffin nail or an old rusty nail.

1. Hammer the nail against the rock. The goal is not to pierce the rock but merely to score it three times across the face. Visualize what you are dispelling while you hammer.
2. Bury the stone far away.
3. Carry the nail in a red mojo bag, together with some crossroads' and/or graveyard dirt.

✳ Banish Negative Energy

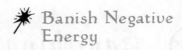

Occasionally what requires banishing is more ambiguous than unwanted guests, mean spirits, or vermin: burn chicory to banish negative emotions from the premises as well as negative energy, regardless of the source.

Banishing Powders

The art of the enchanted powder reaches its finest point with banishing spells. Various Banishing Powders exist, of varying intensity. Some are created from common kitchen ingredients, while others are mixed from more exotic components. Experiment and see which formula works most powerfully for you.

Remember that powders are intended as a subtle form of magic. There's no need to leave a large suspicious pile; a discreet sprinkling is typically sufficient.

Any of the Banishing Powders below may be used to create a Banishing Oil.

Banishing Oil

1. Grind the ingredients together to create a Banishing Powder (see below).
2. Cover this powder with castor oil, shaking vigorously to distribute.
3. If castor oil is too thick to flow adequately, dilute with jojoba oil.

Banishing Powder (1) Basic Banishing Powder

Black pepper
Cayenne powder
Cinnamon
Sea salt
Sulfur

Banishing Powder (2) Begone! Banishing Powder

Chopped bay laurel leaves
Black pepper
Cayenne pepper
Powdered hydrangea blossoms
Sea salt

Both formulas above are similar in intensity and may be used in the same manner:

★ *Sprinkle the Banishing Powder on clothes, especially shoes, belonging to anyone you'd like to see gone*
★ *Sprinkle the powder on the ground, so that the target of your spell is forced to step on or over it*
★ *Banishing Powder will enhance the power of any other banishing spell. Sprinkle as an accompaniment, particularly around and over candles*

The above Banishing Powders are made from what are more or less household ingredients, with maybe a little extra investment. Although not everyone keeps sulfur powder or powdered hydrangea as a kitchen staple, they are both easy, inexpensive items to purchase from an herbalist or spiritual supply store.

The following Banishing Powder has a more complex set of ingredients: obtaining them may take greater effort than the previous formulas. It is, however, considered a stronger, more defiant, and perhaps ultimately a more malevolent banishing agent.

If you enjoy working with figure candles, black devil candles are considered powerful banishing agents:

Black Devil Banishing Spell

1. Hold a black devil candle in both your hands to charge it with your desire.
2. Dress the candle with Banishing Oil and burn.

Botanical Banishing Spells

The following botanicals possess a banishing effect. Incorporate one or (ideally) a combination of them into banishing spells: angelica, asafetida, basil, bay laurel, citronella, cloves, cumin, devil's bit, dragon's blood, elder, fleabane, fumitory, garlic, heliotrope, horehound, juniper, lovage, mistletoe, mullein, mugwort, oleander, pepper (both black and hot chili/cayenne), yew.

★ *Use in any combination to formulate your own banishing spells*
★ *Living plants grown in quantity around the home discourage uninvited visitors*
★ *Several of the above plants, like oleander and yew, are poisonous. As a general rule of thumb, those plants with toxic properties are used in banishing spells, to varying degrees. However, this may not be appropriate for those with children or animals present*
★ *Poison Gardens are discussed in depth in the* Protection Spells *section; however, if it's safe and appropriate for you, a Poison Garden may provide the privacy-minded with a protective banishing shield*

Change or Else!

This banishing spell targets a trouble-maker. Unlike most banishing spells, which simply encourage the person to depart, this one offers another option. The target of the spell can either reform or else leave peacefully.

1. Add essential oils of patchouli and vetiver to a blend of olive and castor oils.
2. Rub this on the door-knobs of your target's home.

Coffee Grounds Banishing Spell

The most effective way to perform the following spell is via subterfuge. Invite the target of your spell over to your home and serve fresh-brewed coffee. For maximum effectiveness, offer to read their coffee-grounds, turning over their cup. Then when they've left, immediately gather your spell materials.

1. Gather the dirt from your target's footprints or, alternatively, gather the dirt from under a chair in which they were the last person to sit.
2. Combine this dirt with cayenne pepper, ground sassafras, and used coffee grounds. (The most potent coffee grounds are those from the target's own cup.)
3. Sprinkle this on the target's front doorstep.

Foot Track Banishing

Traditional methods of spell disposal are not always possible any longer, for a variety of reasons, ranging from ecological to legal restrictions. In some cases, substitutions are easily made which will not adversely affect the desired outcome, but this is not always the case. The following is a very simple banishing spell, common to various parts of the world such as North Africa, the American South, and Romany-influenced Europe. The disposal of the ingredients effectively *is* the spell: sending your target's footprints downstream causes the banishment. If it's not possible to perform this spell exactly, then try another.

1. Follow the target of your spell discreetly, observing their footprints.
2. When you see a clear, distinct left print, dig it up in its entirety.
3. Take it home in a bag, then transfer the dirt to a glass jar or bottle, being careful not to lose or spill any of it.
4. Seal the bottle very tightly shut, adding a wax seal, if you like.
5. Take this to running water flowing away from you.
6. Turning your back on the water, throw the container over your left shoulder without looking, taking care not to hit anything you shouldn't.
7. Walk away without looking back once.

Four Thieves Banishing Spells

An excellent example of how magic travels and evolves, **Four Thieves Vinegar** arrived in New Orleans, brought by either French or Italian immigrants, who valued it for its illness-banishing properties. In New Orleans, another use was discovered: **Four Thieves Vinegar** is an excellent banishing agent for unwanted people. From New Orleans Voodoo, this use of Four Thieves entered the modern Wiccan and Pagan magickal community, many of whom are unfamiliar with its original use as a healing agent.

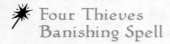

Four Thieves Banishing Spell

To avoid debt collectors or others in hot pursuit of you:

1. Place their business card inside a shot glass.
2. Fill the glass with **Four Thieves Vinegar**.
3. Leave the glass standing in a discreet place as long as necessary.

If a business card does not exist or you cannot obtain one, make one up: write the target's name on a business card-sized piece of paper and place this in the shot glass.

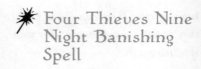

Four Thieves Nine Night Banishing Spell

An extra-strength banishing spell:

1. Each night for nine consecutive nights (ideally timed with the waning moon but cast the spell as necessary) write the target of your spell's name on brown paper, together with a brief, explicit message, something like *"Go home!"*
2. Sprinkle one of the banishing powders over the paper.
3. Add one of the target's hairs, a nail clipping, or a thread from their clothing.
4. Burn everything; place the ashes in a bottle of **Four Thieves Vinegar**.
5. Following the ninth night, wrap the bottle tightly in black fabric, securing it with cord.
6. Make nine knots in the cord reiterating your desire for banishment with each one.
7. Throw this bottle into running water or a cemetery and return home via a circuitous route.

Four Thieves Quick Banishing Spell

This is a quick-fix version of the Four Thieves Nine Night spell above.

1. Add some banishing powder (any one you like) to a bottle of **Four Thieves Vinegar**.
2. Write the target of your spell's name on brown paper and put it inside the bottle, too.
3. Shake the bottle, then leave it upside down in the corner of your closet or behind your bed overnight.
4. Wrap it in black fabric, securing with cord in which you tie nine knots, reiterating your wish for banishing with each one.
5. Throw the bottle in a garbage can at a distance from your home and return via a circuitous route.

Garlic Banishing Spell

Hang a braid of twelve garlic heads over the door to banish jealous people and, by extension, the Evil Eye.

Get Lost and Far Away!

Lost and Away Powder has various uses, in addition to banishment. It's also used to establish personal and psychic boundaries, as well as to prevent someone else from encroaching on these boundaries.

1. Write your target's name thirteen times on a square of paper.
2. Sprinkle **Lost and Away Powder** on this paper.
3. Fold the paper up, always folding away from you.
4. Seal it with sealing wax, preferably red.
5. Bury this paper but mark the spot.
6. Leave it buried for thirteen days, watering daily with **War Water**.
7. On the fourteenth day, dig it up and burn it.

Hit the Road and Don't Come Back Spell

1. Fill your pockets with salt in anticipation of the person's departure.
2. Accompany the person as he or she departs, walking just a step behind to the edge of your property, discreetly sprinkling salt in their wake.
3. When the person has gone and can no longer see you, take a broom and sweep the salt away, always sweeping away from your home or the area you wish protected from their presence.
4. Simultaneously murmur your

target's name, alternately praying and petitioning that he does not return and commanding and compelling him never to return.

Variations on this spell suggest adding black and/or cayenne pepper to the salt.

Another mode of administering Banishing Powder is via a gift.

✳ Out of My House Banishing Spell

The following spell is excellent for ridding your home of an unwanted guest, or perhaps even a family member who needs to depart. The spell presumes that you have access to the target's clothing and personal items. Surely you're doing their laundry? The more personal the items are, the more effective the spell.

1. Construct a small doll using personal items belonging to your spell's target.
2. Write the target's name on a small slip of paper. Cross over the name by writing an appropriate message, something like "*Out of my house now!*"
3. Pin this to the doll like a name-tag.

4. Soak the doll's feet in one of the Banishing Oils. (Exodus Oil is particularly appropriate; however, use whichever resonates strongest for you.)
5. Wrap the doll in dark fabric, folding away from you. Keep it in a safe place, anointing the feet daily and secretly telling the doll exactly what you'd like to tell the target of your spell.
6. As soon as the banishment has been effected, destroy or dispose of the doll. Do not keep it in your home.

✳ Purple Candle Banishing Spell

Burning a purple candle in the following spell indicates your power over the target of your spell. However, a black devil candle may be substituted if you prefer.

1. Write the name(s) of those whom you wish to banish on a square of brown paper.
2. Cover the name(s) with your own, effectively crossing the first name out.
3. Chant:
   *I cover you, I cross you
   I command you, I compel you*

[Name], *child of* [Name]. *Get out of my house now!*

4. Dress a purple candle with Banishing Oil.
5. Place the paper on a dish, beneath the purple candle.
6. Burn the candle.

Adapt the chant to your particular situation.

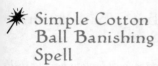

Simple Cotton Ball Banishing Spell

Soak a cotton ball in Banishing Oil. Then slip it into your target's pocket.

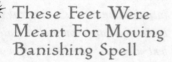

These Feet Were Meant For Moving Banishing Spell

Drizzle Banishing Oil over your target's shoes. Alternatively, massaging the oil into their feet, if you can somehow manage this, can also produce desired effects.

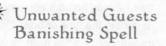

Unwanted Guests Banishing Spell

Sprinkle tormentil under the bed to encourage unwanted guests to move on.

Banishing Bad Habits

Although these spells may be used to target any type of behavior, the term *"bad habits"* is often understood to refer euphemistically to dangerous and/or undesirable addictions. It may be necessary to combine several spells for maximum effect.

Amethyst Anti-Intoxication Spell

Legends surrounding the beautiful purple gemstone, amethyst, suggest that it may be used to prevent intoxication. This is not exactly true: if you're really determined to get drunk, there isn't a crystal in the world that will stop you, nor will drinking from a cup cut from amethyst, the original spell instructions, provide long-term obstruction. What amethysts can do for you is bolster attempts not to drink, whether this means drinking at all or merely to excess. Amethysts reinforce your personal determination and provide a measure of protection.

The amethyst is sacred to Dionysus, Spirit of Ecstasy and Intoxication. It is his power that one witnesses shining through the gemstone. Even gods of intoxication can sometimes be bad drunks, though, as the mythical history of the amethyst points out. Once upon a time, on a morning after, a long, long, time ago, Dionysus, suffering from a hangover and headache, wished to avoid all company. Bothered by every sound, he announced that he would terminate the very next person to cross his path. Who should be passing through the woods at that moment but the lovely young nymph Amethyst, on her way with offerings to present at Artemis' shrine? But before Dionysus could carry out his threat, Artemis stepped in and saved Amethyst by transforming her into a luminous clear crystal. Abashed and ashamed by his bad temper, Dionysus approached with a glass of wine. Pouring it over the now crystallized nymph, Amethyst turned her characteristic purple color. Dionysus swore that whenever he saw this gemstone in the future, he would become an ally in preventing the ill-effects associated with alcohol.

★ *Amethyst's anti-intoxication powers are strongest if one drinks out of an* amethyst cup. *An amethyst-colored cup may be sufficient*

★ *Wear an amethyst as a ring or over the throat chakra. Remember to charge the gemstone and cleanse it periodically*

★ *Amethysts also have a cleansing effect: metaphysically they will help remove and assimilate toxins, including alcohol*

☀ Bury Bad Habits Spell

Among the most famous hexing spells are those involving miniature-sized personalized coffins left on the spell target's doorsteps. This coffin spell is traditionally as much an act of sheer intimidation as it is a magical spell, however it can be put to less malevolent uses. Use the little coffin spell below to lay issues to rest and, in particular, to bury addictions.

1. Create a small coffin. You will need a little box. You can find one or make one, however the imagery should be very clear: there should be no ambiguity regarding the type of box. Inspiration, or a box itself, may be taken from Mexican *Day of the Dead (Dia de los Muertos)* handicrafts.

2. Paint the outside of the box black. Decorate with purple glitter glue if desired.
3. Traditionally the box contains a small doll, which may or may not be personalized so that the identity of the target is clear. Consider how to personify your addiction.
4. Accompany and reinforce this spell with intensive candle burning.
5. The doll may be pierced with pins. Add candle stubs, leftover spell wax, graveyard dirt, asafetida, and banishing powder, especially **Lost and Away Powder**.
6. Dress everything with Banishing Oil.

Traditionally the coffin is left on your target's doorstep. Consider appropriate places to leave it, or bury the little coffin within a cemetery.

You may find just making the box therapeutic in itself. In which case, reserve the box for ritual use or destroy it.

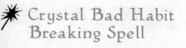

Crystal Bad Habit Breaking Spell

Use double-terminated crystals to help break old habits and destructive patterns, and to heal addictions.

Other beneficial stones include amethyst and kunzite, which interestingly contains lithium, used medicinally to treat depression and bi-polar syndromes.

★ *Carry the gemstones in a conjure bag*
★ *Lay the stones on or around the body*
★ *Use the stones as a focal point for visualization and meditation spells*

Eucalyptus Banish Bad Habits Spell

The eucalyptus tree is believed to possess potent banishing properties. If you have a eucalyptus tree, it's simple to make a decoction: place leaves, twigs, and loose bark into a pot and cover with water. Bring it to a boil, then lower the heat and simmer gently for an hour or more. Otherwise, you can create an infusion from dried eucalyptus, available from herbal supply stores. Pour boiling water over the botanicals and let them steep until the water cools.

Either way, strain out the botanicals and add the infusion to your bathwater, to destroy evil ties that bind, whether bad addictions, bad habits, or bad company.

Sometimes the condition that requires banishing isn't yours. Perhaps someone else's drinking is causing your life to be miserable. Spells have evolved to *encourage* others to stop drinking.

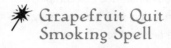

Get Someone Else to Quit Spell

This Pow-Wow technique is used for curing excessive alcohol intake by another, whether he or she wishes to be cured or not.

1. Scrape the dirt out from under the target's fingernails. (Probably best accomplished while they are in a stupor, unless you are in the general habit of providing a manicure.)
2. Secretly add these scrapings to their favorite alcoholic beverage.
3. When appropriate, serve them some. The person will happily drink this beverage. Allegedly the addition should remove future inclination to imbibe.

The modern grapefruit is a relatively new species, having apparently evolved in colonial Barbados. Interestingly this fruit which evolved in a place and time plagued by slavery is among the most potent botanicals for breaking personal shackles.

Grapefruit Quit Smoking Spell

A magical plan to stop smoking:

1. Every time you crave a cigarette, have a grapefruit instead.
2. Here's the catch: you must cut and eat the grapefruit completely by hand. You cannot use a knife to cut it or use a spoon to eat it.
3. Peel grapefruit by hand, and then eat it segment by segment.

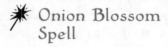

Magnolia Bark Spell

Drinking magnolia bark tea supposedly helps one quit smoking.

Onion Blossom Spell

Burn onion blossoms while making affirmations to help banish bad habits. This provides a magical cleansing effect too.

Banishing Problems and Situations

Although specific spells exist for many different situations, sometimes a problem doesn't fall neatly into any one category. Perhaps no solution exists: the only possible positive outcome is for the entire situation to be eliminated or banished.

Rotten Apple Banishing Spell

1. Cut an apple in half horizontally, so that the star in the center is exposed.
2. Rub one half of the apple with a mint leaf while visualizing what needs to be banished.
3. Put the two halves of the apple back together again.
4. Stick a skewer through the pieces, so that they will remain joined.
5. Tie the pieces securely together with black silk or satin ribbon.
6. Bury the apple. Your problem should dissipate as the apple rots.

You may also name your problem by writing it on a slip of paper. Dip this paper into essential oil of mint and place between the apple halves, before rejoining them. However, by naming the problem on paper, you take the risk of further manifestation. Cast whichever version of the spell resonates for you.

Banish Spirits

Sometimes you need to make the spirits leave. Despite the emphasis on *Summoning Spells* placed in the classical medieval grimoires, the bigger problem is often how to force these spirits to leave once you've achieved your own purposes. A good reason for never dabbling in malevolent magic is that it is typically easier to summon than to banish. Exu Marabo, for instance, a powerful yet dangerous spirit, warns that once summoned, he can never be forced to leave.

In many cases, malevolent magic attracts the attention of equally malevolent spirits. Feeling at home, they move right in, regardless of your desires. Once present, bored and restless, they cause destruction and grief.

In general, banishing spirits is work for a shaman. The first choice in all situations would be to hire an effective, knowledgeable professional. That said, hiring a shaman isn't an option for many people in most circumstances. When all action must be taken in your own hands, the following spells are reputed to be extremely potent.

☀ Bamboo Banishing Spell

House spirits are supposed to be helpful; every once in a while a malevolent one turns up. This Korean spell helps banish unwanted house spirits.

Burn bamboo sticks. Allegedly the sound of bamboo's popping knots scares house demons away.

☀ Banishing Incense

The following incense formula allegedly drives away even the most powerful of evil spirits. The ingredients include:

Asafetida
Bay laurel leaves
Galbanum
Olive leaves
Rue
Saint John's Wort
Salt
Sulfur

1. Crumble all the ingredients.
2. Blend them together, grind, powder, and burn on lit charcoal.

☀ Banishment Bouquet

A bouquet of garlic blossoms an angelica flowers, tied up with re and blue ribbons, repels maliciou spirits.

☀ Bell, Book, and Candle

This phrase, the title of a popula play and film as well as the give name of numerous metaphysica stores, evolved from traditiona Roman Catholic rites of exorcisn and excommunication. This metho of banishing malevolent spirits pre dates Christianity, however, an may be used as a framework fo exorcists of any spiritual orienta tion. In order to effectively cast banishing spell, you must be familia and comfortable with your tools.

1. The bell is the simplest part of the spell. Bells invoke the combined primal powers of male and female generative energy; the ringing of a metal bell disturbs

most malicious spirits. An iron bell will repel most negative entities.

2. The book refers to sacred texts, the introduction of something so sacred that there is no room left for evil to co-exist in the space; hence it's squeezed out. The key is to employ whatever fills you with sacred grace. These might be sacred texts, Gregorian chants, or gospel music, or may even derive from what might be perceived as profane sources: soul music, for instance.

3. Not just any candle will do; the fragrance of beeswax allegedly repels evil. Alternatively rub candles with oils of benzoin and frankincense.

☀ Botanical Spirit Banishing

The following plants allegedly make malevolent spirits feel unwelcome: juniper, maize corn, mugwort, Saint John's Wort, vervain, wormwood, and yarrow. Keep living plants near your home or any area that needs protection, or hang these dried botanicals near doors and windows as amulets.

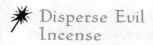

☀ Disperse Evil Incense

Burn benzoin, frankincense, and juniper as a triple threat and triple protection: evil spirits cannot abide any of these fragrances, let alone the combination.

Exorcism Spells

Sometimes spirits attach themselves to an individual rather than merely haunting an area. The spirit may speak through the individual, refusing to leave. Encouraging or forcing them to leave is a shamanic technique. However, should you find yourself dealing with a case of possession without an exorcist in the neighborhood, the following spells may be attempted. In general, you will still need a ritual assistant to help achieve your magical goals.

☀ Exorcism Spell (1)

1. Use intensive cleansing methods to purify the area.
2. In addition to whichever methods are employed, ring bells, cymbals, and sistra loudly.

3. Invoke benevolent protective spirits, like Archangel Michael, Kwan Yin, and/or Isis.
4. Draw up talismans of protection.
5. Summon the demons, demanding that they come forward and depart.
6. Observe for signs of departure. Dramatic spirits will let you know they've gone. Otherwise use divination techniques to determine whether your methods have been effective or, if not, what further action should be taken.
7. If you're sure they've departed, burn the talismans.
8. Mix a teaspoon of the ashes into cooled boiled spring water. Have the person drink it.
9. Close the ceremony.

Exorcism Spell (2)

1. Fill a new pot with freshly drawn water.
2. Pour some olive oil over the water.
3. Whisper Psalm 10 over this water nine times.
4. Dip a new towel into this liquid to bathe the afflicted person.

Ginger Banishing Spell

It's traditionally believed that low-level malevolent spirits can enter the body through food. This is the source of many fairy tales where evil is swallowed. Certain foods, such as ginger, guard against this as well as expelling any previously swallowed demons. Add it to food to expel and prevent demons.

Poltergeist Banishing: Fumitory/Earth Smoke

*Burn **Fumitory** (Earth smoke) to banish poltergeists, demons, and any manner of malicious spirit. (This was the solution allegedly favored in the famed ninth-century geometric gardens of Saint Gall.)*

Sage Banishing Spirits Spell

Burn sage—especially white sage—to rid an area of evil spirits and negative entities.

☀ Sweet Spirit Oil Spell

This Sweet Spirit Oil is safe for use by most people and smells beautiful. Wearing it endows you with a personal protective aura. Evil spirits will allegedly leave you alone, even if they are lurking nearby.

Blend essential oils of frankincense and vetiver, together with honeysuckle absolute and rose attar into a base of sweet almond oil. Add the oil to bathwater before retiring for the night, or massage it onto the body, to keep malicious spirits far away from you.

☀ Sweet Spirit Powder Spell

To repel evil spirits, while simultaneously beckoning benevolent, kind, protective ones:

. Grind the following botanicals together to produce a fine powder: frankincense, honeysuckle blossoms, roses, and vetiver roots.

. Sprinkle the powder onto lit charcoal and burn incessantly, until you're convinced the danger is over.

☀ Tree of Life Banishing Spell

Arbor vitae: *the name given to this tree means "tree of life." The smoke from its burning leaves allegedly disperses unwanted spirits and sends them packing.*

☀ Witch Balls

Witch balls are globes of iridescent colored glass. Place them around your home and property to disperse malicious spirits.

Banishing Vermin

No, not bad boyfriends. Try the regular banishing spells at the beginning of this section for them. Or look through the *Love Spells* for some tips on effectively ending relationships. These vermin are the little creepy crawly kinds that seem to possess magical resistance toward efforts to remove them.

☀ Banishing Powders

The Hoodoo summoning powder called **Drawing Powder** *should contain nothing more than powdered confectioner's sugar. To demonstrate its powers of summoning, sprinkle* sugar on the floor and watch ants and other bugs miraculously appear. Yet Drawing Powder is intended to summon people. Try the spell's converse and see if this works on bugs, too. The various Banishing Powders are meant to banish people, just as Drawing Powder summons them: sprinkle Banishing Powder around your home to see if this works as well.

☀ Eucalyptus Banishing Spell

Botanical methods of banishing may work, too. The scent and presence of eucalyptus allegedly repels cockroaches.

1. Add essential oil of eucalyptus to a bowl of cool water.
2. Soak a cloth in the water.
3. Leave the cloth wherever you'd like to banish the roaches.

If this proves successful, add essential oil of eucalyptus to a spray bottle filled with water and spray wherever needed.

☀ Khonsu's Banishing Spell

The Egyptian lunar divinity Khonsu may be invoked to banish cockroaches.

1. Hold a scarab in your left hand to charge it with your desire.
2. Place it in the light of the Full Moon.
3. Warm essential oil of frankincense in an aroma burner and tell Khonsu what you need.

☀ Magic Chalk Anti-Ant Circles

Stores in New York's Chinatown sometimes feature Magic Ant Repelling Chalk. The magic may be very effective, but the chalk is just plain chalk. Use white chalk to draw boundary lines and protective circles around your home. Allegedly the ants will not cross these boundary lines.

☀ Valerian Rat Banishing

Allegedly valerian is what the Pied Piper of Hamelin used to lure the rats away from that besieged town. If reports are true, he carried the herb in his pocket. You may, however, wish to try burning it in a portable incense burner or censer. Create a magical path for the rats to follow. Rats, like cats, allegedly enjoy the fragrance and will follow it where it leads them.

Better Business and Professional Success Spells

Although many of these are money spells, they solicit money from a specific source. These aren't spells for conjuring up money from out of the blue; you'd like the opportunity to earn this money. Magic provides financial inspiration, added opportunity, and protective buffering from the inherent instability of the marketplace.

Better Business is Hoodoo terminology for more than just increased business, although the desire to stimulate healthy cash flow inspires a large selection of spells. This category also includes anything specifically affecting business, money earned through work or business, employment, and career issues. It is a particularly ancient and universal category: no matter where people come from, they understand the necessity of earning a living, together with its attendant pitfalls, risks, and dangers.

The concept of the "*marketplace*" serves as yet another metaphoric, magical spiritual crossroads, especially if one considers ancient town markets. Roads converged in the marketplace; it was an area of swirling energy and great opportunity for success, loss, transformation, and adventure. More than mere buying and selling of goods went on; diviners, traditional healers, and entertainers including conjurers and professional story-tellers all plied their wares in the marketplace. It was where you went to hear news. Before copyright laws,

★ Better business spells whose goal is increased profits often rely heavily upon the creation and correct placement of special charms
★ Powders and oils are used to encourage out-going money to return "home"

books were "*published*" by being read aloud in the market square. In many traditional African philosophies the marketplace is a crossroads particularly associated with women's power and opportunity for success.

☀ Allspice Better Business Spells

Allspice berries allegedly enhance the fortunes of business ventures. They are also reputed to magically help turn around regrettable investments.

★ *Carry them in a charm bag*
★ *Pierce and string the berries. Wear them as a necklace or more discreet ankle bracelet*
★ *Add allspice berries to a bottle of* **Bay Rum**. *Massage this enhanced* **Bay Rum** *into your hands and body*

☀ Almond Tree Better Business Spell

1. Find an almond tree that you can climb.
2. Offer the tree a libation and gift.
3. Murmur your desires to the tree; state your goals and aspirations.
4. Climb the tree.
5. Linger as long or as little as you like; when you come down, offer the tree another libation.
6. Your success will allegedly be achieved; if so, plant another almond tree.
7. Repeat as needed.

Basil Better Business Spells

Basil is the botanical most associated with attracting wealth and prosperity. Large, fresh, vivid green basil leaves are believed to resemble cash bills. In addition, basil is strongly identified with various spirits of wealth and good fortune. The presence of the botanical beckons these spirits, together with their blessings of prosperity.

Basil belongs to Maitresse Ezili Freda Dahomey, Vodou spirit of luxury, and features in many of her rituals. Tulsi basil, also known as holy basil, belongs to Lakshmi, the popular Hindu goddess of good fortune.

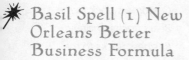 Basil Spell (1) New Orleans Better Business Formula

Maitresse Ezili Freda Dahomey emerged in a region of West Africa known either as Dahomey or Benin. Originally a water snake spirit, she traveled with enslaved devotees to the Western hemisphere, taking root in Haiti, where she has achieved great prominence as the pre-eminent female spirit in the Vodoun pantheon. During the journey, Maitresse Ezili shed her snakeskin to emerge as the breathtakingly beautiful lwa of wealth, luxury, dreams, and love. New Orleans Voodoo stands firmly on the shoulders of Haitian Vodou, although the more religious aspects may or may not be emphasized. Basil is a major component of New Orleans-styled better business formulas, although the original connection to Maitresse Ezili may be overlooked.

1. Shred approximately one half cup of fresh basil leaves.
2. Cover the basil with approximately one pint (560 ml) of boiling water. (Play with proportions to achieve the quantity and intensity you desire.)
3. Let the basil steep in this water for three days.
4. On the fourth day, strain out the water, reserving the liquid.

Sprinkle this liquid over the entrances and thresholds of your business, in corners, behind doors, and near the cash registers—basically in any spot that might be perceived as vulnerable. It allegedly attracts customers and prevents theft.

✳ Basil Spell (2) New Orleans Quick Fix Better Business Formula

There are two methods of creating this quick-fix version. The most preferred is to add twelve drops of essential oil of basil to one pint (560 ml) of water. This isn't as potent as regular New Orleans Better Business Formula but it's fast. It can be whipped up in seconds. An alternative method is to pour boiling water over one tablespoon of dried basil. Allow it to steep until it cools, then strain and use.

The dried herb lacks the potency of either the fresh herb or the highly concentrated essential oil. However, neither the dried herb nor the essential oil possesses fresh basil's distinctive fragrance. Both Quick Fix solutions lack the visual component of the original spell, too: the soaking basil leaves look a lot like cash. Compensate by adding extra focus and visualization to the spell.

Basil hydrosol may also be substituted. Use it by itself or add it to rinse water. Again, because so little effort is required to use this, compensate by added focus and visualization.

✳ Basil Spell (3)

Fresh basil smells so inviting yo may not wish to reserve it for th floor.

1. Chop fresh basil into fine threads
2. Warm honey gently over the stove. (A double boiler or bain-marie is recommended, as honey scorches easily.)
3. Add the basil to the honey and simmer.
4. Remove the basil-enhanced honey from the source of heat and murmur over it something like this:

   Flies flocks to honey
   Customers flock to me
   Bears flock to honey
   Business flocks to me
   Ants flock to honey
   Contracts flock to me
   (Adapt to your specific situation.)
5. Run a warm bath for yourself.
6. Rub the honey over your body, and then enter the bath.
7. Soak in the water for a while. When you emerge, before you drain the water, reserve some of the used bathwater.
8. Toss this on the grounds of your business.

Basil Spell (4)
Personal Business Magnet Spell

Sometimes you are your business. Traditionally prostitutes have bathed in infusions of fresh basil to lure customers toward them, a custom believed to originate in Spain, although it has since traveled around the world. Sex workers aren't the only ones whose prosperity is dependent upon selling themselves. This spell is beneficial for anyone whose business depends upon his or her own personal magnetism.

1. Add strong infusions of fresh basil to your bath, together with fresh basil leaves and some basil hydrosol.
2. For extra enhancement, after bathing and air-drying, dust the body lightly with either **Lodestone Body Powder** or Drawing Powder Personal Dusting Powder.

Better Business: Charm Bag

1. Select one or more of the Money Drawing or Luck oils.
2. Use the oil(s) to anoint five cowrie shells, a High John the Conqueror root, and a matched pair of lodestones.
3. Place these into a red flannel drawstring bag. Carry it with you or place it strategically within the business.
4. Anoint with more oil periodically to reinforce the mojo's power.

Better Business: Commanding Spell

Command and compel business to improve. This spell encourages you to radiate confidence, and others to wish to please you. Rub a drop of **Essence of Bend Over** *or another* **Commanding Oil** *between the palms of your hands just before conferences or when meeting colleagues, bosses, employees, or clients. Shake the target's hand or find an excuse to touch their bare hand.*

Better Business: Drawing Incense

Blend dried basil, benzoin, and ground cinnamon and burn as a business-drawing incense.

Better Business Floorwashes

Floorwashes are a traditional—and discreet—method of casting spells. The botanical infusions are used to radiate magic power, drawing or repelling your desire as the case may be. Floorwashes are used to scrub front steps to provide spiritual protection and attract free-spending customers. Within a building, the term "*floorwash*" is somewhat deceptive; in general, this is more of a "*floor final rinse.*" It is assumed that the floor is clean prior to applying the spell floorwash: the floorwash isn't rinsed off, but should be allowed to dry and radiate its fragrance and power. The physical labor involved in applying the floorwash also enhances the casting of the spell: your effort transmits your intentions and desires.

Applying Better Business Floorwashes

★ *Scrub the walkway and the doorway of your business, beginning at the street and moving toward your front door, just the way customers should*
★ *Scrub the front steps*
★ *Cleanse the interior floors, beginning at the front door and corners and working towards the center of each room*

Floorwashes may be created with any of the following or a combination:

★ *Boiled cooled salted water*
★ *Pure spring water (bottled water)*
★ *Strained, collected rainwater*
★ *Plain tap water*

Better Business Floorwash (1)

1. Combine ground cinnamon, brown sugar, and red brick dust.
2. Add this to a bucket of water, together with some white vinegar.

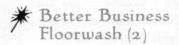
Better Business Floorwash (2)

1. Combine **Florida Water, Indigo Water, Van Van Oil**, and ground cinnamon.
2. Add to a bucket filled with salted water, together with white vinegar.

Better Business Floorwash (3)

Add essential oil of citronella to a bucket of water and white vinegar and use as a floorwash. This allegedly drives away negative spiritual entities while drawing in customers to fill the void.

✴ Better Business: Nutmeg Spell

1. Drill a hole through a nutmeg and string it onto green thread.
2. Add one pierced Grain of Paradise, a Jezebel root and a High John the Conqueror. (It may also be necessary to drill a hole through the High John, a particularly hard root.)
3. Tie the thread together and hang over the front entrance to the business.

✴ Busy as an Ant Better Business Spell

This is a modern adaptation of a Talmudic-era spell. Jewish spells, like ancient Egyptian spells and modern Chinese magic, often rely heavily on the power of the written word. The original spell might have included sacred words of power, acronyms, notarikon, and specially chosen biblical phrases. Incorporate these as you will. There is, however, no substitute for anthill dust.

1. Collect dust from an anthill.
2. On a piece of parchment paper, write your business goals in the present tense. For instance: *"I sell one million units every week."* Use an image or photograph in addition to words, if you wish.
3. Fold up the paper into a very tight little square, always folding toward you.
4. Place the paper, the dust, and a lodestone into a small charm bag.
5. Hang this discreetly in your place of business.

Drawing Powder

Spiritual supply stores sometimes sell really cute little bottles filled with some kind of powdery substance and labeled *Drawing Powder*. It's better business for them if you purchase a few vials, however, it may be better business for you to take a trip to the grocery store instead. Although that name may be used to label a complex, sophisticated Money Drawing Powder full of rare ingredients, technically plain old Drawing Powder is powdered confectioner's sugar. Not sure if it works? Sprinkle some on the floor in a warm climate and watch armies of ants miraculously appear, magically beckoned to draw close to the powder.

To attract customers and financial success:

★ Sprinkle a path of *Drawing Powder* from the street to the front door of your business
★ Sprinkle *Drawing Powder* into your cash register to beckon fresh cash to draw near
★ Sprinkle *Drawing Powder* into and over invitations to your place of business as a magical inducement

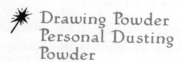

Drawing Powder Personal Dusting Powder

Drawing Powder may be used to draw business toward you yourself, too.

1. Blend powdered confectioner's sugar into cornstarch.
2. Lightly dust this on your body with a powder puff to magically attract personal attention—and open pockets.

For added enhancement, sprinkle the blended powder with essential oil of basil before applying to the body.

Financial Crisis Better Business Spell

This increased power business bath is considered an emergency spell. It allegedly provides temporary relief in times of crisis. Save it for use during truly hard times and crises. It is most powerful when coordinated with the New Moon. Do not be tempted to perform this spell at every New Moon by rote: it loses its effectiveness when used too frequently.

1. Make a strong infusion from the following materials by pouring boiling spring water over them:
   Dried basil or shredded fresh basil
   Dried parsley or fresh parsley
   Coriander seeds and/or fresh coriander leaves
   Cinnamon
   Brown sugar
   Grated fresh orange zest
   Fresh orange leaves (optional)
2. Allow the liquid to cool.
3. Fill a bathtub half full.
4. Strain out the botanical materials and bring the liquid to the bath.
5. Stand naked in the bathtub and toss the infusion over yourself.
6. Sit or recline in the water, soaking for seven minutes. Pray and petition for help and prosperity for the entire period. Visualize your prayers fulfilled.

7. After seven minutes, drain the water and allow yourself to air-dry.

First Dollar Spells

The first dollar earned by a new business venture is perceived as especially charged with magic power.

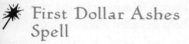

First Dollar Ashes Spell

1. Reserve the first dollar earned in a new business.
2. Grind and pulverize it.
3. Blend with frankincense and gold copal.
4. Burn atop a lit charcoal.
5. Reserve the ashes: carry them in a conjure bag.

First Dollar Candle Spell

1. Reserve the first dollar earned in a new business.
2. Sprinkle it with magnetic sand, sugar, and salt.
3. Place a green candle on top of the dollar and burn it.
4. Bury most of the remnants on the property; reserve a few pieces in a conjure bag and hang it near the entrance.

First Dollar Ginseng Spell

1. Reserve the first dollar earned in a new business.
2. Wrap it around a ginseng root with green and red thread.
3. Hold it in your hands and charge it with your hopes and desires.
4. Place it in a conjure bag and keep it in or beneath the cash register to generate further income.

Garlic Better Business Spell

Garlic provides a combination of increased business with space protection.

1. Make or purchase a wreath formed from heads of garlic.
2. Fill tiny plastic packets or little red flannel pouches with salt. Fill others with yellow mustard seed. (Staple plastic packets shut; sew flannel pouches securely together.)
3. Attach these to the wreath. Decorate with other lucky charms as desired: small horseshoes, crystals, lucky roots, or tiny image cards. Should you have a dried

snakeskin, it's considered especially fortuitous.

4. Hang over the entrance to your business.

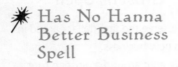 Has No Hanna Better Business Spell

*Make **Has No Hanna** incense from dried jasmine and gardenia flowers, peppermint leaves, and tangerine zest. Burn on lit charcoal and pass business, corporate, or legal documents through the smoke for success.*

Magic Coin Better Business Spells

An entire school of Chinese magic is devoted to the use of coins. (The use of currency as spell components derives from many traditions, however the Chinese school is most complete and cohesive and also remains extremely vital.) Detailed information may be found among the *Money Spells*. In short, coins are used to draw good fortune, protection, and increased prosperity toward you or toward an area. Although any metal coin may be used, traditional Chinese coins are best. Beyond the complex metaphysical reasoning, they are simpler to use than most coins: the square hole cut into the center of each coin lends itself to easy stringing, wrapping, and hanging. String the coins together yourself for added magical input as this type of spell also relies heavily on knot magic and beautiful, intricate magical knots are incorporated into each spell charm. However, coins may also be purchased already strung and knotted (and if you purchase from a master, blessed) in a variety of numerical combinations from feng shui suppliers and traditional Chinatown vendors.

Magic Coin Better Business Spell (1)

1. String three coins together or purchase them already linked.
2. Place these strung-together coins on top of a yellow or golden cloth.
3. Sprinkle magnetic sand over the coins.
4. Anoint with essential oil of bergamot.
5. Roll and fold the cloth toward you, forming a packet.
6. Tie securely with a red silk ribbon.

7. Place this packet inside or near your cash register for increased business and wealth.

your business premises to encourage cashflow.

Magic Coin Better Business Spell (2)

Two Chinese coins strung together with red thread represents Zhao Gong Ming, Lord of Wealth—someone every establishment would like to welcome as an honored, long-staying guest. Hang this charm above a shop window to attract wealth and good fortune to the business.

Should the actual coins be unavailable, an image depicting this amulet possesses similar powers. Post this instead.

Magic Coin Better Business Spell (3)

Place two coins strung together with red thread underneath the telephone to generate business.

Magic Water Spells

Magic Water Spell (1) Angel Water

*Sprinkle **Angel Water** (or substitute an infusion of myrtle) around*

Magic Water Spell (2) Glory Water

1. Place frankincense tears (small pieces of frankincense) inside a bottle.
2. Cover them with orange blossom water or hydrosol.
3. Add a few drops of essential oil of bergamot.
4. Asperge **Glory Water** through the premises to increase business, attract blessings and customers, and overcome challenges.

Malachite Merchant Spells

Malachite is the merchant's stone. It's green, like money. It's a stone associated with the astrological sign Libra, the scales. Use malachite to tip the scales in your favor.

★ *Place it strategically in your cash register*
★ *Hang it in the corners of your business*
★ *Wear it as jewelry while at work*
★ *Carry it in a charm bag*

Malachite gem essence may also be beneficial:

★ Add it to your bath
★ Massage it into the soles of your feet before bedtime
★ Add it to floorwash
★ Add it to a spray bottle filled with spring water or magical formula water and spray into the corners of your business and over its threshold

Commercial houses of prostitution descended from and emerged alongside ancient temples dedicated to spirits of love, life, and fertility. With strong ties to spirituality, magic, and financial need, bordellos have traditionally developed their own better business tricks.

 Maneki Neko's Magic Spell

Although it's doubtful there will ever be definitive surveys, Maneki Neko, the Japanese beckoning cat, appears currently to be the single most popular amulet on Earth. This distinctive feline image emerged relatively recently in magical history: Maneki Neko was unknown until the end of the nineteenth century. According to one legend, Maneki Neko's career began in the window of its namesake a struggling cat house. After Maneki Neko arrived, business improved drastically and Maneki Neko's reputation was set. She now appears in the windows of even the most respectable stores and businesses all over the world. A Maneki Neko with an upturned left hand beckons increased business. (The right hand signals the desire for cash.) Although she's very cute and you may wish to look at her face, Maneki Neko works by beckoning others to come to you: place her so that she draws business to you.*

★ *Place Maneki Neko in the window, facing outside*
★ *Place Maneki Neko so that she faces the front door*
★ *Although a Maneki Neko in any color will generate income, gold Maneki Neko's allegedly serve most powerfully for this purpose*

New Orleans Fast Luck Oils

Sometimes you can afford long-term business plans and sometimes you need better business *NOW!* New Orleans-style *"fast luck"* oils provide quick fixes of good fortune. These are short-term solutions; if you discover that these oils work well for you, then reapply consistently and constantly.

Red Fast Luck

Essential oil of cinnamon bark
Essential oil of wintergreen
Vanilla absolute or pure vanilla
extract

As its name states, this oil must be red. There are three ways to achieve this:

★ *Blend the ingredients into Turkey red oil*
★ *Blend the ingredients into sunflower and jojoba oils, then use alkanet, a botanical dye to color it. Alkanet bestows its own blessings of good fortune but achieving the correct color is time consuming and labor intensive*
★ *The quick fix method: blend the ingredients into sunflower and jojoba oils, then add red food coloring*

Use Red Fast Luck Oil to anoint anything associated with drawing money into your business: tools, machines, stationery, ledger books, etc. Most especially, anoint all money in your cash drawer, so that it

returns to you on the double. If you don't work with cash, then discreetly anoint a corner of all checks paid out.

Red Fast Luck may be used to anoint any other better business charm, to provide enhancement and speed.

Double Fast Luck Oil

Red Fast Luck isn't fast enough? Turn it into Double Fast Luck Oil! Double Fast Luck Oil is used exactly like Red Fast Oil, however it allegedly produces twice the effects at double speed. Double Fast Luck combines the colors green and red. Traditionally red represents luck and life, while green represents growth and prosperity. However, modern associations factor into this oil's power as well. Green and red have evolved into Christmas colors: the goal of this oil is to make every day seem like Christmas. It is an excellent device for shopkeepers and manufacturers who'd like to maintain those Christmas Eve-level sales throughout the entire year.

1. Create a green water infusion. This is most powerful if done with cash-drawing botanicals like

basil, parsley, or mint. However, this will produce a subtle green. If you have visual expectations of bright green, use green food coloring, either alone or as color enhancement.

2. Gently pour this infusion over Red Fast Luck Oil. When at rest, the oil and water should separate, providing two distinct layers of color. Shake it up, dispersing the layers when you wish to use oil.

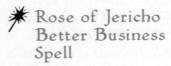

Rose of Jericho Better Business Spell

Among the Rose of Jericho's many blessings are increased business and cashflow. Re-hydrate the rose by placing it in a dish of spring water. Although marketers assure that the rose will bloom overnight or within 24 hours, it is very normal for the process to take several days. Once the rose has bloomed, change its water every Friday (the old water becomes **Rose of Jericho Water** *and has many uses), accompanied by the murmuring of psalms or other sacred verses.*

Rue Better Business Path

Because rue possesses extremely potent protective powers, this spell guards your business's well-being too. Grind and powder rue. Sprinkle a path to your business, using this powder to attract customers.

Employment Spells

Many better business spells presume that you own your own business, are an independent contractor, or somehow have a share in the business's fortunes. Maybe all you really need is a job.

Employment Spells are less financially oriented than *Better Business Spells*—at least less directly so. Employment Spells encompass enchantments needed to find a job, keep a job, and achieve professional success and happiness. There are also spells for finessing a difficult boss or supervisor and getting along with co-workers—or not, as the case may be.

Boss Fix

Is going to work a less than satisfying experience? Perhaps it's not the job that's the problem; maybe you have a supervisor or boss who persecutes you, picks on you, is never satisfied with you, and generally makes going to work the equivalent of going to hell? You don't want to leave your job; you'd just like your boss to leave you alone.

The Hoodoo solution is **Boss Fix Powder**.

According to its most extravagant promises, this spell allegedly causes supervisors to consider you with love and favor. At its more realistic, it offers a boundary line so that at least you'll be left alone to perform your job in peace.

☀ Boss Fix Powder

1. Empty the tobacco from one cigarette. (In order of preference: a cigarette that actually belonged to your boss, his or her favorite brand, any cigarette.)

2. Combine it with some shredded newspaper. (In order of preference: your boss's actual newspaper, a copy of a newspaper he or she favors, any newspaper.)

3. Add some chili powder and grind all the ingredients together into a fine powder.

4. Make sure the powder is fine: this is intended to be a very discreet spell. Your boss already doesn't like you!

5. When the opportunity arises, sprinkle just a tiny bit of powder on or around your boss's chair. If

that's too much of a risk, drop a little over the threshold of the office, so that he or she will inevitably step over it.

This is a highly individual spell, tailored toward one target. If more than one person persecutes you, make fresh Boss Fix for each person.

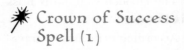 Boss Fix Candle Spell

This spell, cast to receive a raise or promotion, may be a safer, less stressful method of using Boss Fix Powder.

1. Carve and dress a figure candle to represent your boss or supervisor.
2. Place it on a tray covered by aluminum foil and surround the candle with a circle of Boss Fix Powder.
3. Carve and dress another candle to represent you.
4. Dress this candle with a Commanding oil. (Women should also incorporate **Martha the Dominator Oil**; men, use **High John the Conqueror Oil**.)
5. Place this candle on the tray but elevate it so that it is looking down at the first candle.
6. Burn both candles.
7. Sit behind the candle that represents you, facing the other candle. Speak to that candle; tell it what you need.
8. Move the boss candle so that it's resting atop the powder. (Ideally, if possible, dispose of the remnants of this spell in your boss's trashcan.)

Crown of Success Employment Spells

Crown of Success Oil assists you to find a job, land the job, and retain the job. It's also used for professional success and advancements, including obtaining promotions and greater financial benefits. **Crown of Success** may be used to enhance any other employment charm or spell: it is an entirely benevolent formula.

Crown of Success Spell (1)

Crown of Success may be applied to the body so that by radiating its magic, you serve as a charm. Add Crown of Success to your bath, or massage it on to your body, especially your hands and feet.

Crown of Success Spell (2)

1. Dress a lodestone with **Crown of Success Oil**.
2. Place it in a red drawstring bag and carry it with you, at work or while searching for employment.

Devil's Shoestrings Employment Spell

Despite its name, devil's shoestrings, there's nothing satanic about this root charm—quite the opposite in fact. Devil's shoestrings, the roots of the Viburnum *species, earned its name because it allegedly has the power to trip the devil up, proverbially tying his shoelaces together. Devil's shoestrings has an affinity for locating and maintaining employment. Use it to find a job or to improve conditions at the current one.*

★ *Carry it in your pocket*
★ *Pin it within your clothing*
★ *Carry it in a conjure bag*
★ *Attach it to a cord and wear it around your neck*

Don't Sabotage My Success Spell

Are you being set up? Perhaps your boss is unhappy with you or you haven't received your just rewards because you've been maligned and slandered by hostile or jealous co-workers. Although you may wish to supplement with additional Protection, Evil Eye and Unblocking Spells, this particular spell targets co-workers who sabotage your road to career success. Allegedly it will foil any malevolence directed toward you. Prepare a separate mojo for each person who appears to sabotage you.*

1. Write the co-worker's name on a square of brown paper three times.
2. Write your own name over each of the co-worker's names, saying: *"I cross you and I cover you."*
3. Anoint the corners of the paper with essential oils of bergamot, clove bud, and lavender.
4. Fold up the paper, placing it inside a red flannel drawstring bag, together with a devil's shoestring root and some cumin seed.
5. Maintain this discreetly in the workplace, feeding daily with a drop of essential oil of lavender for reinforcement.

Dream Job Spell

1. Write up an advertisement for your dream job.

2. Anoint this "ad" with **Come To Me Oil**.
3. Place it in a conjure bag and carry it with you until your dream is realized (even while employed elsewhere).
4. Anoint with additional oil weekly.

✳ Employment Conjure Bag

1. Fill a charm bag with three garlic cloves, nine distinct crumbs of bread, a lodestone, and some magnetic sand.
2. Dress with a touch of **Magnet Oil**.
3. Wear or carry to job interviews, adding a new drop of oil prior to each one, if possible.

✳ Employment Protection Spell

Tie red ribbons under your desk to provide magical protection at work.

✳ Essence of Bend Over Professional Happiness and Success Spell

Essence of Bend Over, the most concentrated of the Commanding condition oils, takes commanding and compelling into the realm of domination. Indeed, among its other functions, this oil is used in sexual domination spells. However, one of its primary uses is to turn the tables on an employer, particularly for those in menial or service occupations, where continued employment may depend upon the boss's whims and personal satisfaction. Essence of Bend Over enables the employee to discreetly switch the balance of power, so that he or she is able to set professional boundaries and dictate terms of service, although the employer may not realize that this is the case. This is not meant as an evil spell but as a method of preserving a much-needed job and curbing potential abuse and humiliation. And the oil's name? The goal is to have someone else bend over and bow down to you for a change.

Rub the oil onto doorknobs, so that those who open the doors fall under your spell. Or you could rub a drop between your palms and immediately touch the target of your spell.

✳ Find a Job Spell

This is a bit of an arts and crafts spell.

1. Designate a figure candle to represent you.

2. Do basic candle carving (name, identifying information) but then keep going: carve and scratch the wax to represent you in work mode. Create a badge on the candle's chest or scratch the image of a briefcase into the wax.

3. Meanwhile create a model of your ideal workplace from an open-topped box. It can be as specific as you wish or as general. Decorate and embellish as desired. Make sure to create a door large enough for the candle to enter.

4. Have the figure face the workplace.

5. Burn the candle in thirty-minute increments for six consecutive waxing moon days, moving the candle ever closer to the *"job."*

6. On the seventh day, bring the candle within your "workplace" and let the candle burn down completely.

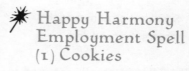# Gravel Root Employment Spell

Gravel root has an affinity for those who must earn their living. Carry it within a conjure bag to find and preserve employment.

Happy Harmony Employment Spell (1) Cookies

To create a harmonious relationship with bosses and co-workers, rather than to achieve domination, bake cookies for everyone. Murmur your intentions over the batter, focusing on your desires during each step of the baking process.

Happy Harmony Employment Spell (2) Sweetgrass

Burn sweetgrass to encourage co-workers to operate harmoniously, without jealousy and backbiting.

Hot Foot It Out Of My Work Place Spell

If there is still conflict within your office, despite your best efforts to foster harmonious working relationships, encourage unpleasant co-workers to seek other employment, or at least leave you alone, with Hot Foot Powder.

1. Grind equal quantities of black pepper, cayenne pepper, salt, and sulfur together.

2. Sprinkle it on or around the target's chair and desk.

The following spells are used to enhance probabilities of success during employment interviews.

Job Interview Success Spell

1. Charge sea salt with your desire: hold the salt in your hand and murmur your desires into it.
2. Place a little salt in your pocket prior to the interview.
3. If possible, sprinkle a tiny bit of salt on your interviewer's clothes without being observed. (Have a good explanation handy, just in case you are caught!)

If you're unable to sprinkle the person, try and sprinkle a little salt over the threshold to the office or even in the office, preferably near the interviewer's desk or chair.

It is not worth taking undue risks: in theory, merely carrying the salt in your pocket enhances your probability of being hired or promoted, although sprinkling as directed will maximize the effects.

Job Interview Self-Confidence Bath

The following magical bath enhances self-confidence and personal magnetism, and increases chances of success. Take the bath either just prior to the interview or the night before. Remember to allow yourself to air-dry and leave the botanicals in the infusion, for utmost power, if at all possible.

1. Place allspice berries, cinnamon sticks, cloves, whole nutmegs, and pieces of sandalwood in a bowl.
2. Cover with boiling water and let the botanicals steep for a while—at least an hour.
3. Meanwhile, draw a bath for yourself.
4. Stand in the tub and toss the now lukewarm infusion over your body.
5. Soak and steep yourself in the bath.

Magic Mirror Office Harmony Spell

A magic mirror may be used to counteract jealousy, backstabbing, and general negative energy: the proverbial evil vibes. This spell requires a bright, sunny day. Although it is a

Chinese-derived spell, it may be understood in the context of the Egyptian spirit Sekhmet, who both heals and destroys with laser beam solar rays.

1. Bring a small round mirror to the scene of the crime or the place of misery. Ideally this is a mirror that can fit into the palm of your hand, for utmost discretion.
2. Slowly, without drawing undue attention to yourself, circulate throughout the room, with the mirror in your hand, reflecting everything in the room for at least several seconds. Include individuals, too, if you feel this is necessary. This spell removes malevolent energy and intent: it causes no harm. You are essentially vacuuming negative energy out of the room and people.
3. The mirror will store these reflections. When you've completed collecting reflections, face the mirror downwards or wrap it in dark fabric.
4. When the opportunity presents itself, take the mirror outside.
5. Hold the mirror up to the sun for no longer than nine seconds. Negativity is burned away and replaced by positive solar energy.

Note: Before performing any solar mirror spells, read the safety tips in the Ritual Tools and Techniques *chapter.*

✳ The Nine Day Employment Spell

Allegedly this spell produces results within nine days; however, it must be accompanied by intensive efforts to locate work.

1. Tie a High John the Conqueror root and a cinnamon stick together, with green, red, or gold thread, knotting your desire and intention into the charm.
2. Dress the botanicals with **Three Kings Oil** and place inside a red flannel drawstring bag.
3. Each morning, before starting that day's job hunt, anoint the charm with additional **Three Kings Oil**.

Should your situation remain unchanged and unimproved after nine days, this indicates that it's time to reconsider your plans and assess alternatives.

Orange Candle Job Spell

1. Write a description of your dream job and/or your employment expectations on the back of a copy of your CV/resumé.
2. Brush the CV with honey and sprinkle it with magnetic sand.
3. Fold the CV nine times.
4. Anoint an orange candle with **Van Van Oil** while you visualize your employment dreams come true.
5. Roll the candle in gold sparkles.
6. Place it atop the folded CV and burn, coinciding with the New Moon.

Pow-Wow Career Enhancement Spell

Pow-Wow Power Potion may be used for career enhancement as well as for psychic enhancement. Its vivid golden color and sweet fragrance provide encouragement and self-confidence, as well.

1. Massage the oil over all your body or just your hands prior to employment interviews or any stressful meetings.
2. Not only is your personal power boosted but the oil can also sharpen that sixth sense so that you'll know the right thing to say at the right moment.

Saint Joseph's Employment Spell

Saint Joseph is the patron of the unemployed, fathers, and step-fathers. He is traditionally appealed to for assistance with finding employment. Should you require work in order to feed a family, he may be helpful and sympathetic.

Although there are various depictions of Saint Joseph, for employment spells he must be shown holding the baby Jesus.

1. Post the appropriate chromolithograph.
2. Keep a vigil candle burning.
3. Request his assistance and search for work.

Seven Knob Employment Search

Green seven-knob candles are beneficial for employment magic.

1. Charge the candle with your desire.
2. Scratch a wish or goal on each knob. The name of a prospective employer may also be scratched into the wax.
3. Burn one knob daily for seven days.

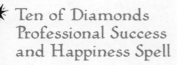

Ten of Diamonds Professional Success and Happiness Spell

Playing and tarot cards may be used to influence your future as well as foretell it. The key, in both cases, is to choose the right cards.

1. Remove the ten of diamonds from a new deck of playing cards and lay it on a dish.
2. Sprinkle it with **Crown of Success Oil** and **Magnet Oil**.

3. Add a handful of coins and/or paper money and/or spirit money.
4. Carve a green candle with your identifying information.
5. Dress the candle with **Crown of Success Oil** and **Magnet Oil**.
6. Place the candle atop the card and burn.
7. Once the candle has completely burned, gather up the ashes, coins, whatever is left of the playing card (it may or may not burn), and any fortuitous-looking wax remnants. Place them in a red mojo hand. Carry with you or keep it in a safe place.

Cleansing Spells

Isn't the house clean enough? I take a daily shower, isn't that sufficient?

Magical cleansing spells have little to do with actual cleanliness, as defined by the absence of dirt, dust, or disorder, although there are spells that accomplish both sorts of cleaning simultaneously. Even the most slovenly, disorganized witch will maintain a regular schedule of psychic cleansing.

At their most basic, cleansing spells remove psychic and spiritual debris. A certain level of this debris accumulates constantly. As you become more psychically aware, you may become more conscious of this and feel a greater need to remove it on a regular basis.

Cleansings remove low-level spiritual entities that are attracted to ritual, if only to feed parasitically off the generated energy. Knowingly or unknowingly, these entities obstruct and weaken your psychic work, lessening your chances of success. In addition, cleansings welcome and make room for more benevolent, helpful spirits.

How do you know when you need to cleanse?

★ *Although it may not be necessary for every quick-fix spell, formal rituals begin with cleansings*

★ *Spells and petitions directed toward spirits are the equivalent of inviting an honored guest to enter your home. Spiritual cleansing beforehand is a measure of respect*

- ★ *Many magic workers perform cleansings on a regular schedule to suit their specific needs, whether daily, weekly, or monthly*
- ★ *If a room doesn't feel right all of a sudden, if your dog suddenly refuses to enter a room, this may indicate the need for cleansing rites*
- ★ *Cleanse any areas that feel oppressive, slightly off, or creepy. Let your inner voice guide you. Any area that has been the scene of violence or a violent emotional altercation needs cleansing*
- ★ *Areas that are frequently and/or consistently the scene of violence or altercations need extra-strong cleansing, followed by protective rituals*
- ★ *Cleansings remove any sense of taint, replacing it with purification and sacredness*

Areas, people, ritual tools, or other objects may be cleansed. Various methods and tools of varying intensity exist for cleansing. This is very personal magic: the results are apparent immediately. You must *feel* cleansed. Choose the methods that resonate most powerfully for you. Your spells will be most effective and potent if accompanied by visualization, affirmation, and/or the chanting of sacred texts.

If at any level you perceive that magic is inherently evil or bad, yet you continue to cast spells, your need for cleansings is even greater than most. At the simplest level, cleansings remove the proverbial bad vibes. On a more serious note, cleansings provide healing and soothing wherever there has been violence, excessive anger, humiliation, and defilement.

Area or Space Cleansing

Any area may be cleansed, from a tabletop altar area or the inside of a magic circle to an entire home or office building. When cleansing a large area, certain spots are believed to require extra care and attention. Vulnerable areas include doors, windows, and other thresholds. Corners, especially dark ones, and the area behind a door, especially one that's consistently propped open, are considered favorite resting spots for malevolent spirits, as are dark closets, bathrooms, and any area that feels *creepy*. Do you recall how children often resist sticking fingers and toes out of the covers for fear that something under the bed will nip them? Dark spaces under the bed can accumulate more than dust bunnies. These are all areas requiring extra attention.

Anyone actively involved in the space cleansing process or exposed to the cleansing materials automatically receives personal cleansing as well, although certain personal cleansing methods cast a more direct and intensive spell.

Asperging Spells

Asperging means sprinkling with liquid in order to effect spiritual and magical cleansing. These are ancient rites: just like burning loose incense, these are techniques known to our earliest ancestors. Asperging spells direct the elemental cleansing power of water and other liquids toward a specific area. Depending upon what is used to direct the water, the elemental cleansing power of Earth may also be incorporated, through the use of botanicals.

★ *Use ritual tools or botanicals to asperge*
★ *Use your fingers to flick the water where it's needed*
★ *Weave an asperging wand of cleansing plants: vervain, lavender, hyssop, and rosemary are favorites. This technique can also incorporate knot magic*

Asperging is the most popular method of liquid-based space cleansing. It is more discreet than smudging or any sort of smoke-based method. Burning botanicals inevitably leaves a lingering fragrance. By definition, it is the aroma of the burning botanicals that provides the cleansing: the inclination of the cleanser is inevitably to strengthen the aroma. This provides the confidence in the effectiveness of the cleansing and its long-term effects. However, aromas tend to evoke highly personal reactions: fragrances favored in cleansings may or may not meet with your neighbors' or housemates' approval.

The issue of fire safety always looms too. Because something is done for positive spiritual purposes does not guarantee that accidents and tragedies will not occur. With water-based cleansings, you are able to maintain tighter control over safety and fragrance. However, different methods resonate for different people: for an intensive cleansing ritual, you may wish to combine several methods.

The most basic cleansing liquid is sea salt dissolved into spring or rainwater. Any of the following formulas also will provide space cleansing. Check the *Formulary* for recipes:

★ *Holy Water*
★ *Florida Water*
★ *Indigo Water*
★ *Marie Laveau Water*
★ *Notre Dame Water*

★ *Pollution Water*
★ *Rose of Jericho Water*
★ *Tar Water*
★ *War Water*

Disperse them through an area. You can intensify the power by combining formulas. **Florida Water**, in particular, empowers any other formula to which it's added. For instance, combine **Florida Water** and **Indigo Water**. Sprinkle through the home or area daily as maintenance cleansing.

✴ Ocean Water Asperging Spell

Unless you live by the sea, this spell may involve more work and preparation than sprinkling with salted fresh water, however the potential power is also greater.

1. Carry ocean water to the area to be cleansed in a glass or metal flask. (For maximum effect, request permission and offer thanks to the Spirits of the Sea.)
2. Asperge as needed, ideally with a rosemary or sea lavender wand.

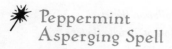
Peppermint Asperging Spell

Create an infusion by pouring boiling water over peppermint. Strain and use a peppermint branch to asperge as needed.

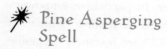
Pine Asperging Spell

Soak pine needles in warm water and asperge as needed.

Ti plant is a sacred and integral component of Hawaiian magical and spiritual traditions. Using a leaf as an asperging tool adds elements of protection to purification rituals. (Ti plant is not the same as either the Australian or New Zealand tea tree but a completely distinct botanical species, despite the similar names.)

Broom Cleansings

You thought witches' brooms were only for flying? Or perhaps they're for ambience? Think again: a broom is as effective a spiritual cleanser as it is a household cleaning tool. Some maintain special ritual brooms, for magical use only. Some spells call for *really* special ritual brooms, intended to be used only once then destroyed, while other spells utilize any available broom, including the one you use for regular daily sweeping.

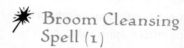
Broom Cleansing Spell (1)

1. Use any broom to sweep the dust from the west to the east.
2. Burn this dust and toss the ashes outdoors.
3. Complete the ritual by mopping the floors with a magical floorwash (formulas follow on pages 217–18), followed by a protective incense fumigation.

Broom Cleansing Spell (2)

This spell incorporates a single-use magical purification broom.

1. Use one or any combination of the following botanicals: broom, cedar, fennel, hyssop, rosemary, sage, vervain.
2. Arrange the botanicals and tie them to the bottom of a branch with raffia, visualizing, charging, and knotting. (Any branch

may be used, however an ash branch is considered particularly powerful.)

. Sprinkle with salted water or any preferred purification formula.

. Sweep the area.

. Disassemble the broom outside, away from the cleansed space.

. Bury the components in the ground or toss them into living waters, flowing away from you.

✳ Broom Cleansing Spell (3)

Any broom may be used in this spell, homemade or commercial, however it must be discarded at the conclusion of the spell.

. Add an infusion of lemongrass and some white or rice vinegar to a bucket filled with water. (If you have time to make lemongrass vinegar, this is even more effective than the infusion.)

. Dip a broom into the bucket of floorwash and sweep the area from the center, working your way outwards. This does not need to be a commercial broom. A branch with attached stiff herbs is fine, however a mop may not be substituted.

3. When complete, dump the wash water outside and discard the broom at a crossroads.

Candle Cleansers

Candles deliver the magical space-purifying effects of fire, without the intensity of smoke or the fragrance associated with fumigation cleansings.

✳ Blessing Oil

Create Blessing Oil by adding frankincense and benzoin to a blend of olive and jojoba oils. Use either the ground resin or essential oils. Dress white and blue candles with the oil and burn to purify the atmosphere.

✳ Coconut Candle Cleanser

Coconuts possess an aroma that many find pleasing, sensuous, and evocative. Releasing the scent of coconut into the air provides long-term spiritual purification in a relaxed, fragrant manner. Unfortunately what is commercially available is almost invariably synthetic; thus the fragrance may be pleasing but the power is nonexistent. *Make your own coconut candles.*

The simplest method is to use pour-and-melt wax from the craft store. White or brown are the preferred colors. If you are a skilled candle maker, however, choose any method or wax you prefer.

1. Prepare the candle shell prior to melting the wax. You may use any type of container you choose; however, a hollowed-out half of a coconut shell is ideal.
2. Melt the wax until liquid.
3. Stir in pure coconut extract. The quantity depends upon the desired intensity of fragrance.
4. Make sure that the wick is attached securely to the container, either by holding it in place until the wax hardens or by attaching it to a pencil or stick laid across the top of the container.
5. Pour the scented wax into the container.
6. Allow the wax to harden.

Supplement the fragrance with a few drops of ginger, frankincense, or lemon essential oils.

Cleansing Powders

Powders are sprinkled through an area to radiate a cleansing effect as well as to absorb malignancies in the air. Sprinkle lightly: typically the powder will disperse into the atmosphere quickly. If any powder is still visible after seven days, vacuum it up and replace. If this occurs consistently, you are either applying too much or stronger cleansing methods are needed.

 Exorcism Powder

Despite its name, rather than performing actual exorcisms, this powder helps eliminate negative emotions, vibrations, and low-level spirit emanations.

1. Blend the following ingredients together and grind into a fine powder:
   Dried basil
   Frankincense
   Rosemary
   Rue
   Yarrow
2. Blend this powder into arrowroot powder.
3. Sprinkle as needed.

Cleansing Spirits

Sometimes you need someone else to clean for you. Calling in the spirits to perform a cleansing is like hiring a deluxe cleaning service. They perform a better, more thorough job than the average person could; they are capable of removing spiritual dirt and debris that you weren't aware even existed.

Like a cleaning service, these spirits expect to be paid. Some demand specific gifts or offerings. Others, like the angels, expect a certain atmosphere of respect and reverence: angels feed off the fragrance of precious resins. Fill the room with their aroma—it will enhance the cleansing.

As anyone who's ever hired a cleaning service knows, you must clean prior to the spirits' arrival. Do some basic cleansings first to prepare the area for their presence: smudge sticks or asperging cleansing waters are appropriate.

Four Archangels Cleansing Service

Summon the archangels; they may arrive alone or leading hosts of lesser angels. The four archangels may be invoked to initiate all rituals and also for the cleansing and protection of ritual space. Angels, most especially the archangels, are not the cute little cherubs one sees depicted on Valentine's Day cards. These are beings of power and majesty. Their presence may remain invisible or they may manifest in various forms, however a typical vision of angels involves a being so bright they remain visible even with your eyes closed. Their presence as cleansing agents burns like purifying fire, yet they leave holiness in their wake, rather than devastation.

1. Cast a circle, with a sword, crystal-tipped wand, flaming torch, or other tool.
2. Pause at each cardinal point and invoke the appropriate archangel:
   Raphael to the East
   Michael to the South
   Gabriel to the West
   Uriel to the North

Make the invocation as simple or as elaborate as you choose. Different schools posit which angel has dominion over which direction. If you are familiar with other directions, choose what resonates for you.

Whether the following ritual began in Africa, Haiti, or in New Orleans itself is unknown, however it emerged in New Orleans as an adaptation of Haitian ritual. Extremely popular, it passed into general American magical usage and is now familiar all over Earth. It is difficult to find a botanical, occult, or spiritual supply store that will not teach you this spell. However, while many are aware of the mechanics of the ritual, few understand the spiritual context of this spell.

The ritual calls upon extremely powerful and prominent lwa to provide cleansing and protection. Although their names are invoked, their identities are forgotten: for many people, this spell is a modern equivalent of the litanies of ancient, forgotten words of power invoked by medieval magicians. However, these are no forgotten spirits: these lwa remain active and vital, invoked daily in Vodoun ritual. If you call them, they may come. If you take the time to understand *who* you're calling, this spell becomes even more powerful.

New Orleans Voodoo Spirit Cleansing Service

This spell may also be used purely as a spirit-banishing spell, however it does a potent job of cleaning up all negative vibrations and debris. It is best performed at midnight during a waxing moon. Be sure proper ventilation is available: the smell of sulfur is pungent and potentially irritating.

1. Place a square of red paper onto a small metal or stone plate. You will need one plate plus its contents for each corner of any room you wish cleansed. Most rooms require four sets.
2. Place a pinch of sulfur on top of each paper.
3. Place each plate in a corner, so that there is one in each.
4. Light the sulfur.
5. Simultaneously, address the four lwa invoked in this ritual, turning to face each new corner as each name is uttered.
    Granbois!
    Baron Carrefour!
    Baron Cimitiere!
    Damballah!

*I invoke you! With the power of
your names, I command and
compel all evil spirits, spells,
and vibrations, any negative
entities, to leave me and my
home and never return!*

5. Withdraw from the room,
maintaining a vigilant eye on fire
safety.

Cleansing Through Smoke

Burning botanicals releases their
powers into the air, releasing
various magical effects. What is
actually being released depends
upon what is being burned. This
is true in areas outside magic too:
up until World War I, French
hospitals burned juniper and
rosemary in order to release the
volatile oils to provide antiseptic,
antibacterial effects.

Smoke cleansings are considered among the most potent of
cleansing spells. Their effect
lingers as long as you can smell
any vestiges of the botanical
aroma. Strong, fragrant, visible
smoke that shoots straight up is
considered especially powerful
and auspicious.

In order to cleanse an area
effectively, the aroma of the
burning plant material has to

permeate the air. In theory, if
the quantities of the botanical
cleanser are great enough, there's
no need to waft the smoke
around. Hence the huge mounds
of frankincense and myrrh
burned in ancient temples, as
well as the traditional Midsummer and Beltane bonfires. If you
want to burn such quantities,
however, be aware that not only
will every corner of your own
area be permeated with fragrance, but that aromas spread
and are difficult to contain. Your
neighbors will be calling to
either complain or to thank you,
as the case may be.

Few, however, have access to
such quantities of botanicals.
Therefore, most cleansing smoke
needs to be directed toward what
needs to be cleansed. Burning
releases the magical properties
into the atmosphere: actual
cleansing comes from direct
exposure to the smoke.

☀ Basic Botanic Fumigation Spell

*Burning specific botanicals provides
magical and spiritual antiseptic
effects. These botanicals include:
aloes wood, benzoin resin, bloodroot,*

cajeput, cinnamon, cloves, dragon's blood resin, eucalyptus, frankincense, garlic, harmel (Syrian rue), juniper, mastic, mugwort, myrrh, onions, rosemary, sage (especially white sage), Saint John's Wort, sandalwood, thyme, wormwood, and yarrow. Burn them alone or in any combination.

Many of these plants also radiate a protective aura: maintaining them as a presence, particularly as living plants but also as dried amulets, can only be beneficial. Whatever else these plants do (and many, such as frankincense, dragon's blood, and wormwood are extremely versatile magically), they always radiate a cleansing, purifying aura. Although certain methods of use intensify their cleansing effects, those effects are constant: the more these botanicals are used, the more consistent their cleansing power.

The simplest of all smoke-cleansing methods is the smudge stick. A smudge stick is a small wand made from dried botanicals. Although today the most famous smudge sticks derive from Native American tradition, this is basically a very simple, universal tool. The old English lavender wand is, in effect, a smudge stick, albeit one that is not frequently burned.

Smudging is the process of using directed smoke to cleanse an area, person, or object. Smudge sticks are popular occult tools and easily purchased, but they can be just as easily created.

1. Dry bunches of herbs.
2. When they have completely dried, bind them together with thin cotton thread.
3. When needed, the stick is lit and the smoke directed toward and over whatever needs cleansing.
4. A feather fan is often used to direct the smoke, although you may also use your bare hands.

Be aware of fire safety: smudge sticks tend to smolder long after the flames appear to have died out.

Although a smudge stick may theoretically be created from any dried botanicals, for cleansing purposes, the following are most potent and practical:

★ *White sage or common garden sage*
★ *Juniper*
★ *Desert sage (a different species from the sage above: an* Artemisia, *not a* Salvia)
★ *Rosemary*

The smudge stick has certain advantages: it's neat, compact, easily controlled, discreet, and mobile. Loose incense, however, is also extremely effective and offers you the luxury of a wider selection of botanical material.

Many of the most potent cleansing materials are gum resins and wood chips that do not lend themselves to binding into a wand. These are usually burned on charcoal, which is placed on a dish, iron pan, or incense censer so that the cleansing smoke may be directed as needed.

Specific cleansing formulas have evolved:

Birch Cleansing Incense

Burn birch bark and twigs to remove negative energy.

Cast Out Evil Incense

This powerful formula provides cleansing for areas profaned by evil and/or violence:

1. Blend and grind the following ingredients together into a fine powder:

Camphor
Cinnamon
Frankincense
Myrrh
Sandalwood

2. Sprinkle onto a lit charcoal and burn.

Cast Out Evil Extra Strength Spell

For areas that have been truly profaned and need extra-potent cleansing:

1. Do an initial moderate cleansing of the area.
2. Prepare the room by closing all windows and sources of ventilation.
3. Prepare an incense burner with lit charcoals.
4. Place a substantial quantity of Cast Out Evil incense onto the burner.
5. Position the burner in the center of the room.
6. Let it remain there for a minimum of an hour, and overnight at longest. While the incense burns, the room should be closed to all outside ventilation. If it's possible for someone to stay in the room, to attend the incense, they will be rewarded with a powerful

personal cleansing. If this is not possible and the incense will be temporarily unsupervised, be extremely vigilant as to fire safety.

7. When sufficient time has passed, open windows, provide ventilation, let the fresh air in.

 Garlic Cleansing Spell

1. Place the reserved garlic peel in a mortar and pestle and add brown sugar.
2. Pound and grind them together.
3. Sprinkle the result onto lit charcoal or burn it on a cast iron pan.
4. Waft the fumes over the areas to be cleansed, allowing the aroma to permeate and settle.

Old Affair Removal Cleansing Incense

There aren't only spiritual reasons for cleansing spells; sometimes they're necessary to set the stage for new love by removing all vestiges of the past. Burn myrtle and dried rose petals.

Pine Cleansing Incense

Grind dried pine needles to powder and sprinkle on lit charcoals to cleanse an area of negative energy and entities.

Sacred Purification Incense

This cleansing formula incorporates the botanicals most frequently used in sacred rites. It removes the negative and the tainted, leaving an aura of holiness behind.

Benzoin
Dragon's blood
Frankincense
Myrrh
Sandalwood
Sea salt

1. Blend and grind the ingredients into a fine powder.
2. Sprinkle onto a lit charcoal and burn.

Cleansing Through Sound

Music plays many magical roles. *Charms*, in the most ancient sense of the word, were meant to be sung. Traditional Finnish magi ians were famed for their ability to sing things into existence or to heal via songs. Experienced magicians were expected to possess songs that could halt bleeding.

Like botanicals or crystals, perhaps every musical instrument has its magical uses. Violins and flutes are used to cast love spells, while the sounds and reverberations of drums and percussion instruments provide extremely powerful cleansings.

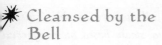

Cleansed by the Bell

Among the reasons bells are traditionally incorporated into churches is that bells are powerful space cleansers. Although any bell may be used, the most effective for cleansing purposes include silver bells, iron bells, and brass bells.

Maneki Neko is the amuletic Japanese beckoning cat. Usually a free-standing figurine, Maneki Neko bells cleanse personal and spatial auras, in addition to their traditional function of attracting prosperity and protection.

Ring bells whenever you feel cleansing is required. Hang bells in a breezy spot so that their activity can be consistent.

Bells are interesting cleansers because, unlike other methods, they can operate spontaneously. Should a typically silent bell suddenly ring, especially without obvious cause, pay attention. Further cleansing or protective rituals may be needed.

The Serene Yet Powerful Method: Singing Bowls

The harmonies created by Himalayan singing bowls are used to wash space. Ideally, the goal is to achieve a perfect balance of yin and yang energies. This method is particularly beneficial before ritual. It has a soothing effect on participants as well: beyond cleansing, it is also used to balance and harmonize energies—excellent for the initiation of group ritual.

The singing bowl is a round metal bowl made in varying sizes. It is portable, so that it may be carried directly to any area needing cleansing. Traditionally, the finest singing bowls are crafted in Nepal from seven metals: gold, silver, copper, iron, tin, lead, and zinc. Each metal corresponds to one of the seven visible planets and thus incorporates its energies and blessings.

A small wooden mallet is used to tap the bowl, typically three times for maximum effect. Different sounds are produced depending upon whether the bowl is tapped, rubbed, or hit. Try using your fingernail or the tips of your fingers instead of the mallet. Adding varying amounts of water to the bowl also alters the sound. Experiment. Find the sounds that please you, that literally resonate with you. Harmonize the sound of the bowl with your own ears and intuition to achieve the correct sound for your purpose and space.

1. Place a small cushion beneath the bowl as it's carried. A round cushion is traditional. This is not merely a formality: the cushion improves the sound, lengthening the tone.
2. Walk with the bowl, directing the sound as needed.
3. For heavy-duty cleansing, place the bowl on its cushion on a table in the center of a room. Strike it, letting its sound reverberate and radiate.

Like any other occult tool, given the opportunity, an individual singing bowl can develop a rapport with an individual person. A fine singing bowl is an exceptionally receptive tool.

It will become attuned to anyone in frequent contact with it. Store the bowl in soft, heavy fabric such as velvet when not in use. Singing bowls improve with age, becoming more powerful with frequent use.

Singing bowls are also used for empowering, energizing, and replenishing space following any kind of space cleansing.

Cleansing Vapors

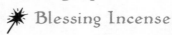

Blessing Incense

Not all incenses are dry. This is liquid, steam-based incense formula from Yemen.

1. Gently warm rose water or hydrosol.
2. Add sugar, stirring until the sugar is completely dissolved.
3. Add some or all of the following: aloes wood, rose petals, sandalwood powder, black tea leaves, attars of jasmine, rose, sandalwood, and henna.
4. Simmer, until steam rises.
5. Use the steam to bless and cleanse an area, people, and/or objects.

☀ Chinese Vinegar Steam Cleanser

Steam is the result of the merged powers of water and fire; it is an extremely effective spiritual cleanser. This Chinese formula is recommended for a weekly standard cleansing:

1. Boil rice vinegar in a shallow pan until it's steaming (a paella pan or similar is ideal).
2. Very carefully, so as not to burn yourself, carry the steaming pan of vinegar through all the rooms of the home, letting the vapors cleanse corners, closets, all and any areas that don't feel "*right.*"

Floorwashes

Floorwashes don't sound as glamorous as incense and asperging, however they are an integral component of the Hoodoo and Conjure magical traditions. They combine actual physical house cleaning with spiritual and magical work, effectively killing two birds with one stone. They are potent yet discreet and perhaps the single most effective use of multi-tasking within magic.

Although the liquid is called *floorwash*, technically it refers to the final rinse used to clean a floor or other interior surfaces. It should not be removed but allowed to air-dry, so that its power radiates into the surrounding atmosphere. In other words, the floor should be clean *before* applying the floorwash. The radiant power of the botanicals is what is crucial: floorwashes are a component of many spells for a variety of purposes, including protection and romance, in addition to their obvious value as a space-cleansing device.

There are two standard methods of making a floorwash. Choose which suits you:

★ *Fill a bucket with warm water. Add the magical infusion together with some white vinegar*
★ *Create the infusion and pour it into an empty bucket. Pour enough boiling salted water over it to fill the bucket. Add some white vinegar*

☀ Angelica Floorwash

In addition to its cleansing abilities, angelica possesses a strong protective aspect.

1. Make a strong infusion from dried angelica.
2. Strain out the herbs.
3. Add the infusion, together with some white or rice vinegar, to a bucket of wash water to cleanse floors and surfaces.

 Aura Cleansing Floorwash

Agrimony repels and sends back hexes. Peppermint is an aggressive cleanser that beckons the presence of helpful, benevolent spirits. Combined, these botanicals create a particularly potent floorwash.

1. Make a strong infusion from dried agrimony and peppermint.
2. Strain out the herbs and add the infusion liquid to a bucket of water, together with white or rice vinegar.
3. Cleanse floors and surfaces.

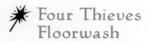 Four Thieves Floorwash

*Add **Four Thieves Vinegar**, black salt, and rosemary to a bucket of floorwash.*

New Home Floorwash

This is recommended for a prelimi nary cleansing when moving into new home. This removes old vibra tions and emotions lingering from past residents and allows you t begin with a fresh slate.

1. Make a strong infusion from basil, hyssop, and pine needles.
2. Strain and add to a bucket of rinse water, with vinegar.
3. Cleanse floors and surfaces as needed.

Post-cleansing Spell

*After other Cleansing Spells ar complete, add **Cascarilla Powde** to a bucket of salted water. Was down floors and walls to seal an enhance your previous efforts.*

Full House Cleansings

Special techniques may be needed should you wish to magically cleanse an entire building Although many cleansing spells assume that a home is being ritually cleansed, these spells may also be used for workspaces or any other type of building.

Coconut Cleansing Spell

1. Bring rum, **Cascarilla Powder**, and a whole coconut to the corner of your home furthest from the main entrance.
2. Take a mouthful of rum. Don't swallow it; instead spray it over the whole coconut.
3. Next sprinkle **Cascarilla Powder** on the coconut.
4. Roll the coconut through your home, out the main entrance.
5. Pick it up and bring it to a four-way crossroads at a distance from where you live, a remote crossroads, not one that you pass frequently.
6. Circumambulate the four points of the crossroads, dropping offerings of fruit, coins, and candy as you pass each one.
7. Bring the coconut into the center of the crossroads and throw it to the ground, making sure that it cracks open.
8. Leave it there. Return home via a circuitous route without looking back.

Intensive Space Cleansing

1. Take an entire bunch of peppermint and rub it vigorously against walls, furniture, objects, and whatever else needs to be cleansed.
2. When the cleansing is complete, wrap the peppermint in brown paper and remove it from your home immediately.
3. Dispose of it far from home, returning via a circuitous route.

Jessamine Flowers House Cleansing Spell

Botanicals don't have to be burnt to cleanse: spread day Jessamine petals throughout the house for spiritual cleansing and to remove the residue of any malevolent spells cast against you.

New Home Major Cleansing Spell

This cleansing ritual may be used for individual rooms or for an entire house and is an excellent cleansing method prior to moving into a new home.

1. Blend essential oils of frankincense and sandalwood into olive oil.
2. Use this to dress a blue candle.

3. Place this candle onto a disposable saucer or plate.
4. Place this saucer on top of some spread-out sheets of newspaper or a disposal tablecloth.
5. Cast a large circle with sea salt on the paper around the candle and saucer. The circle must be large enough for you to maneuver comfortably within it.
6. Enter the circle; you may either stand or kneel on the paper, and light the candle.
7. Close the doors and let the candle burn out. (Always maintain an eye on fire safety.)
8. When the candle is finished, fold everything up securely inside the newspaper. Do not spill even one grain of salt.
9. Take it to a moving body of water. Slide all biodegradable materials into the water. Throw everything else into a trashcan at a distance from your home. Walk away and don't look back.
10. Repeat in every room that you would like cleansed.

✳ Salt Cleansing Spell

1. Make an infusion by pouring boiling water over High John the Conqueror roots.

2. Sprinkle the infusion on salt. (Only moisten the salt; don't melt it.)
3. Allow the salt to dry out.
4. Sprinkle the salt around your home to absorb negativity.
5. Reserve the remaining High John liquid and refrigerate. Repeat the spell as desired, daily or weekly.

Stationary Cleansers

Certain objects are perceived as being similar to magical vacuum cleaners. They absorb malevolence and negativity, removing it from the premises. As a general rule, white foods may be used in this manner.

In general, when the object is full, like a vacuum cleaner bag, it needs to be removed from the premises and discarded. Crystals are the exception: they may be cleansed, effectively emptying them of debris, so that they may be used over and over again.

Stationary cleansers are typically left unsupervised in an area; if children and/or pets are present, make sure a safe method is used.

✳ Amethyst Crystal Cleanser

Place large amethysts in room corners to serve as spiritual vacuum cleaners. When they look dull, cleanse and recharge them. Other crystal gemstones recommended for space cleansing include clear quartz crystal and malachite.

✳ Basic Stationary Cleansing

Sprinkling directs the cleansing, however liquids may also be used as stationary cleansers:

1. Place any of the cleansing formulas recommended in Asperging Spells above (but especially **Florida Water** and **Notre Dame Water**), in shallow uncovered pans.
2. Situate them strategically through an area, to absorb negative energy and provide a cleansing effect.
3. Replace weekly. If the liquid starts to look odd or smell strange, however, replace it immediately.

✳ Onion Space Cleansing Spell

1. Chop one onion into quarters and place one piece in each corner of a room. Don't peel the onion. Don't use a food processor. Chop it by hand.
2. Allow the onion pieces to remain in place overnight.
3. Bury them outside the following day.
4. Repeat the process for a total of five consecutive nights.

✳ Vinegar Cleanser

Plain vinegar is cheap, easily obtainable, and among the strongest cleansing agents of all.

1. Place a cup or bowl of vinegar in every room that needs cleansing.
2. Replace weekly.

*For intensified cleansing, add a square of camphor to the vinegar. To improve the fragrance, add a few drops of essential oils of frankincense, rose, or sandalwood, or blend with **Florida Water**.*

Personal Cleansings

Personal cleansings are done in preparation for rituals and spell-work. They have an empowering effect and will remove accumulated psychic debris that obstructs full expression of personal power. In addition, many who delve into spiritual work perform regularly scheduled cleansings, usually once a week, as general magical maintenance.

Stronger cleansings are needed in special circumstances: they provide psychic healing following violence, violation, or humiliation. Personal cleansings can also provide relief after trivial, unpleasant experiences. Should you ever feel somehow *tainted* or *unclean*, to any degree, that's the signal that some sort of personal cleansing ritual is needed. Choose the rituals that resonate, most strongly for you.

Personal cleansings have an advantage over many other types of spells: their effects are readily apparent fairly immediately. A successful cleansing spell leaves you feeling refreshed, renewed, and *clean*.

Many personal cleansings, particularly the baths, may be performed for oneself. However, some cleansing techniques require that one person performs the cleansing for another. To some extent, that's because many are survivals of shamanic rituals. Shamanic healers provide profound cleansing and soul restoration, beyond the scope of the average layperson. Once upon a time, unlike today, shamanic healing was common and accessible (according to many anthropologists and historians, the true oldest profession is that of the shaman). Perhaps it will be so again: cleansing spells do not replace the need for shamans. However, their methods have been adapted to household use: make sure you choose ritual assistants and cleansing assistants wisely.

☀ Basil Cleansing Bath

In addition to standard cleansing effects, this bath is excellent for removing negative emotions caused by extended exposure to very controlling people. Basil also enhances luck and the potential for prosperity.

1. Pour approximately one cup of boiling water over one heaped teaspoon of dried basil.

2. Allow this to stand until the water cools, creating a strong infusion.
3. Add this to your bath.

✳ Citrus Bath

1. Obtain as many kinds of citrus fruits as possible: lemons, limes, oranges, tangerines, and so forth.
2. Draw a bath, quarter each fruit, squeeze the juice into the bath, and toss the fruit in the water.
3. Add yarrow hydrosol, as much as you like.
4. Get into the bath and rub the fruit over your body.
5. Let yourself air-dry. (You may be sticky but let it remain for as long as possible.)

✳ Cleansing and Energy Balancing Bath

The botanicals frankincense and myrrh are perceived as happily married, perfectly balanced, and a matching couple, as are vetiver and patchouli. In addition to aura cleansing, these botanicals also balance yin and yang energies.

1. Add a cup of salt to a dish.
2. Add two drops each of essential oils of frankincense, myrrh, patchouli, and vetiver. (You may add more if you wish, but keep proportions equal. Add additional drops in even-numbered combinations.)
3. With your fingers, blend this into the salt.
4. Add this to a tub of running water.
5. When the bath has filled and the temperature is correct, adjust the fragrance, if you like, by adding a few more drops of any of the essential oils directly to the water.

✳ Cleansing Oil

Sometimes cleansing means adding something rather than removing it. This Mediterranean formula has a purifying effect. Using either essential oils or fresh herbs add basil, rosemary, and thyme to olive oil and massage this into the body.

✳ Destroy All Evil Bath

1. Add at least one cup of **Florida Water** and at least one cup of sea salt to a tub filled with water.

2. Add a generous splash of **Four Thieves Vinegar**.
3. Just before you enter the water, when the temperature has already been adjusted, add nine drops of essential oil of rosemary.

Reinforce and enhance the bath's potency by keeping a large quartz crystal in the water while you bathe.

 Garlic Personal Vacuum Service

Sometimes someone else really needs cleansing. If negativity emanates consistently from a single individual, tainting the mood and atmosphere, take matters into your own hands: perform an indirect cleansing. Use a clove of garlic as a personal vacuum cleaner.

1. Peel and crush a single clove of garlic.
2. Place it under the person's bed, chair, or under the carpet where they are sure to stand.
3. Remove and burn after twenty-four hours.
4. Replace as needed; an improvement in attitude should be observed shortly.

Herbal Magic Cleansing Bath

Make an infusion by pouring boiling water over fresh lavender, mint, marjoram, oregano, and rosemary. Add the strained liquid to your bath.

Kitchen Herb Bath

Magically powerful plants masquerade as common kitchen herbs. Make a strong infusion by pouring boiling water over fennel, dill, and chervil and try adding it to your bathwater.

Lavender Bath

Lavender derives its name from "lavare," meaning "to wash." Laundry comes from the same root source. This bath may be dedicated to Hecate, for whom lavender is a sacred plant. Add essential oil of lavender, lavender hydrosol, or an infusion to the bath for spiritual as well as physical cleansing.

Mother Holle's Cleansing Bath

Mother Holle, Germanic Queen of Witches, leads the Wild Hunt. These herbs are traditionally gathered on

Midsummer's Eve and used for intensive cleansings between the winter solstice and January 6th.

Blend the following botanicals:

Avens
Chamomile
Elder
Elecampane
Heartsease
Mint
Mugwort
Mullein
Saint John's Wort
Southernwood
Vervain
Yarrow

Make an infusion by pouring boiling water over the botanicals. Let it steep, then strain and add to the bath. For maximum spiritual cleansing and happiness, float heartsease (wild pansy) blossoms in the water.

 Nine Flowers Bath

1. Place three white roses, three white carnations, and three white lilies in a dish and pour hot water over them.
2. Strain out the liquid, reserving the flowers, and bring them to the bathtub or shower.
3. Scrub from head to foot with one flower at a time until that flower falls apart.
4. When all nine flowers have been used, get out of the water and air-dry.
5. Dress in clean clothes; don't clean the bathtub immediately. Wait several hours or have someone else do the job.

Personal Fumigation Spells

Personal fumigation means using directed smoke to spiritually cleanse the body and the personal aura. This is also a very ancient method of applying perfume. Perfume literally means *"through smoke."* Although modern perfume is liquid, this is a relatively recent development. For centuries, people stood over burning aromatic materials, wafting it strategically, hoping to permeate skin, hair, crevices, and clothing with healing, protective, or seductive fragrances, as the case may be.

Most purifying botanicals also possess a protective aspect. Depending upon which botanicals are used, there may also be a sensual component. For all of their protective and purifying powers, for instance, sandalwood and frankincense are also luxurious, fragrant, even aphrodisiac substances. Cleansings can be sensual rather than medicinal and still be very effective, although this also depends upon personal expectations and preferences.

In ascending order of strength, try these methods:

★ *Have someone else cleanse you with a smudge stick or directed smoke. White sage, desert sage, frankincense and benzoin resin are particularly effective*

★ *Place the incense burner on the ground and straddle it, directing the smoke upwards around the body. Kneel down and direct it over your head. You need greater quantities of botanicals for this to be truly effective*

★ *You can also burn the incense in a small, closed room such as a bathroom. After the room is permeated with the smoke, get undressed and enter the room so that you can bathe in the smoke*

Purification Bath

1. Make a strong infusion by pouring boiling water over nine bay laurel leaves and two tablespoons of anise seeds.

2. Let it reach room temperature.
3. Strain out the botanicals and add the liquid to your tub of water.

Quick Fix Aura Cleanser

*Add one cup of salt and one cup of vinegar to a bath. Lemon vinegar is most potent, however apple cider or rice vinegar is also very effective. Homemade **Four Thieves Vinegar** is also powerful and very effective, but its fragrance is pungent rather than light and relaxing.*

Rosemary Anisette Cleansing

This personal cleansing invokes the healing powers of massage. Someone else must perform this cleansing on you. The subject of the cleansing focuses on his or her goals or on prayer and petition, while the other person performs the massage.

1. Soak rosemary stalks in anisette.
2. The person to be cleansed lies down comfortably on the floor, bed, or on a massage table.
3. The massage is initially performed only with the hands: this is a gentle, easy massage, not a vigorous one. The goal is aura

cleansing, not muscle manipulation.

4. With the fingers, repeatedly and rhythmically form the sign of the cross, pentacle, and/or other sacred, protective symbols on the body. Start with the palm, and then journey up the arms. Go to the soles of the feet and up the leg.

5. Remove the rosemary wands from the liqueur, shake them out gently and use them to lightly massage the body.

6. Simultaneously request assistance from your favorite spirits. Order any evil entities to leave. Affirm your safety.

☀ Sage Cleansing Spell

Plain garden sage is a profound spiritual cleanser.

1. Dry the sage.
2. Grind it into a fine powder with a mortar and pestle.
3. Sprinkle the powder onto a charcoal and use it to fumigate the body.

Salt Cleansing Spells

Salt is the single most powerful and consistent aura cleanser. Sea salt, processed as little as possible, is most powerful, although many magical traditions, not necessarily Jewish, prefer kosher salt, as it bears the aura of being blessed. However, *in extremis*, any type of salt is effective.

☀ Salt Cleansing Bath

This is a quick-fix cleansing, perfect for spontaneous needs:

1. Add at least one cup of salt to a bathtub filled with warm water.
2. Soak thoroughly, allowing yourself to air-dry, when the bath is over.

☀ Salt Scrub

A salt scrub provides a more concentrated cleansing. For maximum effect, add bath salts to the water and then apply the salt scrub directly to the body.

The Standard Salt Scrub formula consists of a blend of approximately one cup of salt and one half cup of oil. The actual quantity depends, however, upon the desired consistency and the sensitivity of your skin: if you'd like a softer, less abrasive scrub, increase the proportion of oil.

Because salt is purifying and protective, every salt scrub inherently provides aura cleansing. However, the purpose and added effects of a salt scrub may be adjusted through the addition of essential oils. Rosemary, clary sage, frankincense, manuka, benzoin, thyme linalool, and sandalwood all intensify the cleansing effect.

✳ Seven Flowers Miracle Bath

This bath is ideal for when you're very tired, very jaded, very drained, or very bitter. Seven different fresh flowers are required for this bath, the magic number associated with hope and miracles. Choose whatever flowers are available or whatever flowers appeal to you. Float the flowers in the bathtub and soak while focusing on regaining innocence and optimism.

✳ Seven Roses Bath

This spell requires:

Seven red roses
A handful of sea salt
A splash of vinegar
A squeeze of lemon juice
A splash of pure spring water or substitute a splash of either **Marie Laveau** or **Notre Dame Water**.

1. Fill the tub with water.
2. Throw all the ingredients into the tub.
3. Spend seven minutes in the bath, rubbing yourself with the roses, submerging yourself periodically and focusing upon your goals.
4. Dry off with a clean towel, white or unbleached cotton if possible, and put on fresh clothes.
5. Don't clean the tub out right away; let it sit for at least an hour while your aura cleansing stabilizes.

✳ Seven Waves Ocean Cleansing

Immerse yourself in ocean waters to achieve aura cleansing. When seven waves have passed over you, the cleansing is complete.

✪ Death Spells

Death spells are not hexes nor are they meant to cause death. There are no "*killing curses*" here. Instead, "*death spells*" as a category revolves around the topic of death, death's aftermath, and death's magical effect on both the departed and the living left behind. Although magical practitioners may be buried with their ritual tools, for a variety of reasons, most typically death spells are spells for the living. Ghosts, vampires, and other denizens of the next-world will have to discover their own new repertoire of enchantment in the Summerlands.

This was not always the case: ancient traditions from Egypt and Tibet for instance required that spells and rituals be learned in life so that they could be performed after death. The books, known in English as *The Tibetan Book of the Dead (The Book of the Great Liberation)* and the *Egyptian Book of the Dead: The Book of Going Forth by Day*, record these traditions. Spiritual adepts trained for years, so that they would be prepared and show no fear when they finally faced their after-life examinations, sort of like the application process to a university with extremely tough admissions standards. Although eventually in Egypt this practice degenerated into merely being able to present the appropriate spell or sacred text. Thus the wealthy were buried with *Books of the Dead* as amulets—or glorified hall passes!)

This is another of those spell categories that fall along the razor's edge between religion, spirituality, and magic. Cast these spells (or adapt them) as they correspond to your personal spiritual realities.

Many of these spells are extremely ancient, so many presume that preparations for the dead person will be conducted at home, typically by someone who is either familiar with the deceased or familiar with correct magical procedure. However, for modern people in industrialized nations, death is primarily a topic to be avoided at all costs. Death has become a mystery, tended to by professionals. People no longer die at home: they die in hospitals or hospices. Families and loved ones no longer prepare the body: professionals whisk away the corpse and perform all functions discreetly away from the eyes of loved ones left behind. It is perhaps the area where magical cultures diverge most strongly from surrounding conventional ones. Magical cultures are concerned deeply with preparation of the body and the funeral rites. This is an extremely important threshold; if errors are made, there are potentially disastrous consequences for both living and dead:

★ *Incorrect or absent funeral ritual leaves the soul of the deceased vulnerable to capture by a sorcerer who may use the soul as a tool for nefarious ends or as a work-slave. This belief dates back at least to ancient Babylon and survives in the duppies of the West Indies*

★ *The spirit of the deceased who cannot transition properly to the next realm has nothing better to do than hang around this realm and, depending upon their frustration level, make life miserable for the living. This applies particularly to unidentified homicide victims*

★ *In many cultures, the "next life" means becoming an ancestor and serving and protecting descendants. If proper burial rites as well as later propitiatory offerings aren't available, neither is the potential power of an ancestor, leaving the dead angry and frustrated and the living vulnerable and unprotected*

Death Spells

Death Spirits or *Spirits of Death* sound so threatening compared to a *Healing Spirit* or a *Spirit of Love*. This isn't mere modern squeamishness but an attitude shared with the ancients. Death Spirits, although they play a necessary function, made our ancestors nervous, too.

Death Spirits tend to fall into one of two categories:

★ *Spirits who are involved in the dying process or who serve to ease the transition to the next life*
★ *Spirits who are guardians of the dead, who preside over the realms of the dead, or who rule cemeteries and cremation grounds*

Many Spirit Guardians of Death's Doors remain unnamed. As with Disease Spirits, there's some reluctance to name many of them, just in case they actually come when called, thus epithets and euphemisms are frequently substituted. Often, a Death Spirit's true name remains secret. Hades literally means *"the unseen one."* Should that name become too familiar, other euphemisms may be substituted: Polydegmon means *"the hospitable one"* because,

after all, *everyone* is welcome in his realm. Pluton means *"wealth,"* because ultimately he owns everyone and everything.

Despite the fear they instill, these spirits can be very needed, helpful, and welcome—at the right moment, of course. Their assistance is incorporated into many spells for a variety of reasons and purposes.

Guardians of the next world and of the cemetery gates include:

★ *Baron Samedi, leader of the Vodoun Ghede spirits, and his consort, La Grande Brigitte*
★ *Dongyue Dadi, Lord of Tai Shan (China)*
★ *Erishkigal/Lamashtu (Mesopotamia)*
★ *Hades, Persephone (Greece)*
★ *Hella (Norse)*
★ *Kali, Shiva, Yama (Hindu)*
★ *Mictlantecutli and Mictecacuiuatl (Aztec Lord and Lady of the Dead)*
★ *Osiris (Egypt)*
★ *Oya (Yoruba)*
★ *Yambe Akka (Saami)*

Appeal to these guardian spirits to protect the souls of the dead, and also to maintain control over the souls of the dead, keeping them in line, so to speak. Petition them also for access to the spirits of the dead, should this be desired.

Psychopomps

Psychopomp means *"conductor of souls"* in Greek. The term refers to a specific type of spirit, entrusted with a specific type of function. These are the spirit guides who lead the soul between the lands of the living and the dead. (In addition, they sponsor, protect, and guide shamans who journey back and forth between the realms.) You will recognize them in your dreams or waking visions by the attributes they carry; traditional emblems for this class of spirits include a key, a cutting instrument, and/or a torch. Culso, an Etruscan psychopomp, for instance, awaits the arrival of all souls. He carries scissors in one hand to sever ties with the realm of the living and a bright flaming torch to light the way toward new adventures.

Psychopomps include:

★ *Angels: Gabriel, Azrael, and the unnamed "Angel of Death" (Jewish)*
★ *Anubis, Hathor, Wepwawet (Egypt)*
★ *Baron Samedi, Baron La Croix and Baron Cimitiere (Vodoun)*
★ *Culso (Etruscan)*
★ *Freya and the Valkyries (Norse)*
★ *Giltine (Lithuania)*
★ *Hecate, Hermes (Greece)*
★ *Jizo (Japan)*
★ *Mother Holle (German)*

Animals serve as psychopomps, too. The most famous are dogs, jackals, and other canines. Many spirit psychopomps manifest in these forms. These include Anubis and Kali (jackals), Hecate (dog), and Wepwawet (wolf). Other animal psychopomps include butterflies, snakes, and birds, especially ravens, crows, hornbills, and frigates. It is considered extremely auspicious if any of these creatures make a spontaneous appearance at a funeral or similar post-death rites. This indicates that the escort service for the soul has arrived and is intended to comfort and reassure the living.

Psychopomps may be petitioned to ease the travails of the dying, by the dying person or their loved ones alike.

✳ Angel of Death Intervention Spell

Foil the angel of death by changing a person's name! Death angels in Jewish tradition, similar to Chinese death spirits, possess a bureaucratic nature. Instructions must be followed to a "t," thus they come prepared with a magical warrant naming the specific person whose soul is scheduled for harvest. (It's believed dangerous to have too many people— like more than one—bearing the same name in one family. The Angel of Death might get confused and take the youthful one instead of the aged.)

1. In case of life-threatening illness, should a visit from the Angel of Death genuinely be feared, change the afflicted person's name. Traditional choices are Raphael for a boy, interpreted to mean *"The Creator heals,"* or Eve for a girl, which literally means *"life."* Other options are names of animals, especially *"Bear,"* *"Lion,"* or *"Wolf"* because these creatures are perceived as holding onto life particularly fiercely and tenaciously.
2. Should the illness and threat of death abate, it's considered wise to maintain the new names, even

changing names legally, on the off chance that the Angel is still searching.

✳ Baron Samedi's Appeal for Life Spell

There are many magic spells for healing illness. From a certain perspective these may be understood as spells that indirectly seek to prevent or forestall death. There are very few spells, however, that openly and directly target prevention of death, perhaps because most magical philosophies understand death as part of the process of life.

In an emergency, however, a rare exception is an appeal to Baron Samedi. The Ghede are the Vodoun spirits of death and the guardians of the cemetery. They control the cross-roads between life and death. Baron Samedi is their leader, owner of the metaphoric and literal cemetery; ultimately no one can die if Baron Samedi refuses to "dig the grave." You'll have to have a very good explanation of why a life must be spared, however Baron Samedi has been known to be sympathetic to appeals made on behalf of dying children.

1. Offer Baron Samedi a piece of dry toast, a cup of black coffee, and some dry roasted peanuts. He drinks rum in which 21 very hot peppers have been steeped. Cigarettes and cigars are appreciated as well.
2. Give the Baron a pair of black sunglasses, with one lens popped out, demonstrating that he can see in two worlds, the realms of the dead and the living. (Once you've given the gift, they're his; don't put them on afterwards.)
3. Set up an altar, make your offering and start talking, explicitly, respectfully, and frankly about what you need and what will be offered in exchange for a miracle.

2. If possible, set up her offering by the central cross in a cemetery or under a willow or elm tree. Given the choice, the most auspicious day to petition her is on a Wednesday.
3. Light a white or purple candle for Maman Brigitte, make your appeal, and explain why it should be considered.

☀ Burial Protection Spell

Drive or carry the deceased around the cemetery sunwise (either one or three times is recommended) before burial, for protection and luck during the next journey.

☀ Brigitte's Appeal for Life Spell

If you perceive that a woman may be more sympathetic, appeals may also be made to La Grande Brigitte, Maman Brigitte, Baron Samedi's Scottish-born wife. She co-owns the cemetery with the Baron.

1. Offer La Grande Brigitte nine purple eggplants together with a glass of red wine.

☀ Epidemic Lock and Key Spell

There's only so much one family should have to bear; however, epidemics are greedy and know no boundaries. This spell can only be performed after at least one member of a family has succumbed to an epidemic. It must be cast during that person's burial in an attempt to protect other members of the immediate family. Someone in the family casts the spell.

1. Lock a padlock while focusing on your desired goal.
2. Throw the closed padlock into the grave so that no further members of the family will follow the deceased into the grave.
3. Bury the padlock under Earth together with the coffin. It must not be removed under any circumstances, nor ever opened.
4. If there is a key, put it in a small bag filled with stones and drop it into a river, arriving and leaving via a circuitous route, without looking back.

Escort Service to the Beyond Spell (1) Tarot Card

To request this sort of escort service, either for yourself during the dying process or for a loved one immediately following death, remove the Moon card from a Rider-Waite tarot deck or a thematically similar deck.

1. Place it where you can meditate on the image. The two canines are the awaiting psychopomps; the crab or lobster is the soul beginning its next, long journey.
2. Try to go into the card, jump inside and see what happens. Practice jumping in and out of the card; it's important to the success of the ritual that you're confident that you can emerge safely. The subject of death is a mystery and so to some extent is this spell.
3. Enter the card and see what assistance you can bring back with you.

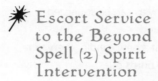

Escort Service to the Beyond Spell (2) Spirit Intervention

If, for any reason, the soul of the deceased seems to be lingering or doesn't seem to be in a hurry to make the next journey, appeal to one of the psychopomps to provide an immediate pick-up service. Any of the spirits may be petitioned, although one dear to the deceased would be the kindest choice.

If you're unsure what to do, burn white candles and provide one of the fragrances that call in spirits best: benzoin, cinnamon, frankincense, or sandalwood. Call the spirit by name and request that it comes to collect the recalcitrant soul quickly.

Fiery Ring of Protection

1. Until funeral rites occur, maintain lit candles around the body to create a fiery wall of protection.
2. Irish tradition designates a dozen candles steadily burning; other traditions suggest two (one each at head and foot), four (marking the body's cardinal points), or as many as can be squeezed around.
3. Light a new candle, every time one burns out.

Guardian of the Dead Spell: Osiris

Osiris, Lord of the Dead, presides over the Western Lands, the ancient Egyptian after-life. He may be petitioned to guard the soul of a loved one. Burn frankincense and gum arabica in Osiris' honor; light black and green candles. Osiris accepts offerings of spring water, flowers, and grain.

Iris Spell

Popular Greek mythology indicates that Iris was a messenger for the Olympian spirits until she was supplanted by Hermes. Iris had other roles, too: she served as psychopomp for women's shades. Plant purple irises on women's graves to ensure Iris' help and blessing.

Funeral Cleansing Spells

Once upon a time, the first magic spell one encountered, immediately after birth, was an enchanted cleansing bath. One's final Earthly magical activity (at least in this body) was similarly a magical bath. Just as childbirth rituals frequently incorporate cleansing spells (specifically, cleansing baths), so last rites usually incorporated a magical/spiritual cleansing bath. The body is bathed, typically with spiritually cleansing, protective materials. Incense may also be burnt to cleanse and comfort.

Chervil Incense

Chervil, also known as Sweet Cicely or British myrrh, was among the ancient Egyptian funerary herbs. Remains of the herb were found within Tutankhamun's tomb. Burn the dried herb as incense to comfort the bereaved and also to enable them to contact the deceased if desired.

✳ Copal Incense

Copal is traditionally burned during Mexican Day of the Dead rituals but it may be used anytime. Its fragrance allegedly pleases, pacifies, and honors those who have passed on, while protecting and cleansing the living at the same time.

✳ Funeral Garland (1)

This garland offers immediate comfort and spiritual cleansing. Each tear is charged with blessings and may be burned at a later stage for protection or in attempts to contact the deceased. Pierce tears of frankincense and myrrh and string onto thread. Give the garlands to funeral attendees to take home as a talisman to burn as needed.

✳ Funeral Garland (2)

Pierce cloves and string them onto a necklace. Wear or hang to comfort the bereaved.

✳ Hyacinth Spell

Fill the home with fresh hyacinths to comfort the bereaved and assuage their grief.

✳ Jasmine Incense

Burn jasmine incense to protect and purify, comfort the bereaved, and honor the deceased.

✳ Ocean Cleansing Spell

Life emerges from salt water, both metaphorically speaking and literally. Each person begins their Earthly incarnation swimming in their mother's salty amniotic fluid. Ocean water is also used to signal rebirth in the next realm.

Gather ocean water; add essential oil of lavender and bathe the deceased's body with this liquid. If real ocean water is impossible for you to get, place as much salt in spring water as possible, preferably Dead Sea salt, and use this instead.

✳ White Sage

Burn white sage to comfort the bereaved and to provide simultaneous spiritual cleansing.

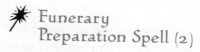

Funerary Preparation Spell (1)

Create an infusion by pouring boiling water over myrtle, mugwort, and rue. Use this liquid to bathe the body.

Funerary Preparation Spell (2)

Place a fresh sprig of basil over the deceased's chest to provide safe passage to the next realm.

Funerary Preparation Spell (3)

Place fresh rosemary in the deceased's hands, for protection against any coming dangers.

Funeral Protective Spell

Amulets and travel-charms may be sent along for the journey, for luck and protection, as exemplified by the ancient Egyptians who filled the tombs of the wealthy with every object needed to maintain the lifestyle to which the dead person was accustomed, including magical models of people to serve them and do their bidding in the next life. Even the poorest person, however, was buried with basic protective amulets and an eye-makeup palette, necessary for magic as well as maintaining appearances.

The Egyptians cultivated a magical science of amulets and talismans for a variety of purposes. There were over thirty styles of funerary amulets alone. These included:

★ *Djed amulets (Pillar of Osiris)*
★ *Eyes of Horus*
★ *Scarabs*
★ *Tet amulets (Buckle of Isis)*
★ *Vulture-shaped amulets*

Ghost Prevention Spell

1. Immediately following a death, brew substantial quantities of bayberry (*Myrica cerifera*) tea, in order to follow a Seminole recommendation to prevent ghosts.
2. Family and friends of the deceased should drink this tea, as well as bathing their heads and arms with it for three days following the death.

Hair Girdle Spell

It is customary in many traditions to remove a lock of the deceased's hair as a keepsake or memento. An Australian aboriginal custom suggests the metaphysical origins of this tradition. Think of "girdle" in terms of a magic belt or "girding your loins," rather than as a figure-shaping undergarment.

1. When a man dies, his hair is cut off by a male relative.
2. It's woven into a belt and presented to the deceased's eldest son. Wearing this magic belt transmits all the positive masculine qualities of the deceased and enhances the wearer's psychic skills.

Madame Death Spell

Central Europe's Madame Death is a unique spirit. When she arrives, she actually teaches you how to die, demonstrating how to do it, and then serves as escort during the transition. If it's time to contact her, look for Madame Death sitting at the crossroads or in apple and pear trees. It's unnecessary to bring her gifts or offerings, and you can't see her until she's ready to see you.

Passport to Death

In many disparate magic and spiritual traditions, a tattoo serves as the passport to the next world. The tattoo serves as an identifying mark for the psychopomp and gains one admittance to the afterlife, in the sort of way some clubs and museums stamp one's hand when allowed entrance. It's believed that this reason was among the initial stimuli for the concept of permanently tattooing the body.

This tattoo is applied when one is still living, usually on the hand or inner wrist. Geometric patterns are typical; however, consider what your passport should look like. If you're not sure but would like one, turn to the Divination Spells to help you determine what sign is needed.

Petrified Wood Past-Life Spells

Pieces of petrified wood are typically sold alongside crystal gemstones. Like crystal gemstones, they're believed to retain memory and are used to help access those buried within you.

Petrified Wood Past-Life Spell

Hold a piece of petrified wood in your hand during conscious attempts at past-life regression.

Sandalwood

Burn sandalwood to stimulate past-life recall.

Wisteria Past-Life Spell

Hang wisteria over your bed to access past-life memories while you sleep.

Following removal of the body, it's recommended that any rooms where it was kept be swept out completely.

Post-Death Cleansing Spell

1. Sweep the house thoroughly using a single-use ritual broom or any other broom that you're not sorry to lose.
2. Dispose of any dust and debris outside the house, ideally by burning.

3. Dispose of the broom immediately, outside the home, preferably at a crossroads unless, of course, you'd like return visits; then keep the broom as a summoning device.

Rest in Peace Aloe Vera Spell

Plant aloe vera on the gravesite in order to soothe the deceased, ease any sense of loneliness or abandonment and prevent their longing for the living.

Rest in Peace Chamomile Spell

A carpet of chamomile planted over a grave encourages the dead to sleep and also eases their passage to the next realm.

Rest in Peace Floral Spell

Cover graves with a carpet of daisies and bluebells to bring peace to the deceased and joy to the bereaved, and to invite the presence of benevolent guardian spirits.

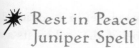
Rest in Peace Juniper Spell

Burn juniper berries at the gravesite during the funeral to ward off any malicious or mischievous spirits.

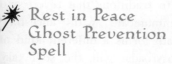
Rest in Peace Ghost Prevention Spell

Drive iron arrowheads into the ground at the foot and head of the deceased's body to prevent the forma-tion and return of a ghost.

Rest in Peace Sleep Well Spell

To encourage the dead to sleep peace-fully and deeply, strew wild poppy seeds throughout the cemetery.

Rest in Peace Final Amends Spell

Ideally one has the opportunity to say a final farewell to the deceased and depart on good terms. This is not, unfortunately, always the case. This can stimulate great pain and regret for the one left behind. According to a Romany tradition, however, it's never too late to make amends. This spell should relieve your heart and

also forestall any possible difficulties with a testy, still-resentful ghost.

1. Go to the grave.
2. Offer a libation of spring water or whatever would be the beverage of choice. A small gift of some kind might not be a bad idea either.
3. Talk to the person. Be frank and familiar. The standard speech goes something like this:
   I forgive you. Don't harm me, don't haunt me.
   I behaved badly toward you [or specify the situation]
   Please forgive me. I forgive you.

Ideally a response is received shortly, in dreams if not in waking life.

Rest in Peace Food of the Dead Spell

Although it's customary in many traditions to spend time at the gravesite, cleaning, caring, and sometimes bringing offerings of food and drink, a more direct method was used in ancient Greece.

Create a blend of olive oil, honey, and spring water. This may be poured directly onto the grave, or poured through a tube into the grave. Mean-while, the living should picnic nearby.

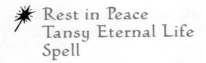

❋ Rest in Peace Tansy Eternal Life Spell

Tansy is described as an herb of life everlasting. It allegedly comforts the bereaved while assuring the dead that they will not be forgotten. Sprinkle ocean water or **Holy Water** *over the deceased's body using a tansy branch as an asperging tool.*

Ghosts

The understanding of what constitutes a ghost depends largely on what one believes happens to the soul after death or, in fact, on how one views the soul during life.

To discuss the human soul as singular contradicts many metaphysical beliefs. Many believe that each person has multiple souls, each with a special function. Thus the dream soul travels and wanders, when released by sleep. Perhaps one of these souls or facets of the soul lingers on Earth after death.

Perceptions of souls and what happens to them following death vary according to spiritual tradition and individual belief.

As one example, in traditional Hmong belief, the soul exists as a kind of trinity: one part stands guard at the grave, another journeys to the realm of the dead, while a third part is subject to reincarnation.

In traditions that revere and communicate with ancestors, death forms a different kind of crossroads: will the soul take a positive turn and accept the responsibilities of an ancestral spirit or will it transform into a ghost? If it does transform into a ghost, will this be a helpful benevolent or at least unobtrusive, quiet ghost content to linger near the living, or will it transform into a malevolent spiteful, resentful, mischievous trouble-making ghost?

The road taken at that crossroads may depend on the actions of the living: were proper funeral rites given? Was the body treated with respect and care? Were any needed spiritual precautions offered?

Among many traditional philosophies, those who die violently far from home or whose funerals and/or graves are neglected have the capacity to evolve into wandering semi-malevolent ghosts or worse.

It is never too late to lay a ghost, however, and many rituals exist worldwide for propitiating those who were laid to rest without proper rites. For example, the Festival of Hungry Ghosts: during the seventh month of the Chinese lunar candle, paper offerings are burned for one's own personal ancestors. However, extra offerings may be given to placate any hungry, wandering ghosts. In Mexico, November 2nd, the Day of the Dead, is a national holiday. Families congregate in cemeteries, visiting loved ones, repairing and caring for graves. In addition to offerings made for ancestors and relatives, many add candles for forgotten souls, those who have no one to welcome and care for them. These candles, with additional offerings, may be placed on the family altar or as independent offerings by the roadside, for passing ghosts.

If a ghost isn't causing trouble, how do you know it's there?

★ *Candles that burn dim, low, or blue may indicate the presence of a ghost*
★ *An unexpected chill in the air may indicate a ghost*

A frequent observation is that the presence of ghosts is indicated by a significant decrease in temperature—a cold spot
★ *Ghosts may signal their presence through specific fragrance, a sort of aromatic calling card*

Peaceful, mutually beneficial coexistence may not require any spells. Many homes feature the presence of a ghost who wants nothing more than to linger in the presence of loved ones. If the ghost isn't bothering you, there is generally no need to exorcise it; actions to do so may in fact antagonize the ghost and cause trouble.

There are basically two types of ghost spells:

★ *Spells to provide protection from troublesome ghosts and keep them far away*
★ *Spells to obtain access to ghosts and their powers*

☀ Samhain Hungry Ghost Spell

Samhain, the Celtic roots of Halloween, marks the beginning of the dark, incubatory half of the year. It's also the moment when the veils between the realms of living and dead are sheerest. Thus it's the time around the world to contact one's ancestors, pay tribute and honor to them, and engage in necromantic practices of various kinds. Hungry ghosts are also believed to abound— those without family or friends to feed and remember them.

Place offerings of milk and barley outside under the stars to ease the ghosts' hunger, prevent their mischief, and to accrue their blessings.

☀ Boneset Ghost Spell

Boneset guides ghosts elsewhere, attracting protective, benevolent spirits instead. Boneset may also be used to protect people and animals from "ghost sickness," the illness that some believe may emerge after extended contact with the dead. The most potent boneset is found growing on or near graves. Supplement it with white pine for added enhancement.

Hang fresh boneset branches over doorways, or burn young boneset branches and twigs within a cauldron to drive away existing ghosts.

☀ Get Away Ghost Spell Backwards Candles

1. Light a white candle after dark.
2. Carry it in your right hand while holding a handful of salt in your left.
3. Walk backwards through every room of the haunted house from bottom to top, sprinkling salt through your fingers. (Keep additional salt in your pockets for refills if your house is large: do not backtrack.) Simultaneously tell the ghosts to get lost, aloud or silently as you deem appropriate.
4. At the topmost, furthest point of the home, extinguish the candle.

☀ Get Away Ghost Bean Spell

Scatter beans around your property to deny entry to ghosts for a year. (If plants result, this banishing effect may last even longer!)

✳ Get Away Ghost Coffee Spell

Tell those ghosts to wake up, smell the coffee, and leave! Burning ground coffee (rather than brewing it, although you can try that, too, having a cup in the process) allegedly repels ghosts as well as malevolent spiritual entities. It's important to use real ground coffee, the stronger the better, and especially not decaffeinated.

✳ Get Away Ghost Pine Trees

According to Hildegard of Bingen, ghosts hate pine trees and avoid places where they grow. If it's not possible to surround your home with living pines, bring small living trees within it and situate them strategically. Decorate with images that resonate strongly of life: ankhs, hexagrams, and imagery (abstract or otherwise) depicting human genitalia. (In case you weren't sure what to do with that Thai penis amulet, this is the perfect opportunity.) This allegedly drives away the ghost, or at least makes it feel extremely unwelcome.

✳ Get Away Ghost Tiger Lilies

Tiger lilies planted near doors and windows allegedly prevent the entry of ghosts.

✳ Get Out Ghost!

If the ghost has taken up residence in your home or within another building, hanging alyssum up in every corner of a house will allegedly exorcise it.

✳ Ghost Co-existence Spell (1) Lilies

Do you have ghosts? Can't get rid of them, no matter what you do? Keep lilies in your home and garden. They won't repel ghosts or banish them but they will keep the ghosts well behaved, preventing them from causing harm or mischief.

✳ Ghost Co-existence Spell (2) Incense

Keep ghosts happy and good-natured by maintaining the fragrance of benzoin and sandalwood in the home.

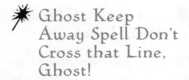

Ghost Keep Away Spell Don't Cross that Line, Ghost!

Create a boundary line over which ghosts allegedly will not cross.

1. Place three peeled cloves of garlic in a bowl, together with one handful of sea salt and one handful of fresh rosemary leaves.
2. Grind and mash the ingredients together.
3. Sprinkle them to create a boundary, as needed.

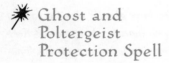

Ghost and Poltergeist Protection Spell

To provide relief from destructive and mischievous ghosts and poltergeists:

1. Maintain fresh bay laurel branches and/or leaves within the home.
2. Replace them as their green color fades.

Haunted House Prevention Spell Anti-Ghost Garden

Ghosts may be prevented from haunting houses by surrounding the home with specific botanicals. Create an anti-ghost garden by maintaining a substantial quantity of bay laurel trees, rowan (mountain ash) trees, and lilies.

Pacify Ghost Halloween Spell

At midnight on Halloween bury apples at crossroads to feed hungry ghosts.

Rest in Peace Spell (1) The Unknown Ghost

An ancient Greek method to lay a ghost to rest is especially beneficial if not only the identity but also the gender of the ghost is unknown.

1. Make distinctly male and female dolls from wood or true earthen clay (not synthetic substitutes as typically found among art supplies). It's crucial to the success of this spell that the dolls

be formed from biodegradable materials, so that they can decompose entirely without leaving traces.

2. Give the dolls a feast, a party in their honor. Have real food and drink, real fun.

3. When the party's over, explain that their wanderings are over, too. Bury them in uncultivated land, where they are unlikely to be disturbed for a long time.

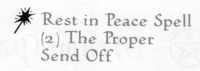

Rest in Peace Spell (2) The Proper Send Off

Restless ghosts may be laid to rest by giving them the proper funeral they may never have had.

1. Place a small doll in a tiny coffin.
2. Have a great send-off.
3. Bury the coffin in a remote area or even in a cemetery itself.

⊕ Dream Spells

It's only a dream, some say, implying that something is ephemeral, unreal, unworthy of attention. Those subscribing to that notion are not occultists. For the spell-caster, nothing holds more significance than a dream. Dreams are your passport to magical realms and the ticket to your own power. Because dreams come naturally doesn't mean that dreaming isn't also a skill that can be learned and enhanced. From a magical perspective, dreaming isn't a passive state. Dreaming is a primary activity of the soul. Dreams aren't something that happens *to* us; dreaming is something we *do*. Magic spells encourage you to consciously guide and control the dream process.

Dreams are how we most frequently receive communiqués from other realms. Spiritual entities communicate in dreams, as do guardian angels, animal allies, ancestral protectors, and those who have departed. Dreams are where we receive responses to petitions, where we receive the answers to oracles. Spells are cast in dreams, healing occurs, spontaneous past-life regressions and visions of the future are achieved. Dreams replenish our psychic ability and strengthen our personal power.

During the dream state, divisions between psychic knowledge and conventional wisdom grow thin or even disappear. Psychic receptivity increases. Without dreams psychic power is minimized or even curtailed, physical health suffers; we are cut off from needed spiritual advice and intervention.

Everyone dreams. Like a running cinematic program, the average person with sufficient sleep has approximately five dreams every night. The last dream, the one that occurs just at the threshold of awakening is usually the most spiritually and magically significant.

You object: you're sure *you* don't have any dreams at all, let alone a series of five.

Most likely you're wrong. Few of us truly don't dream, although it's very common not to remember dreams. Some people, unfortunately, only remember unpleasant dreams, leading to negative associations and fear of sleep. This fear, as well as trauma and stress, sometimes result in dream suppression.

True failure to dream frequently derives from chronic lack of sleep, or sometimes from medication, especially, ironically, medication taken to enhance sleep. That irony is furthered when one considers the possibility that the whole function of sleep may exist so that dreaming occurs. In other words, it's not *sleep deprivation* that's potentially a problem; it's *dream deprivation*.

Because dreams are so crucial to the magic process, an occult science has evolved to control, nurture, and enhance dreaming. If you think you don't have dreams, there are botanicals that will coax them out of the shadows. You can produce the dreams you need and desire, teach yourself to recall your dreams, and receive visitations from desired persons and spirits alike. You can control and understand nightmares so that they no longer plague you.

What actually happens during dreams?

Although there are various scientific explanations, according to many spiritual/magical traditions, each person has not one but multiple souls, including a distinct dream soul that can journey during dreams and have true experiences before returning to the body when it awakens. The dream soul then sleeps when the body is awake. This dream soul can pursue information, journey to other realms, rendezvous with other dream souls, and have magical adventures impossible when awake. What happens in dreams, thus, really occurs, at least in that special realm, Dreamland.

Dreams serve as the bridge between daytime reality and Dream land, offering information to assist us during waking hours, to improve life, and provide protection.

Dreams cannot always be taken literally: they are fluid, hallucinatory, full of secret codes, private languages, and inner jokes. Dreams can be overwhelmingly joyous and ecstatic. There are those whose most transcendent sexual, spiritual, creative, and magical experiences occur in dreams. I play the piano beautifully in dreams—an ability I cannot reproduce in waking life.

Dreams can also be a source of terror: horrible things happen in dreams, worst nightmares and deepest fears are realized. Suppressed memories emerge—or are they *just dreams?* Loved ones turn into enemies in dreams; we engage in behavior we would never countenance while awake.

The Talmud states that, *"An uninterpreted dream is like an unread letter."* According to general worldwide metaphysical wisdom, dreams may be harbingers or omens; however, they rarely, if ever, cast a sentence of inevitable doom. Instead dreams carry warnings, messages of protection from watchful ancestors and guardian spirits that must be interpreted correctly in order to avert danger and disaster. Looked at from this perspective, even a bad dream may be welcomed; clues in dreams often indicate your best attempt to fix or preempt an unhappy situation. Nightmares signal some sort of imbalance or else a potentially dangerous situation, of varying degrees: usually imbedded in the nightmare are clues for preventing or remedying disaster, as opposed to submission to the inevitable.

Dream Spells

According to the Talmud, three kinds of dreams come true:

★ The dream in the morning
★ The dream that someone else has about you
★ The dream that is interpreted by another dream

Spell-casters' Dream Tools

Mugwort

If an alarm clock is a dream's worst enemy, then mugwort is a dream's best friend. Mugwort is a member of the *Artemisia* family, botanicals named in honor of the Greek lunar deity Artemis. Artemis protects women, wild nature of all kinds, fertility and creativity, witchcraft, magic, and psychic ability. No other plant has more powerful associations with magic in general and dreams in particular.

Mugwort doesn't give you psychic ability; instead it unearths what's hidden within you and drags it, kicking and screaming if necessary, to the surface. Mugwort is not a gentle plant. It is not for everyone, for a variety of reasons. *Mugwort should not be used by pregnant women or those actively attempting to become pregnant.* A traditional medicinal herb for stimulating menstruation, mugwort may cause violent uterine contractions. Nor is it for children's use. Children typically produce vivid-enough dreams, without further stimulation.

Mugwort doesn't produce dreams for you; instead it flings open the gates to Dreamland. Even if you swear you *never* dream, mugwort will very likely stimulate the process. Most commercial herbal dream teas, baths,

and products contain mostly mugwort. Other ingredients are required, not to enhance mugwort's magic powers, but to make it palatable. Like its close cousin, wormwood, mugwort is among the original bitter herbs.

Mugwort stimulates the production of dreams. It also enhances clarity, vividness, and your ability to remember dreams. In addition, dreams allegedly linger longer: you may receive a little extra time to hold onto the dream and record it. Because mugwort simultaneously enhances and stimulates psychic power, your ability to understand dreams may also be enhanced. Mugwort also provides spiritual protection during dreams, encouraging acts of bravery and daring you might not otherwise attempt.

Despite these benefits, not everyone likes mugwort. Some find dreams produced under its influence too vivid, too intense, or too frequent. Some complain that all that dreaming prevents a good night's sleep! Experiment and test your personal reactions. Mugwort may be most valuable for jump-starting the dream process: a psychic enhancement to be used only as needed.

Mugwort, as is true for many plants, is available in a variety of forms. Even more than for most other plants, these forms are not interchangeable. In other words, the flower remedy, dried herb, and essential oil all produce different effects.

★ **Essential oil of mugwort, also marketed under its French name, "Armoise," is not safe for use by anyone.** Mugwort's chemical constituents are more highly concentrated in the essential oil than in any other form: it is potentially neurotoxic

★ The dried botanical herb is safe in moderation for most people, other than pregnant and nursing women, women actively attempting to conceive, and children. A general rule of thumb for mugwort, long considered to be a woman's herb, is that if you're not old enough to menstruate, you are not old enough for mugwort. The dried herb is used in teas, baths, herbal pillows, and various spells. An infused oil may be made from its blossoms

★ Living mugwort plants are a powerful dream and magic ally. Mugwort, which grows rampant on wasteland, is not necessarily an easy plant to cultivate, just like its namesake goddess. If it grows for you, this indicates the plant's willingness to work magic with you and to encourage your psychic powers. Mugwort may be grown from seed; however, it is best propagated by taking cuttings or by root division in the fall. Surround your house with it; grow mugwort in pots indoors. A witch's garden isn't complete without this witch's herb

★ Mugwort flower essence remedy is the safest, most accessible method of use. However, be cautious: a bottle of mugwort essential oil is easily mistaken for the flower remedy. Be sure you have the right product, especially if you plan to take the flower remedy internally. Follow the manufacturer's directions for internal dosage or add to baths and massage oils

Dream Stimulation Flower Essence Remedies

Flower essence remedies are strongly beneficial for the dream process because they work upon soul and emotions most easily expressed through dreams. The effects of any flower essence remedy may be perceived through dreams, but the following specifically stimulate and facilitate dreaming.

★ *Apple (FES)*
★ *Chokecherry (Pegasus)*
★ *Gum plant (FES)*
★ *Jimson weed (Pegasus)*
★ *Mugwort (FES, Pegasus)*

Take in combinations of up to six remedies at a time, as per manufacturer's directions. Place a few drops in a glass of spring water and drink before going to sleep, or rub flower remedies into the thin skin between your thumb and forefinger.

Dream Stimulation: Holed Stone

Humble holed stones facilitate dreams as much, if not more, than precious gemstones. Should you find a naturally perforated pebble or small rock, treasure it: it's a priceless gift from Earth. These stones provide protection, and clairvoyance, and enhance all facets of the dream process.

To access a holed stone's dream power:

★ *Wear it around your neck*
★ *Attach it to the headboard or bed post*
★ *Post it on the wall above the bed*
★ *Tuck it under the pillow*

Dream Baths

These baths are intended to be relaxing, sensuous, and soothing. Don't toss botanicals over your head; just relax in the tub. Warm water is generally more conducive to sleep and dreams than either hot or cold. Simultaneously burning candles and dream incense in the bathroom may facilitate the process, too.

Take these baths just prior to going to sleep. Add essential oils to a bath after the water has been drawn and the temperature has been adjusted. Unless advised otherwise, adjust quantities to suit your nose, but remember: when using essential oils, *less is always more.*

Dream Bath (1) Dream Stimulation

This dream-stimulation bath doesn't work on a regular basis. It's for use as a single-use jump-start only. This bath is most beneficial for the following purposes:

★ *To initiate your first forays into the dream-world*
★ *To stimulate a specific, new course of dreaming*

★ To initiate a new dreaming process, after an extended period of not having or recalling dreams

★ To kick off any dream healing, dream oracle, or intensive dream spell

Add twenty to thirty drops of mugwort flower essence remedy (never, never, never the essential oil!) to a bath before bedtime. Follow the manufacturer's recommendations for internal use also, if so desired. This dosage is for single-use only. If you'd like to continue using the flower remedy in the bath, reduce the dosage to no more than five drops after the initial foray.

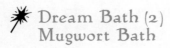 Dream Bath (2)
Mugwort Bath

Bathing in mugwort tea may be more pleasant than drinking it and equally effective.

Pour boiling water over one teaspoon of dried mugwort. Allow the infusion to cool to room temperature, then strain and add to the bath. Enhance by adding a few drops of mugwort flower remedy to the water, too.

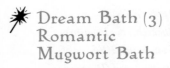 Dream Bath (3)
Romantic
Mugwort Bath

A plain mugwort bath is potent but medicinal. This bath packs an equivalent punch but is sensual and romantic, too, not to mention excellent for enhancing love-dream oracles and erotic dreams. Take:

One handful of dried hibiscus
   flowers
One tablespoon of orange
   blossoms
One tablespoon of red rose petals
One teaspoon of dried mugwort
Three dried bay leaves

1. Place the botanicals in a bowl and cover with boiling water.
2. Allow this infusion to cool.
3. Strain the botanicals, if desired, and add the liquid to the bath.

Dream Incense

Dream incense is *not* burned while you sleep and dream; the burning process should be complete just prior to actually going to bed.

1. Close doors and windows prior to burning the incense, to intensify its effects and fragrance.

2. Place the incense burner on a nightstand or on a safe area near the bed.
3. Burn the incense.
4. When the incense has completely burned, provide ventilation by opening doors and/or windows as appropriate and then go to sleep. Don't wait too long or the fragrance may dissipate.

Dream Incense (1) Dream Herb

Mugwort derives from the Eastern hemisphere. Other plants served similar purposes in the Western hemisphere, including one that earned the nom de plume, "Dream Herb." Calea zacatechichi is a native of the Mexican rainforest. Burning dream herb as incense extracts its power.

1. Burn it in the bedroom before going to sleep, allowing enough time for the incense to burn completely.
2. Do not go to sleep until the incense has completely burned, inhaling the aroma instead and concentrating upon the dream adventures one wishes to experience.

3. Keep doors and windows closed while the incense burns, but then immediately provide ventilation before going to sleep.

Dream Incense (2) Next Realm

Burn the following incense in your bedroom before going to sleep in order to contact someone who has passed over into the next realm or just to see them in your dreams.

Acacia leaves
Myrrh
Star anise

Mash the botanicals up in a mortar and pestle and burn before going to sleep.

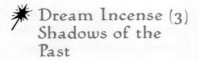

Dream Incense (3) Shadows of the Past

Sometimes the dream you need to incubate doesn't pertain to the future; the information you require is buried in your past. These botanicals are specifically used to facilitate past-life recall and also to access this lifetime's hidden memories:

    Chopped bay leaves
    Honeysuckle blossoms
    Lilac blossoms
    Juniper

Burn the powdered ingredients on lit charcoal before bedtime.

Dream Incubation Spells

Dreaming can be an adventure; one never knows what will happen, who we'll meet, what adventures we'll have. Although that can be very exciting, sometimes we need more from our dreams. We need dreams to be a source for specific information that we're unable to access in any other fashion.

A dream incubation spell requests a specific dream. The technique of dream incubation becomes easier with practice; initially it may be challenging. Do not give up if the dream doesn't occur on first attempt; persist, repeating as needed. Different dream incubation spells work for different people. Play about and experiment until you find those that work for you.

Dream incubation is an ancient technique, pioneered in early temples of healing, Earth's first hospitals. Following spells, rituals, counseling, and healing, one went to sleep within the shrine with expectations of receiving a healing dream: either an actual healing within the dream, a visitation from the resident spirit, often in the form of a snake, individual diagnoses, or treatment recommendations. Dreams may be incubated for any purpose, however.

Two types of spells for requesting dreams exist:

★ *Spells cast to receive a specific dream. The dreamer knows exactly what dream or what type of dream is needed: Dream Incubation Spells*
★ *Spells and procedures to increase clairvoyance and psychic ability. Dreams are prophetic; however, the dreamer is content to receive dreams as they appear, not specify the exact one. These spells are classed among Prophetic Dreams*

Dream Incubation (1) Archangel Michael Dream Oracle

Michael the Archangel's flaming sword illuminates dreams and provides safety as you linger in Dreamland. This dream oracle affirms whether a spiritual petition or request is appropriate or not. This spell is based on surviving remnants of Alexandria's Magical Papyri. The request for the dream is made using a magic lamp.

1. Cleanse and purify yourself thoroughly, using whatever methods you prefer.
2. This spell doesn't assume that you have a special ritual lamp. Oil lamps were once common household articles, like a table lamp is today: it wasn't a big deal back then for a spell to suggest using one, any more than a modern spell's request for a spoonful of salt is an inconvenience. An "*everyday*" magic lamp may be used, or create one following the instructions in the *Ritual Tools and Techniques* chapter.
3. Light the lamp.
4. Speak to the lamplight, observing it, reacting to it, until it burns out.
5. Repeat the following incantation periodically throughout the vigil, and it must be recited at the very conclusion:
   Lamp, light the way to Archangel Michael,
   If my petition is appropriate, show me water and a grave,
   If not, show me water and a stone.
6. Be silent, go to sleep, and dream.

The symbols of water and grave and water and stone were used at the dawning of the Common Era. Use them if you like or select others that suit you better; just announce explicitly the identities of the symbols.

Dream Incubation Spell (2) Artemis Assistance Spell

Divine assistance may be requested to receive the dreams you need.

1. Build an altar for Artemis.
2. Decorate it with images of the moon and the animals she loves, especially dogs, wolves, and deer.
3. Light silver and/or white candles.
4. Sprinkle dried mugwort onto lit charcoals and burn as incense.

5. Describe the type of dream you need to Artemis.
6. Go to sleep.

Should you receive your dreams, Artemis accepts gifts of toy animals, your old childhood toys, living Artemisia plants, and moon-shaped cakes lit with candles.

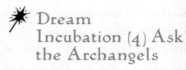

Dream Incubation (3) Ask the Angels

Russian magic favors beautifully poetic incantations. These incantations follow specific formulas, usually placing the spell-caster in the heart of a mythological dreamscape (an island in the sea, the hills of Zion) before incorporating information pertaining to the specific spell. Although this formula may be used to incubate any dream, it's believed particularly beneficial for diagnosing and identifying mysterious health ailments.

1. Place an object under your pillow that pertains to the question you need answered in the dream.
2. Chant aloud:
   I lie on the hills of Zion
   Three angels surround my bed
   One hears all
   One sees all
   One tells me what I need to know.
3. Conclude the chant by incorporating your question, as succinctly and specifically as possible.
4. Go to sleep.

Dream Incubation (4) Ask the Archangels

Sometimes you need dreams to get in touch with the spirits. Sometimes you need spirits to help you receive the right dream. This dream divination is based upon traditions from Alexandria, the great Egyptian city of Alexander the Great, and dates from the first centuries of the Common Era. It invokes assistance from angels and clairvoyance from bay laurel.

1. Write the following incantation on bay laurel leaves:
   I call upon you Uriel, Michael, Raphael, and Gabriel
   Don't pass me by
   Don't disregard me
   As you bring your nightly visions, please enter and reveal to me what I wish to know.
2. State your wish clearly, concisely, and explicitly.

3. Place the leaves beside your head and go to sleep.

Dream Message Spell

Send a message via dreams. The goal of this German spell is to magically induce someone else to have a specific dream.

1. Determine the exact dream that needs to be transmitted in as much detail as possible.
2. At the New Moon, place a clear quartz crystal within a glass of spring or **Holy Water** and create lunar-infused water by leaving it exposed to moonlight overnight.
3. During the waxing moon, dress your bed with clean white sheets and sprinkle the lunar water over them.
4. Place yarrow, wormwood, and thyme inside a muslin bag or tie up within a handkerchief.
5. Hold the herb packet in your hand; concentrate on the person for whom this dream is intended.
6. Place the packet within your pillowcase; as you go to sleep visualize the dream you'd like to send as if you were watching a movie.

Dream Oil

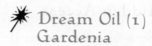

Dream Oil (1) Gardenia

The fragrance of gardenias inspires abundant, prophetic dreams, beckons benevolent spirits, and enhances psychic ability. That's the good news. The bad news is that the scent of genuine gardenia is rare. Commercially available products are almost invariably synthetic; what's in the bottle smells like gardenia but doesn't actually possess the botanical's magic powers. If at all possible, if you possess fresh gardenia petals, create your own gardenia-infused oil to spark intensely powerful dreams. (The alternative is the Tahitian gardenia-infused coconut oil known as monoi.)

1. Infuse gardenia petals in coconut oil. (It may require as many as six weeks to achieve the desired intensity of fragrance.)
2. Strain the infused oil and discard the flowers.
3. Reserve the oil. Add approximately one tablespoon to a bath before bedtime to stimulate prophetic dreams.

✳ Dream Oil (2) Hidden Access

This oil is infused from honeysuckle blossoms and lilac blossoms. The fragrance of lilac unlocks the door where hidden memories, from this lifetime and those long past, are stored. Unfortunately there is virtually no version of commercially available lilac fragrance that is not synthetic. If you'd like to access lilac's power, you'll have to infuse your own oil.

1. Follow the instructions in *Elements of Magic Spells* for making flower petal-infused oil.
2. When the oil is finally complete and all botanical material has been strained out, for added enhancement add a few drops of mugwort flower essence remedy (FES).
3. Massage onto the body before bed or add to the bath to unlock buried memories from this lifetime or others.

Dream Pillows

Dream pillows are an excellent venue for botanicals to stimulate and enhance dreaming. Botanicals are placed within a bag, which is then either laid under the cheek or placed beside you on the pillow. The bag should be smooth and comfortable. Botanicals are ground to a fine powder so that nothing protrudes and irritates. A dream pillow that prevents you from sleeping defeats its purpose.

Dream pillows serve all sorts of uses:

★ *Basic dream stimulation*
★ *Incubation of specific types of dreams: erotic dreams or financial dreams, for instance*
★ *Sleep enhancement*
★ *Nightmare prevention*
★ *Spiritual protection while you sleep*

Specify your goal by adjusting the botanicals stuffed within the pillow. Every botanical has its own power: select those that correspond to your desire. Crafting the dream pillow is a spell: remember to charge and consecrate materials as desired. Focus on your desire and intent while you're crafting. Every knot tied is an opportunity for an individual knot spell.

The typical dream pillow is made from muslin or some other soft material. Natural fabrics breathe better, allowing better access to the pillow's fragrance. The pillow's power is delivered to you via its aroma. The standardized dream pillow is 12 inches by 8 inches (30 cm × 20 cm) and requires approximately 8 to 10 ounces (around 300 g) of dried herbs. However, craft whatever pillow suits you best. A small sachet made from highly absorbent material works beautifully. Resist the temptation to stuff the pillow with herbs in the mistaken belief that increased quantity always means increased power: a flat, loosely filled pillow is more comfortable, more conducive to sleep, and thus most likely to be more effective.

☀ Basic Dream Pillow Instructions

For the pillow, cut two matching pieces of fabric and sew them up together on three sides.

Fill the bag from the open end, and then sew this last side up, too.

1. Botanicals must be completely, thoroughly dry before sewing into the pillow or sachet because otherwise they may rot, producing an acrid fragrance liable to stimulate nightmares, rather than the desired dreams.

2. Unless they are very soft, grind ingredients to a fine powder. Comfort is the key element: rose petals are preferable to buds, which are pointy and must be finely ground. Bay leaves are superb dream enhancers but must be at least crushed. Otherwise they will protrude from the pillow and are liable to poke you in the eye.

3. If adding essential or fragrance oils, blend them into the dried material well, using a twig or wooden chopstick. Allow the material time to dry *completely* before sewing into the pillow.

4. If adding charms or harder roots, place them carefully in the center of the pillow and surround with softer material.

5. Ideally, if only for maximum effectiveness, the pillow's fragrance should be pleasing to you. Dislike of any botanical's aroma may signal that this plant is not beneficial for you. Irritation is liable to keep you awake, defeating the purpose. At the very least, make sure you find the fragrance neutral. Adjust the fragrance to suit your taste, keeping in mind that when you're lying in the dark, deprived

of other stimulation, especially if unable to sleep, the fragrance may be more intense than initially realized.

✳ Crystal Dream Pillows

Many crystals enhance dreaming, but because they must be cleansed periodically (for maximum potency but also in the aftermath of disturbing visions and nightmares), don't sew them up inside a pillow or sachet.

1. Place a crystal on a clean white handkerchief together with some dream herbs.
2. Tie it together with a blue silk ribbon.
3. Sleep with this under your pillow or cheek.
4. Take it apart and cleanse as needed.

✳ Quick-fix Dream Pillow

Sometimes you have the herbs but lack the time or patience to sew. Maybe you just really hate sewing. In that case place dream botanicals in a white handkerchief and tie them up in a bundle with a red, blue, or silver ribbon. This is not as comfortable to

sleep with as a smooth, flat pillow, and the herbs do have a tendency to spill out. However, purely from a spell-caster's perspective, this is equally as effective as a full-blown dream pillow.

Alternatively, fill a drawstring bag with dream herbs and use it as a dream pillow. Muslin is preferable to flannel, as the fragrance is released with greater intensity.

✳ Dream Pillow (1) A Basic Dream Pillow

The simplest dream pillows contain one ingredient only: mugwort. Fill a pillow with dried mugwort to stimulate your dreams.

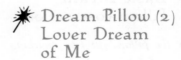

✳ Dream Pillow (2) Lover Dream of Me

Sometimes it's not your own dreams that are so crucial. Give this dream pillow as a gift to someone whose dreams you'd like to enter.

1. Grind allspice berries and orrisroot to a fine powder.
2. Place them in a bowl together with dried honeysuckle blossoms, red rose petals, and hibiscus flowers.

3. Add a lock of your hair.
4. Dress with one drop of essential oil of pine and one drop of essential oil of sandalwood.
5. If you'd like, add one drop of menstrual blood.
6. Stir gently to blend thoroughly.
7. Allow the mixture to dry completely.
8. Use this blend to fill a small dream pillow and present it to the one you love.

Pillows covered in red silk or satin are most powerful.

Dream Pillow (3) Prophet's Pillow

Stuff a dream pillow with heather for prophetic and financially insightful dreams.

Dream Potions

Don't confuse magical dream potions with medicinal sleep aids. Most of these potions are ancient recipes; whether or not they've since been discovered to have sedative properties is incidental. Their goal is to promote dreaming, not to forcefully sedate you into sleep. In general, drink these potions just before bedtime.

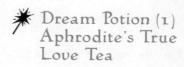

Dream Potion (1) Aphrodite's True Love Tea

Aphrodite's sacred tree is the apple and thus its fruit is the fruit of love.

Make apple blossom tea. Sweeten it with honey and bring it to bed. Before drinking make an invocation to Aphrodite, requesting that true love dreams be sent to you.

Dream Potion (2) Basic Mugwort Tea

Plain mugwort tea is very potent. A cup before bedtime should stimulate dreams. Unfortunately it tastes so unpleasant few will drink it. Adding honey may be sufficient to sweeten the taste for some.

Place one teaspoon of dried mugwort in a cup and cover with boiling water. Allow this to steep for ten minutes, then strain and drink.

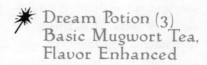

Dream Potion (3) Basic Mugwort Tea, Flavor Enhanced

A more palatable blend:

One tablespoon dried mugwort
One teaspoon dried lemon balm (melissa)

One teaspoon dried hibiscus

1. Place the ingredients in a tea pot. (This is more herb than necessary for a single cup of tea. Adjust quantities to suit your needs.)
2. Pour boiling water over the herbs and let them infuse for ten minutes.
3. Strain and drink.

Sweeten with honey if desired.

Dream Protection

While some perceive the dream-state's hallucinatory fluidity as an opportunity for spiritual growth, excitement, and adventure, others fear sleep and dreams. Surrender of consciousness leads to feelings of extreme vulnerability. That *anything* can happen in a dream may be an invitation for some, a nightmare for others. That sense of exposure and vulnerability is no illusion: all sorts of defenses are surrendered together with consciousness when you lie down to sleep. Standard physical precautions are taken: doors are locked, windows bolted, the stove turned off, and burning candles extinguished to avoid danger and risk. Special magical security measures may also be taken to provide spiritual safety while you sleep—a wise plan for nervous and intrepid dreamers alike.

These spells are specifically designed to ward off spiritual night dangers rather than scary dreams or nightmares.

✳ Dream Protection (1) Basic Botanicals

The following botanicals enhance sleep, or at least won't disturb it, while simultaneously creating a spiritual shield to protect you while you sleep:

Angelica
Anise
Black mustard seeds
Cloves
Henna
Mugwort
Purslane
Rosemary
Rue
Saint John's Wort
Southernwood
Sweet Annie
Sweet flag (calamus)
Vervain
Wormwood
Yarrow

Use one or any combination of the above to fill a dream pillow.

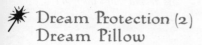 Dream Protection (2) Dream Pillow

Fill a small dream pillow with coriander seeds and dillweed to enhance sleep and dreams, and to provide spiritual protection at the same time.

✳ Dream Rendezvous

This spell assists dream assignations. This spell may be easier to accomplish if the people wishing to meet in Dreamland work out the dream details in advance. (In other words, make plans where to meet.)

Grind and powder linden flowers and blend with rice flour. Both parties must dust their bodies from head to toe with this powder before going to sleep.

Erotic Dreams

Aphrodisiacs create erotic enhancement while you're awake; certain botanicals stimulate sensual dreams and pleasures while you sleep.

The following botanicals provide that special effect:

Aloes wood
Anise
Cardamom
Catnip
Cloves
Coriander seed
Damiana
Gardenia
Henna
Hibiscus
Jasmine
Myrrh
Orchids
Rose
Tagetes-marigold
Tuberose
Vanilla
Vervain

★ *Fill a dream pillow with any one or combination of the above herbs*
★ *Instead of filling a pillow with the herbs, place them loose in a covered box kept by your bedside. Inhale this potpourri before bedtime*
★ *Make an infusion from any combination of these botanicals, except tagetes, and add to your bath*
★ *Dried plants aren't necessarily more effective. Place a bouquet of cut flowers on the nightstand or keep living plants close enough to waft their aroma over you while you sleep*

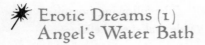

✳ Erotic Dreams (1) Angel's Water Bath

*Add substantial quantities of **Angel's Water** to your bath for aphrodisiac effect and to provoke erotic dreams.*

✳ Erotic Dreams (2) Aphrodite's Dream Bath

If a real lover isn't in your bed, summon a dream lover instead. Aphrodite's favorite botanicals incite dreamtime revels. Allow yourself to air-dry; the botanicals will linger on your skin and attract real-life lovers, too.

Use six drops of essential oil of myrtle and six drops of rose attar in your bath.

✳ Erotic Dreams (3) Honeysuckle

Some erotic dream-inducing botanicals are particularly powerful. Honeysuckle, in particular, is strong enough to create the desired reactions independently.

★ *Add honeysuckle flower essence remedy (Bach flower) to the bath before bedtime*

★ *If you're fortunate enough to possess real honeysuckle, place some on your pillow or by the bed so that its aroma wafts over you*

✳ Erotic Dreams (4) Honeysuckle Bedtime Foot Massage

1. Gently warm a little hazelnut oil.
2. Remove the oil from the source of heat and add one or two drops of jasmine absolute and a few drops of honeysuckle flower remedy (Bach flower).
3. Massage this into your feet and ankles when you get into bed.

✳ Erotic Dreams (5) Rose Bath

One cup of rose hydrosol
Five drops of rose attar
Five drops of neroli or essential oil of petitgrain
Five drops of honeysuckle flower essence remedy (Bach flower)

Add all the above "ingredients" to a tub filled with water and luxuriate before bedtime.

For maximum effect, float fresh rose petals and/or orange blossoms in the bath, too.

Lucid Dreaming Spell

Lucid dreaming is the technique of staying conscious while dreaming, thus being able to actively navigate through Dreamland rather than being the passive recipient of dreams. Various methods teach mastery of this shamanic art; however, many people have spontaneous, if brief, lucid dream moments.

Jasmine's fragrance encourages this spontaneous lucid dreaming. For maximum effectiveness, maintain living jasmine plants in the bedroom. If this is not possible, incorporate jasmine attar into a pre-bedtime massage, or sprinkle the sheets with jasmine water.

Marriage Dream

This is more than a soul mate or true love dream. Bridewort has an affinity for marriage; allegedly this spell produces dream visions of the one you'll marry.

Create infused oil from the blossoms of the Druid's sacred plant Queen of the Meadow, also known as bridewort. Rub it on your body before bedtime to dream of the one you'll marry.

Prophetic Dreams

The floodgates of psychic ability are completely open while we sleep. Stimulate prophetic dreams, enhance and encourage clairvoyance with various spells. Experiment to discover which ones best enhance your own innate power. Many of these techniques also encourage dreams to linger, be more vivid, and more easily recalled.

Prophetic Dreams (1) Basic Psychic Enhancement

Certain botanicals stimulate clairvoyance, psychic perceptions, and prophesy:

- Angelica
- Anise
- Basil
- Bay laurel
- Copal
- Dittany of Crete
- Dream herb (zacatechichi)
- Gardenia
- Mimosa
- Mugwort
- Peppermint
- Roses
- Sandalwood
- Syrian rue (harmel)
- Wisteria
- Wormwood

Use any one or combination of these herbs to stuff dream pillows. Or place any combination of them in a conjure bag, to be worn around the neck at night.

✳ Prophetic Dreams (2) Botanical Blast

1. Choose any combination of the prophetic-dream botanicals listed above.
2. Place the loose botanicals inside a covered box, kept beside your bed.
3. Uncover or inhale this potpourri before sleeping, to receive a blast of its power.

✳ Prophetic Dreams (3) Lucky Mystic Powder

A Hoodoo formulation said to induce psychic dreams:

1. Grind dried basil and vetiver root together, creating a fine powder.
2. Blend this powder with silver magnetic sand, until you achieve a fragrance and appearance that pleases you.
3. Sprinkle this powder around your bed before bedtime.

✳ Prophetic Dreams (4) Rose Tea

Roses are often heavily sprayed with pesticides making them unsafe to drink. Make sure your roses are organic, and drink a cup of tea brewed from them before bedtime to stimulate clairvoyant dreams.

Remembering Dreams

The dream was desperately needed. Perhaps you needed to see your true love's face before you accepted what might be the wrong marriage proposal. Maybe you needed a dream consultation with your grandmother regarding some vital family secrets. You ground the dream incense by hand, forced yourself to drink that bitter, bitter mugwort tea, and surrounded yourself with dream charms and pillows. You tried and practiced for weeks and finally you had the *exact* dream you needed! You were so excited you promptly woke up—and forgot the dream.

It's happened to all of us. A dream is so vivid, so vital, so important we swear we can never forget it even if we try. We're so sure of this that we see no reason to record the dream and within hours precious details are gone forever.

Dreams are by nature elusive: if you move abruptly when you awake, you will lose all or part of your dreams. Nothing prevents dreams from being recalled more than a loud, sudden alarm clock. Dreams are always retained and recalled better if one wakes naturally, whenever one is ready. If you must wake up *on time*, gently transitioning awake, perhaps to soft music, rather than being abruptly jolted awake, increases the likelihood of retaining your dreams.

Keep pen and paper by your bedside. Some prefer a special dream journal. As you become an experienced dreamer, you may awaken briefly following every dream, in order to record it, before returning to sleep. This shouldn't disturb your rest: "*awaken*" may be the wrong word. A sort of half-sleep state is achieved, just awake enough to fuzzily perform the function of writing. This semi-comatose state is the best state in which to recall and record dreams. Some learn to write in the dark, some learn to write with their eyes closed. Dream pens are sold containing tiny lights, so as to provide just enough to write by.

As long as you can understand your own writing later, it's not important to write neatly now. Transcribe dreams into a proper journal later.

Record dreams immediately: even minutes later, details disappear forever from memory. Don't believe me? Experiment: when you awake, write down your dream immediately, then go back to sleep or about your business. Several hours later, without reading what you've written, recall your dream or write it down again. Go back to your first record: most will discover that the initial description included details, some crucial, no longer remembered.

Other methods assist dream recall too.

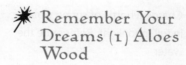

Remember Your Dreams (1) Aloes Wood

Aloes wood (not aloe vera, a different plant) is believed to deepen sleep and to create access to other realms while dreaming. It is also supposed to enable you to better remember your dreams. Aloes wood is rare: burn splinters of it at a time, while wishing for profound, magical dreams.

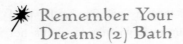

Remember Your Dreams (2) Bath

This fragrant bath encourages dreams to linger longer so that you can remember them better.

Four drops essential oil of juniper
Four drops essential oil of
    lavender
Four drops essential oil of
    mimosa

Add the essential oils to a full tub of water.

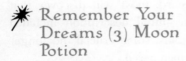

Remember Your Dreams (3) Moon Potion

This enhanced method not only helps you recall dreams but also promotes understanding and clarification.

1. Charge a bottle of spring water in full moonlight. Refrigerate the water.
2. Before going to sleep, pour a small glass of water.
3. Take a few sips; leave the rest beside the bed to sip as needed.
4. Reserve a little bit to drink just before recording any received dreams.

Stop Dreaming

Because sometimes you've had enough: hang a sprig of lemon verbena around your neck to halt the dream process, should you need to take a break.

Sunflower Truth Spell

If you suspect lies have been told, have the truth revealed in your dreams.

1. Before taking the next step, talk to the sunflower plant and explain what is about to occur and why.
2. Pull up an entire sunflower and gently shake it free of dirt. Otherwise leave the plant whole.
3. Place an offering (coins, honey, tobacco) in the hole left by the plant.
4. Place the sunflower beneath your bed. The truth should be revealed within your dreams.

True Love Dream Spells

Fairy tales are filled with princesses determined to wed none but their one true love, their soul mate. They've never actually met he guy, but he visits frequently n dreams. Perhaps the princesses ried one of the following spells:

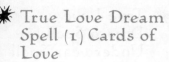

True Love Dream Spell (1) Cards of Love

. Remove all four playing cards corresponding to the gender of the person you desire from a deck of playing cards: kings for men, queens for women.
.. Place the four cards under your pillow to dream of your true love.

f for any reason, one card, not neces-·arily a court card, holds special ·omantic significance for you, substi-·ute that card instead.

True Love Dream Spell (2) Daisies

After you've established whether or not he loves you by pulling the petals off daisies, place daisy roots beneath your pillow to dream of your true love.

True Love Dream Spell (3) Dinner for Two

After everyone has eaten dinner and left the table, discreetly pick up a knife and some salt and bread that have been left behind. Place these under your pillow to dream of your beloved.

True Love Dream Spell (4) Dumb Cakes

Cast this dream spell on a solitary evening. However, it's a lot more fun to cast it the traditional way: during a sleepover party with sisters or good friends.

1. Combine one cup of flour, one cup of salt, and a sprinkle of fireplace ashes. (Scrape any ashes from out of the fireplace, but leftover ashes from some love incense or from a fireplace romance divination are most powerful.)
2. Add enough water to form a "batter."
3. Ladle the batter onto a heated, greased griddle, so that there is one dumb cake per participant. Pretend you're making pancakes. Flip them with a spatula.

4. Before each dumb cake is completely done, scratch a name or initials or some identifying mark onto the cake, so that everyone knows to whom each cake belongs.

5. Each time you flip a cake, add an additional sprinkle of salt. (If there's a party, make sure everyone gets the chance to flip a dumb cake.)

6. What's the next step? Eat them? Oh no, that would be too cruel! Instead, each person must place her dumb cake under her pillow to dream of her very own true love.

Why are these called dumb cakes? Not because these pancakes taste so bad you'd have to be severely intellectually challenged to eat them, but because the ritual demands total silence (not a peep!) from anyone involved, from start until the conclusion the next morning after all dreams have been recorded!

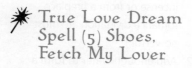

True Love Dream Spell (5) Shoes, Fetch My Lover

1. Sprinkle a pair of your beloved's shoes with spring water or **Angel's Water**.

2. Place a sprig of thyme in one shoe, rosemary in the other.

3. Place a shoe on either side of your bed.

4. Crawl in and dream.

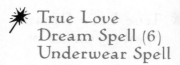

True Love Dream Spell (6) Underwear Spell

This spell, at least from Step onwards, is cast under a Full Moon

1. Obtain an undergarment appropriate for the gender of the one of whom you wish to dream

2. Perform appropriate personal cleansing spells.

3. Take a bucket of pure spring water or **Angel's Water** and go outside at midnight under the Full Moon. (The traditional recommendation is that you should be naked, however adapt to your needs and circumstances.)

4. Gaze at the moon: make a petition for true love and a request to see your lover in your dreams. Show the moon the underwear.

5. Toss the bucket of water over your left shoulder.

6. Go to bed without looking back.

7. Place the underwear under your pillow and say aloud: *"Lover, come get your underwear!"*

8. Go to sleep.

Reserve the underwear afterwards. The spell may be repeated, as needed. Should your dream lover arrive, fumigate with Dreams of Delight or other erotic incense and have him or her wear the item for you.

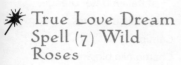

True Love Dream Spell (7) Wild Roses

Drink a cup of tea made with wild rose petals before bedtime to conjure a vision of your true love.

Insomnia

If you can't sleep, you can't dream, it's that simple. Of course, chronic insomnia causes other troubles too: you're grouchy, irritable, and inefficient at work. Unable to sleep when you want,

you may find yourself unable to stay awake at inconvenient moments. Your immune system may suffer. Because so much growth and healing occurs during sleep (or is it during dreams?) you may find yourself feeling stagnant and blocked. Many turn to sleeping pills, which can force sedation but tend to suppress dreams. Is this a problem? Consider whether you wake up feeling refreshed and ready to go and you'll have your answer.

There are sleep scientists and dream researchers who consider that the whole reason for sleep is to provide an opportunity for dreaming. It's the dreaming part that's really the necessity. Without ample rest and sleep, one's psychic and magic powers suffer and weaken. Because sleep and dreams are so crucial

These are traditional magical remedies; they may or may not also have sedative or other sleep-enhancing properties. However just because remedies are magical doesn't mean that they don't also have profound physical impact, particularly botanical-based spells. Insomnia can be an adjunct of various physical ailments; discuss your remedy plans with your professional health-care provider before initiating any course of action.

to magic, a host of magical remedies exist to ease your way into Dreamland.

Insomnia Bath

This bath provides the soothing equivalent of milk and cookies before bedtime. Its power is proportionate to the quantity of milk used.

1. Gently warm goats' or, ideally, sheep's milk (as in counting sheep).
2. Blend true almond extract and several drops of essential oil of lavender into the warm milk so that the fragrance pleases you.
3. Add to a tub filled with warm water before bedtime.

Insomnia Incense

Blend pine, juniper, and ledum, and burn as incense. This soothes an insomniac to sleep while stimulating prophetic dreams at the same time.

Insomnia Spell (1) Basic Botanicals for Sweet Sleep

The following herbs allegedly promote sound, deep sleep:

Bee balm *(Monarda didyma)*, also sometimes called bergamot or bergamot mint. It is not a true mint nor should it be confused with essential oil of bergamot, which is extracted from a type of Italian bitter orange.

Calendula blossoms
Catnip
Chamomile blossoms
Henna
Hops
Linden blossoms
Marjoram
Mullein
Patchouli
Poppies and poppy seeds
Tuberose
Valerian
Vervain
Vetiver

Place any one or combination of these herbs in a dream pillow.

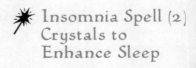
Insomnia Spell (2) Crystals to Enhance Sleep

Crystal gemstones can stimulate sleep as well as dreams. Blue crystals in general are particularly beneficial. Other stones believed to encourage sleep and dreams include amber, amethyst, emerald, jet, and smoky quartz.

Charge the crystal with your desired goal prior to its initial use. Crystals' magic power may be accessed in any of the following ways:

★ Place one or more crystals under your pillow
★ Wear as jewelry against your skin while attempting sleep
★ Create sleep charms: hang them from your bedposts or keep a larger stone on the nightstand

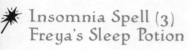

Insomnia Spell (3) Freya's Sleep Potion

Beautiful Freya rules love, sex, and magic. Queen of Witches, original sponsor of Scandinavian shamans, Freya journeys through the sky in her falcon-feather cloak. Simple cowslip, a wild primrose, ranks among her sacred plants. It allegedly permits dream visitations from the land of the fairies, too.

Steep cowslips in wine or milk, and drink this before bedtime. Back in the good old days, wine was actually made from cowslip, ostensibly to prevent and heal insomnia. If you have some, try it!

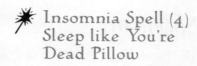

Insomnia Spell (4) Sleep like You're Dead Pillow

So tired and sleep-deprived, you're starting to look at the cemetery with envy? The following botanicals have earned the nickname graveyard dust because they allegedly encourage you to sleep as soundly and peacefully as the dead: patchouli, mullein, and valerian.

1. Grind the botanicals together to create a fine powder.
2. For extra enhancement, add another botanical strongly associated with sleep—poppy seeds—the first anesthesia.
3. Fill a dream pillow with the botanicals and sleep.

For enhanced dreaming, add chopped-up bay leaves too.

Insomnia Spell (5) Violet Wreath

Make a wreath from violet leaves and/or flowers; wear it for a sound night's sleep.

Nightmares

The problem isn't that you *can't* sleep; you're just too scared to close your eyes.

Going to sleep, a welcome relief for some, a palace of delight for others, is the living equivalent of going to hell for those afflicted with chronic nightmare. Because sleep is a place of persecution and misery, those afflicted with nightmares often avoid it at all costs, driving themselves to stay awake as long as possible. Temperament suffers, work suffers, health suffers, and magic power also suffers as a result.

Everyone has a bad dream once in a while. The occasional disturbing dream may be a warning signal of some sort, worthy of attention and careful interpretation. For those afflicted with chronic nightmare, every dream is a horror, the only good night a dreamless one. What should be a source of pleasure and power feels like being cursed and haunted instead.

There are various magical interpretations for nightmares. In some cases, it is perceived as a haunting or curse. The actual word *"nightmare"* derives from the German *"mara,"* a type of evil spirit, which squats on a sleeper's chest, causing frightening dreams and the sensation of suffocation. Spirits haunt Dreamland, sometimes from good intent but sometimes not. Ghostly visitations may be desirable after that necromantic ritual you performed because you need to ask Great Aunt Maud that important question which only she can answer, but nightmarish when the ghost makes the first move. Then there are assorted vampires, incubi, succubi, etc.—creatures of the night that revel in creating nocturnal disturbance. Sometimes spiritual portals are accidentally opened, allowing us to witness things we should not. Sometimes, as we will see, an act of malice allows one person to send another a frightening dream.

Typically chronic nightmares indicate some sort of spiritual and emotional imbalance (magic, a holistic system, cannot separate the two) or even some kind of extended, unpleasant spiritual test. Avoidance of sleep and suppression of dreams isn't the solution. Dreams must be analyzed (by professional dream diviners, if necessary), untangled, and faced, so that they will disperse and make room for sweeter, more desirable dreams.

Dreams deliver messages to us, from Earth, from spirits, from ancestors, allies, other dreamers, and our own subconscious. What happens if someone tries to call you on the phone and can't get through? Sometimes the caller gives up, but if it's important and the caller is responsible and persistent, they'll keep trying. If you fail to pick up or properly understand a dream message, that dream or recognizable variations will repeat itself until you do.

Next time someone chases you in a dream, whether loathsome ex or fearsome creature, turn around and confront it. Calmly, firmly, ask it what it wants. Odds are those animal dreams involve an animal ally trying to get in touch with you. Animal allies come in all forms, not just cuddly bunnies. Deep fear is as much an indication of an alliance as deep love and attraction. The ally may misunderstand your reactions in the same way that you misunderstand theirs. Anxious to reach you, the more you run, the faster they chase and the more eagerly they await your return to Dreamland. The creatures don't necessarily

mean to scare you; they may even mean to assist you.

Yes, this sounds easier said than done, but it can be accomplished, although taking control of your dreams may take time. As usual, there are magical tools to assist, to provide protection, and to place bad dreams in perspective and abeyance.

 Nightmare Spell (1) Anti-Nightmare Garden

Why start a nightmare protection plan in the bedroom? Target the whole house. There's a reason everyone in Sleeping Beauty *slept so soundly. That wild overgrowth of surrounding botanicals banished bad dreams. This isn't a suggestion to banish the gardener, too. The plants can still be manicured if you wish; however, certain botanicals provide nightmare blocking. Cast a living circle around your house.*

The primary botanical nightmare-repellant is rosemary. Given the opportunity it flourishes and grows wildly. Other suggestions include:

Mimosa
Mint
Mugwort

Poppies
Roses
Rowan
Saint John's Wort
Snake plant
Wormwood

6. If possible, dispose of the ashes immediately through an open door or window. If not, place the ashes inside a brown paper bag and dispose of it outside the house as soon as possible.

✴ Nightmare Spell (2) Banishing

This spell is most beneficial immediately after a nightmare although it can be used to disperse lingering effects long after the dream is over, too. If possible, keep a window open for the duration of the spell, to encourage dream visitations to fly away.

1. Write the nightmare down in detail on a piece of fresh paper.
2. Light a white, silver, black, or red candle.
3. Hold the paper in the flame until it catches fire.
4. Let the paper burn down in a saucer or cauldron.
5. Cover it if necessary with a second upside-down plate so that the ashes don't escape into the house. This is tricky because you can put the fire out. If so, just light it again. It's vital that the entire dream is burned to ashes and removed from your home.

✴ Nightmare Spell (3) Candle

1. Charge a yellow or golden candle with your desire for sound, peaceful, untroubled sleep. Place a glass of spring water beside it while it burns.
2. When you're ready to sleep, place this glass of water beside your bed to absorb any bad dreams. (There's no need to keep the candle burning.)
3. In the morning, flush the water down the toilet, whether you recall bad dreams or not. Repeat as needed.

✴ Nightmare Spell (4) Crystals

Certain crystal gemstones repel and relieve nightmares:

★ *Blue crystals in general, especially angelite, lapis lazuli, and turquoise*

- ★ Black crystals, with the possible exception of onyx
- ★ Chrysolite
- ★ Citrine
- ★ Topaz

How to access the crystal's nightmare-repelling powers:

- ★ Wear while sleeping so that they are in contact with your skin
- ★ Place one or more on or beneath your pillow
- ★ Put one or more in a small flannel drawstring bag; wear it like a shield across your chest or place it beneath your cheek for comfort
- ★ Cast a circle around your bed or on your bed around you with crystal gemstones

Onyx is a stone that evokes unpredictable personal reactions. Although it is used to halt nightmares, it occasionally causes them. If you habitually wear onyx and also habitually have bad dreams, remove the stone(s) and observe any reactions.

Many magical approaches to nightmares consider the long-term results: spells for banishing them, preventing them, understanding them, and minimizing them. What action can you take when you've just awakened from a nightmare? Nightmare dispersal spells are intended to disperse and nullify a specific nightmare's effects immediately upon waking.

✳ Nightmare Spell (5) Dream Catcher

Spiders weave dreams as well as spinning webs. In the indigenous traditions of the Native American Plains, circular webs resembling a spider's web, known as "dream catchers," are hung over the bed to facilitate the arrival of desired dreams while preventing disturbing dreams from reaching the dreamer. Not only are nightmares prevented, but the dreams received are happier, more vivid and exciting.

Charge the dream catcher with your desires and needs before hanging over the bed. If disturbing dreams suddenly start arriving, it may be time to cleanse the dream catcher (emptying out the vacuum bag, so to speak) by passing it through cleansing incense smoke.

the Evil Eye

Oh, that Evil Eye! Is there really such a thing? Is it a constant dire
threat, a secret universal force, or nothing but cliché, the worst use of
magic and superstition as a repressive force? And is there really an
eye involved?

The answer is a qualified yes to all of the above.

Although it may be delivered by people, the Evil Eye is not the
same thing as a malevolent spell. A malevolent spell is targeted deliberately and intentionally: the spell must actually be *cast*.

The Evil Eye is not a spell at all, although there are many spells to
oppose it. Instead the Evil Eye is an ill-defined, somewhat nebulous,
but entirely malefic force naturally present in the universe—a different kind of magic power. Although there is general agreement on
what constitutes the Evil Eye, who is vulnerable, and the nature of its
destructive effects, exactly *where* the Eye emanates from is subject to
heated metaphysical debate.

Some perceive the Evil Eye as an abstract destructive force, like an
infectious cloud that one must attempt to avoid, ward off, repel, minimize, or remove. Many other traditions, however, believe that *people*
deliver the Evil Eye, sometimes knowingly, sometimes completely
innocently and unintentionally. Sometimes they just can't help it.

From that perspective, the Evil Eye is a destructive force that
emanates from certain or potentially all people. Every one of us

according to some theories, is able to cast the Eye. It is the human ability to scorch with a glance. The Evil Eye is the force of envy, jealousy, and resentment that shoots out of the human soul like a heat-seeking missile.

The Eye reference may be understood in two ways, which are not mutually exclusive:

1. The Evil Eye as omnipresent destructive abstract force, somewhat similar to *The Lord of the Rings'* all-seeing Eye. Try as you may to hide happiness and good fortune, the Evil Eye is attracted, sees all, and spoils it.
2. The Evil Eye is cast with the human eye, either intentionally by those who are jealous, destructive, and malicious by nature, or involuntarily in other circumstances.

There are also two methods of avoiding the Evil Eye:

1. Don't boast, brag, or call undue attention to your good fortune.
2. Protection via the use of magically empowered amulets and spells.

Because the secrets of other hearts are unknown, believers counsel discretion regarding personal matters. What you might never construe as bragging may still invoke the Eye from another. The bereft, lonely, heartbroken woman, overhearing another complain that there are just *too many* men in her life, may involuntarily shoot her with the Evil Eye. The person unable to conceive or whose children have died, overhearing someone complaining about how hard life is because her babies won't sleep at night, may be unable to resist casting that Evil Eye. It just shoots out.

Then there is the southern Italian *jettatura*. This person knows he or she is casting the Eye because they do it all the time. They can't help it; they don't mean to do it. It is just a force that emanates from them: everything they look at turns to disaster. Glance at a building, within 24 hours it burns down. Glance at a champion cow, by night-fall it's sick and dying. Glance at a pregnant woman…

They're not necessarily bad people, these *jettatura*. They may even be very good people. Even a pope was once branded a *jettatura*; people

ran from him, hoping to avoid that fatal glance, no matter how benevolently it was intended. (If you fear you are or know a *jettatura*, don't
worry. There is a magical solution. Keep reading.)

Although anyone may be struck by the Evil Eye, not everyone is
equally vulnerable. Some are more at risk than others: brides, babies,
pregnant women, children, and horses are all exceptionally vulnerable. Men are not inherently vulnerable to the Evil Eye, but their
sperm, genitals, and capacity for fertility are.

The connection with eyes is not limited to the English language.
In Italian, this force is called *"mal d'occhio."* In Hebrew, it's *"ayin hara,"*
literally *"evil eye."* In Arabic it's just *"ayin"* or *"the eye."* Anti-Evil Eye
amulets invariably take the form of eyes, usually, in Mediterranean
lands, blue eyes.

These blue eyes indicate something else about the Evil Eye. People's abstract conception of the Evil Eye, the concept of its existence
rather than the Evil Eye itself, has historically been used to target
minorities and individuals who are different from what is perceived as
mass culture, although one could say that the persecutors are mani-
festing the destructive force of the Eye even as they accuse others.
Thus in the Mediterranean, blue eyes are suspect. In Northern
Europe, dark skin is suspect. Redheads, frequently a minority, are
often targeted as possessing the Evil Eye.

Exploiting the Evil Eye as a tool of discrimination by a dominant culture indicates little true magical knowledge, little understanding of the
Eye as a phenomenon, or else the complete degeneration of a magical
system. The Evil Eye either emanates from the universe and not from
any individual, or else every individual potentially casts the Eye. *Real*
magic makes discrimination and persecution unnecessary. It's a waste of
time, only increasing tension and resentment within a society. Real
magic has much more powerful means to avoid and remove the Evil Eye.

Traditional signs of attack by the Evil Eye include:

★ *Sudden disaster. Everything was going really well and then, all of a*
   sudden … a major problem or series of problems hits like a bolt of
   lightning. A perfectly normal pregnancy suddenly isn't normal any longer.
   A perfectly healthy child suddenly has a health crisis

★ *Not all manifestations are so sudden: the Evil Eye also manifests as malaise, characterized by consistent lack of energy and lack of interest, and by wasting illnesses that resist conventional diagnosis and/or treatment*

★ *Stubborn, persistent head or body lice*

★ *Sudden, excessive biting of the lips, especially while sleeping*

★ *The Evil Eye can also block fertility, although it is but one of many other potential metaphysical reasons given for the inability to conceive or deliver a healthy, living child*

There are several issues involved when dealing with the Evil Eye: *prevention*, so that the Eye cannot be cast; *repelling*, so that even if cast it bounces off the target without causing harm; and the *removal* of the Eye and its effects. There are many methods employed to prevent being a victim of the Evil Eye, probably the most common being the carrying of charms and amulets.

★ *Many Evil Eye amulets also ward off other dangers: malevolent magic, spiritual attack, etc. Each type of disaster leaves you vulnerable to others. There is an entire category of general* Protection Spells; *however, these may not ward off the Evil Eye and they will not remove it*

★ *Because the Evil Eye is typically inflicted during personal contact, most frequently outside the home, many Evil Eye-repelling charms and spells are mobile, like amulets and conjure bags*

★ *Because one can never be sure when the Eye will be cast and from what direction, many magical anti-Evil Eye spells take the form of amulets that, once charged, will repel the Eye independently without further action from the spell-caster*

★ *Anyone (babies, brides) or anything (new cars, new houses) perceived as exceptionally vulnerable to the Evil Eye may be protected before the Eye falls upon them*

★ *Like healing and cleansing spells, Evil Eye removal spells frequently require the participation of another to perform the spell on behalf of the afflicted. Always select ritual assistants carefully. The* "target" *of the spell is generally the person who is afflicted with the Eye*

There is some belief that the Tenth Commandment that forbids *coveting* actually refers to deliberate casting of the Evil Eye.

Body Defiance Spells

Just as certain people and objects are inherently vulnerable to the Eye, certain images, objects, and botanicals are perceived as the Evil Eye's natural enemies, repelling, removing, defying, and destroying the Eye by power of their very nature, none more so than images depicting parts of the human anatomy.

It takes an eye to defeat an eye. Eye-shaped amulets match the Evil Eye's glance, distract it, and overpower it.

Natural stones or crystals that vaguely or literally resemble eyes are valued but rare, a problem when the Evil Eye is so omnipresent, therefore people developed more accessible talismans. Glass beads that look like tiny, perpetually open eyes are favored worldwide, especially blue eye beads. Although this association has caused trouble for the blue-eyed in certain parts of the world the original intention was not to point fingers at certain people or ethnic groups. Instead blue is an important color indicating spiritual protection. Doors, ceilings and amulets are customarily painted blue for the same reason. That blue eye beads protect from the Evil Eye does not indicate that blue-eyed people are any more likely to cast it.

The most famous and accessible blue eye bead is the Turkish "*nazar boncuk.*" These round blue beads may be used independently, one at a time, or they may be strung together to form shapes, especially horseshoes.

Blue Eye Bead Spells

Blue eye beads' power will be enhanced if you cleanse, charge, and consecrate them before use and whenever you perceive that they've "worked" for you.

★ Wear a single bead around your neck
★ Pin individual beads all over using safety pins
★ Sew them onto clothing or anything else that needs protection
★ Hang them from the rear-view mirror of an automobile

If a bead cracks, it's understood to have worked. Its demise is considered death on the field of combat, a direct hit from the Evil Eye. Bury it with honor and replace it.

Chili Pepper Spell

This is among the simplest but most potent anti-Evil charms, recommended especially for guarding sperm count, virility, and male reproductive capacity.

1. Pierce a fresh, firm red chili pepper; ideally it should appear as phallic or horn-like as possible.
2. String it from a cord and wear it around your neck.

3. Its effectiveness lasts as long as it remains firm and hard. A temporal amulet, replace as needed with a fresh one.

Mutiny Against the Eye

Winged phalluses, the symbol of the Roman spirit Mutinus and found in the ruins of Pompeii, serve as a prophylactic against the Evil Eye. Wear or hang as needed.

The shape of the human hand is a ubiquitous, international magical protective charm. The hand depicted may be realistic or extremely stylized; sometimes only the five fingers are implied using five dots, or a pentagon. Five fingers poke out the Eye. These hands are shared with general protective magic, however other hand images specifically target the Evil Eye.

★ The "fica" or fig hand, an ancient Italian amulet, repels the Evil Eye. This amulet depicts a hand, with the thumb poking between the first two fingers. This is intended to duplicate the reproductive act. To make matters more explicit, the word "fig" is ancient slang for vulva. The hand, thus, re-creates the power of the genitals

★ *The* "mano cornuto" *or horned hand, another old Italian Evil Eye charm, displays a hand making the sign of the horns, first and last fingers thrust out from the otherwise clenched hand*

Should you find yourself threatened without recourse to an amulet, take your hands off your belt: it's not necessary to resort to the genuine article. Magical gestures made with the hands ward off the Eye. In general, this is not a confrontational act: the gesture is made behind the suspect's back as they depart from you or under cover, out of sight. The goal is to stop the Eye, not start a fight.

These spells will repel the Evil Eye if you catch it as it's being sent or immediately after; they will not remove its effects, however. Stronger spells are needed.

General Evil Eye Protection Spells

 ## Bean Spells

Grow jack beans or sword beans as a border surrounding your home and property to repel the Eye.

 # Coconut Reversal

1. Carry a coconut to your front door.
2. Hold it in your hands and visualize the forces of evil plaguing you passing from your body out of your hands and into the coconut.
3. Visualize the coconut's eyes as the Evil Eye and the coconut head grinning at you.
4. When you're ready, open the door, drop kick or place the coconut on the floor and kick it out on the street, yelling aggressively, "*Get the hell out!*" or something stronger.
5. Go inside and immediately perform cleansing and protective rituals for yourself.

This may also be used to reverse any kind of malevolent spell.

Conjure Bags

These bags, in general, provide protection from the Eye, a measure of security. They will not necessarily remove the Eye that's already been cast.

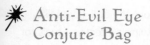

Anti-Evil Eye Conjure Bag

Anti-Evil Eye recommendations from India suggest filling a red bag with some or all of the following:

★ *Crocodile teeth*
★ *Pottery shards or bits of terracotta pottery found in a cemetery*
★ *Protective verses and sacred texts*
★ *Chili peppers, lemons, or limes, to be replaced with fresh ones weekly or as needed*

Wear or carry the bag with you.

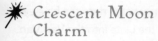

Crescent Moon Charm

Underscoring the similarity between horns and crescent moons, according to ancient Hebrew practice, wearing the crescent moon shape repels the Evil Eye.

Dill Evil Eye Repellant

Hang dill over all entrances and windows to ward off the Evil Eye.

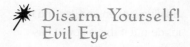

Disarm Yourself! Evil Eye

Are you afraid that you're sending the Evil Eye? To disarm:

1. Unroll one cigarette.
2. Sprinkle the tobacco onto freshly lit charcoal.
3. Stand over this incense or waft it toward you with your hands or a fan, so that the smoke creates a fumigation for you.
4. Repeat as needed.

Dress Spell

The clothing worn when the Eye is encountered can help you remove and repel its effects. This Northern European technique of averting and removing the Evil Eye should be attempted as soon as possible following contact with the Eye. The dress in the spell is understood to be the one you were wearing when you met the Eye.

1. Pull your dress over your head as if you were removing it, but instead, with it held over your head, twirl three times sunwise.
2. Remove the garment.

3. Holding it open and, leaving it inside-out if this is how it has come off, drop a burning coal through it three times.
4. Put the dress back on.

Evil Eye House Protection Spell

Protect your new home from the Evil Eye and other envious glances, particularly while it's under construction.

1. Create a doll to divert the eye. In India, from whence this ritual derives, the doll is usually made from fabric and stuffed with straw; however, what the doll is made from isn't as important as what the doll looks like. The crucial point is that it must be eye-catching. Usually the dolls are vivid in color, funny, or sexually suggestive: long protruding red penises are customary, although this may not play well in the suburbs.
2. Charge the doll with its mission, then set it on scaffolding or hang it above the front door. When observers glance at your house, their eye is irresistibly drawn to the doll; they never see your house.

3. Remove the doll, if you like, following protective rituals for the home.

Evil Eye Oil

Although the concept of the Evil Eye and many anti-Evil Eye spells are ancient, modern versions exist, too. This Hoodoo spell draws upon a blend of Egyptian and British magical traditions.

1. Draw a blue eye onto a white plate using indigo or blue food coloring.
2. Fill a dish with **Van Van Oil**.
3. Using water, rinse the blue eye off the plate into the **Van Van**.
4. Rub the resulting concoction onto your hands and the soles of your feet daily for seven consecutive days.

For best results, accompany with recitation of psalms and/or other sacred texts.

Evil Eye Removal Spells

A typical Evil Eye removal spell involves one person holding something in their hand which is then passed around the victim's head three times. The substance held in the hand must be magnetic and absorbent.

★ *The substance serves as an Evil Eye magnet: it pulls the Evil Eye off the victim*
★ *Because it is absorbent, the Evil Eye goes into the substance*
★ *The substance is then usually immediately thrown into a fire, destroying the Evil Eye and its capacity to harm*

This ritual can be in response to an attack of the Evil Eye, suspicion of attack, or even just as a nightly precautionary method. The person doing the removal (versus the target of the spell, the victim of the Eye) magically concentrates and focuses on removing the Eye and blessing and protecting the victim. The spell may be accompanied by murmuring blessings, sacred texts, and/or defiant comments towards the Eye. Although the spell may work even if done mechanically, it lacks the potency and blessing-quality of a consciously empowered spell.

☀ Evil Eye Removal (1) Black Cumin

1. Wrap an odd number of black cumin seeds in paper or place them inside a small paper bag.
2. Pass this packet around the victim of the Eye three times.
3. Burn it in fire.
4. When you hear the seeds snap, crackle, and pop, you'll know the Evil Eye has cracked too. If no sounds are heard, consider whether further action is needed.

☀ Evil Eye Removal (2) Date Leaves

1. Collect 21 date palm leaves.
2. Knot them together, envisioning your goals and desires as you form each knot.
3. Wave this garland around the afflicted person.
4. Place it in a covered terracotta pot in the corner of the afflicted person's room overnight.
5. Put an old shoe, a broom, or a piece of iron on top of the pot.
6. In the morning dispose of the pot's contents at a crossroads or burn the garland outside the home.
7. Spiritually cleanse the pot before further use.

✳ Evil Eye Removal (3) Egg

1. Pass one egg around the afflicted person three times, muttering blessings, sacred texts, and defiance towards the Eye.
2. Take the egg outside, ideally off your property, and smash it on the ground.
3. Check for signs of blood; if any appear, continued magical action is required.

✳ Evil Eye Removal (4) Iron

1. Heat a bar of iron until it is red-hot.
2. Holding it with tongs, pass the iron bar around the afflicted person three times.
3. Drop the bar into a dish of turmeric water.
4. Leave it there until the water cools, then dispose of the water outside the house.

✳ Evil Eye Removal (5) Is It Gone Yet?

To determine whether the Eye has been removed, follow spells to remove the Eye by dropping three fresh drops of oil into a pan of fresh water.

When the drops remain round and distinct, the Eye is gone.

✳ Evil Eye Removal (6) Salt

1. Prepare a fire.
2. Pass a handful of salt around the afflicted person's head three times.
3. Toss the salt into the fire.

✳ Evil Eye Removal (7) Sizzling Water

1. You need to create a hot surface: either place hot coals onto a plate or heat up a metal plate.
2. Place an overturned jar on top of the plate.
3. Fill a bowl with water. Pass it over the afflicted person. Empty the water over the jar so that it spills onto the plate. (If the water hisses or sizzles or somehow makes noise, it's attempting to communicate with you regarding the spell and the success of the removal. Try to interpret.)
4. Place a metal implement across the now-empty bowl until you can properly cleanse it.

Evil Eye Waters

The following formula waters repel the Eye:

> Holy Water
> Indigo Water
> Marie Laveau Water
> Notre Dame Water

Formulas may be found in the *Formulary.*

Add substantial quantities of one or a combination of these waters to your bath. Alternatively, asperge an area using a rue wand to cleanse the place of the Evil Eye's influence.

✳ Eyebright Evil Eye Repellant

The dark spot in the center of the eyebright flower is often interpreted as an eye. Grow the flower around your home to repel the Eye.

✳ Five Eye Spell

Five pairs of glass beads, each pair in a different distinct color, are required for this amulet. Dizzying colors dazzle the Evil Eye.

1. String the beads in a double row.
2. Arrange them in a circle.
3. Post or wear.

✳ Five in Your Eye!

Sometimes dazzling the Eye isn't sufficient. Just as people attempt to protect themselves from the Eye, so the Eye is believed to possess instincts of self-preservation and will recoil from potential harm. How many times have you heard adults admonish children, "Don't play with sticks! You'll poke someone's eye out!" or "Don't point your finger! You're liable to poke out an eye!" Sharp, pointy objects and plain human fingers serve as potent Evil Eye amulets.

Many Evil Eye spells feign aggressive action and mimic destruction of the Eye. Don't touch or get near anyone's actual eyes! It's that big abstract malevolent invisible force that must be stopped, not anyone's actual glance or their ability to glance.

1. When the threat of the Eye is perceived aggressively mutter or shout, as appropriate, the Moroccan saying *"Five in your eye!"*

2. Add a thrusting motion of the hand with splayed fingers in the direction that the Eye is believed to come from, or straight ahead of you if unknown.

Four Corners Dirt Spell

This quick-fix pan-Semitic spell is extremely effective for removing all traces of the Evil Eye.

1. Take dirt from the four corners of your home.
2. Mix it together and throw it on a fire within the house shouting fiercely "*Get the hell out, Evil Eye!*"

Henna

Amulets are left at home, lost, forgotten, or given to others as emergency protection. Permanent amulets that can't be lost create another option: one of the primal reasons for tattooing is the creation of such a permanent amulet.

Once upon a time, and sometimes still, throughout Africa and Asia, women's faces were tattooed with small blue downward-facing triangles and/or a series of five dots, representing the protective energy of the human anatomy.

North African tattoo designs were particularly intricate, each detail filled with symbolic value. After the Islamic conquest, Berber women were forbidden their traditional tattoos. So that the shapes would not be forgotten, the women turned to henna.

Henna, in itself, is an extremely potent enemy of the Evil Eye. Even carrying the powder in an amulet bag repels the Eye; however its power is magnified when combined with anti-Evil Eye imagery.

Most other botanicals demonstrate their power ephemerally or through aroma. Henna does both and adds visual impact too. Henna creates a temporary dye on the skin. The color ranges from orange to brick red to deep brown, all metaphysically powerful colors, particularly in regards to spiritual protection. Magical, amuletic, and talismanic designs are displayed on the skin. Henna's primary associations with weddings and fertility may derive from its reputation as a potent anti-Evil Eye weapon.

Use the powder to create henna paste in order to decorate

hand and body. (Check the *Formulary* for further instruction.) The most efficacious anti-Evil Eye designs to be incorporated into henna decoration include:

★ *Downward-facing triangles*
★ *Dots grouped together in series of five*
★ *Pentagons*
★ *Eyes, especially an eye inside a triangle*

These designs may also be incorporated into tattoos and other body art.

Home Protection Spell

Envious neighbors? Too many passers-by gazing at your house? This spell is particularly effective when undergoing construction work on a home.

1. Attach a red ribbon to a hand of bananas and some rue. Add Evil Eye beads or a *cimaruta*, the Italian Evil Eye amulet, for maximum effect. (The *cimaruta* is usually crafted from silver or a silver-colored metal, and has evolved into a complex, fabulous amulet.)

2. Hang outside the house until the bananas are completely rotten.
3. Burn or bury everything; do not bring within the home.
4. Repeat as needed.

Horn Charm Spell

Fill a small horn or cornucopia with sage leaves to protect against the Eye. Wear it or situate it strategically.

Iron Anti-Evil Eye Spell

Found nails protect against the Evil Eye. If you find one, pick it up and carry it in a red conjure bag.

Mirror Charm

Supplying your own eye may not be necessary. Mirrors reflect the Evil Eye straight back where it came from and, as with the fabled basilisk, can prove fatal.

Mirrors are incorporated into other amulets. Or they can be strategically arranged so best to repel the Evil Eye; sew small mirrors and reflecting surfaces onto your clothing.

Nine Nail Lemon Charm

1. Pierce a lemon with nine nails.
2. Wind red thread around these nails.
3. Knot the end of the thread around one of the nails.
4. Place this charm above the door to repel the Evil Eye.

Quick-fix Evil Eye Spells

Although many anti-Evil Eye spells and rituals are lengthy and complex, in a pinch, quick-fix anti-Evil Eye spells can be very effective, especially when you need to remove the Eye from yourself without assistance.

Quick-fix Evil Eye Spell (1)

Drip olive oil into water, especially boiling water. Let the water cool, and then bathe yourself with it, focusing on the face, back of the neck, and the soles of your feet.

Quick-fix Evil Eye Spell (2)

Drop glowing coals or lit matches into water. Watch them hit the water. Expose yourself to any steam. Visualize the Eye extinguished.

Quick-fix Evil Eye Spell (3)

Pierce a lemon with iron nails. Visualize yourself simultaneously piercing the Evil Eye.

Remove the Eye Spell

This Italian spell removes the Evil Eye.

1. Add spring or **Holy Water** to a saucer.
2. Add three drops of olive oil to the water plus seven small leaves from an olive branch that has been blessed on Palm Sunday.
3. Dip your finger into the dish, swirl it in the ingredients, then use your finger to make a cross on the victim's forehead, saying:
   Jesus, Joseph, and Mary
   Evil Eye Away!

4. Repeat two more times for a total of three crosses and three chants.
5. Repeat on three consecutive mornings. Here's the catch: oil and water don't mix; if they do, something is wrong. The drops of oil need to remain visibly distinct within the water. Should they at any point disperse completely into the water, dispose of the ingredients. Wait 24 hours and repeat the entire ritual.

An alternative rhyme is sometimes used:

Two eyes have overlooked you
Two saints have enjoyed you
By the Father, Son, and the Holy
Ghost
Evil Eye Away!

 Secret Red Ribbon

Tie a red ribbon to your underwear. (Just wearing red underwear may be effective, too.) For maximum effectiveness, magically charge all items prior to use.

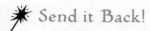 Send it Back!

This ritual either neutralizes the Eye or sends it back from whence it came.

1. If you know or suspect who cast the Eye, secretly cut a small bit of the suspect's clothing.
2. Burn it together with frankincense resin.
3. Brandish either the burning incense or the dish with the cold leftover ashes in front of the suspect with an aggressive gesture.

There's no need to explicitly inform the other person of the intent of the ritual: the effect is subliminal.

Shark's Tooth Spell

Wear a fossilized shark's tooth to repel the Evil Eye. Cleanse periodically by passing through protective incense smoke.

Fertility: Spells for Conception and Contraception

Magic spells are cast to obtain many benefits: wealth, luck, true love or a passionate lover, renewed health, enhanced psychic power. However, the subject they are most primordially and intrinsically involved with is human fertility.

Although it's often suggested that religion and mysticism emerged in response to the mysteries of death, the very opposite may be the case. The earliest religions, characterized by veneration of images of the human genitals, were fascinated by the mysteries of birth and life and generative power. Clues are imbedded in our language: the word "venerate" stems from the same roots as Venus, venerable, and venereal.

This fascination with generation remains crucially integral to magic. After all, what does a magic spell usually attempt to do but create something new, something that previously didn't exist? The Spirits most involved with magic (Hecate, Artemis, Yemaya, Baba Yaga, Freya, Oshun, Aine, and so many others) invariably are involved with human reproductive capacities as well.

Themes of sexual reproduction echo throughout magic. Magical instruments most frequently double as fertility motifs as well: mortars and pestles, sieves, cauldrons, broomsticks, not to mention phallic wands ands staffs, derive their power from associations with human generative power. Humans can generate babies and humans can generate magic.

To some extent, even the term *sex magic* is redundant: ultimately the sexual act *is* a magical act, although like everything else, it can be performed badly, degraded, abused, and unappreciated. Violence and coercion destroy all trace of the sacred.

This isn't to suggest that magic is all about being fruitful and multiplying. The emphasis is on control over reproductive cycles so that the individual retains health and happiness. Magic provides a vast repertoire of spells for fertility. The earliest magical systems are also intrinsically connected to the earliest medical systems: holistic systems don't rigidly distinguish between the two. Great emphasis was also placed on botanicals to prevent and sometimes end pregnancy when it wasn't desired. Many of the most famous and ancient witch-spirits like Hecate, Kybele, Artemis, and Baba Yaga are also master herbalists. Perhaps fertility spells are best understood as reproductive control spells; spells designed to permit conception when and if one desired.

Fertility is a capacity that exists so that it may be drawn upon as desired and when desired. In a sense that capacity for fertility is synonymous with one's capacity for magic. You may not wish to cast magic spells every day but you want the power to do so when you choose. Likewise you may not wish to become pregnant this year or ever, but if you change your mind, you want the capacity to fulfill your desires.

Despite tales of legendary fish with such intense fertility power that even virgins and men who consume them conceive, there is not one spell here for a virgin birth. Fertility magic requires sex: it is a given that any spells are accompanied by the actual act of procreation. No matter how powerful your magic, no matter how splendid and rare your materials, if you're not accompanying fertility spells with well-timed sex, they can't work.

Despite all this talk of sex and procreation, fertility spells aren't limited to people wishing to have children. They may be used to enhance and stimulate artistic creativity as well as actual conception and birth. Adapt these spells to suit your needs.

Spells for Conception

The boundaries between magic and traditional botanical medicine are often fluid; nowhere is this more true or crucial than in fertility magic. Please consult the section in the *Elements of Magic Spells* regarding botanical safety. Botanicals, unlike visualizations for instance, always have an actual physical effect on the body. Many botanicals used to promote fertility in the seriously infertile are unsafe during pregnancy, especially early pregnancy. Be very careful and choose your spells wisely. Topical application of an herb, for instance in baths or massage oils, may have effects as strong as or even stronger than internal application. *As a general rule, essential oils are not safe during pregnancy, especially early pregnancy.*

Animals of Fertility

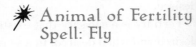

✴ Animal of Fertility Spell: Fly

I know an old woman who
    swallowed a fly,
I don't know why she swallowed a
    fly ...

Well, yes, we do know why. It wa[s] once believed that women could con[c]eive by swallowing flies. Fairy tal[e] heroes are often conceived in thi[s] manner.

    Flies were understood as souls [of] the dead looking for a new incarna[tion]. Souls were once believed able t[o] travel between lives in insect form[.] The original Baal-Zebub, Philistin[e]

spirit and psychopomp, later demonized as Beelzebub, was not only Lord of the Flies but also Shepherd of Souls, leading them to new incarnations.

1. Incorporate this imagery into spell visualization, to help manifest your desires in reality. No, don't swallow real flies: find more appetizing ones.
2. Mold marzipan or chocolate into the shape of flies.
3. Swallow one per visualization and see yourself filled with the soul of the child you desire.

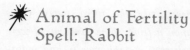

Animal of Fertility Spell: Frog

A more active fertility spell incorporates the use of Zuni carved fetishes. A frog fetish is required; one carved from shell is especially potent for this purpose.

1. Bring the frog to bed with you; otherwise keep it in a jar or bag.
2. Feed it at regularly scheduled intervals to activate and maintain its power. Traditionally corn pollen was offered but bits of food may also be used, or whatever inspiration suggests.
3. Speak to the frog; tell it your heart's desires.

Animal of Fertility Spell: Rabbit

Modern Halloween cards invariably depict the witch accompanied by a black cat, but once upon a time witches' familiars were a varied lot. The most popular familiar during the Burning Times was believed to be a rabbit. This association derives from the rabbit's perceived affinity with the moon (many cultures see a rabbit in the moon) and as the totem animal belonging to many spirits of women's primal power. And we all know the habits of the rabbits...

This is an easy, discreet spell: begin to collect rabbit images. Surround yourself with them. Keep silent about your intent, why you're collecting them. Discussing it weakens the spell. Others collect images of bears, pigs, dwarfs, or fairies, so why not rabbits? The rabbits will eventually begin to come to you, multiplying as rabbits are wont to do. During the Full Moon, take your rabbits outside, cast a circle of them, sit inside, exposed to the moonbeams, and see yourself multiplying, too.

Animal of Fertility Spell: Snake Bag

In the tale of Adam and Eve in the Garden of Eden, the snake isn't

necessarily the third party. Once upon a time, some say, snakes were believed, metaphorically and magically at least, to possess the power to impregnate women and activate conception. Whether that's true or not, snakes remain profoundly affiliated with women's fertility and general reproductive health. A woman's snake power is her fertility power. This amulet bag attempts magical activation.

Very many botanicals are named in honor of serpents, so many they lead to confusion. Many are used therapeutically to remedy various aspects of women's reproductive health; however, this is a magic spell. Merely carry the botanicals, do not consume. Many of these botanicals are unsafe if consumed by pregnant women and no medicine should be used without expert supervision.

Gather as many as you can and carry in an iridescent beaded bag. Botanicals include the two black snake roots—black cohosh and Serpentaria—rattlesnake root, rattlesnake master, adders tongue, snake weed (bistort), snake head, and many others. If you find an unnamed root or twig that resembles a serpent, add that too. Snake charms and carved stone fetishes may also be incorporated. A piece of freely shed snakeskin may be added as well. Carry the bag to enhance and boost fertility and psychic power. Sleep with it beneath your pillow.

Astarte Oil

The name "Astarte" is believed to mean "the filled womb." The name may refer to an independent deity or it may be another name for the Semitic deity, Anat. Either way, the authors of the Bible viewed her with reprobation; she held a notorious reputation for encouraging erotic rites and independent women. The oil named in her honor is believed to promote personal fertility.

Essential oil of coriander
Essential oil of jasmine
Essential oil of myrrh
Essential oil of petitgrain or neroli
Rose attar

Blend all the ingredients above into a bottle filled with sweet almond and jojoba oils. If desired, add cowries or henna twigs and blossoms to the oil.

Because many essential oils are not safe during pregnancy, especially in the first months, reserve this oil for magical uses such as dressing candles and charms.

Astarte Oil Spell (1) Candle Dressing

1. Obtain a human figure candle that represents you.
2. Carve it with your name, birthday, identifying information, affirmations, and desires.
3. Dress the candle with Astarte Oil, particularly the abdominal and genital areas.
4. An optional step is to roll the candle in henna powder.
5. Burn the candle.

Astarte Oil Spell (2) Personal Dressing

Many botanicals that influence fertility appear to create a balance: they encourage fertility if you're not pregnant but can have the opposite effect if you are. If you're sure you're not pregnant, rub the oil on your thighs prior to sex to magically enhance possibility of conception.

All Astarte Oil spells may be accompanied by spiritual petition directed towards Astarte.

Basil Spells

Basil is considered a fertility promoter both physically and symbolically. A tea made from its leaves relieves suppressed menstruation. It is also a traditional component of infertility repair magic spells.

Basil Spell (1) Living Plants

Basil's very presence is believed to enhance fertility. Plant basil around the home or maintain abundant potted plants. Place basil plants in window boxes or beside the door to signal your wish for fertility to Earth's spirit forces.

Basil Spell (2) Basil Boughs

Hang fragrant boughs of basil over the bed to enhance successful conception. Keep the basil fresh, green, and aromatic: replace with fresh boughs as needed.

Basil Spell (3) Fertility Diet

Add basil to your diet—a perfect excuse for pesto. Dine on basil and make love by the light of red candles.

Bed Spells

The bed is the altar on which magical rites occur. Treat it the way you would any sacred altar: spiritually cleansing, ornamenting, and empowering it, demarcating it as enchanted space. Spells incorporate the conjugal bed as a way of promoting fertility.

☀ Bed Spell (1) Fruits and Nuts

A recommendation from the time of the Chinese Han dynasty (206 BCE–220 CE) is to scatter dates and chestnuts on the bed to stimulate conception. The presence of the dates and chestnuts on the bed stimulates the aura of fertility; however, making love on the bed before removing them or changing the sheets can be incorporated into the spell.

☀ Bed Spell (2) Iron

The bed itself can impact fertility. An iron bed offers spiritual protection against all dangers of the night while generating and radiating fertility energy while you sleep.

For maximum effectiveness fumigate the bed with cleansing incense, hang charms and talismans from the bed, and spend a lot of time lying in it.

Botanicals of Fertility

Plants containing extra magical fertility-boosting power often reveal themselves by their resemblance to human genitalia, affiliation with the moon, or by the extravagant quantity of their seeds. These plants include: assorted snake roots, black-eyed peas, corn, figs, jasmine, lilies, lotuses, melons, moonflowers, mugwort, assorted nuts, olives, pomegranates, poppies, pumpkins, roses, and wheat.

☀ Botanical Fertility Bistort Spell

Bistort is also known as dragonwor or snakeweed. Carry the dried roo to promote conception.

☀ Botanical Fertility Bottlebrush Spell

Place bottlebrush blossoms in th bedroom to promote fertility.

Botanical Fertility Candle Spell

Hollow out the inside of a vulva-shaped candle. Stuff it full of a selection of basic botanicals of fertility. (Fruits and vegetables are highly represented among these; use leaves, flowers, and dried seeds rather than the fruit or vegetable itself.) Then burn the candle.

Candle Spells

Candle magic may be used to stimulate fertility and pregnancy. Red candles are typically chosen for fertility spells. Any candle may be used, but figure candles may be particularly appropriate: either an individual human figure, to represent the spell-caster, or a joint male-and-female figure candle. Other powerful candle choices include red cats and red witches as well as snake candles and candles in the shape of hearts or genitalia.

Candle Spell (1) Red Candles

British folk healers recommend burning red candles before, during, and after sex to enhance chances of conception. (If you're really serious about getting pregnant, just keep those red candles burning whenever it's safe and appropriate.) Although you can if you like, it's not even necessary to carve and dress the candles; just keep them burning brightly.

Although this spell stands alone, it can also be incorporated into any other fertility spell as extra enhancement.

Candle Spell (2) Red Witch

The traditional image of the Halloween witch still proudly displays the emblems of women's reproductive magic: womb-like iron cauldron and triangular peaked hat. When witches weren't riding on broomsticks, whose form unites the principles of male and female generative energy, they rode through the sky in mortars and pestles like Baba Yaga, or set sail at sea in sieves, oyster shells, and egg-shells, all images of women's reproductive power, and all components of fertility spells.

Candles in the shape of red witches may represent a literal woman or witch, but they are also used to represent women's primal magical powers, the metaphysical traditions deriving from the mysteries of birth and menstruation. The red witch possesses long-forgotten and suppressed magical secrets that might perhaps assist you in your quest, whatever it is. Burn red witch candles to tap into that power and discover the magical secrets and power hidden within you.

1. Write your deep needs or desires on a piece of paper.
2. Carve and dress a red witch candle, using Astarte Oil or another oil of your choice.
3. Place the paper under the witch and burn the candle.
4. When the candle has burned down completely, bury all spell remnants in Earth or carry them in a mojo bag tied around your waist.

Date Spells

This is a two-part spell for a couple that wishes to conceive. Either part of the spell may be cast independently, but they work best in conjunction.

Date Spell (1)

This allegedly boosts a woman's reproductive capacity: a man feeds dates by hand to the woman he hopes will be the mother of his children. Reserve and cleanse the date pits to be used in Date Spell 2.

Date Spell (2)

The man should now carry the cleansed date pits in a red conjure bag for enhanced fertility and sexual power. (Although a similar spell exists for enhanced virility alone, his fertility is allegedly unaffected unless he has actually put the dates into the woman's mouth.)

Earth Spell

Once upon a time, women engaged in magic ritual to enhance the fertility of the Earth. If you're in need, Earth can repay the favor. However, not all dirt is believed to possess equal fertility-activating magic power.

1. Gather a handful of dirt from near the doorway of a bordello.
2. Gather a handful of dirt that's been dislodged (dug up) by a bull's horns.
3. Gather a handful of dirt that's been dislodged by a boar's tusks.
4. Place them in a red conjure bag and carry with you.

Earth Spell Enhanced

This spell derives from traditional offerings to the Hindu deity, Durga. Durga, warrior spirit of protection, rides upon a tiger, doing battle with demons.

Create the bag as above, but as part of a petition of fertility directed toward Durga. Bring it to one of her shrines or dedicate it to her upon a personal altar.

Egg Spells

Eggs, for obvious reasons, rank among the most ancient and powerful of fertility symbols, and are incorporated into many spells.

 Egg Spell (1) Candle

Create your own strong, powerful egg.

1. First make the candle mold: gently punch a small hole in the large end of a raw egg.
2. Use a cuticle scissor to cut a small circle of eggshell. (Buy a dozen eggs; you may have to practice a bit.)

3. Empty the egg into a bowl: use as desired.
4. Gently wash the inside of the shell with water. The membrane and all contents must be thoroughly removed. Allow it to dry completely.
5. Prepare the wax. (You may also add tiny fertility charms or herbs.)
6. Use the egg carton as a holder. Place the eggshell, hole-end up, in the carton.
7. Pour in liquid wax, reserving a little. (When it's half full, you may add tiny seed beads, charms, or herbs if you choose, although the candle is effective without them.) Let the wax harden overnight.
8. Next day: gently heat the reserved wax until liquid.
9. Gently chip away the shell, exposing your candle.
10. Heat an ice pick or similar sharp thin tool: put it through the center of the candle and quickly thread with a wick.
11. Fill the hole with the hot wax.
12. Decorate. Keep as an amulet or to burn in a spell.

Egg Spell (2)

1. With a pin, carefully pierce each end of a raw egg. (In some

variants of this spell, the male
partner must pierce the holes.)

2. The man and woman kiss.
3. Place the egg between you,
   holding the egg gently in both
   mouths, each taking an end. (No
   hands!)
4. The man blows egg out of the
   shell into the woman's mouth.
   (How easy or difficult this is,
   depends upon egg and people.)
5. She swallows the egg.
6. Carefully set the shell aside.
   (Don't break it.)
7. Have sex.
8. Whenever you're ready—there's
   no rush—take the empty
   eggshell outdoors together and
   bury it in Earth, at least seven
   inches deep. (If not possible, bury
   it in its own flower-pot and
   enhance with fertility plants.)

☀ Egg Spell (3)

*Eating an egg with a double yolk,
if you can find one, allegedly produces fertility. Likewise, finding a
fish within another fish bestows
tremendous fertility power. (And if
there's a magic ring inside that
fish, you're the star of your very
own fairy tale and should expect
miracles to occur!)*

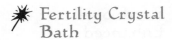

☀ Fertility Crystal Bath

*Fill a bath with as much rainwater
as possible. Place moonstones and
quartz crystals in the tub (make sure
the crystals are large enough so
there's no danger of falling down the
drain!) and bathe, ideally in the
moonlight.*

☀ Fertility Doll Spell

*The use of dolls to magically
enhance fertility and activate conception was once common around the
world, from native North America
to China, Italy to India. Vestiges
of these traditions survive, not least
in the dolls that traditionally orna-
ment the wedding cake. Fertility doll
magic remains most vital, however
in traditional Africa. Although the
style of doll varies, the spell is virtually identical wherever fertility doll
magic is practiced.*

*Create or obtain a doll baby. The
doll does not have to be life-like
unless it's important to you. Dolls
are crafted from wood, clay, nuts,
bones, corn cobs, fabric, metal: any
conceivable material. If working
with a mass-produced doll, embellish it with seashells, beads, seeds
and fertility charms to enhance its
power.*

This doll is your baby. In Africa, dolls accompany their "mothers" everywhere, sometimes discreetly, sometimes not. The doll is fed, bathed, and cared for every day, never left unattended, as if it were a flesh and blood child. This may be understood in various ways:

★ *The doll is the seed from which the actual child grows*
★ *The spell magically stimulates conception*
★ *Your actions indicate your desire to the spirit powers and also demonstrate what a good mother you'll be, given the opportunity*

Like a real baby, the doll is not abandoned, whether pregnancy occurs or not. The doll may be treated as the resulting child's sibling, or given to the child as a toy or amulet. A successful doll may be passed on to another infertile woman to work its magic, while a doll that is not successful may be buried with its "mother" when she dies.

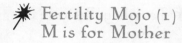

Fertility Incense

1. Gather a pinch of dirt from a fertility shrine or use graveyard dirt from your ancestor's grave.

2. Mix with dried crumbled red rose petals and hibiscus flowers.
3. Sprinkle on lit charcoal and burn.

Fertility Mojos

Conjure bags designed to enhance and empower fertility are treated slightly differently to the standard bag. The standard mojo hand is a red flannel drawstring bag; however, for fertility-enhancing purposes, red silk or beaded bags are most potent. You should wear the bag hanging between your breasts or over the abdominal area, rather than carrying in your pocket, and sleep with the bag beneath your pillow or hang it over the bed in which you make love.

Fertility Mojo (1) M is for Mother

Their first initial isn't what really links these particular botanicals; rather it's their association with fertility and the moon.

1. Add the following to a conjure bag:
   Mandrake
   Mistletoe

Motherwort
Mugwort
2. Wear or carry as desired.

Be cautious with mandrake and mistletoe, both are potentially very toxic.

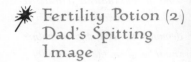

☀ Fertility Mojo (2) Charm Bag

1. Fill a mojo bag with fertility charms: acorns, mistletoe twigs, cowrie shells or pearls, or silver charms in the shape of rabbits or moons.
2. This is a spell-in-progress. Add charms as they appear.
3. Dress with Astarte Oil for fertility and **Van Van** to make your dreams come true.

☀ Fertility Potion (1) Couple

A Romany fertility potion is designed to be shared by prospective parents together. Time this spell to coincide with either the New or Full Moon, whichever suits your reproductive cycles best.

1. Make an infusion with spring water and comfrey.

2. Combine with equal parts brandy.
3. Pour into a single glass, which the man and woman drink together.
4. Drink it in bed; make love immediately afterwards.
5. Repeat three nights in a row.

If it doesn't work, wait until next month's corresponding moon phase before attempting this method again.

☀ Fertility Potion (2) Dad's Spitting Image

A prospective father may choose one of two ways to prepare this fertility potion for the prospective mother of his child:

1. Either drop burning hot coals into spring water or spit into it (think of "spitting image of his father").
2. While the woman drinks the water, the man chants:
   I am the flame, you are the coals!
   I am rain, you are the water!

Fertility Potion (3)
Men

A Moroccan potion to increase male fertility and sexual vigor invokes the fertility-inducing prowess of the egg.

1. Break a raw egg every morning and swallow it before breakfast for 40 consecutive days.
2. Immediately after consuming the egg, fill the shell with olive oil and drink.

Results should be apparent at the conclusion of the 40 days.

If the possibility of salmonella gives cause for pause, a different Moroccan recommendation is for men to drink just olive oil alone to enhance the procreative powers.

Fertility Potion (4)
Rose Hydrosol

True rose hydrosol is used as a woman's fertility potion. You can either drink small portions by itself, or blend rose hydrosol with spring water or champagne and drink.

Fertility Potion (5)
Ruby

1. Place a ruby in a glass and cover it with spring water on the night of the Full Moon.
2. Leave it overnight, exposed to the moonbeams.
3. In the morning, drink the water.

Fertility Spell (1)
Coconut

Place a coconut on an altar or situated in a focal position in the bedroom to enhance female fertility.

Fertility Spell (2)
Fruits

Placed dried longans and lichee fruit under your bed.

Fertility Spell (3)
Poppies

Today, poppies are most associated with opium and illicit drugs, however in ancient days poppies' associations with fertility were equally strong. Poppies demonstrate their affinity for human reproduction via their bulging seedpods.

Dry the seedpods. Pierce and string them onto red cord and wear

or hang over the bed as a fertility enhancer.

Fertility power, like magical energy, is contagious and may be obtained via enchanted methods of transference.

Fertility Tree Spells

Trees are particularly associated with fertility. Any tree may have fertility power because of its phallic appearance rising from Earth (or entering her); however, some trees are more associated with generative power than others.

★ Trees most associated with fertility bear fruit or nuts. The most potent, such as the orange tree, flower and fruit simultaneously. Trees bearing fruits and nuts resembling genitalia or somehow suggesting the sexual act are the most potent of all: figs, peaches, pomegranates, and walnuts for instance. Trees with milky sap also radiate fertility power

★ Willows have particularly strong fertility associations because of their affinity for water, the element most associated with fertility, and also because they are under the dominion of Hecate, spirit of magic, fertility, and healing

★ Certain trees are redolent of fertility because of their associations with specific spirits of fertility; the tree is a conduit to the spirit's power and blessings. Examples include apple trees (Aphrodite) and pines (Dionysus)

 Fertility Tree Spell (1) Basic

To avail yourself of the tree's fertility power, make love under it by the light of the Full Moon. The ritual may be that simple, or you may embellish as you please.

 Fertility Tree Spell (2) Personal Relationship

Enhance and intensify any spell by developing a relationship with a specific tree.

1. Choose an existing tree or transplant a grown specimen.
2. Nurture the tree. Develop a relationship with the tree, or with the resident tree spirit or presiding spirit, however you best understand it.
3. Embellish and decorate this tree.
4. Charge fertility amulets, charms, and spell ingredients by hanging

them on the tree or placing them at its base overnight, especially in the light of the Full Moon.

5. Offer libations to the tree.
6. Sleep under the tree.
7. If possible, make love under the tree.

Fertility Tree Spell (3) Apples

Apple trees are sacred to Aphrodite and figure prominently in all spells that fall under her dominion, especially those for love and fertility. Mix water with apple tree sap and wash your face and hands with it.

Fertility Tree Spell (4) May Pole

The May Pole derives from ancient fertility rites. Create your own rituals with living trees. This spell is extra potent if cast during one of Earth's fertility power days: May Day, Midsummer's Day or Valentine's Day.

. Wrap scarlet ribbons around a tree, visualizing your desire all the while.
. Enhance the spell by ornamenting the tree with fertility-inspired charms, small dolls, or decorated eggshells.
3. For maximum effect, make love under the tree.

Gender Spells

Sometimes conception isn't enough. For one reason or another, a child of a specific gender is desired. Various magic spells attempt to fulfill your desires:

★ *To conceive a boy, place a dagger in your headboard*
★ *To conceive a girl, put a dagger in the headboard with a bay laurel wreath around it*
★ *To conceive a boy, place arrows under the bed*
★ *To conceive a boy, charge a small gold knife charm with other yang materials. Wear it as a charm around your neck*
★ *To conceive a girl, place a spindle under the bed or mattress*

Grow-a-Seed Spell

The most basic fertility spell of all may not seem particularly magical to our jaded eyes: grow plants from seed. What has evolved into a child's kindergarten project was once perceived as an act fraught with mystery

and magic. Do not transfer mature plants or cuttings: it is crucial that you sprout the seeds and nurture the plants. This may be done directly on Earth or in pots within your home.

The choice of plants is entirely up to you; however, plants that are metaphysically associated with fertility will increase the power of the spell. Furthermore, time spent in the presence of plants radiant with fertility power can only be beneficial.

Grow plants that can assist you in the quest for conception or plants that will serve as herbal remedies. By doing this, you set up a symbiotic relationship, a true alliance; each of you depends upon the other. Talk to the plant; tell it what you need it to perform for you. Herbal remedies grown in this manner will be more potent than anything you can purchase. Faithfully keep a gardening diary. Eventually within its pages you may discover parallels and clues to your own condition.

Holed Stone Spells

The precious gem most associated with fertility is the ruby. However, precious gems are not the only potent magical fertility tools. The humble holed stone is a powerful fertility booster.

Holed stones, also called holey stones or hag stones, are pebbles or small stones containing natural perforations. Only Mother Nature can create them. If you have a holed stone, for fertility purposes:

★ Wear it around your neck on a red or silver cord
★ Hang it from your bed on a red or silver cord
★ Carry it in a medicine bag

Holed Stone Spell (1) Extra Enhancement

1. Sprinkle rosemary on a holed stone, especially in the hole.
2. Carry it in a medicine bag or wear it around your neck.
3. Repeat the ritual to coincide with the New Moon.

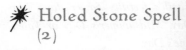

Holed Stone Spell (2)

Not all holed stones are small enough to wear around your neck. Europe and the British Isles are dotted with huge standing stone formations, some erected, some natural, some with holes. These holes have traditionally been used for all manner of healing but particularly for providing and enhancing personal fertility. Getting to one of these fertility power spots may be difficult; the ritual is simple.

1. Journey to a holed standing stone.
2. Make your wish, prayer, and/or petition.
3. Climb through the hole.

Midsummer's Spells

Midsummer's Eve coincides with the Eve of the feast day of Saint John the Baptist. The date also coincides with the Summer Solstice, the height of the sun's powers, and the ancient Roman festival of Ceres, spirit of Earth's generosity. The date has powerful associations with fertility rites, as exemplified by the bonfires traditionally lit on Midsummer's Eve or Saint John's Day.

These bonfires and accompanying fertility rites were once common throughout Europe. Midsummer's Eve is also sacred to the Irish solar deity, Aine, a spirit of love and fertility, and the day has strong Celtic associations. The fertility aspect of the holiday, especially the bonfires, was very popular throughout the Mediterranean, especially in Greece, Italy, and Spain but also across the water in Algeria, Morocco, and Tunisia, although there associations are made with Fatima rather than Saint John.

Among the reasons given for the bonfires during the Middle Ages was that they prevented dragons of the air from their annual revelry, which inevitably concluded in wanton copulation in the skies and the subsequent pollution of springs and wells from drops of dragon ejaculate.

Another theory is that the John the Baptist celebrated amidst fertility rites is not the ascetic John the Baptist who wandered the Judean wilderness wearing his mugwort belt, living on locusts and wild honey, and performing baptisms in the Jordan River. Instead the ancient Semitic fertility spirit Adonis may be lurking underneath, wearing the syncretized mask of the respectable saint.

Although the date itself is propitious for any fertility magic, it's the bonfires, the revelry among them, and the attendant herbs that hold particular value.

☀ Midsummer's Spells (1) Basic

Making love among the bonfires is believed extremely auspicious for fertility. However, as public sex hasn't been condoned in centuries, build your own private bonfire to celebrate the day and conduct private revels.

☀ Midsummer's Spells (2)

Not just any random plants are arbitrarily chosen for the bonfire. Traditionally specific, strongly aromatic plants are used: chamomile, chervil, pennyroyal, rue, Saint John's Wort, thyme, geranium (the fragrant herb, not the bright red flower), and mugwort. When burned, their smoke radiates fertility power.

1. Expose yourself to the smoke of the bonfires.
2. If this isn't possible, choose a selection of Midsummer's herbs, grind and powder them and burn them as Midsummer's Eve incense.

Warning: Make sure that you are not pregnant; several of the herbs may positively influence obstructed fertility but are not safe for use or exposure during pregnancy itself.

☀ Midsummer's Spells (3) Bonfire Wood

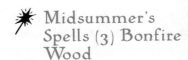

Although bonfires are built from herbs in the Mediterranean region Celtic regions of Europe may build bonfires of carefully chosen wood. This version, for example, suggest nine sacred Druid woods.

Build the fires using the following woods:

Apple
Ash
Birch
Elm
Hawthorn
Hazel
Oak
Rowan
Thorn

Collect the ashes once the fires hav burned out.

Milagros

"*Milagros*" means "*miracles*" in Spanish. It's the term now mos popularly used to refer to th ancient custom of *ex-votos*. Th magical concept of reciprocit figures extremely prominently in the Spiritual petition process:

★ One requests a favor or blessing, sometimes offering a gift to mark the request but always specifying what will be paid for receipt of the requested "miracle"
★ Having received the favor or blessing, one then renders payment

It is wisest to maintain control over two areas of this process: inform the Spirit precisely what blessing or favor is desired. Inform them specifically and explicitly in what form payment will be made and precisely when.

Milagros are used for both purposes. Milagros are tiny depictions, usually but not always formed from metal, of the part of the anatomy that needs repair or healing. These are traditionally brought to the shrine at the same time as a petition is made. The concept of the milagro or ex-voto is ancient. They have been found in Greek, Celtic, and Iberian healing shrines. Prehistoric objects that are dead ringers for ex-votos have also been discovered, although without context or explanation it's impossible to prove what they are. The custom remains most vigorous in Latin America. Shrines typically have an area reserved for you to pin your own ex-voto, either a velvet-covered board or

sometimes on the votive image itself, particularly if the image is associated with miracle cures.

Milagros are also offered to offer testimonial of miracles received. This often evolves into payment for the desired miracle. A cheap metal or wax charm is initially offered, with the promise that if the miracle is received, a golden charm, miniature or life-sized, will be then presented.

Specific milagros represent specific ailments. A pair of metal eyes is donated for eye trouble. A leg or an arm is offered in exchange for healing the appropriate appendage.

Shapes representing fertility and the quest for a child are both literal and metaphoric:

★ Uterus
★ Ovaries
★ Heart (not an anatomically correct heart but the Valentine's Day shape), because it can be synonymous with the vulva and because it represents the love you'd offer a child
★ A baby
★ A hedgehog (because of the old European belief that the womb resembles a hedgehog)

If you have no access or belief in shrines, tie rags or milagros to your own tree or well.

Charge the charms with your desire by any or all of the following methods:

1. Holding them in your hands and concentrating hard on your desire.
2. Sleeping with them under your pillow.
3. Weeping onto them until they're wet from your tears.
4. Carrying in a mojo bag for seven days and nights, until charged with your personal energy.

Nut and Seed Spells

Nuts and seeds represent the property of germination. Eat them if this is healthy and appropriate for you. Carry them in charm bags. Place bowls of nuts in plain sight to radiate fertility power.

Any nuts or seeds may be used in fertility magic, though as usual some are more potent than others:

★ Oak galls, known as serpent eggs, are transformed into magical charms and amulets
★ Acorns gathered at night hold the strongest fertility power. The Full Moon enhances the power; look for an oak with particularly abundant acorns
★ Chinese magic exploits puns and other word games, for instance the derivation of the Chinese name for peanut: "hua sheng." Hua alludes to "great variety," sheng to "give birth." Bowls of peanuts are thus frequently displayed at weddings or in the home to radiate fertility power

 Nut Spell (1)
Jupiter's Nuts

The Latin word for walnuts "juglans," refers to Jupiter's testicles. Walnuts and chestnuts are particularly beneficial for men's fertility magic.

1. Place bowls of nuts in plain sight, to radiate and transfer their energy
2. Eat them as appropriate.
3. Replenish with fresh nuts as needed.

 Nut Spell (2) Bath

The transfer of fertility energy is also attempted via a bath, for the purpose of boosting either male or female fertility.

1. Steep five chestnuts in a pot of water for five hours.

2. Strain, burying the nuts outside, but reserving the liquid.
3. Add this to your bathwater.

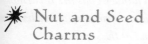

Nut and Seed Charms

Seeds and nuts may also be used for adornment. These simple charms make powerful amulets: the process of making them is as magically charged as wearing them.

1. Make a necklace from acorns, sunflower, pumpkin and melon seeds, and dried corn kernels in a variety of colors: red, yellow, blue, and black.
2. Soak the material in warm water until softened. (At least an hour.)
3. Using a sharp needle, string them on strong thread, ideally red, black, or green. (It may be necessary to drill holes in the acorns.)
4. Pass the charms through the smoke of frankincense and myrrh to further empower, if you wish, although this isn't necessary.
5. Wear your charms.

Ocean Waves Spell

Infertility derives from many causes. Where physical causes are elusive, spiritual causes may be seen. While some spirits heal infertility, others cause it, sometimes one and the same spirit. Ocean water, as well as that from healing springs, is believed to cure infertility inflicted by djinn and other spirits.

Go to the sea. Let seven waves pass over your body to remove evil influences and obstacles. (The number of waves depends upon which side of the Mediterranean you're on. Moroccan magic favors seven. Identical spells exist in Spain but nine waves are required to accomplish the same purpose.)

Pinecone Spells

Pinecones look phallic; they're also associated with Dionysus and Kybele, both powerful providers of fertility. Dionysus' magic wand, the thyrsus, is topped by a pinecone. Pinecones are beneficial for both male and female fertility. Because pine trees are also magically identified with happy marriages, pinecones are especially beneficial for those relationships strained by the stress and anguish of infertility.

Collect baskets of fallen pinecones; look for strong, healthy ones filled with seeds.

Place them in bowls and baskets in plain sight, to radiate their power and transfer it to you.

✹ Pinecone Spell (1)

1. Make a wish on a pinecone. Hold it in your hands and charge it with your desires.
2. When you're ready, toss it into a fire to transmit your appeal to the spiritual powers that be.

This method may also be used to make a petition to either Kybele or Dionysus or both.

✹ Pinecone Spell (2)

1. Collect pinecones.
2. Decorate them by dipping them into wax and glitter.
3. String them onto red cord to make necklaces.

✹ Rainwater Sieve Spell

Although terrestrial water, oceans, springs, lakes, and rivers are perceived as female powers, rain is metaphysically likened to semen. It's difficult to understand at first why masculine "thunder gods" (Zeus,

Baal, Thor, Chango) are associated with fertility. It's not the thunder and the lightning; it's the accompanying showers that fertilize the Earth. Thunder gods are invariably promiscuous: strong rain fertilizes a lot of land at the same time.

Spells that emphasize immersion in the ocean seek to draw on female fertility power. Spells involving rainwater draw on the masculine powers, although both types of spells benefit women in particular. Many spells combine yin and yang, charging rainwater in moonlight, for instance.

Sieves have traditional associations with fertility. They are used similarly in personal fertility spells as well as weather spells to end drought.

1. Collect rainwater.
2. Keep the container tightly sealed in the refrigerator until you have a bright moonlit night.
3. Place the water outside, exposed to the moonbeams.
4. Pour this water through a sieve onto a woman who wishes to conceive. (If she is naked, this is even more potent.)
5. Water may be poured over the head, over the genitals, or directed over the breasts, accompanied by petitions to have a healthy child to nurse.

Saint George Fertility Spell

Saint George's Eve is an extremely potent night for fertility rites. Crusaders encountered Saint George in Semitic West Asia and brought him home to Europe, where he is most famous for killing the dragon. Or did he? And why is he so helpful to women who wish to conceive? Some believe Saint George to be Baal in disguise. Baal, Semitic weather deity and bane of the biblical prophets, exemplifies male thunder gods who rain down fertility on a parched region. The image of the dragon or great snake is often used to represent menstruation, the monthly heartache of women wishing but failing to conceive.

Women once flocked to a Syrian shrine devoted to Saint George. Its attendant priests developed such a reputation for working miracles of conception that suspicious husbands soon forbade their wives to go, preferring no children at all to these "miracle" children.

There's no need to discover the ruins of this shrine: Saint George can assist your quest in the privacy of your own home.

1. Hang a new white nightgown from a fruitful tree on Saint George's Eve.
2. Leave it overnight.
3. Inspect the garment in the morning. If any living creature is found within it, the woman can expect to conceive before next Saint George's Day.

To activate the spell put the nightgown on immediately. Having sex while wearing it wouldn't hurt either.

Contraception Spells

The repertoire of contraceptive spells is far smaller than that devoted to successful conception. Until recently, the emphasis was on being fruitful and multiplying as much as possible, rather than the opposite.

Traditional cultures, the source of so much fertility magic, have also had access to herbal methods of birth control, making magic spells unnecessary. Magic is a mysterious process: you ask for one thing, sometimes you get it and sometimes you get something else. Conventional methods of contraception are usually more reliable and definitely more predictable than magical means.

Magical contraception is intended to supplement and enhance

more conventional methods of birth control, not replace them. Perhaps they should be considered historic spells or what the old Hoodoo drugstores called "*curios.*" Those unable to use other forms of contraception for one reason or another may find these methods useful, although they should still be accompanied by close monitoring of reproductive cycles, if you genuinely care about not getting pregnant.

Bead Spell

1. Mix menstrual blood into clay and form a bead, piercing it with a needle.
2. When the bead is ready, hold it in your hand, and focus upon remaining childless.
3. Keep this bead in a safe place. Don't lose it.
4. Whenever you're ready to conceive, toss the bead into a river or spring and let the water dissolve the bead.

For absolute utmost power, use a girl's first menstrual blood.

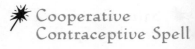

Cooperative Contraceptive Spell

A Moroccan contraceptive spell's success depends upon cooperation between a man and a woman. A few drops of menstrual blood plus either one dried fig or one bead are required.

1. Cut the dried fig lengthwise.
2. Sprinkle the blood into the slit or place inside the bead's hole.
3. The man then hides the fig in a place unknown to the woman. Allegedly a period of sterility will remain for as long as the fig is hidden.

To break the spell, the man removes the fig from its hiding place and with a flourish, displays it to the woman.

Flax Thread Contraceptive Spell

The original spell would have required the woman to spin the thread, in the manner that fates, fairies, and goddesses spin, wield and sever the thread of life. Flax is sacred to such spirits of fertility as Frigg, Hulda, and the Russian

spirit who sometimes masquerades as Saint Paraskeva.

1. Soak flax thread in menstrual blood.
2. Tie ten knots in the thread.
3. Wear it non-stop for nine days and nine nights, sleeping with it at night.
4. When the nine days and nights are complete, bury the thread in a corner saying, "*I bury you for* [insert the time desired to stay pregnancy-free]."

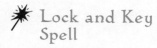

Hawthorn Spell

Tuck hawthorn leaves under the mattress to magically enhance con-traception.

Knot Spell

1. Make knots in a cord for contraception, knotting in your desires, goals, and intentions.

2. Reserve the cord in a safe and private place.
3. Place the cord in a glass of water.
4. Let it soak overnight, then drink the water.
5. When you're ready to conceive, untie the knots.

Lock and Key Spell

1. Place a lock and key on the floor.
2. Walk in the space between them. Turn around. While turning state: "*When I open this lock again, I will successfully conceive.*"
3. Turn the key and lock the lock.
4. Keep the lock and key in a safe place. Prior to attempts at conception, you must ritually open the lock.

Happy Home Spells

Home sweet home. Sounds nostalgic, but nowhere as exciting as gambling, wild sex, fame and fortune—the usual goals of magic spells. That may be true, but when all isn't peaceful on the home front it can be hard to concentrate on anything else. Sometimes what you need more than anything is a peaceful home and a family that doesn't argue. Magic offers advice for pouring oil on troubled waters.

Some Happy Home Spells concern themselves with who's in the home; they allegedly provide peace in the family and create an aura of tranquility. Other spells are concerned with the home—the residence or dwelling—itself. In many cases, in accordance with the belief that it's easier to prevent trouble than fix it, Happy Home Spells are meant to be performed as soon as or before one moves into a new home.

Basil Happiness Spells

Surround your dwelling with fresh basil so as to draw and increase joy within the home, and to stimulate tranquility, harmony, cooperation, and peace.

★ Grow basil in your garden and around the house
★ Place pots of fresh basil by your front entrance and around the perimeter of your home

★ If it's not possible to grow basil, then place fresh basil in a vase in a prominent spot in your kitchen, replacing it weekly or as soon as it starts to spoil

★ Cook with it as much as possible, or incorporate it into spellwork. (Since basil also draws love and money toward you, this isn't a painful, difficult recommendation!)

Blessed Water Spells

Certain magically charged formula waters simultaneously provide house blessings with space cleansing spells.

☀ Blessed Water Spell (1) Notre Dame Water

Notre Dame Water *promotes peace, calm, and serenity; summons benevolent spirits to your home and disperses any malevolent ones lingering about.*

Place a few spoonfuls into open dishes and distribute through the house. Add more as it evaporates.

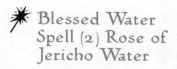

☀ Blessed Water Spell (2) Rose of Jericho Water

Rose of Jericho Water *has many uses including healing, cleansing, and protection. Its presence also encourages serenity and tranquility.*

1. Rehydrate a Rose of Jericho flower, by placing it into a dish and covering it with water.
2. After the rose blossoms, retain the flower but change the water weekly.
3. Don't throw out the old water— it's packed with magic power. Use it to attract blessings of peace, protection, and prosperity to your home.
4. Pour the old water out onto your front doorstep, in an auspicious shape. Choose a pentacle, hexagram, crescent moon, cross, or other. Sprinkle the shape of a sigil or rune, if you prefer.

☀ Blue Bird of Happiness Spell

Rare blue flowers confer peace and protection on a home. Grow cornflowers, delphiniums, bluebells, and hydrangeas. Reserve the blossoms;

dry, grind, and powder them, and then sprinkle the powder discreetly through the home.

Dispel Sadness Spell

When a home is filled with oppressive, contagious sadness, this spell can be very effective.

1. Hold a white candle in both hands while you think of all your sorrows and the causes for them.
2. Write these sorrows onto a piece of white paper. Ideally **Dove's Blood Ink** or myrrh-scented red ink should be used, but don't give yourself further cause for stress and grief. Just use red ink if that's easiest or whatever you have.
3. Anoint the page with honey.
4. Fold it up.
5. Light the candle. Use the candle flame to burn the note, while chanting something along the lines of:
   I give my sadness to the flames
   The Spirit of Fire eats my grief and pain
   (Substitute goddess, god, lady or lord of fire—whatever corresponds to your beliefs. You may also substitute the name of a fire spirit, if you choose.)

Family Unity Spells

The nature of a magic spell, whether positive or malevolent, is determined by intent rather than mechanics. Although many associate hair and nail clippings with malevolent manifestations of magic, vindictive figure spells, for instance, they also have benevolent applications. Although these spells ask for major blessings, they generally use only modest ingredients—typically intimate items, usually collected under a mother's direction, to provide safety, peace, and harmony among family members.

Family Unity Spell (1) Hair Clippings

1. Take a small hair clipping from every member of the family.
2. Roll it up in a leaf, rolling toward you.
3. Fasten it with a strand of the mother's hair (or the father, or whoever is the unifying focal point of the family).
4. Bury it under a tree.

✳ Family Unity Spell (2) Heal Rifts

To heal rifts and maintain the unity of the family, you will need one hair from the head of each person in the family or each person involved in the rift, whatever you deem appropriate.

1. Braid them and tie together with red silk thread.
2. Wrap the braid in more red silk thread, winding it and making seven knots in it.
3. Wrap this in a small square of white silk.
4. Bury this packet at a crossroads.

✳ Family Unity Spell (3) A Peaceful Home Charm Bag

The ingredients for this spell are:

A single strand of hair from each member of the family (add animal hairs from pets if you like, too)
Blue thread
A piece of angelica root
Essential oil of German chamomile
Balm of Gilead buds
Flax seeds
Lavender blossoms
Pink and white rose buds

1. Make a braid with the hair and thread.
2. Use the braid to tie a bow around the angelica root.
3. Anoint the root with one drop of chamomile oil for every member of the family.
4. Place the root together with the other ingredients into a sachet or conjure bag.

✳ Flax Seed Spell

Sprinkle flax seed over the threshold to end dissent and preserve harmony.

✳ Gardenia-Mimosa Spell

1. Make an infused oil of gardenia and mimosa.
2. Rub it on woodwork as appropriate.
3. Soak cotton balls and place strategically in rooms, to promote serenity and family harmony.

✳ Happiness Bath

This one is not for pregnant women!

1. Make an infusion by pouring boiling water over a bunch of parsley.

2. Strain out the parsley while the liquid remains hot and stir in cinnamon honey.
3. Add to your bath.

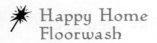 Happy Home

1. Place dried motherwort in a jar.
2. Surround it with family pictures.

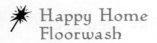 Happy Home Floorwash

Holy Water or **Marie Laveau Water**
Florida Water
White vinegar
Crushed sweet basil leaves
Crushed lavender blossoms
Cascarilla Powder

1. Pour boiling salted water over the lavender and sweet basil.
2. Let the botanicals steep for an hour, then strain out the solids.
3. Add the liquid, together with all other ingredients to a bucket filled with floorwash rinse water.
4. Use this water to cleanse all entrance areas as well as floors and windowsills.

Happy Home Fragrance Blends

Commercially prepared room fresheners are typically crafted from synthetic materials. Who knows what type of powers they possess, if any? Happy Home Spells include what might be considered magical room fresheners; their fragrances range from pleasant to beautiful, though their true goal is the encouragement of happiness, harmony, and cooperation.

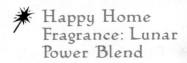 Happy Home Fragrance: Lunar Power Blend

Add essential oils of aloes wood, white camphor, and myrrh to an aroma burner and diffuse through the home to encourage a tranquil, happy atmosphere.

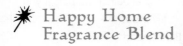 Happy Home Fragrance Blend

Add essential oils of coriander, Roman chamomile, and spearmint to an aroma burner and diffuse the fragrance through the home.

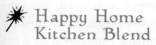

✳ Happy Home Herb Blend

Blend yerba santa, spearmint, and cascara sagrada in an open dish to encourage happiness and cooperative behavior.

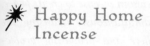

✳ Happy Home Kitchen Blend

Fill the home with the aroma of cinnamon and cloves. Brew the dried spices in water or cider to bring an aura of happiness and tranquility to the home.

✳ Happy Home Incense

Blend frankincense, myrrh, and liquidambar (storax) resins. Burn them to clear away negative energy and to encourage happy spirits, in all senses of that word.

✳ Happy Home Oil

Add gardenia petals, myrrh, and a pinch of five-finger grass to blended jojoba and coconut oil, together with a pinch of salt.

✳ Hearth Spell

That happy feeling of security and contentment so frequently derived from simply sitting beside a burning hearth or roaring fireplace indicates that magically more is going on than just burning some wood. The subliminal conjunction of male and female primal energy is extremely potent, protective, and full of blessings. Examples include nailed horseshoes, hexagrams, mortars and pestles, locks and keys. However, a subtler example was once ever-present: the blazing hearth. The hearth itself, or the fireplace, or its modern replacement the cauldron, represents the female principle; fire represents the male. A roaring hearth fire is thus a magical cauldron of transformation, full of power and blessings. Hence the desperate fear of ever letting the fire go out.

At one time, the hearth was the heart of the home. Various benevolent spiritual household guardians made their homes in or under the hearth. Unfortunately today an ever-present, ever-burning hearth fire is rare.

Light the fire, either in the hearth if you have one, or in a cauldron, and magically evoke feelings of happiness and security. Intensify the blessings by tossing magical botanicals into the fire; include any or all of the following: angelica, anise, pine, rosemary, and wisteria.

Home Protection Oil

Home Protection Oil provides spiritual protection and encourages a serene peaceful atmosphere to prevail in your home.

✳ Home Protection Oil Spell

1. Anoint areas of the home, especially areas perceived as vulnerable or areas that have suffered tension and arguments.
2. Reapply the oil once a week or as needed.

✳ Home Protection Spell

1. Collect rocks and pebbles from your travels, especially places where you felt safe and happy.
2. Charge them in your hands.
3. Keep them in an open terracotta pot.
4. Use to cast circles, for ritual or protection, as needed.

House Blessing Incense

The advantage of incense is that its fragrance permeates an area, leaving a lasting, lingering fragrant aura. Burn sufficient quantities to achieve that effect. Concentrate on troublesome areas first or fumigate the whole home. Benzoin is a resin deriving from Sumatra and Thailand. The ancient Egyptians imported it, favoring it for incense blends they considered "*joyful.*" Benzoin encourages a relaxed, tension-free atmosphere and is frequently the primary component of what are called "*house blessing incenses.*"

✳ House Blessing Incense (1) Basic Benzoin

Burn benzoin incense to create peace, while simultaneously cleansing the atmosphere and providing protection. Benzoin is also reputed to drive off harmful, malicious spirits.

✳ House Blessing Incense (2) Lighten up the Home Front

Which came first, the chicken or the egg? Depression and low energy are contagious. Sometimes people's energy suffers because the energy in the house is listless. Sometimes, however, the general energy of the home may be dolorous because it has absorbed and retained elements of depression

uffered by one or more of the residents. This fumigation simultaneously lightens up the home atmosphere
while helping to relieve an individual's feelings of depression.

1. Combine and blend equal parts
   benzoin, brown sugar, and dried
   powdered garlic.
2. Burn it in a cast iron pan.

Joy and Laughter Oil Spell

*Add essential oils of sweet orange,
lime, and pink grapefruit to a base of
jojoba oil. Dress candles with this oil
and burn throughout the home to
instill joy and laughter.*

Lima Bean Serenity Spell

*This spell is called for following or
in the midst of domestic arguments:
pierce three lima beans and string
them onto red silk thread. Carry
them for three days, then burn the
beans and thread for renewed peace
and harmony and to resolve conflicts.*

Negativity Begone!

*Cast this spell on a happy day, whose
ambience you'd like to preserve*

forever. Blend cumin with sea salt
and scatter a circle sunwise around
the perimeter of your property to
banish negativity and dissension.

New Home Spell

*Lu Pan is the Chinese divine patron
of carpenters, builders, and inventors.
In real life he was a contemporary of
Confucius. Following his death and
deification, Lu Pan provides peace in
the family and builds protection right
into a new home. It is particularly
auspicious to invoke him after building a new home or if you are the first
resident in a new building.*

1. When construction is complete or
   when you are ready to move in,
   have a party in Lu Pan's honor.
2. Burn Spirit Money and incense in
   his honor.
3. Set off fire-crackers to get rid of
   any malevolent spiritual party-
   crashers, who might wish to
   linger in your home. (Loud,
   percussive music works, too. It's
   hard to say which will annoy the
   neighbors more.)

Peace is notoriously difficult to
maintain, while an aura of arguing,
divisiveness, and general unpleasantness spreads all too easily. The

Bible suggests pouring oil on troubled waters. Although the recommendation is usually interpreted as metaphoric, some occultists have traditionally taken the suggestion literally.

✳ Oil on Troubled Water Spell (1) Literal Spell

1. Pour olive oil on the exact spot where an argument, unhappy confrontation, or scene of humiliation occurred.
2. Let it stay for a little, to absorb the tension and negative energy, before cleaning it up.

✳ Oil on Troubled Water Spell (2) Peace Water

This New Orleans Voodoo formula oil derives its inspiration from that same biblical reference to pouring oil over water. However, unlike the previous spell, **Peace Water** *will not increase chances of a broken neck, nor is someone ultimately forced to clean oil off the floor, perhaps leading to yet another argument as to who is responsible for cleaning up.* **Peace Water** *has another advantage. Purchasing most condition oils from*

commercial vendors leaves you won dering what's in the bottle, whethe there are any real botanicals in ther or whether you've been had. **Peac Water** *is a visually distinct oil: on look and you'll know whether it's rea*

Peace Water exists under th premise that oil and water won't mi It should have three (sometimes two distinct layers of oil and blue liqui True **Peace Water** *is visually beau tiful; when looked upon, it shoul evoke a sense of serenity and pleasure*

To provide and maintain peac within the home, keep a bottl of Peace Water prominently dis played in each room of the house, t encourage peaceful, happy coexis tence. In the event of tension, violenc or altercation shake the bottle **Peace Water** *, dispersing the layers Sprinkle as needed, wherever needed*

✳ Peaceful Home Oil Spell

This condition oil allegedly end familial quarrels and encourage reconciliation. An excellent spell t coincide with a family reunion!

1. Create Peaceful Home Oil by grinding brown sugar, bee pollen orrisroot, and peppermint leaves together.

2. Place this in a bottle together with pink rose petals.
3. Cover with sweet almond and jojoba oils.
4. Soak cotton balls in the oil and tuck them strategically through the room.

Onion Vacuum

1. On a Friday night when everyone else in the house is asleep, cut an onion in half.
2. Hold it up, visualize it as a psychic vacuum cleaner. Let it suck up all negativity.
3. Let it rest on a table.
4. Hold up one peeled crushed garlic clove.
5. Leave out for a little while.
6. Put it in a paper bag and dispose of it outside the home.

Relocation Spell: Comfrey Root

Tuck bits of comfrey root into possessions and furniture before loading them onto the moving van, to ensure their safe arrival at their destination.

Salt Spell

Toss a handful of salt into your cooking fire (stove, grill, or similar) every Monday morning to keep your family happy and good-natured.

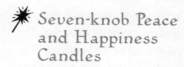

Seven-knob Peace and Happiness Candles

Seven-knob candles draw happiness to you while deleting hardship from your life. Inscribe blessings on each knob of a white seven-knob candle and burn one knob daily.

Sweet Dove Powder

Dove's blood, dove's eyes: magic spells are filled with references to doves. Doves are among the creatures most beloved by spirits of primal female powder, from Aphrodite and Asherah to Maria Padilha's black doves. Grind and powder bay laurel leaves, carnations, cardamom, cloves, marjoram, myrrh, and rose petals. Sprinkle the powder throughout the home to help create joy.

Tranquil Times Oil

Add crumbled white rose petals, cumin, and caraway seed to jojoba oil. Dress blue and white candles with this oil and burn daily or as needed.

Triple Happiness Luck Charm

1. Place three garlic cloves, three yellow rose buds, and three golden coins in a white bag. (The coins must be gold *colored*; anything ranging from real gold to chocolate coins in gold foil works.)
2. Tie the bag up with gold ribbon.
3. Holding the bag, dance around the perimeter of your home three times sunwise.
4. Dance around the perimeter three times counter-clockwise (moon-wise).
5. While dancing envision sealing in love and happiness.
6. Hang the bag over the front entrance using an iron nail.

Vanilla Spell

1. Stick a vanilla bean into a tightly sealed canister of sugar.
2. The aroma will infuse the sugar: use it in your cooking and feed it to your family, to instill feelings of peace, contentment, and happiness.

Wisteria Spell

*Place a piece of wisteria root in a bottle of **Florida Water** or your favorite fragrance. Anoint yourself daily for joy, happiness, and a peaceful heart.*

Yarrow Happy Home Spell

Decorate the home with boughs of fresh yarrow to banish sadness and negativity.

Young Boy Home Barometer Spell

There is a Taoist belief that boys under the age of seven embody so much pure yang energy that simply bringing one into the home and observing his behavior and reactions serves as an atmospheric barometer.

Invite a small boy to visit your home to provide you with a home-happiness diagnosis. Obviously you must choose your boy wisely; however, the following are the indicators to watch out for:

★ *A smiling, happy, playful, energetic, vigorous (but not destructive or overly hyperactive) child indicates positive energy. Things are fine*
★ *A child who falls asleep or is sluggish indicates that the energy in the home needs revitalizing*

★ *A tantrum, crankiness, major hissy fit, destructive impulses, or general bad behavior indicate that something is amiss. Instead of, or in addition to, rejuvenating the energy, some good cleansing spells may be in order*

★ *Temporarily and simultaneously opening all outside doors and windows encourages circulation of air and magical energy*

★ *Consider using the raucous Sound House Cleansing spell to liven up the atmosphere*

How do you revitalize that energy?

★ *Yang energy may be boosted by at least once a day opening blinds and shutters and allowing sunlight to stream in*

Healing Spells

Even those who swear that they don't believe in magic, don't approve of magic, and would *never* participate in magic will make an exception for a healing spell. It's amazing what illness or affliction, especially those that defy diagnosis or conventional treatment, will stimulate us to do.

Healing spells are not intended to be used *instead* of conventional, traditional, or other methods of healing. Instead they work best in conjunction with them, reinforcing other systems, enhancing their power and the likelihood of recovery. Many spells are intended to be cast after one has already exhausted other more conventional resources.

Magical healing spells may be particularly beneficial for those ailments that resist conventional identification because magic possesses a broader definition of the origins of illness:

★ *Illness or disability may derive from purely neutral physical causes*
★ *Illness or disability may derive from spiritual and/or magical causes*
★ *Illness or disability may derive from a combination of physical/spiritual and/or magical causes*

Straightforward physical illnesses are no more than what they appear: you got stuck in the rain; you caught a cold. You ate too much sugar and didn't brush your teeth; now you have cavities. You smoked four packs a day; now you have emphysema. Although the cause of illness is physical, magic may still be used to enhance recovery. In general, however, cure matches source. Straightforward ailments demand straightforward treatment.

Spiritual and magical ailments are more complex. In order to determine the correct course of treatment, it must be determined whether an ailment's ultimate source is human- or spirit-derived.

★ *Magical ailments of human derivation may be the result of a malevolent spell or the Evil Eye*
★ *Spirit-sent ailments are more complex: was illness caused intentionally? Illness may have been sent as punishment, as an attempt at communication, or simply inadvertently*

There's also another magical way to consider illness: health, the state of harmonious balance, is the natural state. Thus illness, by definition, indicates magical workings or spiritual imbalance, the intensity of the illness defining the intensity of the magical or spiritual situation. Sudden surprising severe illness (particularly when fatal) tends to be interpreted as either deriving from human sources (a hex) or from minor low-level spirits. Major diseases, especially smallpox, may be identified with specific well-known spirits. Ailments that are curious, hard to pin down, resist diagnosis, and are incurable (the person never gets better or worse but lingers in a malaise) are also often attributed to major spirits. In this situation, the reason behind the illness may be to stimulate the afflicted person to contact the spirit, not to kill that person. Once spiritual interaction occurs, the illness passes or is controlled.

Healer's Spells

Although concern is focused on the patient, the healer is considered vulnerable during treatment, too.

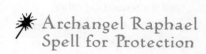

✳ Archangel Raphael Spell for Protection

The archangel Raphael sponsors and protects nurses, physicians, pharmacists, and healers of all kind.

Request his assistance to accomplish your healing and also to protect you before, during, and after.

1. Dedicate a white candle to Raphael.
2. Hold the candle in your hands to charge it with your desire.
3. Place a small silver or iron fish charm near the candle.
4. When the candle has burned completely, carry or wear the fish charm. Reserve any auspicious-looking remnants of wax in a mojo bag or magic box.

Distance Healing Spells

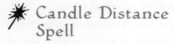

Candle Distance Spell

This candle spell, although intended to assist in another's healing, may also be cast for oneself.

1. Carve a white candle (plain, human figure, cross, or "praying hands" shape) to reflect the person for whom the healing spell is intended. (In other words, carve the other person's name, identifying information, and so on.)
2. Soak hyssop in olive oil and then use the oil to dress the candle.

3. Burn the candle; this is traditionally accompanied by the recitation of psalms or other sacred verses.

Doll Distance Healing Spell

Because once upon a time Chinese women wouldn't undress before a doctor (even today a visit to a traditional Chinese physician rarely involves undressing), beautiful, anatomically correct naked dolls were carved from ivory. These dolls served as a communications device between doctor and patient; pain, illness, affliction, and methods of healing could be demonstrated on the doll with minimum embarrassment. These dolls are still sometimes found in antique shops; reproductions are also available. Use this type of doll or craft or use a less realistic one to perform magical distance healing.

1. Hold the doll in your hands to charge it with your intentions and healing energy.
2. Murmur healing incantations and blessings over the doll.
3. Massage the doll with blended castor and olive oils, scented with essential oil of lavender.

4. Place the doll within a ring of burning healing candles.
5. Repeat as needed until the healing is complete.

Peppermint Distance Healing Spell

1. Place peppermint leaves on top of a photograph of the patient.
2. Charge a blue candle with your desire.
3. Carve and dress the candle as desired.
4. Burn it beside the photograph.
5. When the candle has burned down, dispose of the peppermint leaves.
6. Repeat as needed, with fresh leaves each time.

Psalm Distance Healing Spell

1. Write out a petition of healing and/or blessings of improved health on a piece of parchment.
2. Place this in a dish containing **Holy Water** or **Marie Laveau Water**.
3. Murmur psalms over this dish.
4. When the spell feels complete, remove the parchment, and

allow it to dry. It may be preserved, buried, or given to the spell's target as a protective talisman.

Talisman Distance Healing Spell

To promote distance healing, charge stones with healing energy, then give them to the spell's target as a talisman. Choose any crystal that feels best to you; however, traditionally alexandrite, Herkimer diamonds, lodestones, moonstones, pearls, and quartz crystals are considered most effective.

1. Burn a white candle near Dr. Jose Gregorio's image, or burn a commercially manufactured Jose Gregorio Hernandez seven-day candle.
2. Place offerings in front of his votive image. Cigarettes are perhaps an inappropriate offering for a medical doctor; however, the standard offering of a glass of water or rum would probably not be refused.

✳ Gemstone Shield Spells

Certain crystal gemstones create a protective shield so that the healer may accomplish his or her mission without fear.

1. Carry or wear bloodstone, clear quartz, and/or black tourmaline during healing spells and rituals.
2. Anoint with **Protection Oil** if desired.
3. Cleanse after each magical session.

This is particularly effective for spells or other attempts to heal using body-working therapies, such as massage.

✳ Healer's Spell Crystal Protection

Crystal gemstones can be extremely beneficial in healing; however they are also very appealing to fairies. Do your valued crystals keep disappearing? To prevent the fairies from filching precious crystals:

1. When not in use, keep the crystals safe in an iron box.
2. Fairies can be beneficial in healing too: to remain in their good graces, offer them a gift of glass marbles instead.

✳ Rosemary Infusion of Power

Washing your hands with an infusion of rosemary magically empowers and enhances all healing.

Create an infusion by pouring boiling water over rosemary. Allow it to cool, then strain. This may be done immediately prior to healing or the liquid may be bottled and refrigerated for later use.

General Healing Spells

The following are spells to maintain good health, enhance immunity, provide general healing, and practice preventive magic.

✳ Acorn Good Health Spell

Acorns are sacred signs of life. Carry an odd-numbered quantity of acorns in a green or red charm bag to maintain good health.

Agrimony Bath

This cleansing provides psychic and magical healing.

1. Make a strong infusion by pouring boiling water over agrimony.
2. Let it cool, then strain out the botanical material.
3. Dip a white cloth into the infusion and gently bathe the patient.

Amber Beads
Disease Prevention

Amber beads are perceived as bolstering health; however, not just any amber beads will do. Amber beads carved into the shapes of genitals, whether very literally or just vaguely reminiscent, allegedly provide protection, especially regarding health. Wear or carry as needed.

Banish Affliction Spell

Touch the relevant part of the body, wherever healing or relief is needed, with three fingers: the thumb, middle, and ring fingers. Stretch the other two out straight and chant:

Go away!
It doesn't matter whether you originated today or earlier or anytime
This illness, this pain, this swelling, this tumor, this rash [fill in as appropriate]
I call it out, I lead it out, I speak it out,
I call it gone, I lead it gone, I speak it gone,
I call it vanished, I lead it vanished, I speak it vanished
Through this spell, from my limbs and bones, my flesh and blood
Vanish pain, vanish illness, vanish suffering!

Bloody Stick Transference Spell

According to magical theory, illness may be removed via methods of transference. The following ritual must be accomplished in complete and total silence.

1. Position yourself by a stream so that the water runs away from you.
2. Take a hazel or elder stick.
3. Carve your name into it.
4. Make three small slices into the stick.

5. Fill these slices with your blood, either menstrual blood or a few drops obtained by pricking your finger.
6. Throw the stick over your left shoulder or between your legs into water that must be flowing away from you, ideally rapidly.
7. Walk away without looking back.

✳ Clothing Spell

Among various Dravidian traditions of India, the concept of the contagious aspect of illness extends to the magical. Thus the sick person's clothes and bed linens become impregnated by the disease and are thus dangerous. This is a magical impregnation, beyond what laundering with antibacterial soap can cure.

To counteract, bring fabrics to a place with extreme baraka or benevolent sacred magic power, to regenerate, revitalize, and make them safe. Hang the clothes or linen on a sacred tree, in a holy place, or in a shrine. (This is also beneficial for new linens or ritual clothing. Beyond safety precautions and preventive measures, this creates highly charged talismanic fabrics.)

Once a year, during the month of May, masses of Romany people converge on the French town of Les Saintes-Maries-de-la-Mer, at the shrine of their matron saint, Sarah Kali. Sarah Kali's identity is subject to interpretation. She may be the Egyptian servant who accompanied Mary Magdalene, Mary and Martha of Bethany and Mary Salome to France; she may be a Romany priestess of Ishtar who greeted them upon arrival in Provence; she may be the daughter of Mary Magdalene and Jesus Christ; or she may be the Hindu deity Kali in disguise, having accompanied the Romany from India.

A beautiful statue of Sarah Kali is enshrined within an ancient grotto, believed to have once been a venue for celebrating the mysteries of Mithras. During her festival, the statue is carried in procession to the sea where it is immersed and bathed. Brought back to her shrine, she is then dressed in finery.

It is traditional to bring offerings to the statue in conjunction with petitions asked and received. However Sarah Kali also accepts offerings of clothing from those suffering from illness or in need of healing. The clothing is placed on her body and creates the connection between the deity and the petitioner. As the clothing absorbs the deity's power, the healing is transmitted to the petitioner, who may have attended the festival or may be far away. This principle may also be applied to a personal shrine and a votive image close to your heart.

Color Therapy

Every color has the capacity to heal. Each color has specific magic powers best suited for certain ailments or physical conditions. Expose yourself to concentrated doses of the appropriate color(s) to avail yourself of their healing energy. Surround yourself with the needed color; wear it, gaze, and meditate upon it.

Access the healing magic of color through:

★ *Crystals. Although each crystal gemstone possesses its own specific healing powers, generalities may be drawn based on color. Select crystals in the color range most beneficial for you: use them in*

massage, meditation, and other healing rituals

★ *Color baths. Tint the water so that it coordinates with your healing needs. There are commercially available "color baths." In addition, the nineteenth-century Bavarian cleric and healer, Father Sebastian Kneipp, pioneered a system of hydrotherapy. Although there seems to be no evidence connecting Father Kneipp's theories to color healing, his baths, now commercially available, are vividly colored and may be the most accessible color bath, although this may not have been their original intent. However, you can also tint the water yourself with food coloring and various natural plant dyes. Just make sure whatever you use is safe and non-toxic*

★ *Candle magic. Coordinate candle colors with your particular ailment*

★ BLACK: physical and mental exhaustion
★ BLUE: emotional imbalance, post-traumatic stress, throat disorders, speech disorders, headaches, toothaches, insomnia, susto
★ BROWN: vertigo, disorientation, psychic torpor
★ GREEN: physical healing, cancer, ulcers, high blood pressure, heart trouble
★ ORANGE: bowel and digestive disorders, arthritis, asthma, fevers, bronchitis and related bronchial ailments
★ RED: physical disabilities, blood disorders, HIV and AIDS, anemia, vitamin deficiency, impotence, infertility
★ YELLOW: stomach problems, skin disorders, depression due to heartache

☀ Colored Water Spells

1. Fill clear glass or cut crystal bottles with spring water.
2. Tint the water the desired shade.
3. Place the bottle(s) in a sunny window.
4. Sit, relax, and gaze at the color(s).

☀ Color Spell: Maximum Intensity

Different methods of accessing the magic healing power of colors aren't mutually exclusive but may be used in conjunction. The following combination of colors, candles, crystals, and chants allegedly helps prevent illness as well as overcome it.

1. Choose the appropriate color.
2. Burn candles in the corresponding color.
3. Surround them with color-coordinated crystal gemstones and color-water bottles.
4. This spell may be further empowered by chanting sacred verses, especially Habakkuk 3:3–5.

Convalescence Spells

Maintain the magic during convalescence to speed healing and protect a vulnerable aura.

 Convalescence Spell: Coffee

Coffee allegedly invigorates and empowers magically. Brew good fresh strong coffee. Add an odd number of cups to the bath and bathe.

Convalescence Spell: Rue

Wear a sprig of fresh rue pinned to your clothing during convalescence for protection and to magically speed healing.

 Crossroads Healing Spell

One never knows exactly whom one will meet at the crossroads. Crossroads are perceived as a magic junction full of swirling energies, powers, and spirits. This spell presumes that at least some of these forces will be sympathetic to your plea.

1. Bring bread and a libation to a crossroads.
2. Pour out the libation and place the bread on the ground.
3. Turn in all applicable directions, each time making a request for healing and improved health.
4. Return home without looking back.

Doll Spell Healing Doll Spell

Illness may be transferred by using dolls and figurines. This ancient Assyrian formula, intended to restore good health to someone who is ailing, requires the creation of a clay or wax figurine. It should look anonymous and not resemble either the person suffering from the ailment or anyone else.

1. Someone other than the ailing person is appointed to communicate with the disease spirit. The goal is to entice the illness to leave the human and enter the doll instead. Consider how this is to be accomplished before beginning the spell. Remember, low-level spirit entities, which include many of the lesser disease spirits, are not overly blessed with intelligence.
2. As soon as it's apparent that the disease demon has taken the bait and entered the doll, immediately remove the doll from the premises and dispose of it far from home.
3. Return via a circuitous route.
4. Both the target of the spell (the patient) and the person who communicated with the disease spirit should undergo extensive cleansing and protective rituals.

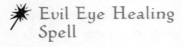

Earth-absorbing Healing Spell

In theory, this spell is dedicated to a deity, the "you" referred to in the chant. Leave it ambiguous or substitute the name of your choice. The spell may also be dedicated to the powers of Earth. The end result is that the illness or affliction magically departs from your body and is absorbed by Earth.

Chant the following, nine times:

I think of you.
Heal my___ [fill in the blank].
Let Earth retain the illness.
Let health remain with me.

Put your hands flat on Earth and spit.

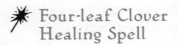

Evil Eye Healing Spell

A method of healing illness caused by the Evil Eye: remove the influence by massaging the body with a whole raw egg, and then bathe the person with **Holy Water**.

Four-leaf Clover Healing Spell

Four-leaf clovers allegedly possess magical healing powers. If you can't find one, create one. This spell is especially beneficial if one person does it for another.

Cut a four-leaf clover shape from paper or a sheet of copper or tin. Empower it with blessings of healing then hang it near the patient or within their line of sight to magically ease pain, bring joy, stimulate healing, and speed recovery.

Fumigation Against Illness and Infection Spell

Grind small amounts of dried juniper and dried rosemary together. Sprinkle the resulting powder on lit charcoal.

For greater intensity, an outdoor ritual may be effected, to transmit the healing fumes into the greater atmosphere. Build a small fire with juniper wood, and feed it with rosemary branches.

Knot Healing Spells

Many healing spells utilize the principles of knot magic. Remember to focus your intent and desire as you pull the knot.

✳ Knot Healing Spell (1)

This spell comes from Central Asia.

1. Spin or obtain a three-colored cord: blue, green, and red.
2. Tie one knot in the cord for seven consecutive days.
3. After the seventh day and the seventh knot, bury the cord in an inaccessible spot. The disease should disappear as the cord rots.

✳ Knot Healing Spell (2)

Sometimes you have to tie, but sometimes you have to untie. Visualize the illness and suffering as you tie the initial knots. You're not wishing the illness—quite the opposite. You're essentially transferring the illness into the knot. Then visualize relief as the knots are untied; the illness's terrible energy dispersing into the atmosphere.

1. Tie seven knots in a string.
2. Make it into a bracelet for the patient.
3. Untie one knot each day.
4. On the last day, unravel the thread and throw everything into running living water, flowing away from the patient's location.

Originally this spell began with the spinning of the thread, accompanied by sincere prayer and the repetition of sacred texts.

✳ Knot Spell: Peony Roots

Peony, the healing plant of the ancient Greeks, is allegedly a plant of divine origin formed from moonbeams. It's associated with the divine healer, Asklepios. According to legend, Asklepios was the child of Apollo and his priestess, a princess. While pregnant she fell in love with a mortal man and attempted to marry him. Apollo, jealous and infuriated, killed her but saved baby Asklepios from her funeral pyre. Or so goes the story. Bad things seem to happen to women who catch Apollo's romantic interest, if we recall some other priestesses, such as Daphne and Cassandra.

In any case, Apollo nurtured his son and taught him secrets of healing. Asklepios became such a good doctor that he revived the dead. This upset the balance of nature and upset the gods; Hades in particular was livid, so Asklepios was immediately killed and deified.

Fashion a necklace from peony roots and have the patient wear it around his or her neck. This allegedly wards off illness and evil and is also beneficial for soothing, preventing, or minimizing seizure disorders.

Milagros

The milagro (Spanish for *"miracle"*) is a magical tool that may be used as a charm, amulet, votive offering, or spiritual communications device. Although milagros may be used in other types of spells, they are most frequently dedicated to healing.

They may also be formed from any material, from precious gems to wax, but most milagros are cut from inexpensive silver-colored metal. The shape of the milagro is chosen to correspond with an ailment or affliction. Milagros take the form of isolated body parts, the most common being hands, heads, feet, legs, arms, eyes, male and female genitals, breasts, eyes, ears, noses, and hearts. Uteruses are traditionally represented by images of toads or hedgehogs, reflecting medieval conceptions of the female reproductive system.

The purpose of the milagro is to either strengthen or heal the corresponding part of the body, to prevent, or to heal a disorder. Milagros may be used in ritual to help extract ills afflicting the

corresponding part, but they are most commonly used as a spiritual communication device.

✳ Milagro Spiritual Petition Spell

1. Determine to whom your petition is to be directed and thus to whom the milagro will be presented. Milagros may be presented at a shrine (many Latin American cathedrals have special areas reserved for such petitions) or upon a home altar. Determine what you will give in exchange, should the healing be effected.
2. Light candles and do whatever is necessary to draw attention toward your petition.
3. Hold the milagro in your hands to charge it with your desired goal.
4. Make your request and your vow.

✳ Milagro Good Health Maintenance Spell

Because milagros strengthen corresponding parts, they may also be used to maintain a state of good health. Collect assorted milagros, corresponding to parts for which you may have concern. Pin them to a fabric-covered board. Maintain quartz crystal

nearby to further empower the mila-gros, just in case any Direct Application Spells should ever become necessary.

✳ Mistletoe Ring

Carve a ring from mistletoe (and wear it!) to ward off illness.

✳ Pearls of Health

An expensive prescription for maintaining good health suggests you keep a bowl filled with real pearls in easy reach. Periodically run your fingers through them. This allegedly enhances the immune system, stimulates health, and encourages longevity.

✳ Potato Health Preservation Spell

Potatoes possess an absorbing quality, similar to eggs or coconuts. Use this spell to maintain good health or to magically absorb and eliminate lingering minor ailments.

. Carry a small potato, such as a fingerling, in your pocket or medicine bag, to ward off disease and other evils.

2. Carry the potato until it begins to smell, rot, or somehow become distasteful. (If you don't want to touch it, then it's time to stop carrying it.) Essentially, it's full like a vacuum bag.
3. Discard and replace.

✳ Radiant Health Oil

1. Grind and powder angelica root, calendula, eucalyptus, lavender, juniper, and rosemary.
2. Cover with two parts jojoba oil to one part castor oil.
3. Carve candles to suit your situation and dress with **Radiant Health Oil** to achieve and maintain a healthy condition.

✳ Rose of Jericho Water Spell

The Rose of Jericho is also known as the "Resurrection Plant" because of its powers of revival. Let those powers be transferred to you. **Rose of Jericho Water** provides general vitality and allegedly prevents illness. Experiment and see what it can do.

1. Once the rose has blossomed, play with it and the water. Touch the rose very gently, let your

fingers play in the water, in the meantime praying, petitioning, and visualizing good fortune and radiant health.

2. Add **Rose of Jericho Water** to your bath or use it in compresses to bathe the brow.

✳ Saint John's Eve Healing Spell

Among mugwort's many nicknames is Saint John's girdle, causing frequent confusion with Saint John's Wort. Allegedly John the Baptist wore a girdle (belt) woven from mugwort while in the wilderness. A similar magic belt allegedly provides you with good health.

In time for Saint John's Eve, weave a magic belt from mugwort, knotting your hopes and intentions into the girdle. Wear it while dancing around the bonfire; at some point before the night ends and the bonfire burns out, toss the belt into the flames to receive a year of good health.

✳ Send the Disease Out to Sea Spell

Every magical tradition on Earth has its personal quirks and predilections that distinguish it from others. Russian magic is characterized by *incredibly poetic, evocative word-charm formulas. They are formulaic because the beginning of the chant i standardized, something like th "Once upon a time" or "Once there was and once there wasn't traditional beginnings for fair tales. When you hear those openings you know you've entered the realm o fairy tales. Similarly, these stan dardized word charms signal tha you've entered the realm of enchant ment. Inevitably the formula allow you an opening at the end to person alize the spell.*

Chant aloud:

On Earth there is an ocean
In the ocean there is a sea
In the sea there is water
In the water there is an island
On the island is land
On the land is a forest
In the forest there are woods
In the woods there are trees
In the trees there is one tree
On that tree is a bough
On that bough is a branch
On that branch is a creature
That creature is a [name it]
Illness! Go into that _____ [name the creature].

(If you want to diminish it eve further, give the creature a parasite.

Stinging Nettles Spell

Keep fresh stinging nettles under the patient's bed. Replace them daily, burning the old nettles.

Sweet Grass Health Protection Spell

Wear sweet grass roots as necklaces or sew them onto blankets and clothing. This Cheyenne charm also allegedly works as a disease preventative.

Three Angels' Health Spell

Chant:

Three angels stand on the far side of
    Jordan
One binds, one resolves,
One cries out, Kadosh, Kadosh,
    Kadosh!

Continue with further chants and recitations of sacred texts. Tell the three angels what you need.

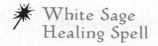
White Sage Healing Spell

White sage, indigenous to North America, is considered one of the most potent cleansing and protective botanicals. Once common, it is now endangered; for maximum benefit and to preserve this botanical wonder, grow and use your own. Burn quantities of white sage to magically drive away illness.

Yerba Santa Spells

Erictyon californicum, a California native, is most popularly known as yerba santa, literally "sacred herb." Another name for this botanical is "bear weed," indicating its use as a miracle healer.

Yerba Santa Prevention Spell

Wear the herb around your neck to prevent illness and injury.

Yerba Santa Healing Spell

Burn yerba santa in the sick room to disperse disease demons and to psychically empower the ailing person.

Specific Ailments

Common Cold

✳ Amber Temperature Control Spell

Minimize and ward off chills by wearing tightly beaded amber necklaces. Amber is believed to absorb body heat and retain it, thus magically creating a balancing effect.

✳ Ruby Water Spell

Astrologically aligned with the sun, rubies are believed to radiate hot red cosmic rays that cure illnesses caused and aggravated by cold. Steep a ruby in a clean vessel filled with pure, spring water. Remove the ruby and drink the water.

Ruby crystal gemstone elixir (Alaska Flower Remedies) may be substituted, although do not exceed the manufacturer's recommended dosage. Wearing a ruby is also supposed to help.

Ruby Water is also recommended for anemia and other ailments associated with blood, including circulatory deficiencies, low (but not high, which it will aggravate) blood pressure, infertility, and (my favorite) stupidity.

Fever

Today, the term "fever" very specifically refers to elevated body temperature. Once upon a time medical terminology wasn't necessarily as specific as it is today. Spells for fever target a whole host of ailments united only by a shared tendency toward elevated temperature. These spells are indicated for any ailment that even loosely falls under that category, including outbreaks of flu.

✳ ABRACADABRA!

Perhaps the most famous spell in the world still retains its mysteries. What does the word mean? Various theories regarding its derivation are offered and hotly debated. Is it related to the Gnostic Spirit, Abraxas, recalled fondly by fans of Hermann Hesse's novel, Steppenwolf? Is it from the Chaldean abbada ke dabra, "perish like the word?" Is it derived from Hebrew Abreq ad Habra, "hurl your thunderbolt even unto death," or is it a corruption of the Hebrew word bracha ("blessing") and dabar ("action, word")? Maybe it's none of the above but the name of a now forgotten spirit.

Despite its modern usage as a joke magical word charm, something like hocus pocus *or* bippety-boppety-boo, Abracadabra *is, in fact, a written charm intended to provide physical healing. It is the most famous of a series of diminishing word charms, most common to Semitic magic. Presumably, as the word diminishes, so does the fever, pain, or illness.*

Instructions appear in the first written reference to the spell in the second century CE, *from Quintus Serenus Sammonicus, the personal physician to the Roman Emperor Septimius Severus. For relief from fever:*

1. Inscribe the word "abracadabra" on parchment or metal lamella.
2. Attach this word charm to a piece of flax long enough to be worn around the patient's neck.
3. The charm must be worn around the neck for nine days then thrown away over the left shoulder into water flowing east.

Tips for writing "abracadabra:"

★ *Write neatly and carefully, focusing on intention as you write. Don't let your mind wander*
★ *The letters are not supposed to touch each other*
★ Abracadabra *is believed most effective when written with Hebrew letters because the word in*

Hebrew contains nine letters, nine being the supreme number of power

There are various methods of using the charm. The inverted triangle is recommended for fever:

```
A B R A C A D A B R A
B R A C A D A B R A
R A C A D A B R A
A C A D A B R A
C A D A B R A
A D A B R A
D A B R A
A B R A
B R A
R A
A
```

An upward-facing triangle is used to heal and relieve asthma:

```
A
A B
A B R
A B R A
A B R A C
A B R A C A
A B R A C A D
A B R A C A D A
A B R A C A D A B
A B R A C A D A B R
A B R A C A D A B R A
```

Abracadabra may also be written as a parallelogram, consisting of two

triangles, for enhanced healing and empowerment:

```
          A
        R   A
      B   R   A
    A   B   R   A
  D   A   B   R   A
A   D   A   B   R   A
C   A   D   A   B   R   A
A   C   A   D   A   B   R   A
R   A   C   A   D   A   B   R   A
B   R   A   C   A   D   A   B   R   A
A   B   R   A   C   A   D   A   B   R   A
  B   R   A   C   A   D   A   B   R   A
    R   A   C   A   D   A   B   R   A
      A   C   A   D   A   B   R   A
        C   A   D   A   B   R   A
          A   D   A   B   R   A
            D   A   B   R   A
              A   B   R   A
                B   R   A
                  R   A
                    A
```

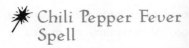

Chili Pepper Fever Spell

1. Break two chili peppers each in half.
2. Place them on an old cloth.
3. Sprinkle them with black mustard seeds and tamarind.
4. Wrap up the packet, knotting it shut.
5. Pass this over the afflicted person three times.
6. Have him or her spit on the bundle three times.
7. Throw the packet into a fire.

Because rubies are believed to have a warming effect on the body, it's recommended that ruby jewelry be removed from those suffering fever.

Headache/Migraine

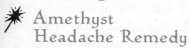

Amethyst Headache Remedy

Because of amethyst's associations with Dionysus and alcohol (see Banishing Spells), presumably this magical cure is especially beneficial for those morning-after headaches.

1. Immerse an amethyst in moderately hot water for seven minutes.
2. Gently pat it dry.
3. Carefully rub the amethyst over affected areas plus the back of the neck.

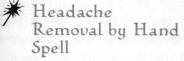

Headache Removal by Hand Spell

Potatoes, coconuts, and eggs are all considered "absorbent" powers used to remove illness and spiritual debris. The human hand has similar properties. Test your powers of healing. See if you can magically remove someone else's headache. Eggs, coconuts, and potatoes are thrown out following use; however, in this case, so as to avoid you being saddled with the headache, other methods of transference and disposal are used.

1. Lay your hand on the brow of the person suffering from headache.
2. Try to draw the headache into your palm but don't allow it to travel past your palm, not up your arm or any farther. You don't want to inherit the headache.
3. As soon as you feel it or the other person expresses relief, immediately drive a nail into the wall.

It's not safe to use this technique for anything other than a minor ailment, without extensive magical preparation. If you fear inheriting the headache, use a lodestone as a tool instead of your palm. Alternatively, use a flat hand charm, such as a hand of Fatima or a hamsa, ideally crafted from silver.

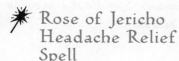

Rose of Jericho Headache Relief Spell

*Soak a white cloth in **Rose of Jericho Water** to create a compress. Place it onto your forehead or the back of the neck to provide relief.*

✴ Stony Head Headache Spell

Pick herbs that are growing on the head of a stone statue. Tie them up with a red thread and place them on the spot where your head hurts. This allegedly removes the pain. Mugwort and/or peppermint are considered the most efficacious of the herbs.

If you suffer from frequent headaches, you may want to train your herbs to grow this way, even if you have to knock the statue's head onto the ground. Both the preferred plants are hardy growers who like stony soil.

✴ Watery Crossroads Spell

For chronic headache take water from the spot where two streams or rivers merge, essentially the water's crossroads. Sprinkle this water on the patient.

Pain Relief Spells

✴ Chestnut Pain Relief Spell

Horse chestnuts are reputed to absorb physical pain, and are especially effective for joint pain:

1. Place a bowl of horse chestnuts in the afflicted person's room.
2. Wash the nuts daily in cool spring water to enhance their capacity to absorb pain, and then dry them well.
3. Should a nut crack, decay, or appear damaged, discard it immediately and replace.

Enhance the power of the chestnuts by ringing the bowl with clear quartz crystal.

✴ Copper Garter Spell

Copper's affinity for healing the aches and pains of arthritis go beyond the popular bracelet. For maximum effectiveness, attach copper charms to a red garter and wear it.

✴ Potato Spell

Place a potato in your pocket to draw out the pain and stiffness of rheumatism.

✳ Stone Pain Removal Spell

1. Hold a rock in your hand and visualize it absorbing your pain.
2. Wrap barley straw around the stone, while maintaining this visualization.
3. Throw the stone into living water flowing away from you.

Toothache/Dental Health

✳ Abracadabra/Sator Full Strength Combination Dental Health Spell

To remedy toothache, chant the Abracadabra spell (instead of writing it) three times, followed by three repetitions of the SATOR square (*see* Pregnancy and Childbirth Spells).

✳ Double Hazelnut Tooth Relief

Find a double hazelnut and carry it within a red drawstring bag to relieve dental pain.

✳ Iron Dental Health Spell

The following is a German recommendation to soothe a toothache. Heat a horseshoe or other piece of iron until extremely hot. Pour oil onto the heated iron. The rising fumes will allegedly ease the pain. If it is safe to do so (there's no need to exchange toothache for a painful scald), bend over the fumes, exposing the tender spot.

Hexes and Their Antidotes

Admit it: this is the first page to which you turned. With the exception of love and money spells, nothing fascinates like a mean, wicked spell. Magic power used so benevolently to draw health, wealth, stability, love, and fertility can also be used as aggressive, punishing conduits of frustration, anger, and resentment toward others, hence the hex. These spells define why some fear magic.

These are not socially respectable spells, to say the least. Lest you take them to represent the state of modern magic, let me emphatically add that in the current cultural climate of twenty-first-century witchcraft, hexes, curses, and other malevolent spells are incredibly *dépassé*. Modern Wicca passionately emphasizes the three-fold law: as you reap, so you shall sow. Whatever magical intention and energy you put forth will come back to you at least three times over, if not seven, nine, or twenty-one times. Many modern Wiccans hesitate before casting a reasonably innocuous love or employment spell on the off-chance that the other party's free will might be compromised. In that context spells that deliberately attempt to cause someone strife, misery, and unhappiness are perceived as abhorrent indeed.

These are the spells that have earned magic its evil reputation—or are they?

In fact ethical considerations of what constitutes *"wicked magic"* date back to that proverbial time immemorial. According to the purest magic theory, power is neutral. Malevolence or benevolence depends entirely upon what is done with this power. Any power can be used for good or ill. This theoretical concept hasn't always satisfied people. Since the very earliest times, there's been debate about *"good magic"* versus *"bad magic."*

Debates about the appropriate use of magic power have existed as long as there has been awareness of this power, and show no sign of abatement. Some fear magic in its entirety, some fear aspects of magic, while others recognize its inherent sacred quality. According to medieval master magician, Cornelius Agrippa, a theologian whose time coincided with European witch hunts, the practice of magic was one of the lawful ways to attain knowledge of God and nature.

At some point, in the Common Era, *"good"* and *"bad"* magic transformed into *"white"* and *"black"* magic, terms that still retain popularity. Those terms are not used in this book. The straightforward terms *"malevolent"* or *"benevolent"* are used instead. At best, it's disingenuous to use those terms (white and black magic) today, pretending that they don't have racial and ethnic connotations. People protest that they don't mean the phrase *that way* but it's difficult to understand how else to interpret it in the context of a world where, historically, darker-skinned minority groups have been discriminated against or persecuted for magical practice and witchcraft by the lighter-skinned majority, whether in Europe (Jews, Romany, Saami), North Africa (Gnawa), North America (Native Americans, those of African descent), or South America (indigenous Americans, those of African descent).

Why would anyone send a hex or a curse anyway?

The first reason is the obvious: bad people do bad things. The destructive impulse can be extremely potent.

Other answers are more complex and ambiguous. In some cases, there may be an extremely fine line between a hex and a justice spell. We're very quick to jump to conclusions these days and automatically brand every hex-caster as evil; however, this perception may derive from the luxurious vantage of comfortable times. People don't create or cast courtcase spells unless there's at least a remote possibility of legal justice. What if you exist in a time or place where you or your loved ones are at the mercy of others more powerful than you and there is no recourse, none, not at all, to justice? What do you do then? Hexes are not an uncommon response. Hexes may be cast as a desperate attempt to end persecution and abuse.

In the same manner that Witch Wars escalate, with witches lobbing spells at each other until it's impossible to determine who cast the first spell, one shouldn't always assume that the hex is the initiating action. It may be cast in response to a terrible violation, crime, or injustice.

Many of the most powerful hexes ultimately call on sacred—or infernal—powers to deliver the punishment. It isn't the mechanical action of the spell that makes the successful accomplishment of a hex possible. It's the passionate anger, hatred, and rage that fuel it. Yet for all that hatred and rage, the spell-caster is plotting a hex, not committing murder. The average hex-caster, or at least those who initially derived these spells, was either not in a position to act on these impulses or was leaving it in the hands of divine justice. Those extreme situations (and there are fine lines; the Justice spell against a rapist could conceivably be interpreted as a hex, as could the Green Devil Spell to regain a cash debt owed) are perhaps the only situations that could justify some of these spells.

Hexes also sometimes serve a function that transcends magic: enforcement of social order. Many of the most malevolent hexes are secret: black candles burned in private or funeral services chanted over your enemy. Other hexes, however, are extremely public: the spell is activated by "dusting" the target's doorstep. Something is left on the target's front doorstep for them to find when they open the door. It's quite likely that by the time the target discovers the hex, all the neighbors and passers-by have already witnessed it. Although these spells are nominally anonymous (the identity of the spell-caster is reputedly unknown), realistically many in the community will know exactly who cast the hex. If someone is behaving in a manner that is perceived as dangerous or undesirable, dusting their doorstep is traditionally a way of informing them that others are unhappy, giving them an opportunity to change their ways or leave. In these cases, hexes may be understood in terms of intimidation rather than magic. And some of them are threatening indeed.

There are essentially two types of hexes:

★ *those created from materials that are inherently malevolent; the fact that the material is even used indicates a hex*
★ *those created from neutral materials or even from material that is inherently sacred, benevolent, and beneficial. The spell-caster's intent is what transforms it into a hex. Thus a handful of graveyard dust may be tossed in someone's wake to provide a blessing or a curse*

IMPORTANT: A WARNING SPELL BEFORE BEGINNING

Should one for any reason (and, of course, yours is a good one) attempt to cast a malicious spell using oils or powders, and should some of that hexing material somehow get onto you, forget about the original spell and focus immediately on cleansing yourself instead.

★ Cleanse thoroughly using rosemary hydrosol or appropriate quantities of the essential oil. (Remember less is always more with essential oils. Don't be tempted to use excessive amounts because you've scared yourself.)
★ Wait at least 24 hours before considering whether to return to the original spell

This cleansing may also be used if you are the target of a malevolent spell.

Black Arts Oil

A traditional condition oil used to cast hexes:

1. Grind up black mustard seeds, black pepper, mullein, stinging nettles, and valerian.
2. Put it in a bottle and cover with mineral (baby) oil.
3. Float whole peppercorns in the oil and if you have a black dog, add one single hair. (Pick it off the sofa or your clothing. Don't bother the dog; annoying the dog will cause the spell to backfire on you immediately even before the Rule of Three kicks in.)

So now that you've concocted this mean-spirited oil, what do you do with it?

☀ Black Arts Oil Spell Candle Spell

Carve a black or purple candle to suit your situation. Dress with Black Arts Oil and burn.

☀ Blueberry Hex

Even something as innocuous as blueberries has been used to cast malicious spells. Create an infusion of blueberry leaves and sprinkle over your target's doorstep.

☀ Bottle Hex

1. Place your target's photograph inside a bottle.
2. Write the target's name on a piece of paper and put this inside the bottle, too.
3. Stuff holly and ivy into the bottle.
4. Add some black ink and **War Water**.
5. Seal the bottle shut and bury it upside down.

☀ Candle Hex Black Cat Crossed Your Path

*The condition oil **Black Cat Oil** is most frequently used for benevolent purposes, to draw protection, good fortune, and attention from the opposite sex. However, it may also be used to turn a trick. The combination of wax and pins requires no doll.*

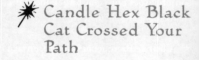

1. Hold a black candle in your hands and charge it with your intention.
2. Carve it with your enemy's name and any identifying information pertaining to that person.
3. Dress the candle with **Black Cat Oil**.

4. Pierce the candle with five pins placed vertically, approximately one inch apart.
5. Light your candle and let it burn until the first pin drops out.
6. Pinch out the candle and reserve it.
7. The following night, light the candle again and let it burn until the next pin drops out.
8. Burn in nightly increments until the final pin drops out.
9. Pinch the candle out yet again but this time take what remains of the candle and throw it against your enemy's front door.
10. Walk away without looking back, returning home via a circuitous route.

Curse Tablets

The most common hex of the ancient world appears to have been Curse Tablets. At least they're the most common artifacts found. Created from metal, curse tablets survive, as no doubt intended, for millennia, unlike more ephemeral wax, paper, and fabric methods. Curse tablets are small sheets of metal, inscribed with specific curses naming the target and what destiny is wished for him or her. Having been inscribed, the tablets were traditionally tossed into wells or springs, and are frequently dedicated to the spirit of the spring as if expecting the spirit to actually carry out the curse. There were professional curse tablet makers; we know this because blanks have been found, standard formulas with spaces left to incorporate a name. However, because soft metal is used and little skill is required, this was always also easy do-it-yourself hexing.

The most favored metal is lead, for two reasons. First, lead is under the leadership of Saturn, a planet with a dour, unforgiving reputation. Saturn, once known by astrologers as the Greater Malefic, is where one discovers life's harsh limits, which is what the target of the spell is expected to discover. Second, and on a more prosaic note, lead is heavy. It sinks and doesn't rise. As the best way to undo a curse tablet is to discover and destroy the tablet, using lead virtually ensures the success of the spell.

In ancient Rome the most powerful curse tablets were believed created on lead stolen from sewer pipes. If you wanted to play around with the form, and a blessing tablet could just as easily be created, curse tablets are even more easily created from tin or wax.

1. Determine the desired effects you wish the tablet to deliver.
2. Cut out a sheet of metal or wax.
3. Inscribe it with your desire, naming your target and his or her identifying information as explicitly as possibly.
4. Traditionally tablets are dropped into springs or wells or attached to sewer walls. A blessing tablet might be affixed to a shrine or altar.

The Cursing Psalm

The power to heal can be the power to harm. Even something as intrinsically good and sacred as a psalm may be used malevolently. Psalm 109 has been called "the cursing psalm." It may be chanted to harm an enemy.

The psalm itself is inherently benevolent. It's your emotion and intention that transform it. Therefore the first step is to be in the right mood. Then start chanting and visualizing.

Cursing Stones

Charging a stone with malevolence is an ancient Celtic method of delivering a curse. Charge the stone by holding it in your hands while allowing yourself to be engulfed by

feelings of rage, jealousy, anger, o hatred. The stone will store th emotion. When charging is complete terminate the process by setting th stone down and consciously chang ing your train of thought. Reserv the stone for future use.

Should one wish to curse someon or something, hold the stone withi your hands, stroking it, while turn ing it counter-clockwise and mur muring curses.

Damnation Powder

Consider whether casting this spell t worth it. Although it's believed to be potent hex, the hex-caster allegedl is left with hell to pay.

*Refer to the Formulary and creat the powder base for **Damnatio Water**. Drop nine pinches o **Damnation Powder**, one at a time into a flaming cauldron, intoning th target's name as each pinch falls.*

Damnation Water Hexes

These are revenge spells, spell: cast from anger. Because **Damnation Water**, like **War Water**, car either confer a hex or break one the emotional intent of the spell caster determines the outcome.

Damnation Water: Basic Hex

*Sprinkle **Damnation Water** on the path where your enemy is sure to walk.*

Damnation Water: Extra Strength

1. Soak parchment in blended **Damnation Water** and **Four Thieves Vinegar**.
2. When the paper dries, write every variation of your target's name on it. (For maximum strength, use **Bat's Blood Ink**.)
3. Carve and dress a black candle against your enemy.
4. Burn the paper in the flame of the candle.
5. Reserve the ashes of the parchment to sprinkle on your enemy's property.

Dog Hex

This spell allegedly destroys your target's peace and harmony, sowing enmity and discord instead.

1. Hang out in a dog park. Eventually, inevitably, some dogs will have a fight. This is what you're waiting for: look for a mass free-for-all, complete with gnashing teeth and wild barking.
2. Don't get between the dogs when they're fighting, but when the battle ends gather up a handful of dirt from where the dogs were fighting.
3. Pick some cat hairs off a cat-lover's sofa or clothing.
4. Grind the dirt and hair together with salt, black pepper, and cayenne or habanero pepper so that a fine powder is created.
5. Sprinkle this powder wherever you wish to sow enmity.

Doll Hex Basic Pins and Needles Doll

The term "voodoo doll" has entered the English language but maligns the Vodou religion. The magical tradition of pierced wax dolls, for both positive and negative purposes, is ancient and international, dating back at least to the days of the Egyptians and appearing virtually all around the world. Here is a Hungarian Romany version:

1. Create a figure to represent your target from melted candle wax.
2. Add bits of the target's clothing and any intimate items that you

may possess—hair, nail clippings, and so forth.

3. When the doll is finished, allow the doll to harden.
4. Prick it with a needle as the spirit moves you but always in a series of three or nine.

Enmity Spells

Sometimes hexes are vague: the spell-caster simply wants the target to suffer. General misery, in any form the universe wishes to dole out, is acceptable. Sometimes, however, a hex is very specific; a specific end result is desired. Frequently the desire is to transform love into its opposite.

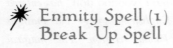

Enmity Spell (1)
Break Up Spell

This spell is intended to cause enmity between two who currently love each other or are closely attached. There may be desire to break up a marriage, a romantic attachment, a business partnership, or a friendship.

Boil a black hen's egg in your own urine. Feed half the egg to a dog, the other to a cat, saying: "As these two hate one another, so may hatred fall between [Name] and [Name]."

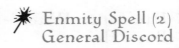

Enmity Spell (2)
General Discord

To sow general discord within a home, bury a found crow's feather in the target's house. (It must be a found feather; take it by force and watch the spell backfire on you.) This spell, from India, derives from a region with thatched roofs and so was easily accomplished. You never actually had to get inside the home. However, any other discreet place in the residence will do. Under the front step, where the target is bound to step over it, should be equally effective.

Enmity Spell (3)
Separation Powder

Black pepper
Cayenne or habanero powder
Cinnamon
Galangal
Vetiver
Metallic sand

Separation powder allegedly does what its name promises: separates formerly devoted lovers or partners. Sprinkle it where the targeted couple will be together.

☀ Empty Wallet Hex

Some hexes are subtle, such as this Romany spell intended to create a negative financial impact.

Give a new wallet as a gift, straight from the store, in a nice box, with nothing in it. Doesn't sound like a hex, does it? The target of the spell will probably be happy to receive it, unless they're sophisticated enough to realize they've just accepted a wish for a perpetually empty purse.

The moral of the story? Always stick at least a penny into a wallet before giving it as a gift—and be wary of gifts received.

Foot Track Hexes

Although foot track magic can be used for positive means as easily as negative, it has something of a bad reputation, one it has retained for millennia: Pythagoras warned against its misuses.

☀ Foot Track Spell (1)
Curse of the Running Feet

Cheating men who've abandoned their sweethearts at the altar should be wary of the vila. If these Eastern European Fairies catch them, they'll dance these men to death as a form of justice. (This is the mythological basis for the ballet, Giselle.) Hoodoo, on the other hand, has the curse of running feet.

Mix the dirt from your target's footprint with cayenne pepper, and throw it into running, living waters. This allegedly causes your target to run from place to place, unceasingly, without rest, ultimately with disastrous results.

☀ Foot Track Spell (2)
Hobble their Steps

A German foot track spell is intended to render someone lame, although whether literally or figuratively is subject to debate.

1. Gather Earth from the footprint.
2. Place it in a pot together with a nail, a needle, and some shards of broken glass.
3. Heat the pot until it cracks.

☀ Foot Track Spell (3)
Walk into Danger

Burn someone's footprint to cause illness or worse. This spell derives from Russia, where for maximum power it would be burned in the bathhouse at midnight, the point

being that it was burned in a sacred yet dangerous place.

To Prevent Someone from Casting a Foot Track Spell on You

These spells are to protect against danger from either foot track spells or any malicious magic absorbed through the feet—powders or secret tricks one walks over, for instance. Their goal is to prevent rather than break an already-cast spell: hex-breakers or spell reversals are required in that unfortunate circumstance.

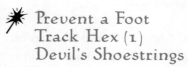

Prevent a Foot Track Hex (1) Devil's Shoestrings

Devil's shoestrings are roots derived from the Viburnum *botanical family. Their name confuses people who think that the roots must be used for evil purposes. Quite the contrary: devil's shoestrings allegedly tie the devil's shoes together to prevent him, or evil in general, from successful pursuit. Worn as an ankle bracelet, devil's shoestrings repel foot track curses. This spell requires nine devil's shoestring roots of equal length.*

They cannot be cut to size but must be chosen carefully.

1. Knot, braid, or weave the roots together to form an ankle bracelet.
2. Attach a tiny piece of real silver, whether a coin, bead, or lucky charm and wear it for protection.

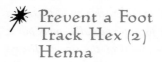

Prevent a Foot Track Hex (2) Henna

Henna creates a protective shield when applied to the soles of the feet. Although beautiful patterns are always a pleasure and decorating with auspicious, protective symbols will no doubt enhance the potency, they're not necessary for the purpose. If you're pressed for time, dip your sole into henna paste for a solid coat of henna.

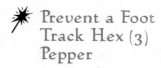

Prevent a Foot Track Hex (3) Pepper

Sprinkle black pepper and cayenne pepper in your shoes. You may also rub it directly into the soles of your feet.

Name Paper Spells

Who needs intimate items when you have a name? Once upon a time (and sometimes still today), it was believed that if you possessed someone's true name you also possessed control over that person.

Name Paper Hex (1) Active Spell

1. Write the name of your target clearly on a piece of paper as well as any other identifying information.
2. Dress it with a drop of **Commanding Oil**.
3. Hold it in your hand, close your eyes, and focus your desire.
4. Now do something to the paper to demonstrate injury to the target. For instance, placing the name paper under drums while they're played allegedly causes the victim to suffer headaches. Can you imagine what taping it inside a pair of cymbals might do?

Name Paper Hex (2) Lemon

A simple piece of fruit may be as effective as a wax image: write the full name of the victim on a slip of paper. Stick pins through the paper into a lemon, to cause bitterness and a sour existence.

✳ Name Paper Shoe Hex

This hex derives from Central American magical traditions.

1. Capture one of your target's shoes.
2. Write the target's name, mother's name, and any identifying information on a slip of paper.
3. Place this paper within the shoe—lift up the sole so it doesn't fall out, if necessary.
4. Do to the shoe whatever you visualize happening to your target.

✳ Peppermint Candle Spell

Peppermint oil, usually a benevolent component of romantic and healing spells, is also used as a hexing agent in candle spells to bring harm and unhappiness to one's enemy.

1. Write your enemy's name and your desires for him or her on a piece of brown paper.

2. Carve a black candle as you deem appropriate.
3. Add some peppermint essential oil to mineral (baby) oil and use this to dress the candle.
4. Hold the candle in your hands, charging it with your intentions.
5. Place the paper beneath the candle and burn the candle.

War Water Spells

War Water, also known as Water of Mars, is a classic formula that harnesses the power of iron to send a hex, repel a hex, or protect against all sorts of malevolent energy. Different recipes may be used to create benevolent or malevolent **War Water**; check the *Formulary* for details.

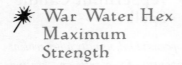
War Water Hex Maximum Strength

*Gather Spanish moss. Add it to the aggressive form of **War Water** and use as desired.*

War Water Spell (1) Basic

*The most common mode of administering **War Water** is to splash your target's doorstep with it. However as this is the most common method of casting any **War Water** spell targeted at another for whatever purpose, it's crucial that while splashing, all of your attention is intently focused on the desired outcome of your spell.*

War Water Spell (2) Houseplant

*A Hoodoo houseplant jinx suggests that the hex-caster sprinkle **War Water** on the leaves and roots of a really nice plant and give it to the target as a gift.*

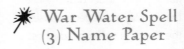
War Water Spell (3) Name Paper

1. Write your adversary's name and identifying information on a strip of brown paper.
2. Place it in a jar and cover it with **War Water**.
3. Seal it tight and hide it in a dark, secret place.
4. Shake the jar periodically.

✳ Weeping Willow Hex

This spell allegedly makes your enemy cry, weep, and moan.

1. Obtain a weeping willow branch.
2. Water it for nine days, retaining any water that doesn't evaporate. (Just keep adding more water.) This gives you nine days to consider and reconsider your plan of action.
3. Pour the water on the front doorstep of your target to stimulate tears in that home.

Reversing Spells

Originally I didn't intend to include hexes in this book because it's really not necessary: if you are angry, frustrated, bitter, or resentful enough, virtually any spell you cast can be converted to a hex. However, for every formal hex or malevolent spell that exists, there are at least two to repel or remove the spell. It is impossible to understand Reversing, Protection, or Uncrossing Spells without considering the malevolence of hexes.

Antidote spells or spells to break a hex take various forms,

although there can be considerable overlap between them.

★ Hex-breakers *generally focus on breaking the malevolent spell only*
★ Uncrossing spells *generally focus on removing the effects of what might be a hex. The effects are real but the cause may be only suspected. If misfortune is indeed caused by a hex, some uncrossing spells will reverse it back to its sender, although if this not the case, no harm will be done*
★ Antidotes *are exactly what they promise to be: they counteract the effects of a specific type of spell*
★ Reversing spells *break the hex and return it to its sender*

Some of these return-to-sender spells are dependent on your knowing the identity of the spellcaster, while others will automatically return-to-sender without that knowledge. You can rest assured that the spell has been returned; however, you may never know the identity of your oppressor—not for sure, anyway.

There is also a spell to transform negative energy sent your way into the positive energy that you truly desire instead.

Beyond the three-fold law and beyond basic ethics, there is

another excellent reason for not engaging in hexes. Should your hex be effective, eventually the target of your spell will suspect that they have been victimized. Although people will swear that they will only resort to hex-breakers and uncrossing spells, if someone gets sufficiently angry and afraid, the standard response tends to be a reversing spell and often the most malevolent kind. What's the difference between many reversing spells and hexes? Well, the reversing spell-caster wasn't the one who initiated the situation and frequently that's about it. After a while, frankly, it can be very hard to remember who actually started the whole malevolent affair. Initiating a hex is rarely a quick-fix, effortless method of removing an enemy. What initiating a hex usually does instead is to initiate psychic warfare—a witch war—with detrimental, damaging effects to all involved as well as their loved ones and many innocent bystanders.

the reason hexes are frequently so effective (particularly intimidating public doorstep ones like coffin spells) is that the target believes him or herself to be doomed and thus wastes away. There may be a grain of truth to this: why is it that so many have a hard time taking love and good fortune spells seriously yet at the same time live in mortal fear of hexes? A hex doesn't necessarily spell doom; it just sets a process in motion. Don't be passive. Just as every poison has its antidote, so does every spell.

These antidotes specifically target a genre of spell; if you're unsure how the spell was cast or if there isn't an antidote to suit your situation, choose hex-breaking, uncrossing, or reversing spells instead.

Antidote: Bewitched Food

To remove and repel a spell cast when you accepted a gift of bewitched food.

1. Throw any remaining food into fire.
2. Slap the fireplace chimney with a broom.
3. Slap all windows with a broom.

Antidotes

According to sociologists and non-magic practicing scholars,

4. Slap all entrance doors with a broom.

5. The removal is complete. Follow up with strong house and personal cleansings.

Antidote: Curse Tablets

This amulet, from Asia Minor, what is today modern Turkey, is essentially an anti-curse tablet. In use around the dawning of the Common Era, the amulet's form, engraved writing on a small metal plate, is known as a "lamella." It's not hard to cut out tin and scratch an incantation into its surface. The original was addressed to a deity or protective spirit. Adapt as inspired.

The ancient text reads something like:

Drive away the curse from [Name] child of [Name].

If anyone harms me in the future, if they attempt to harm me in the future,

Throw that curse back where it comes from!

In alternative version:"Free [Name] child of [Name] from all hexcraft and all suffering and all magical influence by night and by day."

Keep the lamella in a safe, secret place or throw it down a deep well.

Antidote: Foot Track Magic

Obtain your own footprint. Carry it until a windy moment presents itself then toss the footprint down the wind.

Antidote: Iron Curse Basic

*This German spell antidotes curses cast with iron, including **War Water** spells. How do you know whether you're a victim of such a spell? Signs that such a spell has been cast are when a person suddenly and consistently begins to have accidents with small metal implements, such as knives or scissors, which become progressively more serious, graduating to car accidents or industrial accidents.*

This is the bare-bones spell and the version most popularly circulated. The antidote is easy to accomplish any time. The rings may be re-used and many perform this spell as a regularly scheduled preventive measure.

1. Place three small iron rings in spring water overnight or for 24 hours in a serious case. (By

rings, jewelry isn't necessarily meant, although this could be used, but rather any circle formed from iron: hardware stores often sell small metal rings for various purposes.)

2. After the time has elapsed, remove the rings and drink the water.

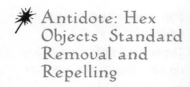 Antidote: Knot Magic

The very simplest antidote to knot magic is to find the string and untie the knots. Should you be unable to locate the string, reciting the Koran's Surah CXIII allegedly undoes any evil worked via knot magic.

Sometimes you can't miss a trick. Has your doorstep been "dusted?" Did you open the front door to discover evidence of a spell laid against you? Tricks may be laid via various powders, **Goofer Dust, War Water,** nasty little coffins, chicken parts, black candle stubs, rotten eggs, or worse. Don't despair; you're not doomed. There are several remedies, which may also be combined for maximum coverage if desired.

Antidote: Hex Objects Standard Removal and Repelling

This Hoodoo spell can be used as a antidote to any type of object–drive hex, whether the items were left o your doorstep, buried in your garde or secreted within your home.

The first step is removal: find a the pieces and gather them up, wrap ping them in a fabric packet an folding away from you. Then tak the packet to a crossroads at mid night, and burn everything.

Antidote: Wax Image Spell Seven Limes

This antidote requires seven lime Although it may be performed fo oneself, it is most effective if you hav an assistant doing the squeezing an bathing.

1. The target of the hex must stand within a large metal washtub.
2. Cut the limes in half and squeeze the juice into the tub.
3. Dump the squeezed-out fruits, the lime peel, into the tub as well.

4. Wash your body with lime juice.
5. When the bath is complete, step out of the tub, let yourself air-dry and put on fresh, clean clothes.
6. Leave the lime peel in the washbasin until evening when it is deposited, preferably in the sea, but at least far from home. There should be no further bathing for 24 hours.

Hex-breaking

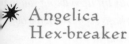 Angelica Hex-breaker

Make an infusion of angelica root. Add this infusion to your bath to remove curses, hexes, and bad spells. Essential oil of angelica may be used instead of an infusion; however, be aware that it has phototoxic properties. Avoid exposure to the sun following use.

☀ Anti-Sorcery Headwash

This is not a preventive measure but is effective if you've already been hit by a malevolent spell. In the traditional Chinese formula, the head is entirely shorn before the head wash. If this is not desirable, make sure the scalp is cleansed as well as the hair.

Wash the scalp and hair with an infusion made from mugwort, garlic, honeysuckle, and broomstraws.

☀ Ash Hex-breaker

Gather fallen ash leaves. Murmur your concerns and fears over them and then take them to the crossroads and disperse them in all directions.

☀ Bamboo Hex-breaker

Inscribe your goal, wish, or prayer onto bamboo wood. Grind it into powder, then burn it to break a hex.

☀ Cayenne Hex-breaker

Sprinkle cayenne pepper throughout the home to break any malevolent spells.

☀ Chamomile Hex-breaker

Sprinkle chamomile around the perimeter of your home and property to break spells against you.

Compelling Curse Breaker Spells

Command that hex to bow down and crawl away! Powerful botanicals, like spirits and people, tend to be multifaceted. Strong Commanding formulas, most frequently used for *Domination Spells* may also be used for hex-breaking, as they also possess a protective aspect. **Essence of Bend Over** is particularly strong but use whichever formula appeals to you most.

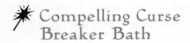 Compelling Curse Breaker Bath

*Massage **Essence of Bend Over Oil** into your skin and then enter a bath containing salted water.*

Compelling Curse Breaker Powder

Use this powder to supplement any other hex-breaker spell as an extra magical enhancement. Grind and powder sweet flag / calamus, licorice root, peppermint, and vetiver. Blend with arrowroot powder and dust your body.

 Curse Removal

Legends tell of individuals innocently obtaining objects, typically ancient idols, jewels, or magical weapons marked with a curse. Ever-worsening misfortune accompanies possession of the object. Sometimes malevolent individuals give gifts like this on purpose. If you are merely the innocent recipient of this curse (in other words, you're not the one who broke into the tomb, stole the object, and activated the curse), this technique may lift it, enabling you to be safe and perhaps even retain the object if you still want it.

Pass a handful of salt around the object three times. Then throw the salt into an open fire, without looking into the fire.

Draw Back Evil!

To rid yourself of evil magic:

1. Bring an offering to the Full Moon. This is based on old Mesopotamian rituals: their offerings might include beer, wine, incense, or perfume. Offer what you feel is appropriate.
2. Tell the moon the deep secrets and fears of your heart.
3. Chant:
   Evil Magic, draw back!
   Evil Magic can't come near!

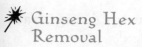

Ginseng Hex Removal

Burn ginseng to break a hex.

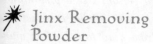

Jinx Removing Powder

This formula specifically antidotes Jinx Powder, but it is also used to remove any malevolent spells, hexes, or crossed conditions:

> Dried ground hydrangea blossoms
> Dried agrimony
> Dried wisteria

Grind and powder all the ingredients together. Blend with rice powder if a more "powdery" texture is desired. Sprinkle throughout your home, over your thresholds, and wherever you sense vulnerability.

Lucky Spirits Oil

Let the spirits break the curse! This oil allegedly sends out an SOS to benevolent spirits. Combine this spell with intensive spiritual petition.

Add essential oils of bergamot, citronella, frankincense, and sandalwood to sweet almond oil. Use this oil to dress candles.

Michael the Archangel Hexbreaker Spell

Archangel Michael vanquishes hexes, demons, and curses with his flaming sword. Have you heard the legend that a spell can't be removed if the one who cast it has since died? Or that a hex can't be removed unless you find the object used to cast it? Michael can remove them.

1. Grind frankincense, dragon's blood, and salt and add them to a base of sweet almond oil.
2. Dress red candles with this oil and burn them in petition to archangel Michael.
3. Add some more of the oil to a bath and soak in it, visualizing yourself surrounded by the cobalt light reflected from Michael's sword.

Ragweed Spell Repellent

Few modern plants have as bad a reputation as ragweed. Once upon a time, its power to stimulate what are now understood as allergies was considered a testament of its magical powers. Fairies were believed to ride upon ragweed, earning its nickname "fairy's horses." Witches allegedly rode upon it as well, just like a

broomstick. *Ragweed will not work with everyone; if its presence makes you ill, the plant is telling you something. Choose another spell. However, if you can, carry ragweed to break hexes and repel them.*

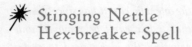

Stinging Nettle Hex-breaker Spell

The princess in the Grimm fairy tale The Twelve Swans *is almost burned as a witch while crafting nettle shirts to break a curse laid on her brothers. It's largely the nettles that condemn her; in Christian Europe, stinging nettles developed powerful associations with witchcraft. Despite the obvious care needed to gather them (wear gloves!), nettles are very beneficial: they are extremely nutritious and can also be used to create a sort of fabric, as in the story.*

If you're willing and able to spin and weave nettles, an effective quick-fix hex-breaker spell exists.

1. Carve a figure candle to represent the afflicted party, whether yourself or another.
2. Spin and weave a nettle shirt large enough for the candle.
3. Literally dress the candle with the shirt and burn *everything* under the light of the Full Moon.

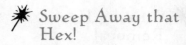

Sweep Away that Hex!

Based on shamanic ritual, someone else must perform this spell on the afflicted person. Use a pine branch complete with needles to sweep the body from head to toe while murmuring affirmations, prayers, and sacred verses.

Thistle Hex-breaker

1. Spin and weave thistles into "fabric."
2. Create a garment from it—any kind—to break a hex. Shirts are traditional, but any garment will do.
3. The entire creation process from start to finish constitutes the spell. The garment is created with *intent*. Once the garment is placed on the body the spell is complete and the hex is broken.

Spell Reversals

Spell reversals do more than just break a hex and remove its effects; these spells create a boomerang effect, returning the spell to wherever it came from.

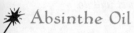

Absinthe Oil

This is not essential oil of wormwood! Essential oil of wormwood is among the most dangerous essential oils and should only be used under the most expert supervision (and most experts avoid it!).

Soak wormwood roots, leaves, and stems in castor oil. (If you really despise your target, use mineral oil as a base instead.) Castor oil does not flow easily; dilute with jojoba or olive oil as needed. This is an oil of revenge, an oil of justice: it sends harm back to an evil-doer. Secretly apply it to the body of your enemy so that the harm they have caused will revert back to them.

Black Cross Reversing Spell

*Dress a black cross (altar) candle with **Uncrossing Oil** and **Flying Devil Oil**. Visualize the hex leaving you and flying toward its original sender.*

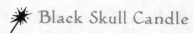

Black Skull Candle

Use a Black Skull Candle to reverse a spell.

1. Carve the candle as desired.
2. Dress with **Flying Devil Oil**.
3. Focus on your hopes and desires as the candle burns.
4. Dispose of the candle remnants outside of your home, returning via a circuitous route.

Blackthorn Reversing Spell

1. Collect five thorns from a blackthorn tree.
2. Create a wax image; it can be a generic image. It doesn't have to represent any specific person. It's not necessary for you to know who wished you harm; if someone did, this spell will find them.
3. Stick one thorn through each hand saying, "*The evil that you have crafted returns to you.*"
4. Stick one thorn through each foot saying, "*The evil that you visit upon me returns back to you.*"
5. Stick the last thorn into the image's head saying, "*The evil that you think and conceive returns to you.*"
6. Burn or bury the image.

☀ Elm Reversing Spell

Elm is a magical tree, associated with both elves and fairies and considered under the dominion of Mother Holle. It may be used to remove and reverse a hex. Grind and powder elm twigs and leaves. Add it to your bath water to break a hex and return it.

☀ Foot Track Reversal Spells

If you know or suspect the identity of the person who crossed you, gather all the dirt from their footprint carefully in a bag. Sprinkle it on whatever has been hexed. This is especially effective when there are actual physical manifestations of the hex—actual objects to sprinkle it on.

If you're wrong in your identification of the perpetrator and that person has not hexed you, no harm will be done.

☀ Hydrangea Hex Reversal

Burn dried hydrangea to reverse spells and remove hexes. Blend the ashes with more dried, ground hydrangea and scatter around the home.

☀ Identity Well Known Hex Reversal

To send a hex back to someone yo[u] know is hexing you, you will nee[d] something that belongs to th[e] person—ideally hair or fingernail[s] but any object will do.

1. Lay down a black cloth.
2. Put a small mirror onto it.
3. Put the jinxer's personal item ato[p] the mirror.
4. Write their name on a slip of paper.
5. Write your own name over that name, while chanting:
   *I cover you, I cross you,
   I cover you, I cross you,
   You put a spell on me,
   Now it returns to you*
6. Cover the mirror and paper completely with sea salt.
7. Wrap it up in the black cloth, folding away from you.
8. Bury it at a crossroads, ideally at sunrise, and ideally under the Ful[l] Moon.

☀ Reversal Candle

A Reversal Candle to reverse a spell cast against you:

1. Get a new seven-day candle.
2. Turn it upside down. Carve the bottom of the candle so that the wick is now exposed and may be lit.
3. Slice the top off the candle so that it can stand.
4. Dress the candle. If you know the name of your jinxer, carve it into the wax.
5. Light the wick and chant:
   "Candle, let the evil done against me reverse itself as I have reversed you."

☀ Revocation Spell of Elegba

"Revocations" recall, revoke, or annul something. In this case, you'd like a curse revoked. Elegba owns the roads, permitting or forbidding passage as he sees fit. So, technically speaking, the hex that reached you did so with his permission. Of course, perhaps that one slipped right by him without catching his attention. Draw his eye toward the hex; explain the injustice and request that he send the curse back to its sender, simultaneously erecting a shield of protection around you.

1. Fill a cup two-thirds full with **Indigo Water**.
2. Top it off with **Florida Water**, **Flying Devil Oil**, **Protection Oil**, **Uncrossing Oil**, and turpentine.
3. As this is being done, petition Elegba, owner of all roads, to send the evil that is afflicting you on its way quickly.
4. Take a small mouthful of rum: hold it in your mouth, then blow it into the cup.
5. Blow cigar smoke into the cup. (If you don't smoke, just waft the cigar smoke over the cup.)
6. Add three nails.
7. Add a camphor square to the cup.
8. Write the name of your enemy, if you know who it is, on a piece of brown paper.
9. Put the paper over the cup with the name facing in.
10. Place a plate on top of it.
11. Quickly reverse the cup so that it is now upside down on the plate.
12. Place this near a door.
13. Knock three times on the floor, calling *"Open the door Papa Legba!"*
14. Place a white candle on top of the cup and burn it. Explain your predicament to Elegba.

Revocation of Archangel Michael

The *Revocation of Archangel Michael provides protection and returns a hex.*

1. Write your enemy's name on a small piece of paper.
2. Place it inside a glass.
3. Cover the paper with sea salt.
4. Fill the glass with spring water, **Carmelite water**, angelica hydrosol, or any combination of these.
5. Cover the glass with a saucer.
6. Turn it over quickly so that it rests atop the saucer, making sure no water spills or leaks out. (If it does, start completely from scratch.)
7. Slice a white candle into nine pieces, pulling out the wicks, so that each becomes a distinct little candle. Every night for nine consecutive nights, place one candle slice on top of the reversed glass and burn it.
8. Petition Michael for assistance while it burns.

War Water Reversal Spell

*Boil pins or nails in **War Water**. Allow it to cool, strain out the soli material and throw the liquid i your target's home to return a ba spell.*

Other Direction Reversal Spell

1. To reverse a reverse, put your clothing on backwards.
2. Walk backwards while concentrating on sending the curse back.

Transformation

Living well is the best reveng against a hexer. There are spell to neutralize malevolent magi There are spells to reverse an send back malevolent magi However, this spell takes th malevolent energy someone h deliberately aimed toward yo and changes it into your chose good fortune.

1. Hold a small black candle in you hand and envision all the negative effects of the curse tha has been laid upon you.

2. When you're finished—and you should really think deeply, even if it isn't pleasant—place the candle on a tray covered with brown paper.
3. Wash your hands by rubbing them with either a salt scrub or dry salt, then rinsing.
4. Hold a white candle in your hands and concentrate on a vision of your life as you would like it to be. See yourself happy, stable, and secure, with all that negative energy transformed into positive.
5. Place this candle on the tray too.
6. Consider what you need to make that happy vision a reality. Write down your requirements or a plan of action on a piece of brown paper.
7. Place a small flat sheet of copper between the two candles, so that one is at each end. (Copper sheets are available through hardware and art supply stores.)
8. Place the paper on top of the copper sheet.
9. Light the black candle and say aloud, something like: "*Negative energy transform into good. Transform into* [name your desire]."
10. Light the white candle and say aloud, something like: "*My dreams and desires are accomplished. Nothing and no one obstructs me.*"

Remember, copper is an excellent conductor of heat and energy!

Uncrossing Spells: Removing a Crossed Condition

New Orleans Voodoo and Hoodoo have incorporated Christian iconography in unorthodox manners. Any visit to a spiritual supply store will turn up white candles shaped like crosses or crucifixes. Magic is in the eye of the beholder. These candles may be used in any way that makes sense to the candle burner and so these candles are frequently used as altar candles; however, they're really intended for uncrossing rituals. The terminology derives from that old metaphor about one's cross being too heavy to bear. In hoodoo terminology—and hoodoo is a genre that loves to play with words—this is known as a "*Crossed Condition.*" Uncrossing candles, oils, and rituals aim to remove that cross *and* uncross that crossed condition.

A crossed condition may derive from any number of sources, although a malevolent hex is most common. The Evil Eye may also cause it. Uncrossing spells are less concerned with where misfortune came from and where it should be redirected than simply making sure it leaves you for good, although some will reverse a spell. All uncrossing spells are most effective when accompanied by hex-breaking baths, prayer, petition, and/or fervent repetition of psalms.

Uncrossing Spell: Basic Candle (1)

*How do you get rid of a cross? You burn it. Dress a white cross candle with **Uncrossing Oil**, light it and burn.*

Uncrossing Spell: Basic Candle (2)

Some manufacturers sell special "Uncrossing" seven-day candles.

1. Dress with **Uncrossing Oil** (drill holes in the top of the candle if it won't slide from the sleeve and drip the oil into the holes).
2. Burn the candle.

Uncrossing Spell: Basic Candle (3)

*Combine a purple candle, indicating personal power, with a white cross candle. Dress both with **Uncrossing Oil**, burn and pray.*

Uncrossing Spell: Black Cat

*Let a black cat uncross your path. **Black Cat Oil** is used to attract the opposite sex, garner luck, and break hexes too! Sprinkle it at all entrances to your home to reverse, repel, and remove malign influences.*

Uncrossing Spell: Rosemary

This spell breaks a curse and will also lift the Evil Eye.

1. Put nine drops of essential oil of rosemary in a glass of rainwater.
2. Add nine drops of **Uncrossing Oil**.
3. Stir it up and place it in the window. Leave it there for three days.
4. On the fourth day, sprinkle this water throughout the house, concentrating on corners, dark spots, and any areas that feel "creepy."

5. At the same time, add rosemary essential oil and **Uncrossing Oil** to your bathwater.

Uncrossing Mojo

Add the following to a red flannel drawstring bag: a scoop of crossroads dirt, a rusty iron nail, a small magnetic horseshoe, and a real silver bead or charm. Dress the bag with **Uncrossing Oil** *and carry with you.*

You can incorporate other charms or religious medals as desired.

Witch Bottles

Spells can be cast within fabric pouches, cigar boxes, and furniture cabinets. Once upon a time, spells cast in sealed glass bottles were very popular. Witch bottles, as these spells are known, derive their name from two sources.

The most obvious is that witches were assumed to cast spells using glass bottles. In addition, witch bottles were a popular method of breaking hexes allegedly cast by witches. Whether witch bottles were ever as popular as some claim is worth pondering. They've largely fallen out of favor because, in general, witch bottles favor extremely dangerous methods. Frankly, you're far more likely to be seriously injured from one of these bottles than from a curse. ***I strongly recommend against casting any of the traditional witch bottles spells.*** Safer, modern adaptations are presented following the old ones.

Witch bottles basically exist for one of two purposes:

★ *To provide spiritual protection*
★ *To reverse a malicious spell*

Protection Bottles

Protection Bottle (1)

To protect against malevolent magic:

1. Place a single castor bean in a small glass bottle.
2. Seal it tightly. Keep one bottle and bean in each room of the house.
3. Replace the beans at every New Moon.

Warning! *Castor beans are poisonous. Do not leave the bottle where a child or animal (or an unknowing adult) has access to it.*

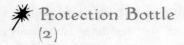

Protection Bottle (2)

1. Fill a tiny vial with mercury.
2. Seal it tightly shut.
3. Place this bottle inside a second larger bottle or jar.
4. Fill this second container with water and seal tightly shut.
5. Place this second bottle into an even larger jar or bottle.
6. Fill this with sea sand, seashells, and pebbles from the beach.
7. Seal tightly shut and bury it. Traditionally this is buried in the hearth or by the home's front entrance.

Warning! Mercury is an extremely toxic substance.

Love Magic

The universal stimulus for magic, there are more love spells, more different types of love spells than any other kind of magic. There are spells to find love, lose love, repair love, and to discourage one love but encourage another. Basic Love Spells are grouped together, followed by more specialized concerns:

★ *Binding Spells*
★ *Break-Up Spells*
★ *Love Potions*
★ *Heartbreak and Disappointment Spells*
★ *Sex and Seduction Spells*
★ *Male Virility Spells*
★ *Summoning Spells*

Some of these spells are a lot of trouble to cast. Some may be perceived as "*disgusting*" or demand that the spell-caster do humiliating or unpleasant things. Although theoretically most spells are cast in secret, in many cases, it's almost impossible for the target of some genres of love spells not to know a spell has been cast or at the very least to think that you're doing something crazy. (Consider the spell that demands that you bathe the spell target's private parts with a potion while they sleep: how can the other party not wake up mid-spell?)

There are two things to remember: first, it can be very flattering to have someone go through so much trouble out of love and desire for you. This may even account for a portion of the effectiveness. And second, spells that are a lot of trouble, particularly those that are a lot of trouble over an extended period of time, invite you to examine the crucial question, is he or she worth it? Particularly with binding spells where you are, in effect, binding yourselves together for eternity, if it's too much trouble, maybe you shouldn't be performing a binding spell.

TIPS FOR SUCCESSFUL ROMANTIC MAGIC

★ TIMING: In general, all things being equal, a Friday coinciding with a New Moon is considered the most auspicious time to perform love spells. Fridays in general are the best days for love spells. The day is named in honor of Freya, Northern Lady of Love. It is also the day associated with other powerful spirits of love, Aphrodite and Oshun

★ COLORS FOR LOVE MAGIC: Yellow, orange, pink, and red

★ NUMBERS:

Two: the standard number, for the obvious reason
Five: if you'd like to invoke the power of Oshun, Orisha of Love
Six: if you'd like to invoke the power of Aphrodite, Lady of Love
Eight: if you'd like to invoke the power of Inanna-Ishtar, Queen of
    Heaven. Eight is also the number of infinity and eternity

★ Bathe your hands with rose water prior to mixing up any love potions or powders to intensify their effects

★ If you find that your love spells are consistently not working, place a strand of your target's hair under a continuously dripping faucet to magically wear away resistance

Basic Love Spells

These are spells to find new love as well as preserve and protect existing romance.

Adam and Eve Root Spells

Adam and Eve is the name given to the roots of the family of orchids that grow from a pair of conjoined roots. The root has two forms, male and female (hence Adam and Eve), believed to resemble the respective genitalia. Once upon a time they were extremely popular, advertised in the backs of comic books and commonly sold as curios in spiritual supply stores. Today, the plants are endangered and the roots are thus very scarce. They are considered very powerful and are featured in many love spells.

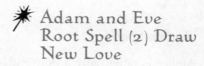

Adam and Eve Root Spell (1) Basic Spell

Carry the roots in a mojo hand. Take them out periodically, hold them in your hand and charge them with your desire.

Adam and Eve roots like their private time together; they don't play well with other botanicals. Don't add other roots or plants to an Adam and Eve conjure bag.

Adam and Eve Root Spell (2) Draw New Love

Begin this spell at the New Moon to draw new love into your life.

1. Choose Adam and Eve roots to represent the appropriate gender and dress them with love-drawing oil, something like **Come to Me Lover**.
2. Place the roots facing each other on opposite ends of a mirror.
3. Each night, dress the roots with an additional drop of oil and move them a little closer to each other. They should be touching when the Full Moon arrives.

If you are unable to find Adam and Eve roots, substitute lodestones or figure candles.

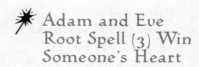

Adam and Eve Root Spell (3) Win Someone's Heart

This is not a spell for casual relationships; it's essentially a commitment charm.

1. Give the appropriate root to one you desire: an Eve root to a woman, an Adam to a man.
2. You keep the other.

Amber Spells

Amber is potentially a powerful love charm, although you may have to activate that potential. Romany magical traditions particularly value amber as a love-drawing charm.

✳ Amber Charm Romany Dreams of Desire

1. On a Thursday night, make a list of the qualities you desire in a romantic partner or visualize and name a specific person. Before you go to sleep that night, leave a piece of amber by your bed or under your pillow.
2. On Friday morning, first thing upon awakening, clutch the amber in your left hand, holding it close to your heart.
3. Close your eyes. Visualize your desire: make it as real and tangible as possible. Take as much time as you need.
4. Kiss the amber and wrap it up in a small piece of silk, wrapping or rolling toward you.

5. Keep this with you for seven days, carrying it by day, sleeping with it at night, beside your heart, between your breasts, wherever.
6. Repeat the process every morning. At the conclusion, you will have a highly charged love-drawing amulet.

The arrows of love go straight to the heart, and arrows are frequent components of love spells.

✳ Arrow Spell (1) Diana's Petition of Love

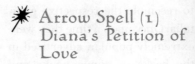

Diana, the Roman lunar goddess and mistress of magic, to whom this spell is dedicated, has excellent archery skills. Don't try this spell unless your skills are worthy of the goddess. The spell requires that you shoot a flaming arrow. This is potentially a dangerous spell for more than one reason. Diana will not look favorably upon your petition if you burn down her forest.

1. Write out your petition of love.
2. Affix it to an arrow.
3. Set the arrow aflame.
4. Quickly shoot it toward the moon.

✳ Arrow Spell (2) Eight of Wands

One of the traditional meanings of the eight of wands tarot card is love at first sight. The eight wands represent the arrows of love.

1. Carve and dress a red candle as desired, using love-drawing oils.
2. Burn the candle.
3. Place an eight of wands card upright near the candle so that it is easily visible.
4. Place a rose quartz beside the card and candle.
5. Once the candle burns down, place the card underneath your pillow so that it can provide romantic insight and inspiration while you sleep.
6. During the day wear the rose quartz in a charm bag, pocket, or tucked into your bra to attract and maintain the love you desire.

Basic Botanicals of Love

Although there are many plants associated with love and romance, the following have all earned a powerful reputation as love-drawing botanicals. In combination they're even more potent. Incorporate them into your spells as inspired: basil, carrots, catnip, chamomile, cardamom, coriander, cubeb, gardenia, grains of paradise, hibiscus, hyacinth, iris, jasmine, lady's mantle, lavender, lovage, mint, onion, orchid, poppy, rose, rosemary, Saint John's Wort, southernwood, strawberries, thyme, tormentil, vervain.

Surround your home with one or more of these living plants as an open invitation to true love.

✳ Basic Botanicals of Love Candle Spell

1. Select basic botanicals of love that please you.
2. Choose a pink, red, yellow, or orange candle.
3. Hollow out the base and pack it full of botanicals.
4. Burn the candle.

Bouquet Spells

Presenting someone with a bouquet of flowers was once a method of delivering a spell right into your target's hands. The "Language of Flowers," whereby each type of flower represents a specific message, originated in the harems of the Middle East, where secrecy regarding roman-

tic intrigues was crucial. That floral code would ultimately be formalized in Victorian England. Some floral bouquet spells, however, transcend any code.

 Bouquet Spell (1) Basic

The simplest, yet extremely effective, love spell is the gift of roses, either one single bloom or a bouquet of a dozen.

Bouquet Spell (2) Enhanced

Combine roses with myrtle for an especially powerful bouquet. Both plants are sacred to Aphrodite, and together they transmit her power and beseech her blessing. For extra enhancement, combine with conscious petition to Aphrodite.

Bouquet Spell (3) Sorcerer's Violet

The addition of vincas, also known as the sorcerer's violet, transforms any bouquet into an instrument of seduction.

1. Sprinkle a bouquet of romantic flowers with dried powdered vinca flowers, the sorcerer's violet.
2. Give them to the woman you want.

Candle Spells

Candle Spell (1) Heart Candle

1. Scratch your lover's initials into a heart-shaped candle.
2. Dress it with love drawing oil and sprinkle with a love drawing powder.
3. As it burns, chant:
   As this candle burns, so your heart burns with love for me
   As this wax melts, so your heart melts with love for me
   When this spell is complete, your heart belongs to me!

Candle Spell (2) New Moon

This spell is most effective if using handcrafted candles, because you can actually embed the magical material into the wax. However, a

store-bought candle may be doctored as well.

1. Prepare the candles so that this spell is ready to begin in conjunction with the New Moon.
2. Make two wax figures or purchase figure candles to represent you and your beloved.
3. Place a few strands of his or her hair in the candle representing the other party. (Pubic hair is most powerful, with underarm hair a close second. However if all you have are a few strands picked off a jacket, this will do.)
4. Place a few of your own hairs in your candle.
5. Begin burning the candles at the New Moon. Face the candles across from each other. Burn them in timed increments, a little bit every night, gradually bringing them increasingly closer and closer to each other.
6. When the candles are finally touching, let them burn all the way down, so that the waxes intermingle.
7. Any remaining wax can be saved as a love talisman, especially if it's melted into an auspicious shape.

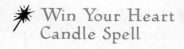

Win Your Heart Candle Spell

This spell allegedly enables you to win the heart of the one you desire.

1. Carve your name and that of the desired party nine times each on one pink seven-day candle.
2. Gently warm honey in a bain-marie and then blend in rosewater and powdered orrisroot.
3. Roll the candle in this mixture and then burn it.

Doll Spells

The description *"doll spell"* tends to invoke images of stereotypical *"voodoo dolls."* However the use of dolls in magical spells is incredibly ancient and fairly universal. Dolls are used for hexing but they're also used for healing, protection, fertility, and romantic spells. The piercing of wax figures with pins goes back at least as far as ancient Egypt, however those pins weren't meant to cause bodily injury. Instead they were intended to stimulate pangs of love and desire from whatever part of the body was pierced. Methods of piercing are frequently more inventive than just sticking needles into the doll.

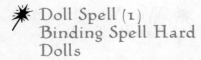

⚹ Doll Spell (1) Binding Spell Hard Dolls

1. Create two small dolls from a hard material: roots, wood, or bone.
2. Embellish the dolls: decorate with beads and fabric.
3. Anoint with love oils and with any available sexual fluids.
4. Bind them together with red cord, creating knots.
5. Hide them safely, for as long as you wish the romance to last.

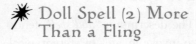

⚹ Doll Spell (2) More Than a Fling

To turn a sexual relationship into something more:

1. Cut out dolls to represent each party from an unlaundered bedsheet, stained with sexual fluids.
2. Personalize as much as possible. Embroider or draw names onto the dolls if secrecy isn't an issue.
3. Fill each poppet with love-herbs: roses, rosemary, orrisroot, heartsease, and vervain.
4. Bind the dolls together, face to face, belly to belly with scarlet ribbons.

5. Wrap the dolls in red or black velvet.
6. Slip this packet under the mattress on the side the other party usually sleeps on.

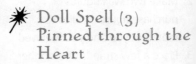

⚹ Doll Spell (3) Pinned through the Heart

1. Make a doll from malleable materials, such as wax, clay, dough, or similar.
2. Personalize it: if you possess any intimate items, incorporate them into the doll. Otherwise, decorate as you please.
3. Scratch a name onto the doll or pin a name-tag on it.
4. Push a brass pin or an ornamented hat-pin (especially one with a romantic motif) through the heart. This pin is thought to open the heart and induce love for the maker of the doll.

⚹ Friendship into Love Spell

Turn friendship into something more.

1. Obtain a Lover's Candle, usually a red candle depicting an entwined naked couple or, if you're a

candle-crafter, create one of your own.

2. Carve the woman's name on the man's body and the man's name on the woman's.
3. Anoint with the love oil you like best (**Amor**, **Jezebel**, **Come to Me Lover!** for instance) and burn the candle.

Forget-Me-Not Spell

Slip a forget-me-not into someone's pockets so that you will remain on their mind.

Garnet Soul Mate Magnet

Wear garnets to attract the love of your life.

Juniper Spells

Juniper is most commonly associated with protection spells. However, juniper berries possess tremendous love drawing and sexuality enhancing powers.

Warning: Juniper spells are not safe for use during pregnancy.

Juniper Spell Woman Seeking New Love

A quicker spell to prepare, ironically it solicits long-term love, romance, and commitment.

1. Soak juniper berries in vinegar for several hours.
2. Strain out the berries, reserving some, and add a generous quantity of the infusion to your bath water.
3. Enjoy your bath. Vividly visualize the end results of a very successful spell.
4. Emerge from the bath but don't drain the water yet.
5. Toss some used bathwater plus the reserved berries outside onto the Earth near your home to signal your desire for love and your available status.

Easy Juniper Spell

Pierce, string, and wear juniper berries to attract lovers.

Lodestone Love Spells

Lodestone's magnetic properties inspire their use in love spells. Lodestones are used to draw love toward you and then keep that love close at hand. According to traditional Chinese mysticism, the luckiest wedding bands are crafted from matched lodestones.

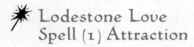
Lodestone Love Spell (1) Attraction

Lodestones are believed to have genders, just like other living creatures. Their gender is determined by appearance: the rounder-looking ones are female, while the males bear a phallic resemblance. Choose lodestones to match your desires. Use one to represent yourself and another to represent the person you would like to draw into a romance.

1. Choose a lodestone to represent you and soak it in **Come To Me Lover Oil!**
2. Sprinkle it with magnetic sand and place it on the edge of a mirror.
3. Choose a lodestone to represent the person you wish to draw into romance. It is not necessary for the lodestones to be of opposite sex; males may draw males, and females may draw females.
4. Soak this one in **Amor Oil**.
5. Sprinkle with magnetic sand and place it on the mirror, on the opposite edge from the first lodestone.
6. Carve a candle dedicated to romance and dress it with **Lucky Lodestone Oil**.
7. Light it, focus on your wish for romance, and move the two lodestones slightly closer to each other.
8. Pinch out the candle.
9. Repeat this daily until the lodestones meet in the middle, then allow the candle to burn all the way down.

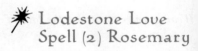
Lodestone Love Spell (2) Rosemary

1. Sprinkle dried ground rosemary onto a lodestone.
2. Carry it in a charm bag to draw love and attract favorable attention.

Lovage Spells

The herb lovage lives up to its name: it allegedly inspires love and amorous attention.

✳ Lovage Spell (1) Bath

1. Draw a tub of warm water.
2. Sprinkle fresh or dried lovage into your bath to attract romantic attention.
3. Let yourself air-dry.

✳ Lovage Spell (2) Food

Sprinkle lovage on food—fish or chicken is recommended—ten minutes before serving the meal to your beloved.

✳ Love Attraction Spell

1. Write your target's name on a small piece of paper.
2. Sprinkle it with the most fragrant fresh flower petals available.
3. Fold the paper toward you.
4. Hide it within your underwear drawer to magically lure the person closer to you.

✳ Love Candle Spell

This spell requires two candles, one to represent you and one to represent the object of your desire.

1. Carve the candles as desired.
2. Dress the candle that represents you with **Magnet Oil** and **Come to Me Lover!**
3. Light that candle; it will remain in one place.
4. Dress the other candle with plain olive oil and sprinkle magnetic sand over it.
5. Burn it in increments, drawing it ever closer to your candle and sprinkling with magnetic sand.

Love Conjure Bags

Create your own bag using romantic charms, botanicals, and symbols, or follow one of these formulas.

✳ Conjure Bag (1) Aphrodisiac

This bag promotes faithfulness as well as romance.

1. Take a whole spikenard root or a piece of one, together with a little bit of hair taken from the tail of a goat.
2. Wrap it in fabric or carry it in a bag.
3. Reinforce periodically by dressing with essential oil of spikenard or a drop of oil infused from the root.

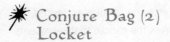

Conjure Bag (2)
Locket

A locket worn around the neck serves as an elegant charm bag. The chain also gives it the air of a binding spell.

Place a photo of your beloved inside a locket together with a strand of hair and a tiny piece of moonwort (Botrychium lunaria).

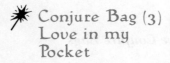

Conjure Bag (3)
Love in my
Pocket

In Romany, a conjure bag is known as a "putzi," literally a "pocket."

Fill a red silk bag with all or some of the following ingredients to draw and maintain love and romance: amber, cinnamon, cloves, acorns, rose buds or petals, orrisroot, a magic ring and an old coin, re-engraved with new sigils.

Love Incense

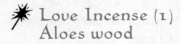

Love Incense (1)
Aloes wood

Burn aloes wood on the Full Moon for a new lover by the New Moon. Repeat as needed.

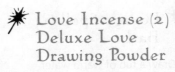

Love Incense (2)
Deluxe Love
Drawing Powder

To find a new love, grind the following ingredients into a fine powder and blend them together. Allow your nose to determine the proportions that are correct for you.

Aloes wood
Camphor
Frankincense
Mastic pearls
Myrrh
Orrisroot
Patchouli
Red sandalwood
Saltpeter
Sandalwood
Vetiver

1. Place this powder in a red flannel bag.
2. Carry it between your breasts for seven days; sleep with it beneath your pillow for seven nights. This may be enough to attract new love
3. If there are no results or promising leads after seven days, burn a pinch of the powder every morning for seven days.

Magically enhance the power of your love letters. For maximum effectiveness cast these spells in conjunction with each other.

Love Letter Spell (1) Bay Leaf

Write an invisible wish on a bay leaf and enclose it in the envelope.

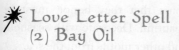

Love Letter Spell (2) Bay Oil

Dab a tiny bit of essential oil of bay laurel onto the corners of the letter's pages.

Love Powders

Once upon a time most perfumes were dry. They were easier to transport, both in terms of trade and in terms of personal use: a conjure bag could easily be filled with perfumed powder and carried with you to use as needed.

Powders are versatile and can be used in various ways:

★ *Dust powders on the body*
★ *Sprinkle them around the bed*
★ *Sprinkle them around a lover*
★ *Cast a circle for a love spell*

Sprinkled on the sheets, any vigorous activity that heats up the bed will simultaneously cause the erotic fragrances to intensify. Sweat encourages the powder to adhere to the skin.

The advantages of edible powder cannot be overemphasized: avoid talc and replace with food quality powder.

Love Powder (1) Do It Yourself Formula

Customize your own love powder.

1. Choose one or any combination of the following:
   Chocolate powder
   Cloves
   Cinnamon
   Cubeb
   Dried ginger
   Essential oil of cypress
   Grains of Paradise
   Orrisroot
   Peppermint
   Rose petals
   Vanilla sugar
2. Grind the ingredients into a fine powder.
3. Blend them with rice powder, cornstarch, potato starch, or arrowroot powder, distributing the botanical material evenly.
4. Use a sifter to help you achieve a smooth, even consistency.

5. Test it on your skin to make sure that you have a comfortable dilution: some of the powder ingredients (cinnamon, cloves) can irritate sensitive skin.
6. Place in a covered container and use.

Aphrodite Spells

The most celebrated love spirit of all, aphrodisiacs are named in her honor. The finest are believed to share in her essence.

Aphrodite most commonly manifests as either a mermaid or as an impossibly beautiful woman. She shines so brightly that she dazzles the eyes. She is the Queen of Wild Beasts and the Lady of Flowers, and she accepts devotion from both men and women. A friendly, sociable although temperamental spirit, she is usually accompanied by a host of lesser spirits as well as her companion animals. She likes a party. Love is her sacrament. To say that you're too busy for love or uninterested in romance is to offer her grave insult. To acknowledge the need and desire for sex and romance is to honor her and acknowledge her authority: request her assistance so that you, too, may worship at her altar.

Aphrodite is at the height of her power during the Summer Solstice. Her planets are the sun and Venus. Her day is Friday. Call her with myrtle, myrrh, and roses. Ancient worshippers offered her triangle-shaped honey cakes. Aphrodite is a versatile spirit and her altars take many forms. The bottom line is that they, like the spirit that they honor, must be beautiful. Decorate with seashells and other motifs from the sea.

✳ Aphrodite Spell (1) Apples of Love

Aphrodite is a bountiful spirit; she has not one but many sacred creatures and a multitude of sacred botanicals. Apple trees are among her favorites, however, and apples figure prominently in Aphrodite's magic spells.

1. Place three yellow apples on Aphrodite's altar and request that Aphrodite bless them.
2. Ask her to charm the fruit so that whoever eats these apples will fall madly in love with you.
3. Give an apple to the one you choose.

This may be considered the most "ethical" love spell of all, as the other

person retains the choice to eat the apple or not.

✳ Aphrodite Spell (2) Enchanted Charms

Have Aphrodite empower your love charms so that they will become romantic talismans to draw, maintain, and protect love.

1. Create an altar for Aphrodite.
2. Consecrate it with offerings to her such as flowers, fruit, perfume, or jewelry.
3. In addition, place upon the altar something that you'd like her to empower for you as a love charm. A belt or waist beads are traditional but any small charm or piece of jewelry is effective.
4. Be very clear and explicit as to what belongs to Aphrodite and will remain hers forever versus what she's empowering for you as a charm.
5. Let the charm rest on the altar overnight. Give it to your beloved as a gift or use it to draw new love.

✳ Apollo Spell

Apollo is a spirit of omnivorous sexuality. His romantic desires for men and women are equally strong; what seems to be the bottom line of attraction for him is beauty, intelligence, and talent, rather than gender. His is a complex myth. Classical Greek mythology paints him as the handsomest, most talented, most clever spirit of all, yet the women he pursues inevitably run from his embrace. Apollo had better luck with male lovers, with whom he had happy, successful relationships. Request his assistance, especially with someone who's hard to get.

1. Carve and dress a large yellow or gold candle and dedicate it to Apollo. Use any of the love drawing oils. **Pow-Wow Power Oil**, although it wasn't intended for this purpose, may attract Apollo's attention because it's so *sunny*.
2. Roll the candle in powdered Saint John's Wort.
3. Burn it and make your appeal.

Apollo's sacred creatures include crows and mice. Significant or surprising appearances may signal your response.

✳ Artemis Spell

Women seeking other women may request assistance from Artemis and Athena.

Artemis' happiest times are spent in the company of other women. She has deep-seated doubts about men, although she's partial to the very few special ones who come along. If you've discovered one of those unique men, Artemis may also be petitioned for assistance.

1. Petition Artemis at night.
2. Offer her cool spring water and white or silver candles. Small images of the wild animals that she loves are appropriate offerings.
3. Tell her that if she will grant your wish you will make a contribution toward the preservation of wild life.

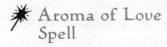 Athena Spell

Athena is a complex spirit, torn between her roots in the ancient Libyan religion of the Great Mother and her later fervent embrace of conservative patriarchy. Appeal to her earlier instincts:

1. Call Athena with a dish of olive oil dressed with olive flower essence remedy and a glass of wine.
2. Decorate her altar with images of snakes and gorgons.

3. Speak to her lucidly and articulately and tell her what you need.

Spells to Make Her or Him Love You

In the same manner that certain medicines or hormone treatments affect men and women differently, so some botanicals have different impacts upon the different genders. With the following spell categories (*Make Her Love You* and *Make Him Love You*), in general the gender of the target of the spell is what is significant. Thus these are spells to attract a man or a woman. The gender of the spell-caster may or may not be significant so unless told otherwise, assume that these spells are equal opportunity spells.

Make Her Love You Spells

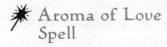 Aroma of Love Spell

Fumigate your clothing with the scent of aloes wood, cinnamon, and myrrh to attract women's romantic attention.

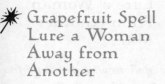

Basil True Love Spell

Hand a woman a sprig of basil. Allegedly if she accepts it, she'll fall in love with you and remain faithful forever.

Grapefruit Spell Lure a Woman Away from Another

1. Cut a grapefruit in half.
2. Write the woman's name and her present lover's name on a piece of brown paper.
3. Write your own name over the lover's name, so that the original lover's name is now illegible.
4. Stick this paper into the center of the grapefruit.
5. Put it inside a disposable pan or baking dish or line a permanent pan with foil.
6. Sprinkle the grapefruit with salt, pepper, and brown sugar.
7. Arrange five golden candles around the grapefruit in the dish and light them.

It's no accident that High John the Conqueror root is called by a man's name. It has powerful associations with men's magic.

Many women find success with it as a charm for luck, money, and general good fortune. When it comes to love and sex, however, this charm works best for men.

High John, like lodestones, is divided by gender: there are male and female High John's. Shape determines gender: the round ones are female; the phallic-looking ones are male. For love, sex, and romantic domination spells, obviously the more phallic the High John the better.

High John has heterosexual proclivities: it draws women to men. Men seeking other men traditionally substitute Sampson snake root.

High John Attraction Spell

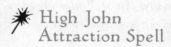

To attract a specific woman:

1. Steep High John in a jar of olive oil for seven days.
2. Remove the root and bury it under the steps of your target's home.

Reserve the oil for use as dressing oil.

✴ High John Love Drawing Spell

1. Obtain a few strands of hair from the head of the one you desire.
2. Wrap them around a High John the Conqueror root, making knots.
3. Anoint with a love drawing oil and place it inside a red drawstring bag.
4. Sleep with this under your pillow, and carry it with you during waking hours.
5. Anoint with one drop of the love drawing oil daily.

✴ High John Sexual Domination Spell

In addition to stimulating sexual generosity, this spell also allegedly produces a compliant nature.

1. Add a few drops of tuberose absolute to a bottle of **Command and Compel Oil**.
2. Use this oil to dress a High John the Conqueror root.
3. Place the dressed root into a red charm bag and sprinkle it with powdered confectioner's sugar and cayenne pepper.
4. Keep this bag under the mattress on the side where the woman usually sleeps.

5. Dress the root once a week with the oil to ensure cooperation. (And also to ensure that she hasn't yet discovered and removed the bag!)

✴ Isis Invocation: To Lure a Woman From Another Man

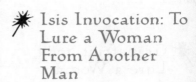

This spell requests assistance from Isis. It invokes famous lovers in the hope that you too will achieve their ecstasy.

1. At midnight on Saint John's Eve, pick a handful of vervain leaves, the plant that allegedly sprang from Isis' tears, when she lost her true love.
2. As you pick them, call on her:
   Isis, Great of Magic!
   Make [Name] daughter of [Name] love me like I love her.
   Make her love me like you love Osiris!
   Make her love me like Penelope loves Odysseus!
   Make her love me like Ariadne loves Dionysus!
   Make her love me like Aphrodite loves Adonis!
   Make her love me like Juliet loves Romeo!

3. From the moment you grasp the leaves, until your arrival home, keep up your chant and petition. Improvise, speak from your heart, invoke other lovers, but don't stop.
4. Carry the leaves home inside your shirt against your skin.
5. Place the leaves in new green silk.
6. Leave this packet in a dry, well-ventilated place for 21 days.
7. Then grind the leaves into a powder. Keep them in a mojo bag. When the opportunity presents itself, dust your hands with the powder. Touch the woman's hands and ideally her face.

✳ Sandalwood Seduction

Men are advised to wear sandalwood to elicit a positive sexual response from women.

✳ Three Hairs Spell

1. Steal three hairs from the woman, one at a time, on three separate occasions, while the woman is sleeping. For maximum effect, the hair should be taken from near the nape of the neck.

2. Braid the hairs.
3. Hold onto this braid for a little while, don't rush this spell.
4. Keep it in a charm bag worn or carried on the body, to absorb your power and desire.
5. When you're ready, push it into a crack of a tree so that it may grow with the tree from then on. (A romantic tree is ideal, such as an apple, other flowering or fruit tree, hazel, ash, hawthorn, or elder.)

Make Him Love You Spells
✳ Baked Goods Spell

1. Bake bread, a cake, or cookies for the one you love.
2. As you knead the dough, press it against your private parts or squeeze it beneath your underarm.
3. If you are baking multiple items simultaneously, mark whatever is intended for your beloved, to avoid confusion and trouble.
4. Feed it to him.

✳ Follow Me Boy!

Follow Me Boy! is the name given to a traditional condition formula. It is considered one of the Commanding formulas but is virtually always used in romantic or erotic situations. Sweet flag creates the commanding effect, which is reinforced further if you add licorice, however damiana is a potent aphrodisiac. He may be forced to follow you but he'll be happy to do it!

The basic formula consists of:

Dried sweet flag (calamus)
Dried catnip
Dried damiana
Optional: add licorice if you like the fragrance. For a more potent seductive oil, also add essential oils of bergamot, sweet orange, and tuberose, plus essences of any red flowers.

1. Powder the dried ingredients together.
2. Add them to sweet almond oil, shaking to blend.
3. Finally add any essential oils.

To use, dip a cotton ball in the oil and tuck it into a bra or pocket.

✳ Shoe Spell

To turn a sexual relationship with a man into something more:

1. Pick up his shoes as soon as he takes them off.
2. Place your own shoes inside his, your left inside his left, your right inside his right.
3. Buckle or tie them together as securely as possible.
4. Leave them like this until morning.

✳ Vetiver Attraction

The fragrance of vetiver allegedly attracts men, whether worn by women or other men. Wear it on the body or soak a cotton ball in the essential oil and tuck it into a pocket or bra.

✳ Wrap a Ring Around You Spell

1. Create a wreath or hoop from vines or love drawing plants, knotting your intentions and desires into the hoop.
2. Burn it.
3. Gather the ashes and sprinkle them around your heart's desire in a ring.

New Love Initiation Spell

Magically signal your readiness for love to the universe. This spell allegedly beckons true love near.

1. Pulverize splinters of acacia and aloes wood together with three hairs from your head.
2. Take the resulting blend to a crossroads on a breezy day.
3. Let the powder slip from between your fingers as you revolve in a circle, murmuring an invocation of love.

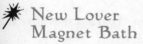

New Lover Magnet Bath

Add cubebs and hibiscus blossoms to your bath. Reserve some of the used bathwater and sprinkle it around your home to signal your magical invitation to a new lover.

Old Love Spell

A proverb suggests that love is wasted on the young. Orrisroot preserves the pleasures and passions of romance throughout one's life. Create this powder by grinding orrisroot and blending with rice powder. Dust on your body and the bed sheets as desired.

Oils of Love

Other oils will be found in the *Formulary*, including **Black Cat**, **Cleopatra**, **Come to Me Lover!**, and **Queen of Sheba**.

Amor Oil

1. Place a balm of Gilead bud and a piece of coral inside a bottle.
2. Cover these with sweet almond and jojoba oils.
3. Add a few drops of either neroli or petitgrain essential oil plus a drop of tangerine essential oil.
4. Add a bit of ground cinnamon or *one* drop of essential oil of cinnamon leaf.

New Orleans-style Fast Luck Oil

As far as love goes, Fast Luck Oil is a pick-up oil. Expect to draw a surprise one-night stand or even a great weekend, but not true long-lasting lingering love. The ingredients are cinnamon, vanilla, and Wintergreen, with a jojoba oil base.

Pansy Love Spell

Look for pansies with little faces that please you. Weave them into chains and hang them in the bedroom to capture the love you desire.

Red Witch Candle Spell

Candles in the shape of red witches are particularly beneficial for love magic.

The imagery is always positive: the red witch may represent the power of the witch as an ally or she can transcend the entire concept of human witches, to represent primordial female power. The red witch is symbolic for the menstrual blood that figures in so many love spells.

Red Witch candles are used to draw love:

1. Anoint her with love drawing oils.
2. Chant your invocation:
   Red witch, red witch
   Bring me my lover
3. Light the candle for a set period of time nightly. Choose a number that has significance for you—six minutes, nine, an hour. What is crucial is that this increment of time be maintained faithfully.
4. Burn nightly until consumed.

This spell may be used for an unknown lover or for someone whom

you already desire. If you know the person's identity, insert their name into the chant.

Red Witch Love Spell

1. Place a beautiful red apple beside a red witch candle.
2. Burn the candle while murmuring incantations of love.
3. Feed the apple to your heart's desire.

Re-ignite Love Spell

"Nothing's cold as ashes after the fire is gone …"

Allegedly vervain can re-ignite spent passions and past love. Create an infusion by pouring boiling water over vervain leaves. Add the infusion to your bath and allow yourself to air-dry when meeting your old love—although presumably for maximum effectiveness one bathes together.

Right Person Love Spell

You don't want just any love; you need the right one. This spell is beneficial for a long-term love search

Add **Attraction Oil** to your bath every Friday until you've found the love you want.

Roses Spells

Roses are a metaphor for the human heart. No flower represents love more vividly. Perhaps nothing does. Roses are sacred to the most powerful spirits of love: Aphrodite, Juno, Isis, Kybele, Maitresse Ezili, and Maria Padilha. Oshun loves yellow roses.

Cleopatra, the living embodiment of Aphrodite and Isis, seduced Mark Antony in a scented bedroom, packed knee-deep with rose petals.

✳ Red Rose Powder

Red Rose Powder is used to heal lover's quarrels.

. Grind red rose petals and peppermint leaves into a fine powder.
. Sprinkle Red Rose Powder on your partner, on a gift of a bouquet of flowers, or on the sheets.

Better yet, add Red Rose Powder to rice powder to create a body dusting powder. Apply it to your own body
with a powder puff so that no one can stay mad at you.

✳ Rose Love Beads

The original love beads are crafted from rose petals.

1. Process rose petals in a food processor or grind them with a mortar and pestle until they form a paste.
2. Roll small amounts into tiny beads with your fingers. Concentrate on your desire as you roll, utter a petition of love as you form each bead.
3. Let the beads dry, ideally on a screen that allows air to circulate.
4. While they are still slightly damp, before the bead has completely dried, pierce each bead with a large needle, so that it may be strung on a cord. Visualize your heart pierced with love as you wield the needle.
5. String the beads on a red silk cord and wear it or hang it over your bed.

✳ Red Rose Spell

1. Place a long-stemmed red rose between two red taper candles dressed with a love oil.

2. Burn the candles.
3. When the candles have burned down, give the rose to the one you want.

Seeking New Love Spells

Spells to initiate love emerge from different needs. Perhaps you await your soul mate, whose identity remains unknown, or perhaps soul mates and true love aren't an issue: you'd just like a companion, a new lover or relationship. Or maybe you have your heart set on someone special, whose identity is known to you. Now if only this person shared your desires…

✳ Seeking New Love Spell

A spell to find new love, particularly following a long period of solitude, loneliness, and bad luck:

1. Add a few strands of hair from your head plus some thumbnail clippings to dried rose petals, Grains of Paradise, and vervain.
2. Burn them over lit charcoal like incense.
3. Stand over the rising smoke wearing outer garments but no underpants. Inhale the smoke's fragrance as it wafts up toward you.
4. Still wearing no underpants, travel to a cemetery.
5. Walk through the cemetery in two directions, forming the shape of a cross, to destroy evil from all directions.
6. Go home via a different route than the one by which you arrived.

✳ Seeking New Love: Grains of Paradise

Grains of Paradise allegedly incite passion, erotic thoughts, and actions. They also possess a commanding element. Originally a popular East African magical ingredient, they are now renowned worldwide.

Use them to draw new love into your life: add an infusion of Grains of Paradise to your bath water; sprinkle the used bath water together with some extra powder around your home to signal your availability.

✳ Seeking New Love Shoe Spell Violet Leaf

Violet leaves resemble hearts. Place some in your shoe to attract new love and to guide you towards the right lover.

Seeking Someone Special Spells

Spells for when you know who you want.

Someone Special: Altar of Love Spell

This is a spell to persuade someone to return your affections. Three candles are required: one to represent you, the second, the object of your affections, and the last candle, the potential state of romance. Use figure candles to represent the people plus a large pillar or heart-shaped candle.

1. Arrange the two figure candles six inches apart.
2. Place the third at the apex of the triangle.
3. Dress the candles, petition, and light.

Someone Special: Heart Spell

1. Write the name of the person you desire on parchment paper seven times.
2. Draw a heart around these names by writing your own name in script, without picking up the pen or pencil. Lengthen each

letter or write your name repeatedly. The key is not to pick up the pen until the seven names are completely enclosed by your own.

3. Chant something like: "*You are in my heart*" or "*My heart encompasses you.*"
4. Preserve this talisman of love in a safe place. (Should you change your mind, rip up the paper, breaking the heart, and destroy it.)

Someone Special: Picture of Love

Cover a small photo of the one you love by wrapping it in strands of your hair. Wrap this up in red thread. Wrap this up in red velvet and bury the whole packet in Earth.

Someone Special: Pin Our Hearts Together

1. Cut two hearts from red wax.
2. Scratch your name on one, your beloved's on the other.
3. Pin them together with three pins and carry near your heart.

Talismans of Love

Fairy tales are full of magic power objects that draw love and good fortune toward their bearers. What the stories sometimes neglect to mention is that you can craft your own.

✹ Talisman of Love: Coral Earrings

In ancient Rome, coral earrings were believed to beckon men and draw love. Wear a pair at strategic opportunities.

✹ Talisman of Love: Red Ribbon Spell

To discover a bit of red ribbon, string, wool, or piece of fabric indicates luck in love and a change in romantic fortunes. Pick it up and make a wish. (If you can't think of one, requesting luck and happiness in love is more than appropriate.) Carry the ribbon as an amulet.

✹ Talisman of Love: Rose Quartz

Rose quartz allegedly draws lovers toward you. Wear it as jewelry or carry it with you.

Should it draw too many, too fast in an overwhelming manner, add an amethyst for a stabilizing effect.

Binding Spells

It's crucial to distinguish between banishing and binding spells, a not uncommon source of confusion.

★ *Banishing spells repel something or someone, removing it from your presence, perhaps permanently*
★ *Binding spells bind another person to you through eternity and perhaps beyond*

Occasionally the term *"binding"* is meant to indicate that someone has been incapacitated (*"bound"*) and is no longer able to harm you. However it is *not* used in that context in this book. Think *"ties that bind"* rather than *"bound and gagged."*

There are two types of love binding spells:

★ *Mutual binding spells that couples cast together to preserve, enhance, and protect love. In a sense these are magical soul weddings, affirmations of true love. These bindings are entered into*

consciously and with free will and desire

★ Binding spells that one party casts on the other, frequently without their knowledge. These bindings are often desperate attempts to salvage a relationship or prevent another from leaving. In a sense, these spells assert romantic ownership over another party. As such, they can be malevolent spells, which rarely work out happily for either party

How do you know if a binding spell has been cast over you? If every effort to leave a relationship fails, there's reason at least for suspicion. Never fear; as with hexes, antidotes exist.

There is a key difference between menstrual blood potions and classical binding spells: a successful menstrual potion causes the other person to love you forever. You, however, remain a free agent. Binding spells bind you as surely as they bind the other party. Use them judiciously.

Wait! Before the binding spells begin below, how do you know you have the right person? Are you binding yourself to true love or to living disaster? These two spells will help you determine the answer.

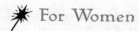 For Women

Rue attracts love but also eliminates women's romantic illusions. **It is not safe for use by pregnant women or those actively attempting to become pregnant**. (In which case, other issues and factors may be at hand.)

Simultaneously burn rue, inhaling the fragrance, while drinking rue tea. Bathing in an infusion of rue, at the same time, will maximize the potential of this spell.

For Men

An amethyst carried as a talisman attracts women. It specifically draws honorable women.

Mutual Binding Spells: True Love Spells

These binding spells are entered into freely and with mutual intent. They produce a magical wedding of souls and affirm commitment to one another. At their best, these are the most romantic spells of all.

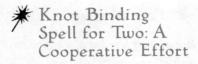

Knot Binding Spell for Two: A Cooperative Effort

This binding spell ensures that a couple remains together. It will also counter efforts to sunder your love, thus serving as a simultaneous protection spell.

1. One partner takes a handkerchief or square of cloth and ties two knots in it.
2. The other partner ties two more knots.
3. Both parties together now take these four knots and tie them together to make one big, tight knot: both parties pull so that the knot is as tight as possible.
4. Keep the charm in a safe place. Dress it with a love oil periodically.
5. If at some point you do wish to separate, untie or break the knot.

Lodestone Binding

The most successful binding spells stem from mutual desire and intent.

1. **Lodestone Oil** is required as well as some privacy.
2. Create Magnetic Sand Dusting Powder: combine rice powder with magnetic sand. You'll need a powder puff or a feather for application. (A shaker bottle will work but doesn't quite have the same effect.)
3. Massage the **Lodestone Oil** onto one partner's body.
4. The other partner should apply the Magnetic Sand Body Powder.
5. Make love.
6. The binding spell is complete; repeat as desired.

Pomegranate Binding

"How do I love thee?" Let me count the seeds ...

To effect a binding:

1. Break open pomegranates; two should be sufficient:
2. One partner eats 220 seeds, the other eats 284.
3. Count them and eat them together.

To Break a Binding Spell

You've discovered that someone has bound you without your knowledge or permission and against your desires. All is not lost. Binding chains can be broken.

✳ Antidote Spell

1. Powdered sassafras bark is required. Take a bit from your own tree and grind with a mortar and pestle or purchase from an herbal supplier. Ground sassafras is also a staple of Cajun cuisine, sold under the name filé powder—think filé gumbo. It may be purchased under that name from spice companies.

2. Add the ground powder to a blend of castor and jojoba oils. (Do *not* use essential oil of sassafras; it is highly toxic.)

3. On seven squares of paper, write the following using **Dragon's Blood Ink**:

   I break your power; I destroy your force [Name], child of [Name]
   You have no control over me [Name], child of [Name]
   You have no power over me [Name], child of [Name]
   I am free from your binding spell.

4. Every morning for seven consecutive mornings, soak one paper in the oil.

5. Tear it into either three or five pieces. Add the pieces to frankincense and myrrh resin and burn them.

6. Every day, as you complete this spell, the power of the other person over you diminishes. It should be completely broken by the spell's conclusion.

Break-Up and Romantic Discouragement Spells

Sometimes the romantic issue at hand isn't attracting or maintaining love, rather it's terminating a relationship. *Break-Up Spells* include:

★ *Spells to terminate an established, existing relationship*
★ *Spells to discourage unwanted attention from strangers and also from those who imagine a relationship exists where it does not. If that attention is extremely persistent and aggressive, check out* Banishing Spells *for those that discourage stalkers*

✳ Anti-Love Potion

Turnips are allegedly the anti-love food. Set a dish of turnips before an unwanted suitor to send them on their way.

Break-Up Powder

Sometimes a significant relationship may have ended for you. Now you're waiting for the other person to come to the same understanding.

1. Grind and powder the following dried botanicals: lemongrass, mullein, patchouli, valerian, and vetiver.
2. Sprinkle the powder in the pockets and shoes of the one whom you'd like to send packing.

*Warning: this is not a secret spell. The ingredients are derived from **Van Van** and (botanical) **Graveyard Dust**. The powder will have a strong aroma. Questions will be asked.*

Post Break-up Cleansing

According to general metaphysical wisdom, any sexual relationship creates vestigial ties that bind, the more intense, passionate, and lengthy the relationship, the more intense, passionate, and lingering the bonds. This cleansing spell is beneficial whenever you wish to sever and erase those bonds, whether from a long-term relationship or a one-night stand.

Gently rub a whole raw egg against your naked body, from head to toe and outwards from shoulders to fingers, with extra emphasis placed on the genitals. When complete, break the raw egg into the toilet and flush it away.

Relationship End Powder

This powder is more subtle than Break-Up Powder.

Grind the following botanicals into fine powder: camphor, pennyroyal, and slippery elm. Sprinkle into the shoes and pockets of the one who should depart.

Warning: Pregnant women or those actively attempting to become pregnant should not handle pennyroyal.

Heartbreak and Disappointment Spells: Pre-Break Up

Do you sense love slipping away? These spells attempt to restore and revive lost or fading love. The relationship isn't completely over; your partner hasn't left … yet. (Under these circumstances, consider *Summoning Spells* to help bring the other party back.)

✳ Baby Please Don't Go Spell

There's no need for a Summoning Spell. He or she hasn't left yet. You, however, foresee with fear and dismay that the date of departure seems imminent. This variation of a floorwash attempts to forestall that departure, revive love and happiness, and make that Summoning Spell you've already picked out completely unnecessary. This is a version of a classic condition formula known as Stay With Me.

1. Pour boiling water over the following ingredients to create a strong infusion:
   Bloodroot
   Cardamom
   Coriander
   Cumin
   Forget-me-not
   Rosemary
2. Strain out the botanical material, and add the liquid to a bucket of water together with some vinegar.
3. Use it to cleanse your home, concentrating on thresholds to the outside and the bedroom.
4. For maximum power, cast the spell in conjunction with many repetitions of the sacred sounds of Lorraine Ellison's recording, "Stay With Me Baby." Sing along or just listen as inspired.

✳ Love Me Again Spell

It matters little that your partner hasn't left; love seems to be gone.

Burn dragon's blood while chanting petitions for love to be restored and resurrected. Keep chanting continuously for as long as the dragon's blood burns.

✳ Stick With Me Spell

"Pega-pega" *is the Spanish name for the botanical* Desmodium obtusum. *Pega-pega literally means "stick-stick" or "attach-attach."*

★ *Add pega-pega to conjure bags to mend damaged relationships and stay together*
★ *Sew it into the other person's clothing*

Heartbreak And Disappointment Spells: Post-Break Up

Sometimes it's not about the other person; it's about repairing and soothing your own broken heart.

Apple Romantic Cleansing Spell

A cleansing spell for when a bad love affair has left you feeling tainted, humiliated, or defiled.

1. Dice an apple and douse the pieces with honey and cayenne pepper.
2. Let it sit until it rots.
3. Flush the pieces down the toilet.
4. Affirm that you will learn to love again but more wisely this time.

Broken Heart Bath

1. Add white rose petals, honeysuckle blossoms, and rose attar to a bath filled with water. Substitute hydrosols for the fresh flowers if necessary.
2. Place a rose quartz large enough not to go down the drain in the bath too.
3. Soak in the scented bath.
4. Following the bath, carry the rose quartz with you. Sleep with it under your pillow until you don't need it anymore.

Heartsease Spell

Heartsease are wild pansies. Their name reveals their secret power to soothe heartache. Float fresh blos-soms in your bath or add the flower essence remedy.

Honeysuckle discourages unhealthy nostalgia and attachment to the past, enabling you to move forward in a whole, healthy manner. These spells require traditional fragrant honeysuckle rather than Cape honeysuckle, which is beautiful but lacks scent.

Oregano Spell

The scent of oregano allegedly helps you forget old lovers. Ordering a pizza may be of some use once in a while, however burning the dried herb as incense or heating a few drops of the essential oil in an aroma burner are much more effective.

Yarrow Heartsease Bath

Among yarrow's meanings in the Language of Flowers is "cure for heartache." Add yarrow hydrosol to your bath water.

Love Potions

At its most basic, the exact nature of the simple love potion beverage is less crucial than your magic power with which you've charged it.

1. Pour out the potion.
2. Whisper and murmur your desires and intentions over the liquid in the glass.
3. Serve it to your lover.

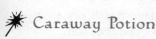

Caraway Potion

Not the alcoholic beverage or herbal tea type? Not to worry. Bake caraway seeds into cakes, breads, and cookies and serve to the one you desire to stimulate mutual emotions.

Chestnut Love Fix

Allegedly hand-feeding someone chestnuts stimulates them to love you.

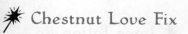

Chocolate Potion

Following the conquest of Mexico, chocolate was exported to Europe. In Aztec Mexico, chocolate was served as a ritual drink, with chili peppers rather than sugar. In Europe, chocolate's aphrodisiac properties were exploited instead. The Inquisition was not pleased: some Spanish women got into trouble for allegedly using hot chocolate

to cast love spells. Interestingly, chocolate is now known to contain phenylethylamine, a stimulant similar to those released during sex. For what it's worth, Casanova's recommended pre-sex menu was a cup of chocolate and a plate of oysters.

Serve hot chocolate to the one you love and see if it works. For extra enhancement, top with powdered aphrodisiac spices, like powdered cinnamon or cardamom.

Dreams of Delight Love Potions

The basic formula includes cardamom, cinnamon, coriander seeds, and licorice root. Two different techniques provide different effects.

Dreams of Delight Potion Fragrant

The aroma of simmering Dreams of Delight may be so inviting that drinking may not be necessary. Merely inhaling the fragrance with its subliminal message of love and seduction may be sufficient for the purpose.

1. Fill a pot with wine.
2. Add the dried botanicals and warm to a simmer.

3. Strain the solids out and serve the warm potion to the one you love.

Elderberry Potion

Fairy tales tell of fairies so infatuated with mortal lovers that they seduce them and carry them away to Fairyland, where no doubt this potion is served. Gather elderberries on Midsummer's Eve, whispering your desires over them. Make them into elderberry wine, or just steep the berries in wine and serve.

Flowers of Love Potion

Add a few drops of hibiscus flower essence remedy to jasmine tea and serve to the one you love.

Lavender Potion

Lavender is one of those interesting substances that may serve as an aphrodisiac—or create the opposite effect. The only way to find out how someone will react is to serve it.

Add fresh lavender to a bottle of white wine. Allow it to steep several hours or overnight, then strain and serve.

Love Potion #2

A potion for two intended to enhance, stimulate, and preserve true love.

1. Pour a bottle of red wine into a pot or cauldron.
2. Add the following botanicals (adjust quantities to suit your taste or that of your intended): cardamom pods, cinnamon sticks, and clove buds.
3. Allow to simmer gently for an hour, then strain.
4. Pour the wine into glasses and add one drop of red hibiscus flower essence per glass.

Love Potion #9

Today any spiritual supplier worth its salt sells some sort of love-drawing oil called Love Potion #9 but, as anyone who's ever actually listened to the song knows, the original was a drink. The earliest Love Potions #9 seem to have been infusions of herbs, i.e. herbal teas or tisanes, relying on aphrodisiacs rather than alcohol to deliver the passion.

1. Choose nine love herbs. Consider these:

   Damiana

   Ginger

   Grains of Paradise

   Hibiscus

   Lovage

   Melissa (lemon balm)

   Peppermint

   Red clover

   Rose petals

   (Other options might include adder's tongue, cardamom pods, catnip, cubeb, lavender, red raspberry leaves, or rose hips.)

2. Make a strong infusion of all the herbs, strain, and serve.

Love Potion #9: Another Version

Lovage, a plant whose associations with romance are indicated by its name, is also known as "nine-stem." Some consider that lovage tea is the true Love Potion #9. Experiment and see which is most effective.

1. Blend all parts of the plant: flowers, stem, leaves, and roots.
2. Grind them into powder (don't make it too fine as it becomes difficult to strain the botanical out of the liquid).

3. Pour boiling water over the ground lovage.
4. Strain and serve.

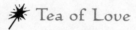

Papaya Potion

Share a papaya. This not only induces erotic feelings but allegedly stimulates true love.

Tea of Love

Simple ordinary black tea allegedly induces lust and erotic inclinations. After all, tea does derive from the beautiful camellia family. Drink it by itself or use it as a base for more complex potions.

Brew black tea from leaves, incorporating fresh mint, rose petals, and/or jasmine blossoms for added enhancement. Add one drop of essential oil of bergamot before serving and murmur your desires into the steaming liquid.

The simplest potion of all is wine. It invokes the blessing of Dionysus, Patron of Intoxication and the only Olympian spirit happily wed to his soul mate. Wine also invokes the precision required by magic: just the right quantity kindles passion and ability. Too much and erotic power is removed, replaced by sleep, obnoxiousness, erectile dysfunction, and general unpleasantness.

✳ Wine Potion (1) Amber and Essence

1. Steep amber in red wine.
2. Remove the amber before serving.
3. Add wild rose (Bach Flower) and hibiscus flower essence remedies (FES, Pegasus, South African Flower) just before serving.

✳ Wine Love Potion (2) Aphrodisiac

1. Steep the following ingredients in wine:
   Cinnamon
   Cloves
   Coriander seeds
   Grated lemon zest
2. Add hibiscus flower remedy (FES, Pegasus, South African Flower) at the last moment, two drops per glass.

Sex, Seduction, and Aphrodisiacs

These are very specific spells: a romantic or true love component may also exist but that's not the main focus of the spell. Just like regular love spells, this category is vast, with spells to suit every taste and desire. A high percentage of *Sex and Seduction Spells*, especially the more ancient ones, are designed to enable men to magically seduce women. This may be because for millennia women's spells went unrecorded or it may reflect historical social sexual dynamics.

During the European witch-craze, the fear of witch-caused impotence reached states of hysteria. In other cultures, other concerns were more prominent. The fear-inducing magical figure of *The Arabian Nights* or Jewish fairytales isn't that notorious female witch, it's the evil male sorcerer intent on seducing young virgins and devout, faithful wives alike with irresistible mystical charms, amulets, and spells.

For happiest results, cast these spells cooperatively.

Basic Aphrodisiac Ingredients

Aphrodisiacs tend to be foods or fragrances. Because they evoke very personal, unique responses, experimentation is required to discover which aphrodisiacs work for you or your lover. Incorporate any one or combination of the following into your very personal spells:

Caviar
Champagne
Chocolate
Coriander
Fruits: apricots, peaches, cherries, grapes, figs, pomegranates
Garlic
Hibiscus tea
Honey
Hot peppers
Mint
Onions
Radishes
Saffron
Shellfish especially, but all fish in general
Spices: cardamom, cinnamon, cloves
Sushi
Vanilla

 ## Cyclamen Spell

In the Language of Flowers, cyclamen represents voluptuousness.

Soak the root in sweet almond oil for three days. Strain and reserve the oil to serve as a dressing oil for charms and candles. Cyclamen flower remedy (Pegasus) may have aphrodisiac properties too. Experiment.

 ## Diamond Spells

Diamond refers to both a gemstone and a shape. In the metaphysical language of geometry, the diamond shape may stand in for the human eye or for the vagina. Is this why Western marriages are typically initiated with diamond rings? Emeralds are the gemstones that attract and stabilize love and fidelity. So why are diamonds such popular engagement rings?

Diamonds, whether carried or worn, promote self-confidence in sexual matters. They relieve root causes of sexual dysfunction. They are a cleansing, releasing, purifying stone in matters of sexuality. These are spells that will, no doubt, please the target:

★ *To stimulate someone to be more sexually receptive toward you, bestow the gift of a diamond, magically charged with your own desires*

★ To heal your own sexual inhibitions and dysfunction, don't wait for someone else to bestow the gift. Provide your own diamond: charge it with your desires, bathe it in spring water enhanced with hibiscus flower essence remedy (FES), and wear it

☀ Dress for Seduction Spell

What does the goddess of love wear to cast a seduction spell? A magic cloak with nothing underneath? Once upon a time, like Aphrodite or Ishtar, she wore a magic girdle but that magical garment seems to have lost some power over the ages. Another item of clothing however, once associated with witchcraft, retains its magic powers of seduction.

Wear a crimson garter belt to enhance your powers of seduction, create an aura of irresistibility (it works without anyone seeing it, unless you want them to), and to discover wells of primal female power.

☀ Erotic Incense

Grind and powder ginger lilies, jasmine, myrrh, and tuberose. (Essential oils may also be warmed in an aroma burner.) Waft the fragrance where desired.

☀ Flowers of Desire Oil

Blend essential oils of jasmine, tuberose, lavender, and ylang ylang to render yourself irresistible and to inspire passionate feelings.

☀ Fruits of Love Spell

Eve seduced Adam with an apple. Or did she? As apples aren't native to that part of Earth, there's been much debate as to the actual identity of the forbidden fruit. Other possibilities include apricots, pomegranates, quince, and figs (hence the fig leaf). A simple display of fruits allegedly magically tempts even someone determined not to be seduced.

1. Find the most beautiful examples of the above fruits you can and place them in an equally attractive bowl.
2. Offer them to the target of your spell. If he or she eats the fruit, they will be yours.
3. If they decline, merely leave the bowl close at hand and see what happens.

Lavender Spells

Lavender is an unusual plant; some find it to have aphrodisiac properties while others find it to be the opposite. Test its effects on lovers.

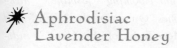

Aphrodisiac Lavender Honey

1. Warm one cup of honey in a bain-marie.
2. Add approximately one quarter cup of fresh or dried lavender blossoms.
3. When the honey begins to bubble, remove it from the heat. (Don't let it scorch!)
4. Let it sit for thirty minutes, then strain out the lavender.
5. Use the honey while warm.

Lavender Irresistibility Spell

Pin fresh lavender to your underwear; allegedly this renders you sexually irresistible. Alternatively, add essential oil of lavender to final rinse water when washing your underwear; this may be as effective and will certainly be more comfortable.

Magic Mirror Sex Spell

1. Purchase a small hand mirror. Many modern mirrors are double-sided; this is an old spell. A mirror with some sort of a back to it is required.
2. Pay whatever is the asking price; don't haggle.
3. Remove at least some of the back of the mirror and write your beloved's name three times in that space. That's the easy part.
4. Now you need to find a pair of copulating dogs. Don't disturb them; just hold the mirror so that their image is reflected within it. Don't look inside it yourself or allow anyone but the object of your desire to gaze within.
5. Somehow you must induce him or her to look into the mirror.
6. Having accomplished this, hide the mirror for nine days in a spot where your beloved is guaranteed to pass by frequently.
7. When the nine days are over, carry the mirror on your person.
8. Allegedly this will now cause the object of your desire to become sexually aroused whenever she or he is in your presence.

✳ New Orleans Parfum d'Amour

1. Blend and gently warm the following ingredients:
   Florida Water
   Rose water or hydrosol
   Cinnamon hydrosol
2. Dissolve honey in the liquid, stirring to distribute.
3. Allow it to cool.
4. Place in a bottle and wear the fragrance.

Peppermint Spells

Persephone wasn't Hades' only love. His true love apparently was the nymph Mentha. This relationship pre-dated his abduction of Persephone and continued after their marriage. When Demeter discovered that not only had Hades kidnapped and raped her daughter, he was also cheating on her, she was outraged and in a classic example of blaming it on the woman, transformed Mentha into the lowly peppermint plant. Mentha had the last laugh: Hades was rendered unable to perform sexually without mint. (Of course, the fact that peppermint was once used as a contraceptive might also have influenced the Lord of the Dead.)

To this day mint is considered among the most potent aphrodisiacs.

✳ Queen of the Night Spell

Night-blooming jasmine's nicknames "Queen of the Night" and "Moonlight of the Grove" indicate its power. Wear fresh blossoms after dark to attract a new lover, romantically hypnotize one you already have, and to transform yourself into a nocturnal queen.

✳ Road of Love

Blend hibiscus and rose petals. (Grind, powder, or leave whole as you choose.) Use these flowers to sprinkle a path to the bedroom or wherever you choose. You may create a lavish carpet or be extremely discreet, as long as the path is unbroken.

Seduction Oils
✳ Arabian Nights Perfume

The compilation of stories known as The Thousand and One Nights *or* The Arabian Nights *is filled with details of magic spells and*

formulas for seduction. Because stories that fall under the broad category of fairy tales are now relegated to children, the erotic material contained in The Arabian Nights is typically excised. Add essential oils of aloes, ambrette, jasmine, liquidambar, myrrh, and rose to your bath in preparation for nights of love.

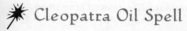

Cleopatra Oil Spell

Place five drops of **Cleopatra Oil** in each corner of the bed and another five in the very center for enhanced erotic enjoyment and powers of seduction.

Jezebel Oil, like the queen in whose honor it's named, is a complex, multifaceted oil. Mainly used in money, love, and seduction spells (and especially those spells that bridge all three concerns), the key to **Jezebel Oil** is that it is used for getting what you want, in the face of all odds. Jezebel root, a cousin of orrisroot, possesses both seductive and commanding properties.

Jezebel Seduction Spell

The spell may be used to initiate a relationship or to hold an already existing lover spellbound. Intensify standard **Jezebel Oil** by adding cinnamon, damiana, jasmine, and/or rose petals. Dress purple taper candles with this oil and burn it in your intended's presence.

Oil Spell (1) Jasmine

Allegedly this oil arouses desire and ability and reduces resistance.

1. Blend a few drops of jasmine attar into sweet almond oil.
2. Use it to massage the one you love.

Powder Spell (1) Better Sex

Grind cubeb peppers into powder and sprinkle it around the bed to magically inspire better sex.

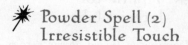

Powder Spell (2) Irresistible Touch

Powder orrisroot and mix with cinnamon powder. Rub just a little bit between your hands and touch the person you desire.

Powder Spell (3) Triple X Powder

Grind Grains of Paradise, damiana, and cubeb peppers together. Sprinkle this powder around your bed to enhance all activities within it.

Sex Sheet Spell

1. Toss a sheet over copulating dogs and then get it back. Don't wash that sheet!
2. Find an excuse to wrap the sheet around the one you desire. This will allegedly arouse amorous feelings.

Sweet-talking Seduction Spell

For sweet, persuasive speech, chew a bit of cinnamon just before speaking.

Peppermint (real peppermint leaves, not breath mints) may work, too.

Thyme for Irresistibility

According to legend, thyme derives from Helen of Troy's tears, and thus shares her essence. Bathe in an infusion of fresh herbs to radiate the

power of a love magnet. Use carefully: remember Helen was kidnapped twice!

Vanilla Seduction Spell

Cast this spell to attract or seduce a lover. Add genuine vanilla extract to your bath. Allow yourself to air-dry, then dust with rice powder blended with a little ground cinnamon.

Virility: Enhancing, Maintaining, Reviving, and Repairing

In addition to general aphrodisiacs, there is a special category of spells designed to enhance, strengthen, and remedy male sexual performance. Male sexual performance spells fall into two categories:

★ *Spells to magically counteract and remedy impotence*
★ *Spells to enhance sexual performance, so as to transform a regular guy into a magically empowered lover*

Spells to Heal and Remedy Impotence

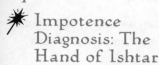

Impotence Diagnosis: The Hand of Ishtar

According to ancient Mesopotamian belief, all-seeing, all-knowing spirits punish a host of infractions, some of which you may not even have realized you had committed until you received the punishment. Mesopotamian deities typically communicate their displeasure by inflicting disease. Each possesses its own specific illness. Thus you will know by the disease, whose displeasure you have evoked. Ishtar, Divine Spirit of Love, Life, and Sexual Delights, punishes via sexual dysfunction. If impotence is a result of her anger, then the only way it can be resolved is through rituals to evoke her forgiveness.

However, a problem of ambiguity exists: impotence may also be the result of malevolent bewitchment cast by another person, or of a mangled Fidelity Spell cast by your wife to stop you playing around on the side. (The notion of a purely physical cause may or may not have existed.)

The root cause of impotence affects the nature of its cure. This diagnostic spell seeks to determine whether lack of sexual ability stems from human hands or from the

Hand of Ishtar. As with many healing rituals, someone else performs the spell for the patient.

1. Form dough from emmer wheat and potter's clay.
2. Use it to create male and female figures.
3. Place one on top of the other, however you're inspired.
4. Place them near the afflicted man's head.
5. Recite an incantation seven times, blessing Ishtar and requesting that the needed information be clearly revealed.
6. Remove these figures and place them in the vicinity of a pig. If the pig approaches the figures, this confirms that Ishtar is responsible for the ailment. A cure may be made through offerings and rituals of appeasement. If however the pig does not approach the figures, if they do not attract its attention, the man has been bewitched by a person. In order to undo the spell, he must find the charm and undo it or take other magical measures.

I've left the ancient spell's original instructions as per materials, on the off chance that emmer has some magical qualities distinct from other wheat and that this ingredient may be possible for some to find. However, feel free to substitute a more convenient wheat if needs be.

Impotence Remedy (1) Dandelion

Early American colonists recommend dandelions to counteract impotence based on magical and folk-healing traditions. Interestingly dandelion leaves have since been discovered to contain extremely high quantities of Vitamin A, essential for production of male and female sex hormones.

A glass of dandelion wine serves as a restorative potion. Alternatively add dandelion leaves to salad. Before consuming, murmur your desires over the food and visualize successful accomplishment of the spell.

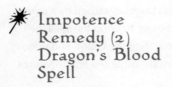

Impotence Remedy (2) Dragon's Blood Spell

Place a chunk of dragon's blood in a red bag and keep it under the mattress, to reinvigorate male sexual prowess.

Iron Spell Iron Key

1. Obtain seven keys, each from a different house, each from a different town.
2. Heat them until red-hot on an anvil. (A cast-iron pan will substitute.)
3. Blend water from seven different sources: the original Moroccan formula requests water from seven different wells, in itself an adaptation of the ancient pan-Semitic miraculous water from seven springs. If either option is a possibility, follow the original directions. Otherwise, seven types of bottled spring water, each deriving from a different source, is a realistic modern update.
4. Pour this blended water over the red-hot keys. The patient is then exposed to the steam. (Be careful not to scald yourself; the goal is to improve the situation, not worsen it.)
5. Catch the water as it comes off the anvil or pan.
6. When it cools off, use it to bathe the afflicted parts.

☀ Strong as an Oak Spell

Oaks are traditionally associated with primal male power. This spell may be used to remedy impotence or just enhance sexual capacity.

1. Look for an older, strong, powerful-looking oak.
2. Talk to the tree: whisper your situation to it, describing your needs and desires. Request assistance.
3. Look down: if the tree is sympathetic, you'll find twigs or acorns on the ground.
4. Actually seeing the twig or acorn fall—or even being hit on the head by one—is a profound assurance of assistance.
5. Leave a gift and libation for the tree; gather up your acorn or twig and carry it with you.

Super Sexual Ability Spells

As the Marvellettes sang, *"My baby must be a magician because he's sure got the magic touch!"* These spells may benefit someone suffering from erectile dysfunction, it doesn't hurt to try; however their real goal is to transform regular sex into nights (and days!) of unflagging ecstasy.

Male Super Sexual Ability Spells tend to take the form of potions or virility charms. In many cases the magic symbolism inherent in these spells evokes female sexual symbolism in order to enhance male sexual ability (almonds, honey, clams, and more).

☀ All Night Long Oil

Add essential oil of jasmine, ideally jasmine sambac, to sweet almond oil. Use this oil to dress candles or the body, to magically fulfill the promise inherent in its name.

☀ Date Super Sex Spell

Make a date with some dates: carry cleansed, dried date pits in a conjure bag, for enhanced sexual ability.

☀ Johnny-Jump-Up Sex Power Spell

Carry dried Johnny-Jump-Up blossoms in a conjure bag to enhance male sexual potency.

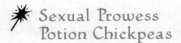
Sexual Prowess Potion Chickpeas

To enhance male sexual prowess:

1. Soak chickpeas (garbanzo beans) in water. They will swell.
2. When they are completely soft and swollen, strain out the chickpeas and drink the water. This allegedly makes a man so virile he can deflower 72 virgin cows in one night.

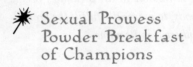
Sexual Prowess Powder Breakfast of Champions

Before breakfast on three consecutive mornings, eat shelled almonds pounded with cinnamon and then mixed into honey. Three mornings is allegedly enough to provide a long-lasting effect.

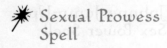
Sexual Prowess Spell

Keep male fern and High John the Conqueror roots stored among your clothing. When you wear the clothing, you will allegedly radiate sexual magnetism.

Virility Charm Horns

Double horns evoke primal female power, reflecting the appearance of women's internal sexual organs; a single horn manifests male primal power and sexual vigor for obvious reasons. Although men aren't inherently vulnerable to the Evil Eye, their sexual power and reproductive capacity are among the Evil Eye's primary targets. Charms representing horns, traditionally worn around the neck, potently protect male genitalia and virility.

Ya Ya Powder

Grind, powder, and blend the following: cinnamon, peppermint, red sandalwood, and vetiver. Dust the sheets or dust yourself to inspire your partner.

Summoning Spells

Summoning spells are exactly what they promise: magic spells to bring someone to you. Most often used for lovers, a summoning charm may be effective for anyone with whom there is a strong soul connection or emotional bond.

In some cases summoning spells beckon a new lover or someone who is a friend, acquaintance, or who has perhaps expressed casual romantic interest but the spell-caster wants more. Usually these spells target someone whose identity is known as opposed to the abstract new-love drawing spells found among *Basic Love Spells.*

Many of these spells, however, are specifically cast to summon a spouse, partner, or ex-partner who has abandoned the spell-caster or with whom there has been a substantial disagreement. Their whereabouts may or may not be known. Many older spells specifically target a husband; women may have been less likely or able to leave or perhaps there were more direct means of bringing them back.

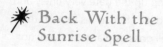

Amethyst Bedroom Spell

Encourage a spouse or lover who has abandoned a relationship to return.

. Charge a substantial amethyst crystal with your desires.
. Attach this activated amethyst to the right side of the bedpost or headboard.

3. Seduce him into sleeping with you in that bed; ultimately he should fall asleep on the left side of the bed.
4. Encourage him to stay. Repeat from Step 3 as needed.

Back With the Sunrise Spell

For the return of an absent lover:

1. Buy peppercorns and coriander seeds from a store that faces west.
2. Burn them at sunset.
3. Turn to the east and let a towel with which you have cleansed yourself after sex flutter in the wind.
4. Pray and petition that when the sun returns, your beloved will return also. If necessary, repeat at sunrise.

Better Sex If You Come Home to Me Spell

This spell was inspired by men who took younger second wives. This is the old wives' retaliation. It may also be used to lure a man back from another lover.

1. Sleep with one date inside your vagina for seven nights. Use the same date; you may remove it during the day, reinserting at night.
2. After this point, the target of your spell is invited for a meal.
3. Chop up the date very finely and feed it to him in his food. If the spell goes as planned, it will not be a brief, businesslike meal.

The spell has two effects: first, to induce him to return to you, and second, to make sex unsatisfactory with anyone but you in the meantime. The second aspect allegedly kicks into action as soon as the date is inserted.

☀ Cleopatra Oil Summoning

*Bring an errant lover back with **Cleopatra Oil**. The oil may be worn as perfume; otherwise saturate a cotton ball with it to wear or carry when you anticipate running into your ex.*

☀ Commanding Doll Spell

1. Make a rag doll to represent the target of this spell or use another kind of doll.

2. Write your beloved's name on a piece of paper.
3. Attach it like a name-tag to a doll.
4. Anoint the doll with **Command and Compel Oil**. Lay it on a piece of red silk or satin. Sprinkle it with **Come to Me Powder**.
5. Chant:
   I command you, I compel you,
   I command you, I compel you.
   I've covered you with powder
   I command you, I compel you,
   I command you, I compel you
   Hear my voice!
   I command you, I compel you:
   Return to me now!
   This very instant, this very
   *   minute, this very hour!*
6. Repeat for three consecutive nights.
7. Following the third repetition of the entire ritual, wrap the doll in silk, and hide it in a dark closet or secret space.

☀ Do As I Say Spell

This summoning spell demand
personal contact with the target.

Create Do As I Say Powder b
grinding and powdering cedar chip
myrrh, sweet flag/calamus, and pep
permint leaves. Sprinkle the powde
on the ground in your target's patl
allegedly this will magically induc
your ex to return to you.

Lover Come Back Spell

This spell allegedly returns a departed lover within twenty-one days. It possesses a protective aspect as well as a summoning one. If the spell doesn't work and he's not back in the prescribed time, this may mean you're better off without him. Start making new plans.

1. Create an infusion by pouring boiling water over damiana and red rose petals.
2. Bathe in it. When you're done, reserve some used bathwater in a bottle.
3. Add a little of your own urine and sprinkle some of this liquid in the front and back of your home for twenty-one days.

Magnetic Summoning Spell

Sprinkle magnetic sand onto a magnetic horseshoe to encourage the return of a lost love.

Rosemary Summoning Spell

. Gather rosemary stalks before daybreak on Midsummer's Day.

2. Light a fire. Add three rosemary stalks.
3. Chant three times:
   I burn rosemary.
   But I'm not burning rosemary.
   What do I burn?
   Your heart—the heart belonging to [Name], child of [Name] that's what I burn
   That he may neither be able to stop or stay away
   Until he comes to be with me and stay

Twenty-seven Day Spell

This spell comes with a time limit; if success isn't shown by the end of 27 days, it's time to consider a new romantic start.

1. Cut out a paper heart.
2. Write your lover's name on this paper nine times.
3. Cross over each name with your own.
4. Place the paper in a saucer or small dish and cover it with sugar.
5. Stick a white birthday candle in the center of the sugar. Burn it. (Make a wish if you want but don't blow out the candle.) Keep the dish with the sugar, paper, and any wax drippings.

6. Add a fresh birthday candle the next day. Repeat for a total of nine times, nine candles altogether.
7. If he's not back by the end of the ninth try, burn the sugar and the paper.
8. Start again the next day, repeating with all new materials. If after nine days and candles, he or she is not back, burn the materials again.
9. If you like, try it one more time, for another nine days.

Three times is the charm: if he's not back after this, he won't be.

Your Absence is Killing Me Spell

This elaborate ritual, intended to force an errant husband's return, pretty much tells the universe that you're as good as dead if he doesn't come home.

1. The deserted spouse lies on the floor, stretched out like a corpse, with funerary candles at her head and feet. Stay in that position until the candles have burnt out. This spell is from Latin America and has a Roman Catholic orientation: it is suggested that the Christian Creed be repeated while waiting for the candles to burn down. Supplement with petitions. Substitute other prayers, petitions, and visualizations as appropriate.
2. Pay attention to your words as the candles burn out. Whatever you're saying when they are actually extinguished must be repeated three times, while pounding on the floor with both fists.
3. Immediately call the spouse's name and demand that spiritual authorities force his return:
   Soul of Tulimeca, you who are in Rome.
   I need you to send me [Name], child of [Name], repentant of all the grief he has caused me Humbled and full of love for me

This ordeal must be repeated for three successive nights.

Luck and Success Spells

Although conventional wisdom frequently depicts luck as an ephemeral quality mysteriously belonging to some but not to others, according to magical perceptions, luck is a distinct commodity to be acquired, squandered, or lost. Luck and good fortune, in other words, can be magically *made*, although it may take some effort.

The Wheel of Fortune, which has its origins in the sacred symbolism of Lady Luck, the Etruscan deity Fortuna, spins constantly. Like hamsters on a wheel, we scramble to stay on top. How fortunate that magic spells exist to acquire, maintain, and preserve luck.

All High Conquering Luck and Success Powder

Use this powder to eliminate obstacles and provide luck and success in the face of all challenges.

Grind and powder High John the Conqueror chips, crumbled bay leaves, *and frankincense. Carry in a conjure bag or sprinkle as desired.*

All Saints Oil Spells

All Saints Oil evokes blessings of good fortune, for success in all your endeavors.

All Saints Candle Spell

*Carve a candle that represents you. Dress with **All Saints Oil** and burn.*

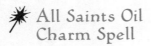

All Saints Oil Charm Spell

*Anoint a clover charm with **All Saints Oil** and carry with you at crucial moments for enhanced confidence, luck, and spiritual protection.*

All Saints Quick Fix Spell

*Don't have a clover or any other lucky charm? Don't worry. **All Saints Oil** stands on its own: soak a cotton ball in **All Saints** and carry it in your pocket.*

Anvil Spell

An anvil serves as a magnet for good fortune. This ritual is most auspicious on specific days of the year, especially Saint George's Day and New Year's Day.

1. Decorate an anvil with fresh tree boughs.
2. Place candles and incense on the anvil as you would on an altar and light them.

3. Chant something like: "Luck come to us! Good fortune draw near!"
4. Offerings of straw are made to the anvil in exchange for good luck and prosperity. This is also an auspicious moment for divination.

Basic Candle Spell

1. Hold a red candle in your hands to charge it with your vision and desire. The candle may be any shape that appeals to you: votive, seven-day, cat, or witch; the crucial element is that it must be red, the color of luck.
2. Carve the candle with your identifying information.
3. Dress it with **Van Van**, **Black Cat**, **Lucky Lodestone**, and/or **Crown of Success Oil**.
4. Burn the candle.

Blessings of Good Fortune Spell

To bless something or someone, scatter elder leaves and berries to the winds, circling sunwise murmuring the name of the person or thing. Scatter some more directly onto the person or thing if possible.

✳ Bread Spell

This ritual derives from petitions to the orisha Babalu-Ayé and is believed to bring good luck. If you incorporate spiritual petition, that luck may be even greater.

1. Nail a slice of bread behind the front door.
2. Fasten a purple ribbon to the nail.
3. Replace as soon as the bread begins to rot or deteriorate, burning the old slice.

✳ Everything's Coming Up Aces Spell

1. Place the four aces from a new deck of playing cards on a plate.
2. Cover them with breadcrumbs.
3. Cover this with sugar.
4. Add seven coins plus metal charms that represent your desires. (In other words, if you're an ice-skater, you'd use a skate charm.)
5. Place a silver candle on top of everything and burn.

✳ Four B's Lucky Incense

This incense's aroma allegedly draws luck, happiness, and prosperity to you while simultaneously repelling evil.

Grind the following into a fine powder:

Bayberries
Bay laurel leaves
Dried basil
Buckeye nuts

Sprinkle the powder on lit charcoal and burn.

Horseshoes Spells

Horseshoes remain among the luckiest charms, although few who carry them today appreciate their ancient associations with the adoration of human primal sexual energy. The luckiest horseshoes have a lucky seven holes. Should you accidentally stumble upon a horseshoe, this is a harbinger of approaching good luck. You'll get a bonus year of luck for every nail still in the shoe.

Horseshoe Spell (1)
Feed the Horse

1. If you find a horseshoe, wrap it in red cloth together with some hay.
2. Tuck it under your mattress.
3. Pay attention to your dreams: they may generate luck for you.

Horseshoe Spell (2)
Wrapped Up in Magic

Latin American magic wraps horseshoes in thread to create magic spells. The horseshoe is the basis of the spell; exactly what is done with it depends upon the spell-caster's goal. The horseshoe spell below generates luck and good fortune:

1. Dip a horseshoe in Lucky Lodestone Oil.
2. Dip it into magnetic sand.
3. Shake off the excess.
4. Wrap red silk thread around the shoe until it's covered completely.
5. Mount the wrapped horseshoe onto a piece of cardboard.
6. Embellish the horseshoe itself and the cardboard with lucky charms like four-leaf clovers and miniature dice. Miniature playing, tarot, or votive cards may be attached, as can seashells. Small quantities of lucky botanicals can be captured in a tiny piece of fabric—a miniature mojo hand—and attached. Place a metal sea-horse charm in the very center of the horseshoe for extra good luck.
7. Post this image so that it will draw good fortune toward you.

Jupiter Spells

Once known as the *"Greater Benefic,"* this huge planet presides over luck and good fortune. The position of Jupiter in your natal chart and the aspects it makes to other celestial bodies determines your luck in this lifetime. Have an astrologer cast your natal chart to analyze what sort of fortune you were born with and how best to manifest that luck. Every person's horoscope charts the gifts and challenges that are present at birth. An astrologer can also calculate your *"Part of Fortune,"* so as best to exploit luck and minimize those challenges.

Jupiter's Angel

Zadkiel, ruler of the planet Jupiter, is the angel of goodness, grace, generosity, and mercy who bestows

benevolence, good fortune, and justice. Burn frankincense to attract his attention and then tell him your heart's desires.

Jupiter's Lucky Charm

The metal associated with luck is tin, as it is the one under the rulership of Jupiter.

1. Cut out a small piece of tin.
2. Engrave it with lucky words, numbers, or phrases.
3. Put it in a lucky mojo bag and carry it with you.

The lodestone may as well be known as the luck-stone. Few things are as associated with the acquisition of good fortune.

Lodestone Spell (1) Basic

1. Dress a lodestone with one or more of the lucky condition oils: Black Cat Oil, High John the Conqueror, Lucky Lodestone, Magnet, or Van Van.
2. Sprinkle it with a lodestone's favorite food, magnetic sand (fine iron shot).
3. Carry with you in a red drawstring bag.
4. Replenish your lodestone's power by dressing and feeding it once a week.

Lodestone Spell (2) Feed the Stone

1. Place a lodestone in a small covered terracotta pot.
2. Once a week, consistently on the same day, remove it from its dish and place it in a bowl of spring water. Let it sit for a few minutes while you express thanks for the blessings that came into your life during the previous week. (Think of some!) Remove the lodestone. Drink the water or add it to your bath.
3. Dry the lodestone; place it back in its pot.
4. Feed it by sprinkling some magnetic sand over it.
5. Keep your lodestone private. Let it know your desires: add a penny or a piece of real silver to the pot for financial luck. For romantic luck, add a photo of the one you love or desire or some other symbol of love.

☀ Lucky Bath

Gather the freshest, most fragrant blossoms you can find. Add them to your bath together with pineapple juice for joy and good fortune.

☀ Lucky Bath: Clover

Make an infusion by pouring boiling water over red clover. Let it cool, strain and add it to a tub filled with warm water so that you're bathing in clover!

☀ Lucky Bath: Spearmint

Make an infusion by pouring boiling water over spearmint. When it cools, strain out the botanical and add the liquid to your bath.

Cats are the animals most associated with luck and good fortune.

☀ Lucky Cat Spell (1) Bastet Candle

Bastet is the Egyptian goddess of joy, luck, love, and the pleasures of life. She is typically depicted as either a cat-headed woman or as a seated bejeweled cat. Candles are sold in the latter shape, however you may also

substitute any green cat candle. (Green is Bastet's sacred color.)

1. Dress the candle with Horn of Plenty Oil. This oil represents Earth's finest fruits and your wish to partake of them. This is a difficult oil to create from authentic materials because your choice of "fruity" essential oils is limited. Use essential oils of lime, tangerine, and pink grapefruit. Supplement with fragrance oils like cherry, apple, or melon.
2. Place a scarab near the candle as it burns.
3. Focus on your wishes, desires, and petitions.
4. When the candle has burned down, carry the scarab as a charged lucky charm.

☀ Lucky Cat Spell (2) Black Cat

Black cats evoke strong reactions. Some fear them and many still subscribe to the superstition that a black cat crossing one's path causes bad luck. Ironically, in many tradition, black cats are associated with good luck. The black cat is believed to epitomize the cat's proverbial nine lives.

1. Hold a black cat candle in your hands to charge it with your desires.
2. Carve it as desired.
3. Dress it with Black Cat Oil to provide good fortune and break all hexes, and then burn.

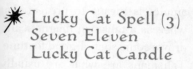 Lucky Cat Spell (3) Seven Eleven Lucky Cat Candle

*Anoint a black cat candle with **Black Cat Oil** and/or **Van Van** or **Magnet Oil**. Burn the candle on consecutive nights: seven minutes the first night, eleven minutes the second, seven the third, and so forth until the candle burns down, by which time you should see a change in fortune.*

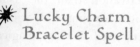 Lucky Charm Bracelet Spell

Charm bracelets go in and out of fashion but their roots derive from magical use, manipulating the secret powers of objects. Lucky charms may be understood as a form of amulet, talisman, or ex-voto.

. Choose a charm that represents your goal.

. At the New Moon place this charm beside a small pink candle.

3. Charge the candle with your desire, carve and dress if you like and burn it.
4. When the candle burns out, attach the charm to a bracelet.
5. Wear it or reserve in a safe place, whatever suits your magic.
6. When this goal is achieved, set another goal.
7. Choose another charm and begin again. (Should you reconsider and change your mind regarding any goal, merely remove that charm and begin again at the New Moon.)

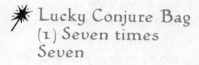 Lucky Conjure Bag (1) Seven times Seven

*Place a staurolite crystal, seven Job's tears, seven tonka beans, and a matched pair of lodestones into a conjure bag. Anoint with **Magnet Oil** as needed.*

Lucky Conjure Bag (2) Lodestone Luck

Carry Grains of Paradise, five-finger grass (cinquefoil), a matched pair of lodestones and one unbroken star anise in a conjure bag for good fortune and protection.

☀ Lucky Devil!

Carry the botanical devil's bit so you'll be a lucky devil, too.

☀ Lucky Golden Handwash

Handwashes are most commonly associated with gambler's magic. However, handwashes may also be used to provide general, all-around good fortune.

1. Place three or seven strands of saffron in a cup.
2. Pour boiling water over it.
3. Let it cool, then bottle and refrigerate it.
4. Rub the liquid on your hands (do not rinse off) to have and maintain happiness and good fortune.

☀ Lucky Incense

Burn incense in harmony with astrological signs to bring good luck in all aspects of life.

1. Blend the following: cinnamon, labdanum, cloves, violets, lemon zest or lemongrass, jasmine, black pepper, ambrette seeds, rose petals, sandalwood, camphor, and dried currants.

2. Burn as incense or simmer to produce aromatic vapors.

Lucky Talismans

Although the words "*amulet*" and "*talisman*" are used somewhat synonymously today, technically an amulet is meant to protect you whereas a talisman magnetically draws some sort of good fortune. Talismans are what are usually meant by the phrase "*lucky charm.*" The term "talisman" also frequently indicates a specific type of lucky charm: engraved precious stones. However talismans of good fortune come in many forms, including metal, botanical, and written charms.

Most talismans require no further activation than the usual charging, cleansing, and/or consecrating used for any magical tool. Talismans are usually worn or carried on the person, frequently in a charm bag. Good luck talismans such as these include:

★ *Devil's shoestrings roots*
★ *A coin minted in your birth year*
★ *High John the Conqueror root*

Some talismans, however, require further activation in order to draw good fortune.

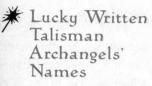

Lucky Written Talisman Archangels' Names

Talismans frequently take the form of written charms. Sacred words and names radiate their own magical power. The creation of the talisman is perceived as a spell. Traditionally, writing a talisman is preceded by cleansing rites and frequently by fasting, and you should choose your paper and ink thoughtfully.

One talisman uses the names of the archangels. Write on parchment paper the names of the seven Hebrew archangels. This is most effective if written in Hebrew script:

Michael
Raphael
Gabriel
Souriel
Zaziel
Badakiel
Suliel

Post the talisman on the wall or carry it within a leather or metal conjure bag.

Magic Box Spells

Magic boxes are especially auspicious for luck spells. Because charms are stored together in these magic boxes, and especially if the box has power too (see *Elements of Magic Spells*) their power is concentrated and symbiotically enhanced. Magic boxes aren't meant to be created to be stored on a shelf. Take the box out periodically and play with the contents. Absorb their power while charging them with your desires. Take one or two out and carry with you as needed, replacing with an equivalent number of alternative charms, always maintaining a lucky seven in number.

Magic Box Spell (1) Lucky Seven Charm Box

Seven is the number of miracles and good fortune. Fill a magic box with seven lucky charms. Some suggestions are:

1. High John the Conqueror.
2. Low John the Conqueror.
3. Small magnetic horseshoe (you could use an actual horseshoe, if your box is large enough).

4. Shamrock or four-leaf clover (real or a charm representation).
5. Lodestone.
6. Piece of Fool's gold (pyrite) or a small piece of real gold.
7. A tonka bean.

Substitute other charms as you like, or maintain a rotating community of charms.

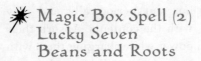

Magic Box Spell (2) Lucky Seven Beans and Roots

Fairy tales identify beans with luck and fulfilled wishes. Roots are frequently the most magically charged, amuletic part of a plant. This magic spell box combines the two for extra good fortune.

Consider filling your box with the following or substitute other preferences:

1. High John the Conqueror.
2. Low John the Conqueror.
3. Lucky Hand root.
4. Galangal root.
5. Tonka bean.
6. Vanilla bean.
7. Black snake root.

Dress the items with essential oils of vetiver and patchouli and sprinkle with powdered nutmeg and mace.

Metal Key Spells

Metal keys attract positive magic into your life, while simultaneously deflecting evil. Magic keys open doors of opportunity. Old metal keys are best: check out flea markets and antique stores—let the keys *and* opportunities find you.

Metal Key Spell (1) Mojo

According to Romany metaphysical traditions, carrying key-amulet charms enables you to learn secrets, have mysteries revealed, and find personal success. Find a special key and charge it with your desire. Place it in a red silk bag and carry it with you.

Metal Key Spell (2) Wind Charm

1. A collection of keys may be strung together onto red thread as a charm or formed into a wind chime.

2. An easy wind chime for the less than artistically inclined may be made from a bent wire coat hanger.
3. Hang the keys in the wind to rustle up beneficial opportunities.

Mirror and Sieve Spell

1. Fasten a mirror to the center of a sieve.
2. Hang the sieve so that the mirror reflects outwards. Good influences are able to pass through the sieve's holes, while the mirror transforms evil influences into good luck.
3. Enhance with a charged magic mirror for extra power or use a "ba gua," the feng shui ritual mirror.

Mistletoe Luck Spell (1)

Twist marjoram and thyme around mistletoe and hang it in the corners of each room to attract luck and fortune.

New Year's Eve Spells

New Year's Eve, the threshold of the New Year, offers the perfect opportunity for a change in fortune.

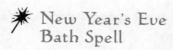

New Year's Eve Bath Spell

*Make an infusion of mucura by pouring boiling water over the herb. Bathe in this infusion in the very first hour of the New Year for luck and protection. (**Note: bathing in mucura is not safe if you're pregnant.**)*

New Year's Eve Bayberry Candle

Real bayberry wax candles are rare and costly: it takes approximately fifteen pounds of bayberries to create one pound of bayberry wax. And so bayberry candles are often reserved for special occasions.

New Year's Eve is such an occasion! Light a bayberry candle on New Year's Eve to draw luck, prosperity, and success in the coming year. Scratch your goals and desires into the candle wax for extra enhancement.

New Year's Eve Lunar Candle

1. Carve a white candle with your desires on New Year's Eve.
2. Reserve the candle until midnight, then greet the

midnight moon by lighting your candle.

3. Make a wish for the New Year as you light the candle.

Peppermint Spells

Peppermint brings joy as well as good fortune. It cleanses stagnation, creating room for opportunity and success.

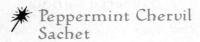

☀ Peppermint Chervil Sachet

Peppermint and chervil, two lucky plants, combine synergistically to bring happiness, luck, and protection.

1. Combine equal quantities of dried chervil and peppermint and sew them into a sachet.
2. Wear it against your skin during the day.
3. Sleep with it under your pillow at night.

☀ Peppermint Floorwash

1. Make a strong infusion of peppermint by pouring boiling water over the botanical.

2. When it cools, strain out the peppermint and add the liquid to a bucket of floorwash rinse water.
3. Add vinegar and a little Cascarilla Powder.
4. Cleanse the floors and threshold areas to radiate an invitation to happiness and good fortune.

Repairing Bad Luck

"If it wasn't for bad luck, I wouldn't have no luck at all," sings bluesman Albert King.

Is he singing the soundtrack to your life? *"Been down so long, it looks like up to me,"* wrote poet/singer/songwriter Richard Farina. Does that sound too familiar, as well?

If you can't even conceive of having good luck, and you'd be content with a respite from the worst luck, don't despair. Magic methods exist to turn your luck around.

☀ Bad Luck Begone Powder

This botanical powder makes no promises about bringing good fortune but allegedly counteracts bad luck and protects from its effects. (Nine, seven and five are numbers of protection

incorporate these numbers into the quantities of botanicals used.)

Blend the following ingredients, grinding them together:

Nine dried bay leaves, crumbled
Frankincense
Juniper berries
Cloves
Dried dill
Dried fennel
Dried tarragon

Make substantial quantities: carry some with you in a mojo hand, while keeping more within the home as fragrant, protective potpourri.

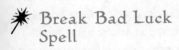

Break Bad Luck Spell

This spell allegedly breaks a spell of bad luck.

1. Carve your affirmations and desires on a white candle and dress it with olive oil.
2. Roll it in ground red pepper.
3. Light the candle, place it securely on the floor and jump over it.

Broken Mirror Antidote Spell

Does breaking a mirror cause seven years of bad luck? It better not; many spells require shards of broken mirror. If the situation causes anxiety, never fear, an antidote exists:

1. Some mirrors break cleanly into a mere few pieces while others shatter into thousands. Be that as it may, gather up all the shards and pieces of the mirror and as much of the glass dust as possible.
2. Wrap it in fabric or a paper bag.
3. Throw the mirror pieces into a river or fast-moving stream, flowing away from you so as to carry away all misfortune.

Drive Away Bad Luck Bath

1. Make a strong infusion of basil and spearmint. You may strain the botanicals out or leave them in for extra strength.
2. Squeeze in the juice of one lemon.
3. Sprinkle with sesame seeds and a handful of flour.
4. Stir in a spoonful of **Command** and **Compel Oil**.
5. Fill a bathtub with water.

6. Carry the bowl with the infusion to the tub.
7. Stand in the tub of water, pour or ladle the infusion over your head, sit down and soak.

☀ Out With Bad Luck, In With the Best Luck Spell

Burn that candle at both ends! Eliminate misfortune and, because nature abhors a vacuum, simultaneously attract something positive to replace it.

1. Obtain one red and black double-action candle. It may be necessary to trim the bottom of the candle, exposing the wick, so that both ends may be burned simultaneously.
2. Carve what you wish to eliminate from your life on the black end.
3. Carve what you'd like to see manifest in your life on the red end.
4. Ideally, place the candle horizontally on a candlestick with a spike. Otherwise drive a long nail or pin through the border dividing the colors. Place the candle horizontally over an open bottle, inserting the pin to provide balance and stability.
5. Burn at both ends simultaneously.

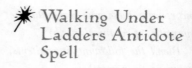

☀ Walking Under Ladders Antidote Spell

Among the most common superstitions is the fear of walking beneath a ladder, and many will go well out of their way to avoid doing so. Should you find yourself forced to walk beneath a ladder there is an antidote to avoid bad luck. This spell must be cast when you walk under the ladder.

1. Cross your fingers as you approach the ladder. (If this isn't possible, a knot may be made instead.)
2. Keep your fingers crossed until a dog is observed. Once you sight that dog, you're home free. Uncross your fingers; untie your knot.

Wishing Spells

Sometimes it's not general good fortune that's required; you need one special wish fulfilled. *Luck and Success Spells* attempt to magically generate general good fortune. *Wishing Spells* tend to have one specific desire in mind. Now anyone can wish: all you have to do is think or articulate it. However, special magic spells and techniques enhance the chances of success, helping transform hopeful wishes into concrete reality.

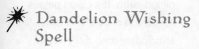

Apple of Desire

With a thorn or pin, scratch your wish into the skin of a beautiful apple. Hold the apple in both hands and contemplate your desire. Dip the apple in cinnamon honey and eat it completely, savoring each bite.

Dandelion Wishing Spell

Make a wish while holding a dried dandelion. Hold that thought in your mind, and then blow all the seeds off the dandelion with one breath. If this can be accomplished, your wish should be fulfilled.

First Star Spell

Starlight, star bright
First star I see tonight
I wish I may, I wish I might
Have this wish I wish tonight

This rhyme has been relegated to the nursery yet it recalls a potent Wishing Spell.

1. Pay attention at twilight; it's easy to miss your opportunity.
2. If you can catch sight of the very first solo star in the sky, gaze at it and make your wish. (The rhyme charm may be incorporated but it's not necessary.)
3. If the first star can't be identified, luck isn't with you: save the spell for another night.

The Four-leaf Clover

According to legend, if you find a four-leaf clover and wish upon it, your wish will come true. Well, nothing is guaranteed, not even if it's legendary, but a special magical technique exists to maximize a four-leaf clover's wish-fulfilling potential.

When you wish upon the clover, count each leaf. Each offers a unique form of good fortune. Visualize how you'd benefit from their promise:

★ *The first leaf to the left of the stem is fame*
★ *The second leaf to the left of the stem is money*
★ *The third leaf to the left of the stem is love*
★ *The fourth leaf to the left of the stem is good health*

Perhaps the first step should be to find a four-leaf clover! However, a metal charm may be used, and may be preferable: its leaves won't fall off while you're counting!

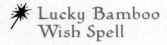

Lucky Bamboo Wish Spell

Carve your wish into a piece of bamboo and bury it in a safe place.

Lunar Wish Spells

Wishing upon the moon is easier than wishing upon a star; however, as with stellar wish spells, timing is everything. The moon is the heavenly body most associated with granting wishes.

Lunar Wish Spell (1) Basic

When you catch sight of a particularly beautiful, evocative moon, stop and gaze at it. Concentrate on your desire, look at the moon and make one explicit well-articulated and defined wish.

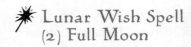

Lunar Wish Spell (2) Full Moon

1. Stand naked in the light of the Full Moon.
2. Go through the motions of bathing in the moonbeams.
3. Gaze at the moon while doing this: when ready, make whatever petition you please.
4. Watch for an immediate response: if the Moon remains clear, it's a positive sign. If the Moon brightens and the light intensifies, this is an extra auspicious sign. If a cloud passes across the moon, you can anticipate some difficulty in achieving your desire. Take some further magical steps or perhaps reassess your desire. Work on it until the next Full Moon and repeat.

Lunar Wish Spell (3) New Moon

The following is a Romany ritual to greet the New Moon.

Greet each New Moon by chanting something like this:

Here is the New Moon.
The New Moon has arrived.
Be lucky for me now
You've found me penniless

Leave me rich and prosperous.
Leave us with money.
Leave us with good health
Leave us with love.

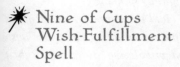

Nine of Cups Wish-Fulfillment Spell

The nine of cups tarot card is traditionally considered "the wish card," a happy card that indicates your wishes will come true.

1. Remove the nine of cups card from a Rider-Waite tarot deck or another deck that illustrates the Minor Arcana. (Some decks only illustrate the Major Arcana.)
2. Place the card upright between a gold and a silver candle.
3. Light the candles; gaze at the card and clearly, distinctly, articulate what it is you truly want.
4. When the candles burn down, place the card under your pillow. Further information may be revealed in your dreams.

Ocean Spirit Wish Spell

Address your request to Aphrodite, Poseidon, Yemaya, or any other ocean spirit you choose, but address it specifically to someone. Don't send out a generic request. Write your request or query on rice paper or some other biodegradable paper. Launch it into the waves and await your response.

Sage Wishing Spell

1. Write your wish on a single sage leaf.
2. Place it beneath your pillow for three consecutive nights.
3. Should this sage leaf appear in your dreams at any time during these three nights, your wish should be fulfilled.
4. If not, what you're requesting is complex and difficult. Bury the sage leaf in Earth, requesting that, if your wish is beneficial, it will grow to fruition. If realizing your dream would be harmful, request that the energy and desire dissipate safely into Earth.

Uninterrupted Happiness Wish Spell

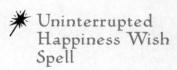

Nine coins strung onto red cord represent "uninterrupted happiness," according to Chinese symbolism. These coins on the cord will also help you turn wishes into reality.

1. Make nine wishes; one wish may also be repeated nine times for extra emphasis and power.
2. Collect nine I-Ching (replica) coins.
3. String each one while concentrating on a wish. Affirm that each wish is received as you tie each knot.
4. When the cord is complete, keep it in a safe, secret place.

✳ Wishing Stones

Make a wish upon a ... stone? Certain stones are believed to have the power to help you achieve your wishes. Preserved in charm bags, they may be taken out as needed, to enhance all wishes and increase the odds of success. Those reputedly most powerful include amber and holed stones. (Yes,

amber is really fossilized tree resin, however because its ancient origins were mysterious, people classified it as a mineral and that ancient classification more or less remains, at least magically speaking.)

Hold the stone in your left hand while concentrating upon your wish and visualizing its success. Rub it with your thumb in a clockwise motion. Keep the stone in your pocket and rub it with your thumb as desired to reinforce this wish.

✳ Yarrow Wish Spell

The very first blooming yarrow that you see is a magical plant that can grant you one wish. Hold the bloom in your hand and make your wish. That night, sleep with the plant below your pillow.

Marriage and Divorce Spells

Because marriage, handfasting, or any ritualized union is one of the major thresholds of life, it's perceived as a time of tremendous power, promise, *and* vulnerability. The entire marriage ceremony, the arrangements preceding it, and post-nuptial celebrations may be perceived as a huge series of magic spells as much as a religious sacrament. In some cases, it's consciously both.

Activate an Engagement Ring

In regards to promoting and pre-serving love and long-term relation-ships, the emerald is by far the best choice for an engagement ring. However the following ritual trans-forms any ring into an enchanted ring of love.

1. First obtain the ring.
2. Tie it to a red silk thread and suspend it into the smoke made from burning frankincense and myrrh, patchouli and vetiver.
3. Wrap it securely in silk cloth. (You may remove the thread.)
4. Wear this packet for nine days and nights against your skin, preferably next to your heart or under your left armpit.
5. Pass it through the incense again.
6. Make a braid from three of your hairs and three of your beloved's.
7. Wrap this around the ring.

8. Wrap the ring with the braid in silk again.
9. Wear it for an additional six days against your heart or in your armpit.
10. On the seventh day, remove the lover's braid and present the ring to your beloved.

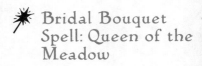

Bride's Anti-Evil Eye Spell

One of the psychic dangers inherent on the Wedding Day is that so much celebration and happiness will inevitably attract the envious eyes of jealous spirits, or the Evil Eye. Among those perceived as vulnerable to the Evil Eye, brides rank highest, right alongside infants and pregnant women. Although many protection spells exist, this one specifically targets the Evil Eye.

The bride holds a coin under her left armpit during the marriage ceremony. Upon leaving the ceremony, the coin is secretly and discreetly allowed to fall to the ground, either as a payment to spirits who will protect from the Evil Eye or as a bribe to the spirits. Whoever discovers and picks up this coin unknowingly obtains a year's good fortune.

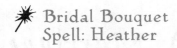

Bridal Bouquet Spell: Heather

Incorporate white heather into the bridal bouquet for luck and protection.

Bridal Bouquet Spell: Queen of the Meadow

Queen of the Meadow's other nickname, bridewort, indicates its affinity with brides. Carry some within the bridal bouquet to obtain all the happiest marriage blessings.

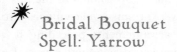

Bridal Bouquet Spell: Yarrow

Incorporate yarrow into the bridal bouquet for seven years of happiness.

Bridal Protection Spells

Because the bride is perceived as so psychically vulnerable, hidden amulets and charms serve as magical bodyguards during the ceremony. Because the distinctive bridal gown so clearly identifies the bride, exposing her vulnerability, so the gown becomes the most common tool of protection. Special spells and charms simultaneously protect the bride while promoting romance and devotion.

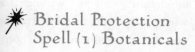

Bridal Protection Spell (1) Botanicals

Sew herbs into the hem and/or belt of the wedding gown to bring love and romance to the marriage. Favorable herbs include clover, elecampane, lavender, and powdered mistletoe.

Bridal Protection Spell (2) Garter

The bridal garter was originally a protective garment, intended to safeguard the bride from spiritual danger. For maximum magical protection, instead of the typical blue garter, wear a red one with a piece of silver attached. Remember to charge it with your desire.

Bridal Protection Spell (3) Mother Goose

Mother Goose rides through the air on a very fine gander. Today, Mother Goose is limited to the nursery, her rhymes intended to entertain only the youngest, least sophisticated children, yet Mother Goose's namesake bird links her to a host of powerful spirits: Aphrodite, too, rides through the air on a goose. The bird is sacred to Egyptian Hathor and Roman Juno, both valiant protectors and advocates for women.

In the Middle Ages, the once sacred goose became associated with witchcraft and disreputable women. Attempts to discredit Lilith and the Queen of Sheba depict them as dangerously beautiful, seductive women, with one goose's foot peeping from beneath a skirt.

Mother Goose's famous marital recommendation echoes an old witch charm:

Something old, something new
Something borrowed, something blue
And a sixpence in her shoe!

Follow Mother Goose's directions in order to provide the bride with spiritual protection and promote romance in the marriage.

Bridegroom Protection Spell (1)

The bride seems to get all the magical attention. Sometimes the groom needs protection, too. Luckily, if he does, the bride can provide it.

In some Slavic ceremonies, just before the ceremony, the groom is wrapped in the bride's cloak, evoking primal female protective power.

☀ Bridegroom Protection Spell (2)

To provide the groom with protection, the bride should circle him sunwise either three or seven times.

Get Engaged Spells: Obtaining Proposals of Marriage

A not uncommon dilemma occurs when one person decides that it's high time to get hitched, while the other party remains unconvinced or doesn't even want to discuss the matter. Reflecting times past, when women's life security was determined by marriage, most spells assume that it's the woman who wishes to wed, although in reality this is obviously not always the case and undoubtedly never was.

There are many spells that contrive to obtain a proposal. They may be used identically by either gender, with the exception of spells that appeal to a spirit that is the guardian of one particular

gender, like Juno, Yemaya, and the Weaving Maiden.

(Maria Padilha is an equal-opportunity spirit, willing to work with women, men, trans-sexuals—basically anyone whom she likes.)

☀ Get Engaged Spell (1) Bride and Groom Candle

Spiritual supply stores sell candles in the shape of a conjoined bride and groom. This particular spell can also serve as a binding spell.

1. Use this type of candle or place two figure candles side by side.
2. Carve and dress the candle(s).
3. Bind them with ribbons, knotting in desires and blessings.
4. Perform a marriage ceremony over the candles, using your name and that of your beloved.
5. When you have pronounced them husband and wife, burn the candle(s).

☀ Get Engaged Spell (2) Elderflowers

Successfully accomplish this spell and English folk tradition say you'll be wed within the year.

1. Pour boiling water over elder-flowers to create an infusion.
2. Allow this to cool, then strain, discarding the botanicals and reserving the infused liquid.
3. Add this elderflower infusion to beer or wine.
4. Contrive to drink from a shared glass.

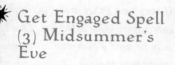

Get Engaged Spell (3) Midsummer's Eve

Dance around nine Midsummer's bonfires to be married within the year.

Happy Marriage Spells

For on-going, ever-present marriage blessings:

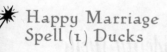

Happy Marriage Spell (1) Ducks

Ducks allegedly mate for life. In any case, their marital success rate is among the best in the animal kingdom, far superior to that of humans, no doubt. A pair of mandarin ducks serves as a lucky marriage charm in the hopes that you'll be able to emulate their devotion to each other.

These ducks epitomize faithfulness and fidelity.

Post an image of mandarin ducks prominently in your home. Or place a matched pair of statues somewhere strategic to radiate happiness there.

Happy Marriage Spell (2) Marjoram Crown

Marjoram is among Aphrodite's sacred herbs. Crown the bride and groom with marjoram garlands to ensure marital happiness and romantic bliss.

Happy Marriage Spell (3) Orange Blossom

1. Reserve orange blossoms from the bride's bouquet or garland.
2. Do not let them whither but burn them, together with a piece of parchment bearing the names of each member of the couple.
3. Put the ashes in a red bag or small bottle, together with a piece of true silver, and store in a safe, discreet place to protect and preserve love and marital harmony.

☀ Happy Marriage Spell (4) Rosemary

The bride and groom should dip a rosemary wand into their first drink as a married couple and sip from a single glass together, to preserve love and happiness.

☀ Happy Marriage Spell (5) Trees

Surround your home with magnolia and pine trees to provide a shield to preserve and protect your happy marriage.

☀ Heartache and Stress Spell

To remedy marital problems:

1. Fill a glass with sea salt, rose water and either **Holy Water** or **Notre Dame Water**.
2. Drop your wedding ring in the glass and let it soak overnight.
3. Recite your wedding vows as you remember them.

☀ In-Law Spell (1)

Trouble with the in-laws? Oregano allegedly keeps meddlesome in-laws away. Greek oregano is allegedly the most magically powerful member of the species.

Don't cook the oregano for your spouse's troublesome relations— fumigate the premises instead. In addition, you may wish to fumigate their photographs at regular intervals.

☀ In-Law Spell (2)

If they won't stay away, perhaps you can inspire some affection. This spell may be used on anyone although it's most traditionally associated with mothers-in-law. It inspires affection rather than passionate love; this is not a substitution for one of the Notorious Potions.

1. Grind up your fingernail clippings.
2. Brew them in a hot beverage, preferably coffee.
3. Serve to your target.

Fidelity Spells

Fidelity is a genteel, pious term for what essentially translates to expected sexual exclusivity. Some have a greater need for it than others; some are better able to provide it than others. Notorious potions may make someone love you forever; binding spells may keep that person by your side forever; however neither guarantees that the other party will be sexually faithful to you, hence development of Fidelity Spells.

There are two kinds of Fidelity Spells. Certain Fidelity Spells magically *encourage* faithfulness and fidelity: they stimulate the other party to *want* to be faithful toward you or at least not to seek out other opportunities. Other Fidelity Spells refuse to take chances but attempt to *enforce* sexual exclusivity, one way or another.

Fidelity Encouraging Spells

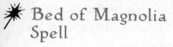

Bed of Magnolia Spell

Magnolia trees represent happy matrimony, so line your mattress with magnolia leaves. Or slip a magnolia blossom under your partner's pillow while he or she is asleep to encourage fidelity. Periodically replace the leaves, burying or burning the old ones.

Be True Charm Bag

This conjure bag incorporates the three "Cs" of fidelity. Two bags may be made and exchanged as a promise of exclusivity.

1. Place caraway, cumin, and coriander seeds in a red charm bag.
2. Add pine needles and an unadorned gold ring.
3. Ideally this should be sewn within your partner's clothing, but it may be placed underneath the mattress on his side of the bed, too.

Clothing Spell

This spell strongly encourages fidelity but also has an aphrodisiac edge to it, so that he'll be kept content while faithful.

1. Obtain an unwashed piece of your lover's clothing, ideally underwear or a sock. You may also use any fabric that has been soiled with his sexual emissions. Cut a piece of the bed linen if necessary.
2. Wear it inside your own underwear for seven days, wearing that same underwear for seven days. Do not launder either your underwear or his item during that time. They can never be laundered again or the spell will be broken.
3. On the eighth day, tie your underwear together with his item, with a red silk ribbon.
4. Place them in a jar and cover with powdered confectioner's sugar,

spikenard, damiana, licorice root, sweet flag, and vetiver.

5. Seal it shut and hide it safely.

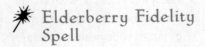 Elderberry Fidelity Spell

Allegedly carrying elderberries and twigs guards against the temptations of adultery. Place some in two conjure bags. Carry one yourself and either give one to the other party or slip it into his or her pocket, as you deem appropriate.

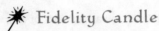 Fidelity Candle

Powder caraway seeds, cumin, and licorice root and add to grapeseed oil. Carve a figure candle to represent your partner; dress with this oil and burn.

Fidelity Wash

Create a strong infusion by pouring boiling water over caraway and cumin seeds and senna leaves. Strain out the botanical material and use the liquid to wash your partner's underwear and socks.

 Footprint Spell

Gather your lover's footprint up in its entirety. (If you miss any, the spell may not work.) Pour the dirt into a bag, which should be placed safely beneath your pillow or mattress.

 Hair Spell (1) Commanding, Compelling

1. Obtain a lock of your lover's hair.
2. Sprinkle it with **Command and Compel Oil**.
3. Place it in a small piece of white linen. Wrap it toward you, knotting it securely shut with blue, red, or gold silk thread.
4. Carry it in your pocket or in a charm bag.

Hair Spell (2) Perfume

1. Obtain two strands of his or her hair and tie them together to two strands of your own.
2. Place these hairs inside a bottle of your favorite fragrance together with an Adam and Eve root.
3. Every morning, ideally before he or she awakes, place a drop of this fragrance under each of your arms

Hair and Ashes Fidelity Spell

This spell, timed to coincide with the New Moon, allegedly keeps your lover true for one lunar cycle.

1. Burn an intimate item of your lover's clothing, reserving the ashes.
2. Braid or otherwise entwine a lock of your lover's hair with your own and place on a white cloth.
3. Blend the reserved ashes with dried crumbled vervain and sprinkle over the hair.
4. Wrap everything up in the cloth, always folding it toward you.
5. Bury the packet under your threshold or doorstep at the New Moon.
6. Repeat as needed.

Heartsease Fidelity Spell

Heartsease, the wild pansy's nickname, reveals its magic power to ease a worried heart. Wrap heartsease in your lover's unwashed underwear or sock. Bury it in Earth.

Hibiscus Fidelity Spell

Sprinkle crumbled hibiscus in your lover's pockets so that he or she will be true.

I Command You To Be True!

Licorice root and sweet flag, the building blocks of commanding magic, also possess romantic, aphrodisiac properties. Thus many of the commanding, compelling condition formulas that incorporate them (**Essence of Bend Over, Do As I Say**) are popularly used to exert one's will in a relationship.

Basic Commanding Fidelity Spell: Discreet Method

Sew a piece of licorice root into the hem of your partner's garment.

Basic Commanding Fidelity Spell: Blunt Method

Soak cotton balls in any of the Commanding Oils: **Do As I Say** *(also known as As You Please) is reasonably subtle;* **Essence of Bend Over** *is most powerful. Slip these cotton balls among the clothes your partner customarily wears when stepping out alone.*

Prized powerful ingredients for fidelity spells may be hiding modestly in your kitchen cabinets. Both caraway and cumin allegedly encourage fidelity and constancy.

Kitchen Spice Spell Magic Diet

Consuming cumin and/or caraway supposedly encourages faithfulness and fidelity. Discreetly add the spices to your partner's regular diet.

Locket Spell

There's a reason "locket" is a homophone for lock it. Wear your lover's picture together with a lock of hair chained in a locket around your neck to encourage faithfulness.

Lodestone Fidelity Spell

1. Place two matched lodestones and some of the botanical skullcap into a sachet. Add lots of the botanical or extra layers of fabric because lodestones are hard and presumably you'd like this spell to remain a secret.
2. Sew this sachet into his pillow.

Martha the Dominator Spell

Make an appeal to Saint Martha the Dominator. Saint Martha epitomizes the able, organized, capable housekeeper, and it is more effective to
request her assistance if you are the wife in an established family than if you are merely a jealous girlfriend. If your husband's infidelities are threatening the stability of your home, marriage, and family, appeal to Martha. She could tame a dragon; you only want her to tame your man. Tuesday is the most favorable day for an appeal.

1. Set up an altar for Martha; most altars display a depiction of the saint and/or her dragon.
2. Carve a green or white candle with your name and identifying, information, simultaneously charging it with your desire. (There are also commercially prepared candles available that are dedicated to Saint Martha. Almost inevitably they depict her with a dragon or snake.)
3. Dress the candle with **Saint Martha the Dominator Oil**.
4. Place an item that belongs to your mate, something that somehow represents his infidelity to you, beside the candle and make your petition to Martha.

Nutmeg Fidelity Spell

This spell depends on the influence of the four elements as well as that of nutmeg, which allegedly promotes fidelity

1. Hold a nutmeg in your left hand and charge it with your desire.
2. Slice it into four quarters. (This is easier said than done; nutmegs can be very hard. Be careful not to slice yourself instead.)
3. Bury one quarter in Earth.
4. Toss one quarter off a steep cliff so that it flies through the air.
5. Burn the third quarter.
6. Make an infusion by pouring boiling water over the last quarter and take one sip.
7. Retain this final nutmeg quarter, keeping it with you at all times, sleeping with it beneath your pillow.

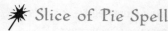 Park Your Feet At Home Spell

1. Offer to give your partner a pedicure.
2. Before moistening the feet, begin by scraping off any dry skin, preferably from the heels.
3. Proceed as you wish, have fun, but reserve that dried skin.
4. When he is peacefully asleep in your bed, bury the skin under your doorstep or a similar safe discreet place.

* Slice of Pie Spell

Serve your partner rhubarb pie to promote fidelity and maintain their romantic interest.

* Shoe Spell

Keep a sprig of myrtle inside a rambling lover's shoes. Peel up the sole, slip the myrtle underneath and glue it down again, if necessary.

* Sock Spell

1. The spell requires a small piece of genuine silver. Once upon a time a dime or silver threepenny bit or similar coin would have been recommended. However, few modern coins really contain silver. Use a pure silver coin, or a small bead or charm.
2. Wrap a hair from your beloved's head around this silver.
3. Write his or her name on a slip of paper, three times.
4. Place this paper plus the hair-wrapped silver inside his or her unwashed sock.
5. Sprinkle magnetic sand over a lodestone and toss that into the sock, too.
6. Close it with two needles or with poultry trusses. (Real silver needles, such as silver

acupuncture needles, provide maximum effectiveness.)

7. Dribble this sock-sachet with a little of your beloved's favored alcoholic libation. (Whatever drink would be most pleasing is what you should feed the sock. However, alcohol has a pacifying effect: if your lover is a teetotaler, simply substitute whiskey.)

8. Hide this sock over your home's rear door. Feed it with a little liquor periodically.

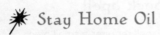
Stay Home Oil

To soothe a restless mate:

1. Steep spikenard root shavings, linden flowers, and yerba mate in sweet almond oil.

2. Strain out the botanicals and add the oil to his or her bathwater.

3. Make a sufficient quantity of oil: periodically reinforce good behavior by using it to anoint shoes, sprinkle over sheets, or even give a foot massage with it.

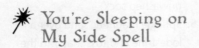
You're Sleeping on My Side Spell

In many metaphysical traditions, the left side is the female side, the right side the male. Because of this percep-tion, many Asian traditions encour-age the woman to sleep on the left, with the right side of the bed, the "rightful" place of the male head of the household.

This Chinese spell assumes, as many do, that it is the female partner who wishes to control the male's rov-ing nature; whichever party desires to enforce fidelity should attempt to sleep on the right consistently. Adjust to your personal situation.

1. To stimulate fidelity and perhaps a little docility too, encourage the male partner to sleep on the left side, with the woman moving to the right.

2. Whether this proves possible or not, tie a piece of amethyst to the foot of the bed on the side the woman sleeps on.

3. Reactivate and re-energize weekly or as needed by placing the crystal in sunlight, moonlight, a dish of rainwater, or all of the above.

Spells to Ensure Women's Sexual Fidelity

You thought only men could be targeted? Think again!

✳ Nine Knot Spell (1) Strap

A woman's nature can be attacked, too, depriving her of desire for anyone but the maker of the charm. Because it lacks any phallic imagery, this spell can be cast by either a woman or a man, although the target must be a woman.

1. Use her garter belt or cut the strap from her bra.
2. Tie nine knots in the strap, focusing with each one on your desire for enforced fidelity.
3. Keep it in your pocket.

✳ Nine Knot Spell (2) Underwear

1. You'll need a red candle to represent you. Choose a red figure candle, a seven-day candle, a red devil, or a red phallus: the choice is yours. Carve and dress it so that it is identified with you.
2. Make nine knots in the woman's unwashed underwear, announcing aloud "You're mine!" or "You have sex with only me" or whatever best expresses your desire each time you tie a knot. Call her name aloud with each knot, too, for a total of nine times.

3. Arrange the knotted panty around the candle. If you have a seven-day candle in a glass sheath, you can tie the panty to it.
4. Spit on the candle and sprinkle a few of your pubic and underarm hairs over it.
5. Announce: "[Name], daughter of [Name], You belong to me!"
6. Light the candle.
7. When the candle has completed burning, take the panty and tie it to a hammer or other metal tool, something heavy in weight and implicitly phallic. Hide it.

✳ Raspberry Branch

An Iroquois spell to keep a woman faithful while you are separated.

1. Find a raspberry branch that has rooted at the tip.
2. Take a small piece of the root from both ends without killing the plant. (This transcends important ecological concerns; killing the plant defeats the purpose of the spell. It won't work. There's no point.)
3. Boil this root.
4. Let the liquid cool. Take one sip of the liquid. Use another tablespoonful to bathe your genitals.
5. Give the rest of the liquid to the targeted woman to drink.

Divorce Spells

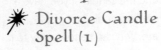

✳ Divorce Candle Spell (1)

A candle spell for the person who would like a divorce while the other party is resistant.

1. Obtain male and female figure candles.
2. Place them back-to-back, ready to go in opposite directions.
3. Dress them with **Command and Compel Oil** and burn in timed increments, corresponding to the number of years you have been wed.
4. For instance, burn them for thirty minutes at a time if you were wed for thirty years. Pinch them out when the time is up. Next day, before lighting the candles again, move them farther apart. When they are finally as far apart as space will allow, let the candle burn entirely.

✳ Divorce Candle Spell (2)

Some spiritual supply companies market what is known as a "Divorce Candle." This is a single candle, usually, although not always, black containing a male and female human figure, back-to-back. This type of candle may be carved and dressed as above but there's no need for incremental burning.

✳ Divorce: Move Out Oil

One person moves out, the other stays—but why do you continue to feel the presence of the departed party? This spell's aim is to banish and remove lingering traces of the other person from the home you once shared. (It is beneficial for any long-term housemate relationship that has ended.)

1. Blend and grind asafetida, camphor, cinnamon, eucalyptus, High John chips, and rosemary.
2. Add the result to sweet almond and jojoba oils.
3. Dress a black candle with the oil. Walk the candle through your home slowly, pausing at areas especially associated with the other person.
4. When your rounds are completed, go outside, pinch out the candle and bury it upside down in Earth.

Money Spells

Certain topics attract more magical attention and spells than others. Weather spells, invisibility spells, and rituals for preservation of animals attract individuals' attention while love, protection, fertility, and healing spells evoke a more universal reaction. Money is another similar universal category. *Everyone* can always use more.

If there were a spell to guarantee an instant fortune, there'd be a lot of rich witches, fortune-tellers, and shamans. Of course, as we all know and as denigrators of magic are invariably quick to point out, this is not the case. On the contrary, the metaphysically inclined tend to be a financially challenged bunch, from the most obscure to the most famous, from Dr. Dee to Dr. John, and from Madame Blavatsky to Count Cagliostro.

That said there are a couple of things to consider. Every individual doesn't win identical prizes; the rewards of the metaphysical life transcend the material. However, because so many brilliant magical practitioners have lived, at least during periods of their lives, from hand to mouth, a wealth of magical money spells exist, suitable for every situation.

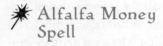

Alfalfa Money Spell

Murmur your financial desires over alfalfa. Burn it and scatter the ashes around your property.

Animal Magic Wealth Spells

Animal Magic Wealth Spell (1) Allies

The animal allies of wealth and financial fortune include the frog, toad, snake, dragon, cat, rat, rabbit, and fish. Surround yourself with their images to generate cashflow and financial inspiration.

Follow the direction given in Elements of Magic Spells for setting up an Animal Ally Altar.

Animal Magic Wealth Spell (2) Chinese Frog

Frogs are universally considered the creature epitomizing increase, generation, and multitude. The ancient Egyptians used the hiero-glyph for "tadpole" to represent the highest number they expressed.

1. Place a money frog amulet on a plate on top of a bed of real coins.

Among the other wealth-generating Chinese animal amulets are the dragon-tortoise, the mongoose, and the cow, all reclining upon a treasure trove. This cow is among Earth's many sacred cows and, according to legend, if she draws wealth toward you, in exchange you must refrain from eating beef. The image of a sow nursing her piglets on a bed of coins is considered particularly beneficial for single mothers and their children.

2. Sprinkle with mingled **Money Drawing Powder** and magnetic sand.

3. Place under your bed, looking toward the door.

4. Sprinkle with more powder periodically.

3. Toss a few coins onto the saucer and make an invocation. Express your needs to the spider.

4. Once a week or whenever the spider comes through for you, toss a few more coins onto the plate.

✳ Animal Magic Wealth Spell (3) Golden Spider

The golden money spider weaves a web of riches. As the old saying "If you wish to live and thrive, let the spider stay alive," reminds us, killing a spider is considered detrimental to one's own good fortune.

. Draw a picture of the spider hidden in its labyrinthine web on red paper with gold ink.

. Place the picture in a corner with a saucer underneath it.

✳ Animal Magic Wealth Spell (4) Japanese Frog

According to Japanese tradition, keeping a small image of a frog in your wallet stimulates wealth. There are two ways of doing this. You can either look for a small Japanese wallet frog charm, flat enough to slide comfortably into a wallet. Charge the frog with your desires and carry it with your cash. Or you can improvise and place a photo or drawing of a green frog inside your wallet.

✳ Animal Magic Wealth Spell (5) Maneki Neko

Although with popularity Maneki Neko, the Japanese beckoning cat, has been adapted to other uses, her primary purpose is to generate cash for her owner. This amulet depicts a seated cat holding one hand up in the gesture that in Japan indicates, "Come here!" Maneki Neko's upraised left hand beckons increased business while the upraised right hand demands cash. Allegedly the higher the hand, the more powerful the amulet.

Maneki Neko comes in a variety of colors any of which is suitable for increased wealth, however a gold cat is believed most powerful for this purpose.

1. Maneki Neko must face the outside world so that she can beckon wealth into your private premises.
2. Place Maneki Neko in the window facing outside or across from the front door.
3. Some Maneki Neko's have a slot in the back as if they were a child's piggybank. Make a wish and place a few coins within as amulet activation.

✳ Avocado Money Spell

Avocado trees serve as money magnets. Transplant an avocado tree and eat the very first avocado that grow on it. Cleanse and dry its pit and carry it as a money charm.

Basic Money Botanicals

The following botanicals radiate wealth- and money-drawing properties. Incorporate them into spells as desired: alfalfa, avocado basil, cabbage, chamomile, chervil clover, coriander, dill, five-finger grass (cinquefoil), lettuce, mint nasturtium, oakmoss, parsley, poppies, and vervain.

✳ Basic Money Botanicals Candle

Hold a green candle in your hand and charge it with your desire. Hol low out its base, pack it full of basi money botanicals, and then burn it.

Basil Spells

Basil is the botanical particularly associated with prosperity and increase. It's used to magically increase fertility and romance and especially to attract and increase wealth. The plant is sacred to two very prominent Spirits of Wealth: India's Lakshmi and Vodou's Ezili Freda Dahomey.

✳ Basil Spell Bath

The scent of basil on the skin allegedly draws financial opportunity toward the wearer. Once upon a time, prostitutes in Spain bathed in basil and rubbed their body with the fragrance to attract free-spending customers. The custom may be emulated regardless of one's profession. Take this bath just before venturing out in pursuit of any financial opportunity. Because basil smells so inviting, this is not a difficult spell to enjoy.

1. Roughly chop most of a large bunch of basil, in order to release the volatile oils, but leave some leaves whole, especially those that most remind you of cash bills.
2. Pour boiling water over the basil and let it steep.
3. When it cools, add the liquid to your bath. Float the whole leaves in the water so that you can visualize yourself swimming in cash.
4. Let the water drain and allow yourself to air-dry.
5. Do not dispose of the used basil leaves (don't throw out the cash!) but either leave them in the tub until your transactions are complete or remove them, place them in a bag, and reserve until an opportune moment for disposal arises.

✳ Bayberry Money Spell

1. Anoint a small piece of silver with infused oil of bayberry.
2. Hold it in your left hand to charge it with your desire.
3. Carry it with you during the day.
4. Place it on your forehead over the Third Eye area for thirty minutes every day. Feed with a drop of bayberry oil weekly.

✳ Buckwheat Poverty Protection Spell

Blend buckwheat hulls with dried basil and parsley in an uncovered glass bowl. Keep this in the kitchen to ward off poverty.

Candle Spells

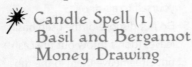

✳ Candle Spell (1)
Basil and Bergamot
Money Drawing

1. Write the precise sum that you require on a square of brown paper.
2. Carve your name, identifying information, and the sum onto a green candle.
3. Dress the candle with essential oils of basil and bergamot.
4. Place the candle over the paper.
5. Burn the candle for increments of fifteen minutes daily until the specified amount has accumulated.

✳ Candle Spell (2)
Seven Knob

1. Write the amount needed on a square of paper.
2. Place it beneath a green seven-knob candle dressed with money oils.
3. Burn one knob a night for seven nights.

✳ Candle Spell (3)
Fast Cash

For fast double financial action, this spell requires a black and green double-action candle.

1. Carve whatever you wish to lose on the black side (debt, poverty).
2. Carve what you need to manifest on the green side. In both cases, be as specific as possible.
3. Trim the bottom of the candle if necessary, exposing the wick so that both ends may be lit simultaneously.
4. Impale the candle horizontally on a spiked candlestick and burn both ends.

✳ Candle Spell (4)
Money Growth

1. Carve and dress a green candle to express your desires.
2. Place it on a saucer.
3. Arrange coins around the base of the candle.
4. Light the candle and chant:
   Money grow, money flow
   Candle burn, watch me earn
   Money grow, money flow
   Flame shine
   What I want is mine!

✳ Cash Boomerang
Spell

*Anoint all your cash with **Magne Oil** prior to spending it, so that i returns to you.*

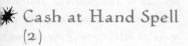

Cash at Hand Spell (1)

A simple spell so as always to have at least a little money at hand: burn onion peelings on the stove.

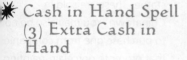

Cash at Hand Spell (2)

Alternatively, burn garlic skins in the kitchen to keep money in the house.

These two Cash at Hand spells are easily combined and reinforce each other.

Cash in Hand Spell (3) Extra Cash in Hand

Rub two drops of essential oil of bergamot between the palms of your hands to attract money. Rub the oil in your pockets, purse, or wallet, too.

Conjure Bag: Lucky Sevens

Fill a conjure bag with seven different pieces of money; you can use coins or paper. You can use assorted national currencies. You just need seven distinct types, for instance: a penny, a nickel, a dime, a quarter, a dollar coin, a two-dollar bill, and a ten-dollar bill.

2. Sprinkle with essential oil of bergamot.
3. Carry the bag for seven days. Allegedly the contents should multiply sevenfold. (Or even seven times sevenfold!)

Conjure Bag: Lunar Blessings

Tuck moonwort into a green charm bag together with a miniature horseshoe, a lunar charm, and either a real or a charm four-leaf clover.

Conjure Bag: Magic Five and Seven

Place a cinnamon stick in a conjure bag together with seven Grains of Paradise and five coins.

Conjure Bag: Seven Coins

Place seven coins in a charm bag, together with violet leaves and a pinch of five-finger grass (cinquefoil), to generate wealth.

✳ Conjure Bag: Smart Ass Mojo

1. Write the amount of money you need on a piece of paper.
2. Anoint it with essential oil of bergamot and/or **Magnet Oil** and place it in a conjure bag.
3. Add magnetic horseshoes plus lodestones plus some smartweed, also known as "*water pepper*" or "*smart ass.*"
4. Feed the bag by sprinkling it with magnetic sand every third day until the money needed is received.

Magnetic sand is sold dyed in inspirational colors. Use gold and/or green (the colors to attract money) to enhance the spell.

✳ Creole Anti-poverty Spell

1. Combine the following ingredients in a bowl: a cup of white sugar, a cup of salt, and a cup of raw white rice.
2. Open a safety pin and stick it into the bowl.
3. Leave it out in full view.

✳ Dragon Spell

The dragon is the traditional guardian of wealth and treasure. Unlike Western stories that paint dragons as hoarding, mean-spirited creatures, East Asian dragons are benevolent and generous. Instead of killing the dragon, the desire is to make an alliance with the dragon, to harness its power to improve one's own quality of life. A dragon can't watch out for wealth with its eyes closed. A Chinese ritual seeks to open the dragon's eyes, in order to activate its energy in your life.

1. You will need a porcelain dragon statue. These are sold in Chinatown. You may also be able to purchase one from companies that promote porcelain-painting parties.
2. The Dragon Hour is between 7 a.m. and 9 a.m. Open the dragon's eyes at this time by dotting the eyes with a new brush and black ink.

Two-dimensional dragons (prints, posters, paintings) should have open eyes in order to promote positive dragon energy. If they are closed or averted, use an incense stick to ritually activate the eyes.

Fenugreek Spells

Fenugreek is known as the plant of increase. It stimulates growth of all kinds. It's used in fertility spells, in spells to enhance the size of one's bust, and in spells to enhance the size of one's bank account, too. Fenugreek provides wealth and protects against poverty.

✸ Fenugreek Spell (1)

1. Place some fenugreek seeds in a jar.
2. Every day add a few more.
3. When the jar is full, bury in Earth and start all over again.

✸ Fenugreek Spell (2)

Scatter fenugreek seeds discreetly around your house and property.

✸ Fern Seed Money Spell

Fern seed allegedly has a magically beneficial effect on one's finances. These aren't the kind of seeds you can buy in a packet, however. Gather ferns and look for the spores that are commonly called seeds. Gently remove them by scraping them off the leaves. Slip them into a sachet and carry for good fortune.

✸ Ginger Root Spell

Sprinkle dried powdered ginger in your pocket or purse to increase your finances.

✸ Golden Magnet Spell

According to the ancient Scandinavians, a tiny piece of gold serves as a magnet for increased wealth. Carry a real gold coin or a small charm in an amulet bag to generate greater wealth.

✸ The Goose is Cooked Spell

September 29th is the feast of Michael the Archangel—Michaelmas. Allegedly if you eat goose on this day you will not lack money during the forthcoming year.

✸ Green Tourmaline Money Magnet

Carry or wear green tourmaline to attract cash.

☀ Grow Some Cash Spell

Plant coins in a pot filled with dirt. (Crossroads dirt is most potent.) Reinforce the spell by adding money-drawing plants to the pot. Ideally this should stimulate your other money to grow.

☀ Has No Hanna Money Spell

*Add a drop of essential oil of bergamot to **Has No Hanna** condition oil. Anoint your wallet with this oil daily so that it will never be empty.*

☀ Horseshoe Spell

1. Wrap a horseshoe with green thread, binding and knotting your desires and intentions.
2. Decorate this horseshoe with images, amulets, beads, and small packets of herbs such as dried basil, High John chips, or fenugreek seeds.
3. Hang it up to bring good fortune.

☀ Incense: Wealth

1. Combine brown sugar, ground cinnamon, and ground coffee.

2. Add powdered (confectioner's) sugar, carnation petals, garlic chives, and cherry blossoms if possible. If cherry blossoms are unavailable, try apple blossoms or the blossoms of any flowering fruit tree. Omit if they are impossible to find.
3. Grind all the ingredients together.
4. Burn it outside the front door of your home or business to attract wealth.
5. Leave the ashes alone for 24 hours to radiate their power, then dispose of them in woods or in living, running water.

☀ Jezebel Root Spell

*Carry a Jezebel root to attract men with money. The root should be sufficient by itself, however just to be sure anoint with a drop of **Follow Me Boy! Oil**.*

☀ Kitchen Money Magic

Trying to cast a discreet money spell? Jezebel root, dragon's blood, frankincense, and five-finger grass may be reasonably conspicuous. They're not exactly standard household items, at least not in most standard households. Never fear.

Some of the most powerful money-drawing plants are innocuous culinary herbs, perfect for subtle kitchen magic for those witches still in the broom closet.

Finely chop fresh basil, dill, and/or parsley. Whisper and murmur your desires over them. Sprinkle onto food as a magical garnish.

Knot Money Spell

1. Comb or brush your hair.
2. Visualize the money that you need. Remember as long as you're visualizing, visualize big.
3. When nine strands of hair have been caught in your comb or brush, stop brushing.
4. Start chanting: "*I need* [amount]. *Please bring me* [amount]." Be specific.
5. As you're chanting, rub the strands of hair between your palms, forming a string.
6. When you've created a long chord of hair, tie nine knots in it, moving from the left to the right.
7. Visualize the money in your hand as you hold the hair. Visualize your debts paid, your purpose fulfilled.
8. When you're ready, either bury the hair in Earth or burn it.

Lucky Buddha Spell

The East Asian deity Hotei conflates a Chinese prosperity spirit with the Buddha. Unlike austere, ascetic Indian Buddhas, Hotei is fat and happy. He's the patron of fortune-tellers, ensuring that they make a living. However, anyone may invoke him for money. Allegedly his large stomach contains his ample money-bags.

Choose an image of Hotei, also known as the Laughing Buddha, that pleases you. His naked stomach should be exposed. Rub his tummy daily for prosperity, luck, and happiness.

Lucky Cat Candle Spell

Lucky Cat candles are used to beckon wealth.

Carve a green or black cat candle with your name, goals, and identifying information. Dress the candle with Money Drawing Oil and burn.

Lucky Money Envelope Spell

Red lucky money envelopes are used during the Chinese New Year to bestow cash gifts. They are used throughout the year for a variety of purposes, including magical ones. The envelope is auspicious and encourages the money contained within it to grow. They are available from feng shui suppliers and in Chinatown.

Place three cash bills of different denominations in a red lucky money envelope. Put the envelope under your doorstep or beneath the doormat to increase cash flow into the home.

 Lunar Money Spell

According to this Pow-Wow spell, the New Moon is a time for growth. So let's put some money in the moonlight and watch it grow. (Okay, this money isn't supposed to literally grow: it's supposed to stimulate other money to grow by proxy.)

1. Put some money on a table by the (closed) window. Be discreet: this is intended to allow your income to increase with the moon, not to invite theft.
2. At the Full Moon, remove the money.

Repeat as needed.

Money Garden

Plant some or all of the following in your garden or around the perimeter of your home to stimulate new wealth, preserve what you've acquired, and generate more: alfalfa, basil, camellia, chamomile, cinquefoil, dill, heliotrope, honeysuckle, jade plant, jasmine, lettuce, marigolds, mints, morning glories, nasturtium, onion, Oregon grape, parsley, or poppies. If you have little or no property, window boxes and potted plants also send out a financial appeal to the benevolent powers of the universe.

Money Growth Spell

According to the old saying, money begets more money. Place two cash bills side by side in a box with a lodestone in between them. Sprinkle magnetic sand over everything. Tell the money to reproduce and keep the box under your bed, feeding the lodestone on a regular schedule.

Money Magnet Spell

1. Anoint a horseshoe with **Magnet Oil**.
2. Hold it in your hands, focus on your desire and make a wish.

3. Still holding the horseshoe chant something like,

   I attract money like a magnet
   I attract wealth like a magnet
   I attract prosperity like a magnet.
   I am a money magnet
   I am a wealth magnet.
   I am a prosperity magnet.

4. Sprinkle with blended magnetic sand and **Money Drawing Powder**.

5. Wrap it in fabric and put it beneath your pillow.

6. Pay attention to your dreams for financial inspiration and insight.

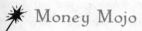 Money Mojo

Slice and dry kumquats, tangerines, or oranges. Add them to a green bag together with nasturtium flowers and dried pineapple peel.

Money Plant Spell

1. Purchase a small plant for your desk. A jade plant or a kalanchoe is ideal.

2. Gently rub prosperity or luck-drawing oil on the leaves.

3. Re-anoint with this oil once a month. Remember to offer libations as needed, especially when the plant seems to be working on your behalf.

Money Powders

Use these powders to create a path for wealth to follow to your door.

★ *Sprinkle them over your checkbooks and ledgers, into your pockets and wallets*

★ *Sprinkle them inside and outside your home*

★ *Sprinkle on your hands*

★ *Sprinkle on candles*

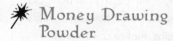 Money Drawing Powder

Grind and powder the following:

Calendula blossoms
Chamomile blossoms
Cinnamon
Cinquefoil (five-finger grass)
Cloves
Ginger
Nutmeg

Money Protection Spell

Cut a sweet flag (calamus) root into pieces. Hide one piece in each corner of the kitchen to guard against hunger and poverty.

My Ship Comes In Spell

A spell inspired by Chinese magic. If you're sick of waiting for your ship to come in, speed its arrival by creating a role model. This spell also works well in conjunction with appeals to Spirits of the Sea and those with sympathy for "poor sailors": Kwan Yin, Mazu, Lord Agwe and La Sirene, Aphrodite, and Poseidon.

1. Stuff a model boat with *"treasure."* Fill it with imitation gold ingots from Chinatown, actual coins, replica coins, glass gems, sparkling beads, and crystals.
2. Strategically arrange the boat so that it's easy to visualize your ship arriving at home port. One thing is crucial: the boat must sail toward you, never away from you!
3. Intensify the effect with candle burning and money-drawing incense.
4. Place a Rider-Waite three of wands Tarot card onto the boat, which shows the ship of good fortune arriving.

Never Empty Wallet Spell

Keep a bay laurel leaf in your wallet to magically protect against poverty.

New Moon Money Spell

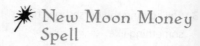

Upon first catching sight of the New Moon, immediately jingle any coins in your pocket to receive an increase in wealth.

Pennies from Heaven

A doorstep message is usually associated with hexes; sometimes, however, it's used for positive intent. Leave coins (spare change, replica coins) on different doorsteps in the magical belief that whatever you put forth will return to you two-, three-, or seven-fold.

Poppy Spell

Place a dry poppy head in the window as a charm to draw money toward you.

Red Paper Money Spell

1. Write the amount that you need in gold ink on red paper.
2. Fold the paper into a square and carry it in your pocket, bra, or conjure bag.

3. When the amount is accumulated burn the paper, together with an equivalent quantity of Spirit Money.
4. Repeat as needed.

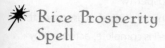

Rice Prosperity Spell

This isn't a money spell as much as a prosperity spell; it protects against poverty.

1. Cook enough rice to serve each spell participant a small bowl.
2. Stir the water sunwise, visualizing the pot always full.
3. Murmur blessings, affirmations, and sacred verses over the rice and then eat it.

Sesame Seed Spell

Keep sesame seeds in an open dish near a window to draw money closer.

Seven-Eleven Money Spell

1. Carve your desires into a black or green cat candle.
2. Dress it with money-drawing oil, and sprinkle it with gold, green, red, and/or purple glitter.

3. If you need a specific amount of cash, write your request on a slip of paper and place it under the cat.
4. Light the candle for seven minutes the first night, eleven the second, seven the third, and so on, alternating between lucky numbers seven and eleven until the amount is received.
5. If the candle burns down completely without receipt of the funds, this too is an answer: the whole situation needs to be reconsidered as well as new alternatives.

Spiritual Financial Aid Spells

Some of the most effective spells aim to put the task in stronger, more capable hands. As befitting a major topic, there are a host of spiritual patrons of wealth. Request some financial aid.

Spiritual Financial Aid Spell Saint Anthony

Saint Anthony is the "bread giver," so keep a small loaf of bread in front of his image, to remind him that you need him to play this role. Keep it for seven days, then replace with a new one. Murmur your wishes over the old loaf and feed it to the birds.

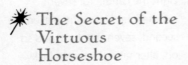

The Secret of the Virtuous Horseshoe

Saint Martin of Tours, in his guise as San Martin Caballero (Saint Martin the Chevalier), brings luck and money. This fourth-century Hungarian was pressed into service in the Roman army but quit to assist the poor. Another miracle-working saint, akin to Saints Anthony and Martha, Martin Caballero is the magical patron of those who are dependent on the kindness of strangers.

"The Secret of the Virtuous Horseshoe," dedicated to San Martin Caballero, is a popular Latin American spell. (Although its more common use is in money-drawing spells, the Virtuous Horseshoe has another guise as a relocation spell.) One may purchase it already made and then simply utter the incantation to activate the spell, however it's easily created for oneself and more powerful that way.

1. Wrap a horseshoe in red silk thread until only the very tips are exposed.
2. Attach the horseshoe to a square of cardboard with the horseshoe turned points down.

3. Decorate horseshoe and cardboard with sequins, glitter glue, and votive images of San Martin Caballero. Maintain your mental focus on your longing for financial stability and prosperity.
4. When the physical aspect of the spell is complete, activate it by repeating the following incantation, reminiscent of the nine magical fruits of plenty, twenty-one times: "*Citron nueve.*"

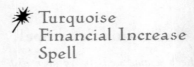

Tulip Spell

Tulip bulbs allegedly protect against poverty. Place one in a charm bag and keep safe and secure in a discreet place.

Turquoise Financial Increase Spell

The instant you first see the New Moon, look at a turquoise to receive an increase in fortune.

Pregnancy and Childbirth Spells

Pregnancy Spells

In general, magic spells target the threshold experiences of pregnancy: conception and delivery. (Spells for conception are contained under *Fertility Spells*). The duration in between is perceived as a vulnerable holding-period, best served magically by protective amulets, talismans, and protection spells requesting assistance from various benevolent spirits affiliated with pregnancy and childbirth.

 Amulet: Crayfish

Not from Louisiana, this is a Central European Romany spell. Crayfish, as depicted on many Moon tarot cards, are emblematic of primal female, lunar, watery power.

Having eaten a crayfish dinner, reserve, cleanse, and dry the shells. Fill a sachet with these shells to bring blessings and protection for a pregnant woman. Pin the sachet into your clothing.

Eye Spells

What parts of the body are most associated with pregnancy? Along with breasts, belly, and all points south, the eye is a consistent anatomical motif. The pregnant woman is believed exceptionally vulnerable to the Evil Eye. The further out the belly extends, the more it draws the Eye. How does the pregnant woman protect herself against the Eye? With amulets in the form of a single eye, which some scholars believe may actually be a euphemism for the vulva, bringing the matter full circle.

Yet the pregnant woman's own eyes also create vulnerability during pregnancy: it's believed that whatever a pregnant woman looks at (consciously or not) for significant amounts of time affects the development of the baby. Consider your immediate surroundings. Surround yourself with whatever are your own sacred images.

Eye Spell Protection

Wear images of eyes throughout pregnancy, especially as your condition becomes more visible. A single blue-eye bead may be safety-pinned to clothing, or wear it as you wish. Egyptian Eye of Horus amulets are very effective, as is any bead or crystal that resembles an eye. A geometric diamond shape fills in for a literal depiction of an eye.

Pomegranate Protection Spell

If you fear that the child in your womb has been exposed to illness, obtain a pomegranate:

1. Cut the pomegranate in half.
2. Rub one half over yourself, especially your belly. Envision any ills or pain or damage being drawn into the pomegranate.
3. When you're finished, bury this half in Earth.
4. Eat every seed of the other half.
5. If you can't get a pomegranate, an apple may be substituted although it's not as magically powerful, nor is consuming apple seeds as easy as eating those of a pomegranate.

SATOR Square

The SATOR magic square was apparently spread through Europe and Britain by the Roman legions. It has many protective uses ranging from fire control to caring for cows, however in general this is either a gender-neutral or even a male-oriented amulet. An exception occurred in England, where Anglo-Saxon tradition favored the SATOR square as an amulet for pregnant women.

Carefully write the magic square on parchment, making sure none of the letters touch and focusing on your desire:

```
S A T O R
A R E P O
T E N E T
O P E R A
R O T A S
```

Place the square in a leather bag or metal case and carry it for protection during pregnancy.

Spiritual Protection Spells

From a metaphysical, spiritual point of view, pregnancy is inherently such a powerful, magically charged situation that various elements of the Spirit Realm can't help but get involved. Malicious, hostile spirits are attracted to the pregnant woman like magnets, as it is a prime opportunity to cause trouble and heartache. Benevolent spirits, in theory at least, also hover protectively nearby, ready to fend off spiritual danger. Some spirits consider pregnancy-protection to be their primary occupation. Instead of trusting to their vigilance blindly, magic spells suggest more active methods of ensuring spiritual pregnancy protection.

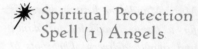

Spiritual Protection Spell (1) Angels

Among the angels known to protect expectant women and newborn children are Ariel (Uriel), Raphael, Gabriel, Michael, and Nuriel. They are sometimes identified as a group by the acronym "ARGAMAN." This serves as an amuletic device to transmit the power and protection of these angels.

1. Carefully, consciously write the acronym on paper. Consider what type of ink and paper are most appropriate.
2. Create two copies: one to travel with you during the day, a second to be posted on the wall near the bed so as to radiate protection while you sleep.
3. Post the amulet on a wall in plain sight.
4. Write it on a small strip of paper and carry in a locket or mojo hand.

Spiritual Protection Spell (2) Mary Magdalene

Mary Magdalene bestows blessings for a happy, successful pregnancy and smooth delivery. The roots of Mary Magdalene's associations with pregnancy are unclear: is it because, as some believe, Mary Magdalene herself was the Holy Grail, the chalice who safely bore Christ's child? Or is it because a Pagan Mediterranean fertility spirit has become so deeply syncretized to the biblical figure as to be inseparable? Regardless of the reason, Mary Magdalene may be petitioned for an easy pregnancy and a happy outcome. Requests may be made anytime but are believed to be most propitious on her feast day, July 22nd.

Display a votive image of Mary Magdalene. Choose whatever pleases you, however images depicting her with the moon or with a closed box are most powerful in this situation. Offer her myrrh, roses, and spikenard and request her blessings.

Tarot Welcome Spell

Lay out the four aces and the Sun card from a tarot deck to issue a welcome to the new soul existing within you, and to ease the path to emergence for both of you.

Miscarriage Spells

Spells for miscarriage attempt to avert it, prevent its recurrence, or provide for the spiritual safety and comfort of the misborn soul.

Anglo-Saxon Miscarriage Spells

These Anglo-Saxon miscarriage rituals are extremely old but the pain, emotion, and determination they reveal remains intensely modern. It's difficult to tell whether they were originally one extremely extended magic ritual or several rituals so commonly performed in conjunction that it became impossible to disentangle them. The rituals are often combined in different orders, or they are performed in separate pieces. Adjust them to suit your circumstances.

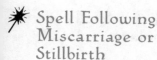

Spell Following Miscarriage or Stillbirth

This spell for a woman involves a progression of rituals, performed over significant periods of time. Originally this was done with the participation of the community; the purpose of the spell was understood, hence the ritual selling of the still-born child.

At the end of the ritual, the unborn child is dedicated to a deity so as to receive that deity's blessings and protection. Pagan Anglo-Saxons chose Frigg; Christian Anglo-Saxons chose Jesus Christ. Choose either, or whoever else is most appropriate for you. There is nothing in the spell that intrinsically calls one, and only one, divinity.

This spell cannot be cast unless the stillborn or miscarried child has been buried. As with other grave-yard dirt spells, there's some ambiguity over exactly what is being dug up. Interpret however this makes sense to you.

1. Take a bit of dirt from the stillborn child's grave, wrap it in black wool and ritually sell it to someone who will not become pregnant, traditionally an elderly woman. This is accompanied by a chant: "*I sell it. You buy it, this black wool and the seeds of this sorrow.*"

2. Soon after, go to the cemetery, step over the grave of a dead man three times, saying these words each time, for a repetition of three:
   This is my help against hateful slow birth.
   This is my help against dreadful sad birth.
   This is my help against hateful misbirth.

3. When the woman next conceives, she steps over a living man (preferably but not necessarily the child's father) in bed three times, saying each time, for a repetition of three:
   Up I go, over you I step!
   With a living child, not a dying one.
   With a full-born child, not a doomed one.

4. Keep quiet about the pregnancy until you're ready for Step 5. Be discreet; don't broadcast the news.

5. At the first signs of quickening—the child's first flutterings in the womb—the ritual is completed by approaching an altar publicly (once upon a time, this was done in church) and saying, "*To* [Deity] *I declare this child in my womb.*"

☀ Ritual to Prevent Miscarriage

Another Anglo-Saxon miscarriage spell, no less complex than the last although more quickly accomplished, may be cast independently or in conjunction with the spell above.

1. Milk from a solid-colored (one color) cow is required. It must be obtained directly from the cow. Take milk in the palm of your hand, drink it but don't swallow. Hold it in your mouth. Without looking around and without swallowing, go quickly and directly to a stream and spit out the milk.
2. With the same hand you used for the milk, take a handful of water from the stream and swallow it.
3. Chant:
   Everywhere I carry within me this great strong one.
   Strong because of this great food.
   This one I want to have and keep and go home with.
4. Don't look around. Don't talk to anyone. Go to a different home from the one where you started this ritual and there, eat a meal.

☀ Jizo's Spell for Solace

"All rivers find their way to the sea."

According to Japanese spiritual traditions, all rivers end in a place called the River of Souls, the home of Jizo. Jizo is the Protector of the Souls of Lost Children. These include still-births and miscarriages. Babies live and play happily in his abode. Jizo is a multi-faceted deity: he protects mothers and children but also serves as a psychopomp, a spirit who guides dead souls to the next realm. Miscarriages, abortions (without judgment), and stillbirths are all under his domain. Jizo comforts mothers in any of the above circumstances, too.

1. Write your child's name (or the name you would have given the child, or the name in your heart for the child) on a slip of paper.
2. Set it on a river to float to Jizo, so that he will watch out for and take care of your baby.

Knot Anti-Miscarriage Spells

Knot magic is used in spells regarding all aspects of reproduction: contraception, enhanced fertility, impotence, and childbirth.

Knots are tied and released as needed. Childbirth rituals all over the world emphasize the untying of knots: everyone within the vicinity of the birthing woman must loosen their hair, for instance. Window curtains are un-knotted in the belief that knots stall delivery. Sometimes however this is exactly what you desire. A knot spell determines to set a safe due date.

Knot Spell (1)

1. At first sign of miscarriage, make a tight knot in a strong cord.
2. Visualize the knot as your baby.
3. Talk to it: *"As this knot holds firm, so you hold firm in my womb. Do not loosen until* [insert due date or select a date]*."*
4. Place the cord in a secure covered container or wrap it up in a baby blanket.
5. Keep it in a safe place. Be sure to untie the cord at the appropriate time.

Knot Spell (2)

If you are prone or vulnerable to miscarriage, incorporate protective knot magic on a consistent, regular basis until the time is safe for delivery.

Incorporate knot magic as much as possible into your life: wear your hair in braids, multiple if possible. Wear shoes with laces and clothing that ties rather than buttons. As you braid, tie, and knot, consciously focus your desire and intent, prayers and petitions.

Miscarriage Prevention Spells

The most popular form of miscarriage prevention spell involves charged stones and amulets that can radiate power constantly. For best success, amulets should always be cleansed, charged, and consecrated before their initial use and then as needed.

A "pile-up" effect is favored when using amulets. Use as many as possible: they empower each other synergistically.

Jewish tradition suggests wearing or carrying an eaglestone to enhance aspects of conception, pregnancy, and childbirth, and especially for the prevention of miscarriage. Unlike amber, rubies, and cowries, this is not something you can buy; it must be *found*— and if it is, it is a sacred gift. Eaglestones are ferruginous pebbles, usually found in a stream. They will be recognized because, when picked up and rattled, the presence of another smaller stone within is apparent: the baby within its mother.

Eaglestones earned their name because, according to legend, eagles gather them into their own nests to assist with conception and delivery.

☀ Miscarriage Prevention Spell (1) Gemstones

Lapis lazuli and rubies are the gemstones believed able to prevent miscarriage or minimize its likelihood. Wear them across the womb for maximum effectiveness, although they still have potency if worn more conventionally.

☀ Miscarriage Prevention Spell (2) Gifts of the Sea

The ocean is the font of Earth's fertility power. Its powers are invoked in many fertility spells but the sea also has gifts to preserve and protect pregnancy, especially regarding prevention of miscarriage.

Amber, coral, and cowrie shells protect pregnancy in general and allegedly specifically prevent miscarriage or minimize its likelihood. For

strongest effect, they should be worn slung around the hips against the skin, underneath clothing.

(Although it's now recognized that amber is fossilized tree resin, ancient people encountered amber lying on the shore where it was tossed by ocean waves. In this context, they perceived it as an oceanic product and those metaphysical, magical associations remain potent.)

☀ Miscarriage Prevention Spell (3) Speedy Labor Charms

Sometimes magic isn't in what you do but in what you don't do. It's crucial to recognize the magical capacity of objects so that they serve your purposes, rather than counteracting your desires.

Emeralds, lodestones, and charms in the shape of downward-pointing arrows all allegedly speed delivery. Do not wear or carry them until the appropriate time.

☀ Post-Miscarriage Cleansing Spell

This bath spell offers spiritual (rather than physical) healing as well as relief from grief. It is recommended

*post-miscarriage whether sponta-
neous or not.*

*Moisten baking soda with **Notre
Dame Water**. Add this to your bath
daily until you feel it's no longer
needed.*

Childbirth Spells

Birth is perhaps the ultimate magical threshold, fraught with simultaneous psychic vulnerability and
primal power. The birthing cham-
ber is the equivalent of the crossroads at midnight, packed with
unseen competing spirits, drawn
by the opportunity for mischief or
the need to prevent it. Magic
spells seek to ease and assist birth.
Spells prevail upon the protective
powers of benevolent spirits, plot
to avoid or foil malevolent spirits,
ease pain, speed delivery, and provide a happy future for mother and
child. The childbirth process is
protected and enhanced through
the use of amulets and special
ritual clothing.

Birth Chamber Spells

Any area or space where childbirth occurs, from hospital delivery room to home bedroom, from
traditional bathhouse to taxi cab,
is instantly transformed into a
tremendously powerful, although
ephemeral, threshold of emer-
gent life, temporarily equal in
magical stature to a crossroads,
cemetery, or shrine. It is also, as
is the nature of thresholds, a
tremendously vulnerable space.
Use protective spells to secure
the birthing room and protect
mother, child, and all other participants in the process.

Birth Chamber Aroma Spells

Aroma is used to create an aura
of protection in the birth cham-
ber. Aroma is created by fumigat-
ing with incense or by warming
essential oils in an aroma burner.

These aromas were tradi-
tionally indicated for childbirth
because of their generally relaxing, pain-relieving effects upon the
mother and because of their magically beckoning, inviting influence
on the child. The person in charge
of maintaining the aroma should
accompany lighting of incense or
candles with blessings for mother
and child.

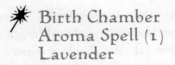

Birth Chamber Aroma Spell (1) Lavender

Diffuse essential oil of lavender through an aroma burner to soothe the mother's fears, welcome the newborn, and stimulate emergence. The scent also beckons benevolent fairies.

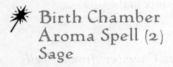

Birth Chamber Aroma Spell (2) Sage

Warm essential oils of clary sage, jasmine, and lavender in an aroma burner to welcome the baby, soothe the mother, and relax all the birth assistants.

Birth Chamber Protection Spell (1) Father's Protective Spell

The father walks deasil (sunwise) seven times around the perimeter of the building where birthing occurs to provide mother and child with magical protection.

Birth Chamber Protection Spell (2) Pomegranates

Hang boughs of fresh pomegranate over thresholds to ease delivery, and also to prevent the entry of malicious spirits.

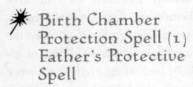

Birth Chamber Protection Spell (3) Umbrella Protection

The origins of the umbrella lie in magical protection spells. Place an umbrella over the bed of a laboring woman to repel evil spirits.

Ease Painful Labor Spells

Components of spells to ease labor may be found, handcrafted, or purchased. These methods may be used in conjunction with each other. As with all object-driven spells, remember to cleanse, charge, and consecrate as needed. The following are said to ease and alleviate the pain of childbirth. (They do not, however, make any promises regarding shortening the process, with the possible exception of Spell 2 because of the incorporation of lodestone.)

☀ Eased Labor Spell (1) Arrow

The use of arrows transcends archery contests and hunting. Arrows also play an ancient and once prominent role in divination, spirituality, and magic spells, especially those for love, protection, healing, and birth. These "medicine arrows," to borrow a Native American term, are traditionally charged, consecrated and/or blessed before use, in the same manner as a candle or amulet. Because they may never be meant actually to fly, these arrows can be embellished with botanicals, charms, runes, and feathers or re-shaped to suit one's magical purposes. The arrow in its quiver also replays the sexual imagery of morter and pestle, sword and sheath.

Place a medicine arrow beneath the laboring woman's bed. Should the pain get very bad, shoot the arrow from east to west, so as to magically carry the pain away. Leave the quiver empty.

☀ Eased Labor Spell (2) Coral and Lodestone

This amuletic charm must be prepared before delivery. Create a necklace of coral beads with a lodestone suspended from it, and wear during the delivery.

☀ Eased Labor Spell (3) Precious Gems

The possibility of easing labor is a nice excuse for an expensive gift: wear emeralds or rubies anywhere on the body.

☀ Eased Labor Spell (4) Raspberry Leaves

Raspberry plants are believed to possess an affinity for childbirth. Wear or carry raspberry leaves in a charm bag to speed and alleviate childbirth.

☀ Eased Labor Spell (5) Red Thread

Wind red silk thread around the laboring woman.

Easy Speedy Delivery Spells

These spells not only allegedly ease labor pains but quicken the process, too. Because these spells are largely object-driven, remember to incorporate petition, conscious visualization and affirmation, magical cleansing, charging, and/or consecration.

Easy Speedy Delivery Spell (1) All Doors Open

To ease and speed labor:

1. Loosen all knots, including braids, shoelaces, and any ties on clothing, in the vicinity of the birthing room.
2. Keep doors and windows open or at least unlocked.
3. Make sure small locks, such as padlocks, are opened for the duration.

Easy Speedy Delivery Spell (2) Crystal Arrow

Clear quartz crystal cut into the shape of a downward-facing arrow and worn during delivery is among the most powerful childbirth amulets.

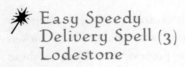

Easy Speedy Delivery Spell (3) Lodestone

Lodestone's very presence is said to encourage delivery. Exploit their drawing magnetic properties by gently massaging the mother's abdomen or aura, demonstrating the suggested route of departure to the baby.

Birth Rituals

Successful delivery signals the beginning of a series of spells and rituals to welcome and protect mother and baby. A host of protective amulets evolved to provide for infants' and children's extreme psychic vulnerability. It is crucial to understand, however, that these amulets were created during a time when fears regarding psychic safety outweighed those for physical safety. The concept of *"infant-proofing"* didn't exist and accidents surely happened. However, this was also a time when babies were rarely, if ever, supervised, infant mortality was high, and when people lived in smaller, more crowded spaces so children were constantly underfoot—and under someone's eye.

Some amulets may not be safe for use as originally directed but must be adapted to suit personal circumstances: they presuppose that someone literally has their eyes on the baby at all times. Once upon a time, the baby was either in a cradle right by an adult, or carried on someone's body. Children were rarely isolated. There's no point protecting against the Evil Eye or malicious Spirits while simultaneously leaving the baby vulnerable to choking.

Infant Protection Spells

Nothing and no one is metaphysically perceived as more in need of magical protection than an infant or young child. Protection spells designed especially for babies fulfill this need. Consider the warnings above, however: many of these spells evolved at a time when babies were never left unattended or unobserved. Their safety precautions are of a much different standard than that of modern parents. The original spells are offered, but consider whether adaptation is required so as to provide a baby with both magical *and* physical safety simultaneously.

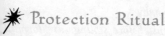 ## Protection Ritual

1. Prepare **Holy Water** for washing the baby.
2. Having cleansed the infant immediately on birth, preserve some of the water.
3. This may be used in the future to remove the Evil Eye by

dipping a piece of coral, the house key, or a ritual key into the water, then hanging it over the baby's crib.

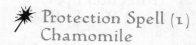 ## Protection Spell (1) Chamomile

Hang bunches of chamomile over the baby's crib for magical protection.

Protection Spell (2) Conjure Bag

A mojo hand to protect a child from harm, this conjure bag is a spell in progress:

1. Place an angelica root together with chamomile and flax seed in a charm bag.
2. Add a coin minted in the child's birth year, together with a small piece of silver. Traditionally the child's initials are scratched into the metal. An initial bead or a charm with the child's name engraved upon it may be substituted.
3. Collect any baby teeth and add them to the bag. It's not necessary to have every single baby tooth; even one is sufficient.

4. Keep this charm bag in a safe place until the child is old enough to inherit it.

☀ Protection Spell (3) Coral Beads Basic

Smooth pink coral beads worn around the neck provide a child with magical protection.

☀ Protection Spell (4) Cradle Charms

The following amulets, believed capable of providing a newborn baby with magical protection, are meant to be attached to the cradle, or else displayed near the cradle. Use one, more, or all of the following:

★ *Antique key*
★ *Blue-eye beads*
★ *Knife used to cut the umbilical cord*
★ *Mirror*

☀ Protection Spell (5) Holy Herbs

"Holy Herbs," *a New Orleans formulation, is used to protect children. Equal parts of seven dried herbs are blended together: catnip,* ground black snake root (black cohosh root), hops, jasmine blossoms, motherwort, peppermint, and skullcap.

1. Grind them together into powder.
2. Reserve them within a tightly shut jar until needed.
3. Should spiritual protection ever be required make an infusion by pouring boiling water over the herbal blend. When the brew cools, strain out the solids.
4. Add the liquid to the child's bathwater or sprinkle it onto the child using an asperging tool.
5. Sprinkle the liquid into each corner of the child's room.

☀ Sibling Harmony Spell

A spell to promote sibling harmony immediately following the birth of a new baby.

Just before siblings are formally introduced for the first time, place a few grains of sugar in the new infant's hand. Elder siblings are encouraged to lick the sugar off the baby's hand. (Never use honey, which contains spores potentially toxic to those under one year old.)

Welcome Baby Spells

Welcome Spells greet the new child and offer blessings as well as requests for spiritual protection.

Welcome Spell (1)
Jamaica

Babies are sometimes born with a natural blue "cross" in the spot over the nose between the eyebrows, which fades as the skin ages and grows thicker. Many traditions consider this mark to be very auspicious: a sign of spiritual protection. Blessings one is not born with, however, can also be consciously, magically bestowed. This bath is traditionally given on the ninth day following birth:

- Add a little rum to bathwater.
- Each member of the family throws in a bit of silver.
- Real indigo is added to the water, tinting it blue.
- Mark a blue cross on the baby's forehead or in the hollow over the nose, between the eyebrows, or else on the back of the neck.
- Offer blessings and prayers for the baby's safety and happiness as you remove the child from the bath.

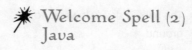

Welcome Spell (2)
Java

This ceremony, or variations on the theme, was traditionally performed when the baby reaches approximately seven months of age or when absolutely dying to crawl, whichever comes first. Its objective: to formally introduce the new baby to Mother Earth.

Until seven months, a baby's existence is considered tenuous. Babies are perceived as hovering in a dimension between spiritual and physical realms, gradually becoming more and more grounded. Until this point, the baby is never placed on the ground but carried in a sling on the mother's body.

1. Form seven moist soft balls of clay, each in a distinct color.
2. Roll each clay ball against the baby's body.
3. Ritually bathe the baby.
4. Place the baby in a large bamboo (wicker) cage or basket together with grains of rice, coins, gold chains, and either feathers or a live hen. (This ritual also serves divinatory purposes: whichever object the child touches first, indicates something about his or her character and destiny.)

5. The baby is slowly lowered to the ground.

✴ Welcome Spell (3) Modern Egyptian

On the seventh day following birth, blend olive oil, salt, and onion juice. (Other optional ingredients include henna and kohl powder.) Dip a feather in the paste and pass it, without actually touching, over the baby's open eyes to make them beautiful, sharp, and healthy.

Protection Spells

Protection Spells are intended to prevent, protect, and repel danger. Many find this category confusing so let's be very clear: there is no magic spell that functions exactly like an armed response guard one might hire from a personal security service. *Magical protection spells provide magical protection.* They create an aura that enhances other protective methods. If you are concerned about actual physical danger, magic reinforces other methods but does not replace them. If you are seriously concerned about your apartment being robbed, for instance, it doesn't matter how many powerful spells you cast, how many amulets you post at the entrance, if you don't also lock doors and windows. Magic doesn't offer license to defy laws of Nature or common sense.

According to occult wisdom, however, there are many kinds of danger in the world. Locking your door may prevent a human thief. However, certain dangers can only be repelled by magical methods. These dangers include:

★ *Malicious spells, hexes, jinxes, magic "tricks," or negative enchantment cast deliberately against one person by another*
★ *The Evil Eye*
★ *Assorted spiritual dangers deriving from a vast variety of spiritual sources. These may be caused deliberately or inadvertently*

Although these dangers derive from magical and spiritual roots, they may manifest in very physical ways, as illness, accidents, and general disaster. However, because their derivation is at least partly magical, prevention and remedies must also be, at least partly, magical.

Anti-bewitchment Spells

Anti-bewitchment spells create a protective shield, an aura of invulnerability against malevolent magic. They prevent the casting of enchantment against you, however they may not remove a hex already cast. Hex-antidotes or reversing spells are required instead.

✳ Anti-bewitchment Spell (1) Asperging

1. Dissolve saltpeter in water.
2. Sprinkle over the thresholds of your home and on people to repel malevolent magic, as well as anywhere you perceive vulnerability.
3. For maximum benefit, use protective botanicals as asperging tools, such as rue, rosemary, or rowan.

✳ Anti-bewitchment Spell (2) Stones

This formula from ancient Mesopotamia to protect against malevolent magic is particularly beneficial if a future personal encounter with evil sorcery is anticipated.

Choose five different stones, including a hematite and a lodestone. (The original Mesopotamian formula suggested different colored glass as well, but what they considered glass might not have been as sharp and jagged as what we call glass. Sea glass might work, or crushed faience.)

. Crush the rocks.

. Blend olive and castor oil and add essential oil of cypress.

. Let this mixture stand outside overnight, exposed to moon and starlight, absorbing their power. Simultaneously there should be spiritual petition, magical ritual, and fasting to bolster the effects.

. At sunrise, massage the body with the oil.

✳ Aloe Vera Protection Spell

Aloe vera's leaves, filled with healing, soothing gel, are shaped like spears. Maintain living plants on your altar for spiritual protection, specially if working with volatile entities or dangerous spirits.

✳ Anti-assault Protection Spell

Carry dried heather sewn up in a sachet to magically guard against rape and sexual assault. (This enhances but, of course, does not replace more conventional safety precautions.)

✳ Aura of Protection Spell

Strategically arrange blue crystal gemstones around the home or area you wish to protect, creating a magical boundary to keep out evil.

Basic Botanicals of Magical Protection

Many botanicals weave an aura of protection, including the ones that follow. Create your own protection spells by incorporating them. Try betony, black cohosh, cactus, calamus/sweet flag, fig leaf, five-finger grass/cinquefoil, garlic, hyssop, lavender, mugwort, peppermint, roses, rue, Saint John's Wort, snake root, stinging nettles, tormentil, vervain, wormwood, and yarrow.

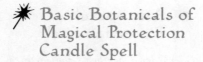

Basic Botanicals of Magical Protection Candle Spell

Hollow out the bottom of a black, blue, or red candle. Stuff it full of basic protection botanicals and burn the loaded candle.

Bay Laurel Protection Spell

According to myth, the bay laurel tree offered the Delphic pythoness Daphne an avenue of escape when fleeing rape. Place at least one bay leaf in each corner of every room to create an aura of protection.

Bell Protection Spell

Bells protect against evil. Their ringing causes many malicious spirits to flee and they are thus a primary component of exorcism rites. It's not only their ringing tones that repel evil; bells, like broomsticks and mortars and pestles, are a discreet metaphor for the reproductive act. Creative acts of life counteract forces of destruction. For this protective ritual, four silver or iron bells are required.

1. Consecrate the bells with **Fiery Wall of Protection Incense**. (Pass the bells through the smoke.)
2. Charge the bells. Hold them and tell them their mission of protection, aloud if possible.
3. Hang one in each corner of the area to be protected.
4. Allegedly the bells will warn when danger appears from that direction by spontaneously ringing.
5. Recharge bells that ring.
6. After an emergency or perhaps a annual maintenance, repeat the entire ritual.

Botanical Guardian Spells

Although different botanical provide different facets of magical protection, certain plants especially in combination, provide a fearsome shielding aura prevailing against evil from all sources.

Botanical Guardian Spell (1) Anti-evil

Allegedly, evil and malevolent force cannot exist in the presence of the following botanicals:

Hyssop
Lavender
Patchouli
Rue

1. Their power is exponentially increased where they are maintained together. Maintain living plants for maximum power.
2. For portable protection, take a sprig of each plant with you.
2. Braid or weave them together, focusing on your desires.
3. Place them in a red fabric bag and carry with you.

Botanical Guardian Spell (2) Nine Herbs

The following nine herbs allegedly withstand and protect against all spiritual and magical dangers:

1. Eyebright
2. Mallow
3. Mugwort
4. Saint John's Wort
5. Self-heal
6. Speedwell
7. Vervain
8. Wormwood
9. Yarrow

Plant them around the perimeter of the area needing protection, ideally in a circle. Maintain living plants in pots that may be arranged in a circle, if and when necessary. In times of spiritual danger, sit within that circle.

Cactus Fence Spell

The equivalent of the thicket around Sleeping Beauty's castle, a boundary of tall prickly cactus around your home casts an aura of protective banishing against humans and spirits alike.

Casting the Circle

An incredibly simple yet remarkably protective spell is accomplished by casting a circle. Children's games, such as tag, often designate an area as *"safe"*; once the child has reached the designated area, the opportunity exists to take respite. Casting the circle is similar: the space within the circle is designated as *"safe."* No malevolent spiritual force can touch or harm you while within the circle. The materials used to cast the circle enhance this power.

In addition to personal protective magic circles, circles are traditionally cast to contain threshold experiences as well as whatever is perceived as potentially vulnerable:

★ Circles are drawn around ritual
★ Circles are drawn around a sickbed
★ Circles are drawn around women in childbirth
★ Circles are drawn around sleeping infants and children

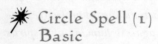

Circle Spell (1) Basic

This is the very simplest protection spell of all. Cast a circle around you. (In other words, stand within while drawing the circle, rather than casting from outside, intending to jump inside when the circle is complete.) Sit in the center until you feel it's safe to come out.

Circle Spell (2) Celtic Quick Fix

Protective materials sufficient to cast a circle large enough to contain you comfortably may not be at hand when most needed. Draw a circle around yourself with a hazel branch. Hold onto that branch so that the circle's boundaries may be adjusted and reinforced as needed.

Circle Spell (3) Wreath

Wreaths are circles, too. The form a well as the material used for con struction contributes to a wreath protective powers. Pick primrose and convolvulus on May Day. Mak wreaths and hang them to protec against evil.

Visible Circles

Visible circles aren't necessarily more effective, however, their clea boundaries may provide additiona peace of mind for the person withi as well as security: you're less like ly to accidentally venture outside the perimeter if you can see it.

Regardless what material i used to cast a circle, it's crucia that the circle be unbroken. Pow erfully protective circles may be cast from the following:

Absinthe
Amber chunks or beads
Chalk
Charcoal
Coral
Cornmeal
Fiery Wall of Protection powde
Flour
Henna powder
Jet

Lava
Pemba
Red brick dust or red ochre
Rice flour
Rum
Salt
Tobacco
Turquoise
Vervain
Vermilion
Whiskey
Wormwood

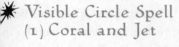

Visible Circle Spell (1) Coral and Jet

Certain circle-casting materials, when combined, create a synergistic, exponentially increased magical effect. Cast a circle of alternating coral and jet. Substitute amber for coral if desired, or combine all three.

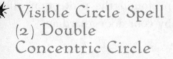

Visible Circle Spell (2) Double Concentric Circle

For extra fortification and maximum power, create double concentric circles: one circle within the other. Fill the narrow border between the two circles with protective amulets or salt.

Crystal Protection Spells

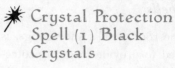

Crystal Protection Spell (1) Black Crystals

Black crystals are used to create a shield against evil and danger. Any black crystal absorbs anger, danger, evil, and malevolence, however black tourmalines are believed to repel it.

1. Hold the gemstones in your hand, charging them with your desire.
2. Wear as jewelry or carry in a mojo bag especially when stepping into anticipated danger.
3. Cleanse these crystals frequently so that their protective power is not hobbled but remains at full strength. (See *Cleansing Spells*.)

Crystal Spell (2) Witch Stones

Holed stones or holey stones—naturally holed pebbles—are also known as witch stones. In magical terms, they are as precious as any rare gem: they provide protection against malevolent magic, famine, storms at sea, and general spiritual disaster.

String a holed stone onto red cord or a silver chain. Wear around your neck during the day, hang onto your walls and bedposts at night.

Devil's Shoestrings Safety Spells

The root, devil's shoestrings, is used to provide magical protection. The following two spells are most effective if cast in conjunction with each other.

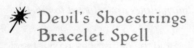

Devil's Shoestrings Bracelet Spell

Nine roots of equal length are required; they can't be cut to size. Knot them into a bracelet, blessing, affirming, and petitioning with each knot.

Devil's Shoestrings Protection Powder

Grind up devil's shoestrings and blend them with arrowroot powder. Sprinkle the powder in your clothing drawers, around your bed, and over your thresholds for round-the-clock protection.

Door Guardians

Thresholds are always places of combined power and vulnerability. The threshold of a home, the front entrance, is particularly vulnerable. Where does both bad and good news most typically enter the home? Right through the front door. Reinforce with protective measures. Door guardians are objects chosen for the protective magic that they radiate. Typically placed by the entrance facing outwards, they stand ready to battle and repel any approaching threat or evil.

With the exception of the Holy Child, under whose deceptively sweet demeanor a primordial spirit hides, these are fierce, threatening, even frightening images—but they're door guards after all. Who gets hired to work as a club bouncer: a cute, little kid or a big bruiser? What type of dog is most typically on guard duty: a miniature poodle or a rottweiler? The fiercer, the more frightening the image, the more profound the protection offered by your door guardian.

Door Guardian (1) Aloe Vera

Place living aloe vera plants over the door, rather than beside it, to provide magical, spiritual protection.

Door Guardian (2)
Blackthorn

Blackthorn is a small tree with profound magical connections. Associated with witchcraft, it's also among the fairies' favorite botanicals. As you're requesting blessings of protection, it's particularly important to request permission from the tree, explain your intent, and offer gifts and libations.

Create a rod from a blackthorn branch. Keep the shape simple or embellish with protective runes, symbols, and sigils. Hang it over the door to refuse entry to mischief, misfortune, and evil and malicious spells.

Door Guardian (3)
Gargoyles

Technically the gargouille was a seventh-century water-spouting (as opposed to fire-breathing) dragon (think "gargle") that lived in the River Seine and was slain upon orders of the local bishop. Although the use of animal-shaped water-spouts dates back to ancient Egypt, Etruria, and Greece, the term "gargoyle" reemerged in eleventh-century Western Europe as the name given to functional but decorative rain spouts, carved in the form of grotesque creatures. Because they most frequently adorn churches and cathedrals, they, like the sheela na gig, are mysterious, evocative, surviving vestiges of paganism. Gargoyles give the appearance of demons but offer spiritual protection rather than harm. It's believed that they are guardian spirits, magically preserved in stone; in the face of evil, however, they will break free to do battle.

In the past few decades, gargoyles have been adapted to serve as door guardians. Free-standing reproductions of famed gargoyles are available. You may also craft your own. Gargoyles do not have to be placed at the front door; consider your most vulnerable points and place gargoyles appropriately. Gargoyles also apparently enjoy each other's company; there cannot be too many. Place them as needed in combinations that evoke a sense of security. According to legend, winged gargoyles can fly; feel free to move them around as desired.

Door Guardian (4)
Tiger

In Asian magical tradition, tigers are the fierce sworn enemies of evil spirits. They are also animals closely associated with warrior spirits and witchcraft: a tiger's magical knowledge is as great as its bravery and physical prowess. All are put to good use when the tiger serves as a door guardian.

According to Chinese schools of magic, it's not advisable to maintain images of tigers within the home; because of their fierce, uncontrollable nature, they have a tendency to stimulate havoc. Instead post an image of one by the entrance door, either a paper image attached to the door or a statue beside the door to provide spiritual protection. The tiger must be looking away from the home searching for danger.

Doorstep Protection Spells

The doorstep marks the literal threshold. It is a particularly vulnerable spot. Many hexes involve what is called "dusting the doorstep." The spell is activated by leaving its remnants or other magic materials at the target's front door.

Many rituals are designed to transform this threshold into a zone of safety. Typically spells are repeated weekly with many involving "cleansing." Because in some cases, although not all, it appears only that you're being very clean and house-proud, this is also a very subtle, discreet style of magic.

(Should your doorstep ever be dusted, check **Hex Antidote Spells** for tips on removing items safely and repelling the spell, but follow up with protective measures, too.)

✳ Doorstep Spell Floorwash

Urine is believed to have fierce magical commanding powers, hence its use in protective floorwashes. If you're genuinely fearful or otherwise passionately emotional, assume that your desires are inherently transmitted; otherwise concentrate on your desire while scrubbing the steps.

1. A bucket filled with some sort of floorwash is required for this spell.
2. Choose any magical floorwash formula or merely fill a bucket with salted water.
3. Add some of your urine to this bucket of wash water and then scrub the step.

✳ Doorstep Spell Red Brick Dust

Red brick dust protects against malevolent magic and repels evil of all kinds.

1. Smash an old red brick with a hammer until sufficient dust is obtained.
2. Add red brick dust to a bucket of floorwash and scrub the front steps and threshold area.
3. Sprinkle powdered red brick dust over the threshold daily before sunrise.

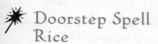

Doorstep Spell
Rice

1. Fill an open jar with raw white rice.
2. Place the jar by the entrance door for protection.
3. Rice doesn't repel evil; it absorbs it. Replace with fresh raw rice weekly.
4. Do not bring the old rice back into your home. Do not cook it. Dispose of it outside the home, whether by burning, throwing away, or scattering on Earth.

Fiery Wall of Protection Spells

Fiery Wall of Protection is among the most famous classic condition formulas. Its name invokes the power of Archangel Michael's protective flaming sword. The formula may be consecrated to the archangel.

Fiery Wall's basic ingredients include such powerful protective agents as salt, frankincense, and myrrh. Its red color, the color of protection, derives from dragon's blood powder. See the Formulary for specific instructions: the dried powder may be used as incense or magic powder. When the powder is added to oil, **Fiery Wall of Protection Oil** is created.

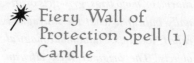

Fiery Wall of
Protection Spell (1)
Candle

*Carve a red or white candle with your name, identifying information, hopes, and desires. Dress it with **Fiery Wall of Protection Oil** and burn. Consecrate the candle to the Archangel Michael if desired.*

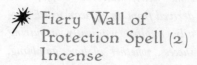

Fiery Wall of
Protection Spell (2)
Incense

*Protect against a threatened curse by burning **Fiery Wall of Protection Powder** as incense. To intensify the protection, add powdered agrimony and/or vervain.*

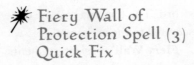

Fiery Wall of Protection Spell (3) Quick Fix

*Soak a cotton ball in **Fiery Wall of Protection Oil** and carry it in your pocket or tucked into your bra.*

Gris-Gris Protection

The term "gris-gris" derives from West Africa. Now frequently used as just another synonym for conjure, charm, or mojo bags, gris-gris originally indicated what the Portuguese called "fetishes:" handmade magical objects. The original West African gris-gris often took the form of dolls; modern New Orleans gris–gris are often a cross between a mojo bag and Vodou paquets-Congo, although doll-shaped gris-gris still exist.

For those who care about magical semantics, subtle, subliminal distinctions exist, however. Mojo, also derived from an African word, usually implies magically acquiring success, whether in love, gambling, money, employment, or legal matters. Gris-gris implies protection; the gris-gris bag thus tends to cover the spectrum between benign protective spells and hexes.

1. The traditional New Orleans Voodoo bag contains an odd number of magically charged items, from as few as a single prized talisman to as many as thirteen.
2. Gris-gris serves a specific purpose; consider your goal and choose items accordingly. Items may include botanicals, stones, bones, and intimate items including hair, nail clippings, or a scrap of fabric soaked with sweat.
3. Charge items on an altar with all four elements represented. Petition and dedication to lwa or other spirits may be incorporated.
4. If your goal is personal protection, carry your gris-gris; if protection derives from adjusting someone else's behavior, typically the gris-gris is left on the doorstep of the other party's property.

Guardian Animals

Animal allies may also be petitioned for safety. As usual, the most potent allies are always your personal allies. If you are unaware of their identity, request them to make their presence known in your dreams and visualizations or obtain professional shamanic/spirit-working advice. In the meantime, certain animals provide magical guardian services when requested.

Guardian Animal Spell: Dog

Dogs provide magical protection as well as the mundane type. This protective spell benefits an entire community.

Create paper dogs so that you are ready to cast this spell on the fifth day of the fifth month of the Chinese lunar calendar (coinciding with Midsummer's Eve). Charge them with their mission and throw them into living waters (rivers, lakes, springs) so that they'll bite and incapacitate any evil attempting to emerge.

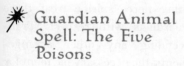

Guardian Animal Spell: The Five Poisons

In general, magical guardian animals are fierce. This makes sense: the Doberman is a more popular guard dog than a golden retriever. Chinese magic contemplates what it perceives as the five most venomous creatures and groups them together to provide magical protection, especially protection against animal attack, poison, and spiritual harm.

Create an image or collage of the five poisonous creatures: centipede, lizard, scorpion, snake, and toad. (The toad, source of powerful venom (think poison-arrow frog) is sometimes replaced by the spider. Use whichever frightens you more.) Images may also be purchased in Chinatown or from feng shui suppliers, however the image created for oneself is always most powerful. Wear to protect against spiritual danger, poison, venomous creatures, and animal attack in general. The image is regarded as particularly beneficial for protecting children and infants.

Guardian Snake Spells

Snakes are renowned for possessing divine powers to ward off evil. Think of a hidden jungle temple guarded by protective serpents. Legends of buried treasure or hidden magical valuables traditionally have snake or dragon (considered metaphysically to be a closely related species) guardians.

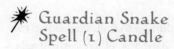

Guardian Snake Spell (1) Candle

Spiritual suppliers sometimes sell candles in the shape of coiled serpents.

1. Hold the candle to charge it with your desire. If you wish, look the snake in the eye and charge it with its mission of protection.
2. Burn the candle to release the snake's guardian powers.
3. Burning the candle is sufficient, however its power is enhanced by being dressed with **Protection Oil**.
4. Burn at regularly scheduled intervals so as to define protective boundaries.

✴ Guardian Snake Spell (2) Personal Bodyguard

Snakes can serve as personal magical bodyguards. Methods of tapping into snakes' protective powers include:

★ *Wear snake armlets on the upper arms*
★ *Snake rings offer protection as does snake imagery in henna designs*
★ *Permanent vigilance is provided by snake tattoos*

In addition to their traditional role as guardians of treasure, snakes and dragons have discovered new realms to protect in the twenty-first century. Snakes and dragons have become the metaphysical protectors of computers and the treasures contained within.

Guardian Spirit Spells

Although there are many benevolent, powerful, protective spirits, your own strongest ally is always your personal guardian angel. If you're unsure of his or her identity, consider that although there are spirits that offer protection, it's best to call on someone you can count on. Call on whomever has helped you in the past, whomever you feel you have a relationship with. That said, there are spiritual experts in the world of protection, just as there are human security experts.

It takes a fierce spirit to defeat other fierce spirits: treat these guardians with respect. Transcending any other arrangements, the necessary payment for protection is respect.

✴ Sign of Protection Spell

Images of the following guardian deities may be used to exorcise or drive off all manner of evil. Not only do they protect from the evil

done by humans, they also guard people against danger threatened by less benevolent spirits.

★ *Archangel Michael*
★ *Bes*
★ *Durga*
★ *Hanuman*
★ *Kali*
★ *Medusa*
★ *Ogun*
★ *Saint James the Major*
★ *Saint Martha the Dominator*
★ *Set*
★ *Shiva*
★ *Taweret*
★ *Various Tibetan and Chinese guardian spirits*

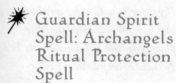# Guardian Spirit Spell: Archangels Ritual Protection Spell

This spell is particularly effective for providing protection during ritual. However it may also be used any time spiritual protection is perceived as necessary.

1. Designate four candles, one for each archangel: Michael, Raphael, Uriel, and Gabriel.
2. Dedicate each candle to one archangel; carve the angel's name or sigil into the wax if you prefer.

3. Place one candle in each corner of the room or make a circle with the candles on your altar.
4. Encircle anything you wish to protect with a ring of these candles, including yourself.
5. Burn the candles, replace as needed.

Archangel Michael Spell

Although the archangels (and potentially any angel) can provide tremendous protection, the archangel Michael is the very personification of protection. Always ready and alert, Michael the Archangel is charged as humanity's guardian and defender. That's his mission, his raison d'être. Put him to work if his services are required. Although Michael the Archangel will respond to any call for help, he is a particular vigilant defender against rape and sexual assault.

The aroma of frankincense summons Michael, however calling his name, particularly when desperate, may be sufficient. Call him with his invocation:

Michael to the right of me,
Michael to the left of me
Michael above me

Michael below me
Michael within me
Michael all around me
Michael, with your flaming sword of
    cobalt blue please protect me
    today.

Herbal Protection

Gather dillweed, Saint John's Wort, and vervain within white handkerchiefs. Either tie the packets closed with blue ribbon or create sachets using blue thread and hang these strategically throughout the home for spiritual and magical protection.

Hyacinth Antidote Spell

Carrying a hyacinth (jacinth) crystal gemstone allegedly protects one from poison.

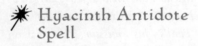

Iron Spells

Iron repels evil of all kind. Most malevolent spirits cannot bear to be in its presence. In addition to providing protection, iron enhances and stimulates the growth of one's personal magic powers, so that you are stronger and better able to protect yourself,

requiring less outside spiritual protection. Iron also invigorates general vitality and energy.

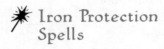

Iron Protection Spells

Iron provides protection 24 hours a day, whether you are asleep or awake.

★ Bend a used horseshoe nail into a ring
★ An iron bracelet reinforces the magical protective capacities of the hand
★ String iron beads and wear around neck and ankles
★ For protection while you sleep, slip a knife or horseshoe under your pillow
★ If you prefer not to keep anything that hard in bed, a sword or fireplace poker can be kept under the bed
★ No need to keep anything in or under the bed: sleeping in a bed crafted from iron creates an island of safety, reinvigorating health, creativity, and fertility while you sleep

Iron Spell: Spoken Word

The power of iron is so strong that even if you don't have any, just shouting out the word "iron" allegedly routs evil spirits.

Iron Spell: Simple

Ironworkers create intricate, complex amuletic designs for fences and gates. Of course, professional talent, extensive training, and skill are required. Simple spells can also be very powerful. Pow-Wow draws on potent household magic: a safety pin serves as a protective amulet. Wear one discreetly on your sleeve to repel dangers.

Living Boundary Spells

In fairy tales, witches' cottages are surrounded by magical gardens. A garden creates a living altar that is cultivated to achieve your desired goals. A protective garden creates an aura of safety around the perimeter of your home.

Living Boundary: Basic Protection Garden

Maintain a protective aura of safety around your home. Include as many of the following as possible: angelica, cactus, clover, dill, elder, flax, gardenia, garlic, holly, juniper, mugwort, nettles, oregano, roses, rosemary, rowan, rue, Saint John's Wort, southernwood, thyme, vervain, wormwood, and yarrow.

Living Boundary: Circle of Trees

Grow or transplant as many of the following protective trees as possible: ash, bay laurel, birch, cedar, ceiba, hawthorn, hazel, iroko, juniper, oak, olive, and rowan. Arrange the trees in a circle, if possible.

Malicious Spirits Protection Spell

Should you hear someone call your name when no one is visibly present, and should you fear that this is a demonic ploy to lure you into trouble, take advantage of low-level spirits' legendary low IQ: respond with a contradictory message. The classic Russian answer is something like "Come again yesterday," but the more clever and creative your response, the more you'll leave the spirits scratching their heads and impotent to hurt you.

Mean Spirit Repelling

This spell is particularly beneficial following banishing spells when you fear that malevolent spirits will attempt to re-visit the scene of their crimes. The aroma of this potion repels hostile, troublesome, malicious spirits and prevents their entry.

Place rotten apples, wine galls, vinegar, and sulfur in a cauldron. Add myrrh and red sandalwood and warm to a simmer.

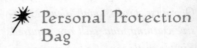 New Year's Protection Spell

This spell comes from Scandinavia; it is diametrically opposed to many Chinese New Year's spells that instruct not to clean on New Year's Day because you may accidentally sweep all your luck away, leaving you none for the year ahead. How you feel about cleaning will determine which magical philosophy is most appropriate for you.

1. Clean the house completely on New Year's Day, removing every speck of dust.
2. Carry the sweepings to a crossroads and discard them.
3. This renders the home immune to bewitchment and malevolent magic during the year to come.

Protection Bags

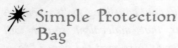 Simple Protection Bag

Entwine mugwort and Saint John's Wort and place within a red bag. Hang over every door and window for powerful magical, spiritual protection.

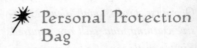 Personal Protection Bag

This protection spell may be cast for yourself or for another.

1. Put together a bag of your own or another person's intimate items (hair, nail clippings, bits of fabric cut from a garment soaked with sweat, etc.).
2. Place them within a charm bag.
3. Attach it to the wall in a very discreet area by hammering in an iron nail. Simultaneously invoke blessings.

Protection Baths

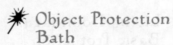 Object Protection Bath

For empowering and protecting specific objects or ritual tools:

1. Place marjoram, peppermint, rosemary, and sage within a bowl.
2. Make a strong infusion by pouring boiling water over them.
3. Sprinkle the infusion as needed or add the strained, cooled liquid to a spray bottle and apply as needed.

☀ Protection Bath: Basil

This spell repels malevolent magic targeted toward you, repairs a damaged aura, and helps erect a personal protective shield.

1. Make a strong infusion by pouring boiling water over fresh basil leaves. Once it cools, strain the leaves out and discard.
2. Bring the bowl of basil-infused water to the bath or shower. Stand naked in the tub or shower. Dip a clean white cloth (a handkerchief or hand towel) into the infusion and, wiping downwards and out, cleanse your body.
3. Repeat daily for nine days. After the final bath, throw any remaining water (and make sure there is some!) out the front door with an aggressive motion.
4. If this isn't possible toss liquid into a pot filled with Earth. Remove it from your home and dispose of it immediately, preferably at a crossroads.

Salt Spells

Although any form of salt provides intense spiritual and magical protection, sea salt is believed most potent. Hoodoo tradition favors

kosher salt because it has been blessed. In a pinch, any salt may be used although the closer it is to its natural state, the less it has been processed and essentially tampered with, the more magical protection and power salt can provide.

☀ Salt Bath: Basic

Add salt to the bath to simultaneously provide spiritual cleansing as well as creating a powerful psychic shield. For a quick fix, just toss handfuls of sea salt, as many as desired, into a tub of running water. Stir to dissolve and soak.

☀ Salt Scrub: Basic

Bath salts are added directly to the water; salt scrubs are applied with either a gentle or a vigorous circular motion to the body. The oil causes the other ingredients to cling to the body, even after rinsing. This is an extremely powerful way to create a cleansing, protective shield.

1. The basic formula is one cup of salt to one half cup of oil, however you may wish to play with these proportions until you achieve a desired texture. This produces a fairly substantial quantity: store in

an air-tight container such as a mason jar. Salt scrubs will last indefinitely, providing water doesn't get into the container.

2. Add more oil if you'd like a gentler scrub. Finely ground salt is less abrasive.

3. Castor oil is the most protective carrier oil and should be added to the scrub, however it's extremely thick and doesn't always blend well. Add other carrier oils and play with proportions until it pleases you.

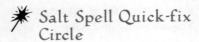

Salt Spell Quick-fix Circle

A potent quick-fix spell, particularly valuable when spiritual danger suddenly threatens to overwhelm you. Cast a circle using salt or black salt. Sit within the circle until you feel that it's safe to come out.

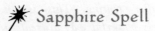

Sapphire Spell

Sapphires allegedly serve as a protective talisman against violence.

Silver Spell

Silver is perceived as a spiritually incorruptible metal that radiates an aura of protection. Place a small piece of real silver under the hearth. Once upon a time a coin would have been used, but once upon a time dimes were real silver. A bead or charm would be very appropriate.

Spell-breaker

This ancient and simple spell breaks any impending enchantment: consciously chew on your left thumb.

Sulfur Spells

Sulfur protects against malevolent magic and repels evil entities. In North African magic, it is sometimes considered equal to salt as a protector against evil. Sulfur is a primary ingredient in exorcisms and banishing spells, where it is typically burned. This is traditional but not necessarily advisable: inhaling sulfur fumes is potentially very irritating. However there are other methods of use, particularly beneficial for protective magic.

Sulfur Spell Eye of the Amulet

1. Make a paste by adding a bit of gum acacia or similar to sulfur powder.

2. Stick a little bit of this yellow paste into the center of any amulet to transform it into a vehicle of protection. This is particularly effective for hand amulets or geometric-shaped amulets, such as triangles or diamonds. Although they are already potent, the sulfur effectively becomes the "eye" of the amulet, further activating and empowering it.
3. Point the eye in the direction from which danger is feared.

Sword of Protection Spell

This symbolic sword is carried to fend off hurtful words and harmful actions.

1. Cut a piece of paper from a clean paper bag.
2. Draw a sword on it.
3. Place it within a leather pouch or metal amulet bag, together with a pinch of cayenne or habanero pepper and a pinch of sulfur.

Tiger Lily Spell

Tiger lilies serve as the botanical equivalent of tigers. Plant them near the home to prevent the entry of mean spirits.

Witch Ball Hex-breaker

"Witch balls" are large, beautiful, iridescent glass balls, resembling colored crystal balls or gigantic Christmas tree ornaments. They are traditionally hung from windows or placed atop pedestals in the garden to catch and absorb any approaching curses. Whether the witch ball reverses the spell is subject to debate; however it's generally acknowledged to shield and protect from malevolent bewitchment.

Arrange witch balls strategically around the property; near the front entrance and any other perceived vulnerable spots. (This is easy to implement as witch balls are so attractive, non-magical observers will assume they are merely garden ornaments.) Despite their ornamental value, witch balls are magical tools. Magically cleanse them on a regular schedule by bathing with mugwort-infused spring water.

Witch's Bottle Protection Spell

Glass, ceramic, stone, or metal bottles may be used for these spells against hexes and for protection against malicious spirits; don't use plastic.

1. Place three pins, three needles, and three nails inside a bottle.
2. Fill the bottle with salt.
3. Add three drops of menstrual blood or prick your smallest left finger and let three drops of blood flow into the bottle.
4. Seal the bottle securely and bury it under the hearth or next to your home.

Yin-yang Protection Spell

Create a protective amulet with magic beans. Yin-yang beans are the large gray seeds of the bonduc tree. They allegedly serve as the balance between male and female energy.

String a pair of beans onto a cord, together with one contraveneno bean, to provide spiritual protection. They guard against spiritual and psychic danger. Allegedly, if they are forced to do their job, the contraveneno will split into four pieces along the cross that marks one side of this black bean.

Spells to Protect Against Enemies

Many *Protection Spells* target evil in general, regardless from where it derives. Sometimes the source of danger is very clearly from another human. *Spells to Protect Against Enemies* take various approaches to the situation, from disarming one's enemy to transforming enmity into amity.

Alyssum Anger Management Spell

Offer a small bouquet of alyssum to one who resents you and bears you hostility and malice. Disarm them; literally place the bouquet in their hands. This magical transaction allegedly cools off their anger toward you quickly.

Box of Chocolate Spell

Chocolate allegedly possesses the power to transform enmity into friendship. Make a peace offering with a box of fine chocolate. This will only work, however, if the other party will eat real chocolate, dark and bitter-sweet.

Cast Off Evil Oil

Cast off malevolent thoughts, intentions, and hexes from those who resent you. (Although this is really a *prevention spell, it does possess a hex-breaking aspect.)*

1. Blend asafetida, crumbled bay leaves, hyssop, rue, and yarrow.
2. Add the botanicals to castor oil.
3. Soak cotton balls in the oil and leave them in the vicinity of the one who hates you (in the office or elsewhere). This is not a spell you can hide: the fragrance, depending on the quantity of asafetida used, can be very unpleasant; however it can be cast anonymously if you're discreet.

Convert an Enemy Spell

Fill a small charm bag with cloves, or actually incorporate the cloves into a spice necklace. Wear the charm around your neck to inspire feelings of affection and friendship.

Melt Your Cold, Cold Heart Spell

A Pow-Wow spell to warm some-one's cold heart: place a plate of snow or an icicle near a fire (fireplace, stove, or candle) and watch it melt while envisioning all the hostility melting away too.

Put the Anger on Ice Spell

1. Write the angry person's name on a slip of paper.
2. Drop the paper into a small, unbreakable container filled with water.
3. Seal the container shut. Keep it in your freezer.

If you have a lot of enemies, line them up in an ice cube tray.

Rose Quartz Transformation Spell

Rose quartz transforms anger into love, or at least mild affection. Wear it. Give it as a gift to those who resent you.

Sweeten Your Heart Spell

To sweeten someone's heart toward you:

1. Write your target's name on a slip of white paper.
2. Put it into a small jar with a lid.
3. Cover the paper with honey and close the jar tight.
4. Place a small white candle on top of the lid and burn.

Unblocking Spells

In some versions of the *Sleeping Beauty* story, the handsome prince would very much like to save Sleeping Beauty from her hundred years' sleep but is initially unable because the road leading to her castle is obstructed with thorns. The prince can't pass until, frustrated, he takes his sword and cuts his own path. In other versions of the tale, his sword won't cut; he's unable to pass through the thicket until powerful fairies recognize his predicament and cut a road for him.

That's exactly what unblocking or road-opening spells do.

When your life seems stagnant, when opportunities always seem to peter out, when no viable alternatives seem to exist, when no roads open for you, you may have what is magically known as a blocked condition. Blocked conditions stem from a variety of causes:

★ *Blockages may result from insufficient magic power: your magical gas tank is empty; therefore you can't proceed*

★ *Blockages may be the result of a hex or curse. However the emphasis with* Unblocking Spells *is emphatically on repairing the situation at hand: opening the roads. There's little emphasis on who may have placed a hex or on returning it*

★ *Blockages may result because you're desperately in need of magical cleansing: too much accumulated negative debris is weighing you down, preventing mobility*

★ *Blockages may result from spiritual causes*

Unblocking spells remove blocks, obstacles, and hurdles, opening the roads so that you can proceed happily with life. Blockages are the opposite of a crossroads. Crossroads offer possibilities of change, motion, and power. Blockages weigh you down, removing avenues of opportunity and limiting you to travel a path not of your choosing.

There are two aspects to unblocking spells:

★ *Specific spirits, magical owners of gates and crossroads, control access on all roads. They determine who passes and who is blocked. These road-opener spirits may be petitioned to remove your particular blockage*

★ *Other spells take advantage of the power of botanicals and magical items to remove a block*

Abre Camino Spells

"*Abre camino,*" literally "road opener" or "make way," is the name given to a plant (*Trichilia havanensis*) used in Latin American magic to open blocked paths. Carry an abre camino stick with you at all times to keep roads clear and remove obstacles from your path.

Abre Camino: Road-Opener Spell

Bring an abre camino stick to a crossroads. Hold it in your hands, and turn around to face each direction in turn, focusing on removal of all blocks from your pathways. Murmur affirmations, petitions, *and prayers if desired. Burn the stick and leave coins at the crossroads.*

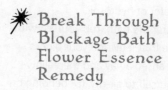

Break Through Blockage Bath Flower Essence Remedy

1. The flower essence remedy chestnut bud (Bach) is indicated when you're stuck, blocked, or trapped in repetitive cycles with no transformation.

2. Initiate use by taking a single intensive bath: add 20–30 drops of the remedy to the bath before bedtime. Pay attention to your dreams for clues on resolving your blockage.

3. Do not add more than half a
   dozen drops to any additional
   baths. Follow the manufacturer's
   recommendations for internal
   administration or apply topically.

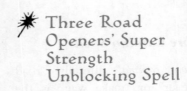

Citrus Unblocking Bath

1. Collect as many types of citrus
   fruits, emphasizing the sour ones.
   There can't be too much fruit in
   this bath.
2. Quarter each fruit, squeeze the
   juice into a tub of bathwater then
   toss in the rind.
3. Add a bottle of orange blossom
   water or hydrosol.
4. Enter the bath, rub yourself with
   the fruit, envision your blocks
   cleansed away and then allow
   yourself to air-dry. (Depending on
   the quantity of fruit used, you
   may be sticky. Leave the fruit
   residue on for as long as possible
   before showering it off.)

Road-Opener Spells

Any powerful and sympathetic
spirit can remove a block. However there is a genre of spirits
known as *"road openers."* These
spirits are said to *"own"* roads;
thus playing the role of a spiritual
gate-keeper they determine who
may pass and who can't, whose
road will be easy and whose will
be obstructed. On the whole,
these spirits possess a somewhat
sardonic sense of humor; they
tend to be volatile tricksters.
Their stomping ground, the place
to meet them, is invariably that
opposite of the blocked road, the
crossroads.

Three Road Openers' Super Strength Unblocking Spell

*To open one's path and clear a major
blockage, invoke Elegba (Exu),
Ogun, and Maria Padilha simultaneously. This offering is made at
midnight at a crossroads.*

1. Sprinkle the ground with anisette.
2. Lay down a red cloth; cover it
   with a black cloth. All offerings
   and candles should be placed on
   these cloths. The two male spirits
   will accept good rum, over-proof
   rum, or cachaca. Maria Padilha
   likes a small bottle of anisette or
   a glass of champagne served in a
   champagne flute. All three
   appreciate fine cigars and
   cigarettes.

3. Make an offering to Elegba/Exu of alcohol, candles, and fine cigars or deluxe cigarettes.
4. Make an offering to Ogun. Give him alcohol and a cigar, and light a red or black candle inside a cauldron.
5. Make an offering to Maria Padilha of red roses, red candles, fine cigarettes, or cigarillos, and a libation.
6. Talk to the three of them and tell them what you need.
7. Back up seven paces before you turn around; leave via a circuitous route. Do not return to that spot for at least seven days.

For the equivalent of magically dynamiting a blockage, repeat this spell at seven different crossroads all in one night.

Road-Opening Spell: Mojo Bag

This bag may need to be contained within a second bag to keep the dirt from slipping out.

1. Gather pinches of dirt from seven different crossroads and place them in a red bag.

2. Add salt, an old key, and pebbles or nails found on or beside train tracks.
3. Carry it with you to keep all avenues open.

Road-Opening Spell: Oil

1. Start with a coconut oil and jojoba oil base.
2. Add true coconut extract, ground allspice, peppermint, and licorice (not the candy, the herb).
3. This oil may be added to the bath or used to dress unblocking candles.

Stimulate Change Spell

To stimulate change, movement, and transformation gather a handful of dirt from each of the following places:

The local police department, courthouse, or jail
The local fire department or blacksmith
A crossroads
A butchery's shop
A place of higher education

You will need five handfuls in all. Place them all in a red flannel bag

together with a High John the Conqueror root to unblock your paths.

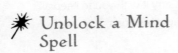 Unblock a Mind Spell

Sometimes what needs to be opened is someone's mind, so that that person will be willing to listen to you, to hear you.

1. Carve a skull candle with the name and identifying information of the target of this spell. Choose the color of the skull to suit your purpose: red for romance, green for financial discussion, black if the person is dense or is stubbornly refusing to consider your position. White may be used for any purpose.
2. Dress the candle with **Command and Compel Oil**. Add any other formula oil that matches your needs.
3. Burn the candle.

Intensify the spell by dedicating it to Papa Legba, Opener of the Ways, Eliminator of Obstacles.

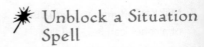 Unblock a Situation Spell

1. Charge a peridot, sardonyx, or quartz crystal.
2. Place it on an altar.
3. Focus your desires on the stone.
4. Carry it with you in a lucky charm bag.
5. Recharge it periodically on your altar.

 Unblocking Spell

Get rid of blocks and bad luck:

1. Go through your home and premises looking for extraneous sharp items: pins, tacks, anything similar.
2. Place them in a jar or bottle.
3. When it is approximately half full, take it outside and bury it, preferably not on your property, but at the least at the absolute furthest edge of your land. Don't dig it up.

Youth, Beauty, and Longevity Spells

Beauty Spells

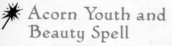

Acorn Youth and Beauty Spell

Three acorns, especially if they're found attached to one another, preserve youth and enhance beauty. A gold or silver charm depicting three acorns will work, too. Charge the three acorns under the New Moon, and wear them in your hair.

A more discreet version: charge three acorns under the New Moon. Wrap them together using strands of your hair and carry them in a charm bag.

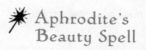

Aphrodite's Beauty Spell

Goats are among Aphrodite's sacred creatures. Soak violets in goat's milk and wash your face with this for beauty.

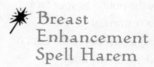

Breast Enhancement Spell Harem

A Turkish harem formula:

1. Pour boiling water over fenugreek seeds to make an infusion.
2. When it cools, strain out the seeds.
3. Use the liquid to bathe the breasts to allegedly increase bust size.

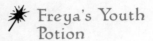 Egg Beauty Spell

Eggs are perceived as magical and powerful. Reserve the water used to boil eggs; let it cool and bathe with it for youth, vigor, and beauty.

Freya's Youth Potion

Cowslips are wild peonies and are said to be Freya's favorite flowers, as well as those of the fairies. Reputedly they magically transmit the beauty secrets of these powerful spirits.

1. Create an infusion, although you may also substitute a hydrosol.
2. Boil water and pour it over the blossoms.
3. When the water cools, strain out the blossom.
4. Apply the potion to your face with a cotton ball.
5. Use the remainder in the bath or elsewhere on the body.
6. You may also refrigerate the remainder for 24 hours.

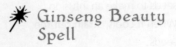 Ginseng Beauty Spell

Tie a red thread around a ginseng root and carry for added beauty and grace.

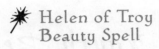 Helen of Troy Beauty Spell

Elecampane (Inula helenium) *was named for Helen of Troy. She allegedly carried it away with her when she fled with Paris. Since then, it's believed to bestow a little of her essence. Carry elecampane root for enhanced beauty, grace, charm, and confidence.*

Lilac Dew Spell

Bathe in lilac dew on May Day for a year of beauty.

Lunar Beauty Bath

The planet of magic, romance, and feminine power, the moon offers the gift of beauty in this Romany spell:

1. Stand naked in the light of the Full Moon.
2. Go through the motions of bathing in moonbeams. Visualize the moonbeams entering you and empowering you. Absorb their beauty.
3. Petition the moon for assistance with whatever troubles you: weight loss, hair growth, perceived imperfections.

4. Now watch for an immediate response from the moon: no change is a positive response; if the moon brightens, this is an extremely encouraging sign. A sudden darkening or a cloud passing over the moon indicates that you should anticipate challenges. Reconsider your request. Work on it until the next Full Moon.
5. Repeat as needed.

Use this ritual for romance and renewed fertility too.

✳ Seven Flowers Bath

A Chinese formula to enhance beauty, vitality, and sensuality: more important, this fragrant bath makes you happy with yourself.

The seven flowers are: rose, jasmine, peony, orchid, lotus, magnolia, and chrysanthemum. Add copious quantities of flower petals to your bath. Watch out for florist's flowers, which are usually heavily laden with pesticides. Substitute home-grown flowers where possible.

Fruit tree blossoms may be substituted for flowers. Peach and plum trees are considered especially auspicious. Vary the colors. If the fragrance is not intense, add essential oils until it suits you.

Hair Growth Spells

✳ Anti-baldness Spell Magic Potion

If you happen to have access to distilling equipment, distill liquor from human hair. Add honey and drink.

✳ Anti-baldness Spell Midsummer's Dew

Dew collected on Midsummer's morning prevents baldness. Collect and apply where needed.

✳ Anti-baldness Spell Onion

An old Anglo-Saxon remedy for baldness: cut an onion in half and rub the half onion vigorously over your exposed scalp, twice daily, morning and evening. If you have too much hair, juice an onion and blend the juice with a shot of vodka and a tablespoon of honey. Massage this mixture into your scalp, leave it for thirty minutes, then rinse it out of your hair.

✳ Facial Hair Spell Watermelon

A Moroccan remedy to encourage male facial hair: rub your chin daily with watermelon.

✴ Hair Growth Spell: New Moon

To promote hair growth, particularly after hair-loss:

1. Three days after the Spring Equinox, go up on the roof (or similar).
2. Smear your hair with a mixture of oil and henna (this can be neutral-colored henna).
3. Comb it out and talk to the moon.
   I gave you my hair
   Now Moon, give me yours.
4. Repeat every third day during this lunar month, until the Dark Moon.

✴ Yarrow Hair Growth Spell

Bathe your head with an infusion of yarrow to magically forestall hair loss.

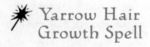

Weight Loss Spells

Spells to affect weight work when they complement more conventional methods (exercise, nutrition); they don't replace them. In other words, burning a weight-loss candle followed by eating a large tub of ice cream is only fooling yourself.

✴ Weight Loss Spell: Candle

This spell may be used for weight loss or for re-shaping one's silhouette.

1. Obtain a naked human figure candle to represent you.
2. With a pin scratch lines into the wax to demonstrate where reduction or re-shaping is needed, just as if you were a tailor making adjustments.
3. Dress the candle with a **Commanding Oil** and charge it with its mission.
4. Burn the candle for fifteen minutes daily. In between burnings, use a craft-knife to chip off wax to reflect your accomplishments and goals.

✴ Weight Loss Spell: Gem Therapy

Wear moonstone or topaz to encourage weight loss or to stabilize weight as needed. According to modern gem therapy, these stones regulate metabolism.

✴ Weight Loss Spell: Milk Bath

Coordinate this spell with a waning moon. Gently warm a carton of milk and bring it to the shower. Pour it

over your head while affirming to grow thinner like the moon.

Longevity Spells

Alchemists through the ages strived to create the *philosopher's stone*, a substance that would enable them to transmute base metals into gold. Kings sponsored alchemists' laboratories and their expensive experiments, dreaming of boundless wealth. However the philosopher's stone possessed another priceless attribute: it allegedly bestowed extended longevity to the point of immortality to its owner. Rumors spread that certain alchemists, such as the Frenchman Nicholas Flamel (born *c.*1330, died ?), had actually created the philosopher's stone. Nicholas Flamel still makes the occasional public appearance.

Western alchemy was born in Alexandria, Egypt and brought to Europe by the Moors. Another alchemical branch developed independently in China: there the quest was more purely focused on longevity, rather than wealth.

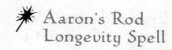 ## Aaron's Rod Longevity Spell

Aaron's rod is the botanical nickname given to golden rod and mullein. Use either plant in this spell. Create an infusion by pouring boiling water over Aaron's rod. Add the strained liquid to a bath to magically enhance longevity.

Amaranth Longevity Spell

Amaranth encourages longevity in the face of illness and obstacles. Carry it in a conjure bag.

Aroma Longevity Spell

Warm essential oils of cedarwood, chamomile, and juniper in an aroma burner. Inhale deeply to encourage longevity.

Beauty Longevity Spell

Like fine wines, certain fragrances grow more beautiful with age: anoint orrisroot with a drop of ylang ylang and/or patchouli oil and carry with you in a red silk bag so that you too will only improve with age.

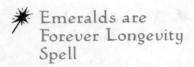

Emeralds are Forever Longevity Spell

Emeralds allegedly inhibit decay: wear them to preserve your youthfulness. If you don't have access to real emeralds, bathe in emerald gemstone essence to receive magical benefits.

Gingko Longevity Spell

Carve gingko wood into an auspicious shape and carry it in an amulet bag. (If "auspicious" leaves you drawing a blank, an ankh is always advantageous for longevity.)

Honeysuckle Longevity Spell

Surround yourself with living honeysuckle to encourage longevity.

Jade Gemstone Essence

Allegedly powdering and consuming green jade enhances longevity. This may not be such a good idea for a variety of reasons; however, jade gemstone essence may have a similar (but healthier) effect. Follow the manufacturer's instructions for internal administration or add the essence to the bath.

Long-life Noodles

As magical insurance, on your birthday eat a bowl of "Long-life Noodles," extra thin, extra long noodles. Be sure not to break any of the noodles while eating; slurp them up instead!

Peachwood Longevity Spell

The ancient Chinese spirit Hsi Wang Mu, the Queen Mother of the West, owns a magical garden containing the peaches of immortality. The Chinese Lord of Longevity also carries a peach. Ordinary peaches may not grant life everlasting, but they are magically associated with longevity. Carry peachwood or a dried peach kernel to magically lengthen one's lifespan.

Shangri-La Incense

According to the legend of Shangri-La, there are hidden valleys in the Himalaya where life and youth are magically extended to the point of immortality—provided you never

eave Shangri-La. *The following
ncense blend magically transports
ou there and magically offers simi-
ar effects, at least temporarily.
3lend spikenard, rhododendron, and
alangal root and burn, wafting the
ragrance as desired.*

☀ Tansy Longevity Spell

*Tansy allegedly increases the lifespan
when used magically. (It is a powerful
erb and is not safe for pregnant
women or many others to consume.)
Vear or carry tansy in an amulet bag.*

☀ Vervain

*Vervain allegedly confers immortal-
ty. Make strong infusions by pour-
ng boiling water over the herb and
adding it to the bath.*

Spells for Youth
☀ Angel's Water Youth Spell

*Not all versions of **Angel's Water**
are suitable for consumption. Create
your own or check ingredients very
carefully for safety's sake. Drink a
glass of **Angel's Water** every three
days to remain eternally youthful.*

☀ Rosemary Youth Spells

*According to European tradition, old
age may be kept at bay by frequently
inhaling the scent of rosemary.*

☀ Youth Dew May Day Spell

*For eternal youth and beauty, rise at
dawn on May Day and roll naked in
the dew.*

✪ Formulary

Charged Waters

Charged waters are charged with magical power and intentions.

Not all charged waters are really *waters*. Some are actually alcohol-based formulas, recalling that the roots of perfumery and liqueurs lie entangled in magic potions, brews, and philters. (Philters are drinks; although some potions are consumed, many formulas are for external use only.) *"Water"* must be understood in the context of perfume designations, such as *eau de Cologne* ("water of Cologne") or of alcoholic beverages like aquavit or whiskey (whose name derives from the Gaelic for *"water of life"*).

The alcohol typically recommended as a base is vodka, no because it may be consumed bu because of its minimal scent Avoid what is commonly callec *"rubbing alcohol;"* the typically strong, unpleasant aroma wil interfere with that of the formula

Angel's Water or Angel Water

The term "Angel Water" may refe either to Jordan River Water, o to an eighteenth-century love potion. This, the most popula version of Angel Water and the one indicated in this book, begar as a sixteenth-century complexior remedy before evolving into a love potion and a popular aphrodisiac

200 years later. Its name may derive from those angels who seduced the *"daughters of man"* with magic lessons in the Book of Genesis.

The crucial ingredient, the one that cannot be replaced if this is to be considered true Angel Water, is myrtle, a small tree native to North Africa and the Mediterranean coast, considered sacred to Aphrodite, whose name inspired the term *"aphrodisiac."*

In legend, when Aphrodite first emerges naked from the sea, she is clothed in myrtle leaves.

The basic formula consists of:

Myrtle
Orange blossoms (Neroli)
Rose

Myrtle is the predominant material. It is substantially less expensive than the other ingredients. Many versions of Angel's Water contain only myrtle. The terms "Myrtle Water" or "Water of Venus" is sometimes used synonymously for Angel's Water.

The simplest method of creation is via hydrosols. This may be best if Angel's Water is to serve as a philter. Homemade floral waters may also be used, as well as infusions of fresh and dried leaves and flowers. Home-grown roses may be preferable to those of florists because of the massive amounts of pesticides used on commercially grown roses. All the basic ingredients are available in the form of essential oils

Angel's Water is typically used externally:

★ *Add to a bath: allegedly the greater the quantities of Angel's Water, the greater the erotic impact*
★ *Blend with alcohol to create a liniment for purposes of massage: administered this way, (and presumably if it's a good massage) Angel's Water reputedly inspires erotic thoughts in even the coldest woman*
★ *Angel's Water may also be used as a love potion, in which case make sure that all materials are safe for consumption*

Myrtle-based Angel's Water was used throughout Europe and the British Isles. There is also a Spanish formula, used for romantic and cleansing spells. This version's basic formula consists of angelica, lavender, rose, and trefoil.

Bay Rum

Technically the "bay" in bay rum does not refer to familiar bay laurel leaves, a staple of so many magic spells, but to the berries of the Caribbean tree, Jamaica bayberry, also known as black or wild cinnamon.

If you purchase bay rum manufactured in Bermuda or the Caribbean, you may receive the original formula. If manufactured elsewhere, you will most likely be purchasing a formula based on bay laurel. Jamaica bayberry does not grow outside the Caribbean and Bermuda; people outside the region are not familiar with the botanical and so assume that any reference to bay must indicate bay laurel. Bay laurel is a plant with profound magic powers and the formula based upon it is potent, although not necessarily for the same purposes:

★ *The original bay rum formula (bayberry) is used for luck, gambling, healing, and cleansing spells*

★ *The bay laurel–derived formula may be used for healing and cleansing, and to enhance divination*

The true substitute for Jamaica bayberry is not bay laurel leaves but allspice berries, a close relative with similar magic properties. However, Jamaica bayberry is available as an essential oil, and a true bay rum is easily created from essential oils.

True Bay Rum

Essential oil of Jamaica bayberry
Essential oil of petitgrain
Essential oil of allspice
Essential oil of cardamom
Essential oil of cloves

1. Dilute the essential oils in fine dark rum and distilled water.
2. Although scent-free alcohol is usually recommended, bay rum is the exception to the rule. Rum, a liquor used in many spells, enhances bay rum's magical properties. Its scent is considered integral to the formula: select the most fragrant rum possible.
3. Jamaica bayberry is the predominant ingredient. Its presence and fragrance should dominate the blend.
4. If you have access to Jamaica bayberries, dried botanicals may be substituted for essential oils. Substitute orange zest for petitgrain.

Bay Leaf-Based Bay Rum

Crushed bay laurel leaves
Ground allspice berries
Ground cardamom
Ground cinnamon
Ground cloves

1. Add the dry ingredients to one pint (half a liter) of fine dark Caribbean rum.
2. Shake it and let it sit for a week.
3. Strain out the solid ingredients.
4. Place some new allspice berries or a whole bay leaf in the bottle.

Carmelite Water

This formula was first created for King Charles V of France in 1379 by the Carmelite Sisters. Its key ingredient, the herb melissa, also known as lemon balm, is another plant closely identified with Aphrodite. Melissa means *"bee."* Aphrodite's priestesses of love were known as bees and according to legend, living honeybees, female worker bees supremely devoted to their queen, are the returning souls of Aphrodite's no less devoted servants. Melissa is a common garden plant; if you grow it, the connection to bees becomes very clear: bees love it and flock to its blossoms.

Melissa is the crucial ingredient in Carmelite Water; its presence, fragrance, and lemony flavor should predominate. Historically, Carmelite Water was a distilled liquor and should you have access to distilling equipment, it may be reproduced as such.

Basic Carmelite Water

Three tablespoons of chopped melissa (lemon balm)
Three tablespoons of chopped angelica root
One tablespoon of cloves
One half teaspoon of coriander seeds
One whole nutmeg
One stick of cinnamon

1. Add the above to four ounces (125 ml) of vodka, along with the juice from one lemon.
2. Allow it to steep for at least seven days, shaking the bottle once daily.
3. Strain and enjoy.

Simpler, quicker, albeit even less authentic versions exist:

★ *Add tincture of melissa to a glass of vodka*
★ *Blend melissa hydrosol with white wine*

Carmelite Tea

For those who eschew alcohol:

1. Roughly chop fresh melissa/lemon balm.
2. Place a small handful into a mug and add a cinnamon stick, five cloves, and one quarter teaspoon of coriander seeds.
3. Make a strong infusion by pouring boiling water over the botanicals.
4. Let it steep for at least five minutes, strain and drink.

Carmelite water was originally intended for healing purposes and may be taken internally. Make sure all ingredients are safe for consumption. A typical dose is the size of a wine glass, consumed with or after dinner. The pioneering physician Paracelsus vouched for its beneficial cardiac claims.

Bathe in Carmelite Water to facilitate the dream process. It allegedly stimulates fun, happy dreams. Carmelite Water is a favorite Pow-Wow potion to cure headaches, protect against poison, break hexes, and as an elixir of longevity.

Damnation Water

The antithesis of Holy Water, Damnation Water is frequently used for malevolent purposes, but sometimes also for protective spells.

Grind asafetida, sulfur, and the ashes of palm leaves blessed on Palm Sunday into a powder. Add this to a base of whichever Holy Water formula you prefer.

Elijah the Prophet Water

Although this is known as Elijah the Prophet Water, it has little to do with the biblical prophet. In Russian tradition, Elijah is syncretized to the thunder spirit, Perun. His feast days are July 20th and July 30th, known as *"thunder days."* Rain falling on these days is believed to have tremendous therapeutic and magical value. Bottle it, refrigerate it, and reserve for magical emergency. Elijah the Prophet Water protects against the Evil Eye, general serious illness, and malevolent magic.

Florida Water

Florida Water was originally marketed as the American version of the original eau de Cologne and should have an attractive, refreshing, light, citrus-rosemary fragrance. Florida Water, however, has also developed into something of a metaphysical staple among the Vodou/Santeria communities, as well as the many influenced by them. It is an intensely powerful spiritual cleanser and protective agent.

Florida Water may be the only charged water whose name is copyrighted. It is officially manufactured and sold by the Murray and Lanman Company, and theirs is an excellent, inexpensive product, easily available in markets that cater to a Caribbean clientele. However, there are *thousands* of versions of homemade Florida Water, and many practitioners pride themselves on their home recipes. Here are two slightly different versions.

Florida Water (1)

Two cups of vodka or other alcohol
Two tablespoons rose hydrosol
Sixteen drops essential oil of bergamot
Twelve drops essential oil of lavender
Six drops essential oil of may chang

Three drops essential oil of rosemary
Two drops essential oil of jasmine
Two drops rose attar

Florida Water (2)

Two cups vodka or other alcohol
Two tablespoons orange flower water or hydrosol
One tablespoon turmeric powder
One quarter teaspoon finely ground orrisroot
Twelve drops essential oil of bergamot
Twelve drops essential oil of lavender
Six drops essential oil of may chang
Three drops essential oil of rosemary
Two drops rose attar
Two drops neroli

Shake this second formula vigorously to distribute the powder.

Florida Water may be added to virtually any cleansing bath or floorwash formula as an added enhancement. It is for external use only.

Flower Waters

Various flower waters are used in a variety of spells, most especially rose water. Although certain spells specifically demand flower water, these waters may also be substituted for regular water in many other spells and formulas, particularly those for romantic or healing purposes, and in magical ink or incense formulas, or for spells that involve dissolving gum resins such as gum acacia.

Rose water and orange blossom water are frequent additions to Indian, North African, and Middle Eastern cuisine and are very easily, and often inexpensively, purchased from specialist vendors. The quality of pre-packaged flower waters is erratic, however; some are excellent, others bear little if any trace of the flower. Fine hydrosols, once rare but becoming more popular by the day, may be the finest source of true flower waters. They may easily be made for oneself, providing one has fresh flowers. In general, depending upon what one wishes to do with the flower water, it's wise to avoid florists' flowers because they tend to be heavily laden with pesticides, which may then be concentrated in the flower water.

Rose/Flower Water: Method 1

1. Remove the petals from a few fresh roses, place them in a small pot, and cover with approximately a quarter of an inch of spring water.
2. Simmer gently until a visual change is observed: the petals will become limp and pallid. (If in doubt, a minute longer may be preferable to a minute less.)
3. Strain and allow the liquid to cool. If not used immediately, refrigerate any left over.

This formula may also be used to create any type of fresh flower water—orange blossom or jasmine, for instance—providing the flowers are not poisonous or toxic.

Flower Water: Method 2

This method is substantially longer, although it is also easier than the method suggested above. No vigilant observation is required. It is suitable for creating lavender water as well as any other flower water.

1. Place petals or blossoms within a mason jar.
2. Cover with boiling water and allow to sit overnight.

3. Strain out the botanical material; if not used immediately, the remainder should be refrigerated.

Lavender Water

The term "lavender water" frequently indicates not a fresh flower water but, rather, steam-distilled lavender blossoms, as first created by Hildegard of Bingen in the twelfth century, hence hydrosols, themselves the product of distillation, are truly the appropriate choice. However a semblance of a distilled water may also be created easily in one's kitchen.

Despite lavender water's associations with the saintly Hildegard, it earned its magical reputation as a potion favored by prostitutes. Lavender water, worn on the body, allegedly attracts sexual interest from either gender while simultaneously sharpening the wits of the wearer.

Two cups of distilled water
Two ounces (100 ml) of vodka or other minimally scented alcohol
Approximately 12–20 drops of essential oil of lavender

For external use only.

Four Thieves Vinegar

The origins of this legendary formula lie in plague-ridden Europe. Many variations on the legend exist: the scene of the crime variously takes place in London, Marseilles, or somewhere in Italy. The situation may have taken place as far back as the time of the Crusades or as recently as the eighteenth century. The basic tale, however, remains the same. Infectious epidemic wracked the land. People were dying, horribly, in great numbers. Quarantine was brutally enforced. In the face of this hardship and tragedy, a gang of four thieves ran rampant, breaking into quarantined houses, even robbing the dead. People were outraged but also intrigued: how did these thieves survive exposure to infection to steal and steal again?

A price was placed on the thieves' heads and eventually they were caught and sentenced to death. They negotiated a trade: their secret formula for a reprieve and one-way ticket out of town. Ever since, Four Thieves Vinegar has been touted for its ability to drive away danger and rescue its user from sure disaster.

Four Thieves Vinegar arrived in New Orleans, transported by either French or Italian immigrants, or perhaps by the wandering thieves themselves. In New Orleans, it was adopted by the Voodoo and Hoodoo communities, who put Four Thieves' illness-banishing powers to other use: it is a crucial component of many banishing and commanding spells.

Four Thieves Vinegar

1. Obtain the best possible red wine or apple cider vinegar.
2. Peel and crush garlic cloves and add them to the vinegar. You cannot have too much garlic, especially if you plan to use Four Thieves for its healing and immunity-boosting properties.
3. Traditionally, each thief contributed one ingredient. Choose one of the following to represent each thief, for a total of four additional ingredients: black pepper, whole cayenne or other chili pepper, coriander, lavender, mint, rosemary, rue, sage, thyme, or wormwood.
4. Allow this to sit for four days, shaking once daily, before using.

If you are using fresh herbs, there is a tendency for the garlic to take on their green color. This isn't harmful but many consider it "unsightly." To prevent this, boil the garlic in the vinegar and allow it to cool before adding the other ingredients.

Glory Water

Glory Water is intended to provide you with glory. It's used in spells cast for success and good fortune. Its key ingredient, the one without which it is no longer Glory Water, is orange blossom water.

> Orange blossom water or neroli hydrosol
> Frankincense resin or essential oil of frankincense
> Essential oil of bergamot

Holy Water

Although many assume that the term "Holy Water" indicates church-blessed water only, this is an oversimplification of a complex concept. The Roman Catholic Church did not invent the concept of Holy Water but adopted it from earlier Pagan use. Various Pagan shrines possessed virtually identical Holy Water fonts. Holy Water is a crucial component of many magical, religious, and spiritual traditions, although what constitutes Holy Water and how it's made varies greatly.

Holy Water may refer to any one of a variety of products:

★ *Jordan River Water*

★ *Church-blessed water*

★ *According to British folk tradition, rain falling on Holy Thursday—Ascension Day—may be gathered and used as Holy Water. Any other day held sacred to the spell-caster may be substituted: Summer Solstice, May Eve, New Year's Day, Samhain, your birthday, a saint's day*

★ *Holy Water may also be made via astrological correspondence. Some believe that waters synchronized with a lunar eclipse or a Full Moon are holy and charged with extra magic power*

★ *Balinese tradition uses a variety of Holy Waters. These may include the water found within unripe coconuts or young bamboo. Ocean water is sometimes used as well*

★ *Modern Wicca has evolved the notion of Holy Water. Various formulas exist: at its simplest, Witch's Holy Water is spring water with salt added. Other covens have personal recipes, including infused herbs (rosemary, thyme, and vervain are particularly popular) or crystals. Designate your own*

★ *Pow-Wow also features various recipes but the mainstay is water with salt and vervain added. Christian Pow-Wows may choose church-blessed waters instead*

As used in this book, "Holy Water" indicates any water that is held sacred or has special significance for the spell-caster. This may be water from a shrine dedicated to a deity or water from a sacred spring. It may be water from the tap of your favorite restaurant. If this concept holds no meaning for you, if all water is the same, then simply substitute pure spring water wherever a spell indicates Holy Water.

Holy Water is used for:

★ *Cleansing and purification, both for individual bathing and for space-cleansing (sprinkle in corners)*
★ *Altar cleansing and blessing*
★ *Healing spells. Holy Water is also believed capable of magically transmitting physical relief, especially for headaches and tension. Use in compresses and massage*
★ *Cleansing and empowering materials and tools: anoint roots and crystals or let roots and minerals soak in Holy Water*
★ *Exorcism and banishing spells*

Balinese Holy Water, church-blessed Holy Water and Wiccan Holy Water (among others) are consecrated via sacred ritual: the ritual activates the water. Other magical traditions consider that the sacred, magical power of Holy Water is such that no further ritual or consecration is needed and may in fact be interference. Obtaining Holy Water may thus be as simple as gathering rainwater or adding sea salt to spring water. Complex rituals may also be designed; choose from among the following ritual elements or adapt and embellish as desired:

Charging Holy Water

1. Collect rainwater, ideally within a stone vessel.
2. Prepare yourself prior to preparing the water: bathe in Fiery Wall of Protection, Dragon's Blood, or at least with lots of salt, while reciting psalms and/or sacred verses.
3. Prepare the water sky-clad (nude) or in clean ritual clothing. Where ritual clothing is not used, fresh, clean clothing, preferably white and made from natural fabrics is favored.
4. Ladle water into a glass or crystal bowl.
5. Place it between two white candles.
6. Light incense first (frankincense, copal, benzoin, and/or white sage) and then the candles.
7. Pass the bowl of water through the incense smoke.
8. Visualize why you're preparing this water. Visualize the results this water will bring.
9. Return the bowl to its place between the candles and leave everything in place until the candles burn out.
10. Bottle the water.

Indigo Water

Until the advent of synthetic dyes in the nineteenth century, indigo was a precious commodity, the botanical source of a beautiful, vivid blue dye. Blue is the color that repels the Evil Eye and confers spiritual protection. With the possible exception of the color red, no color is more strongly identified with protective magic than blue. Hence indigo had powerful magical as well as aesthetic value.

Originally native to India, indigo migrated to ancient Egypt, Greece, and the Yoruba kingdoms of what is now modern Nigeria, where it was strongly identified with the powerful female orishas Yemaya and, especially, Oshun.

In modern Africa, indigo is especially identified with the Tuareg, the traditionally nomadic people of the Sahara Desert. The Tuareg are known as the "*blue people*" because the indigo used to dye their robes its characteristic shade bleeds onto their skin, dying it. This is not perceived as merely an accidental hazard but as a welcome effect, because the protective qualities of the indigo are now transferred to the skin.

Brought to American and West Indian plantations in the seventeenth century, the dye was produced for export. Extracted via a lengthy, complicated, tedious, and malodorous process, indigo was only made profitable by the existence of slave labor. The slaves, many of whom came from Yorubaland and its vicinity, also introduced indigo's magical uses. Indigo Water is used:

★ *To empower charms, tools, and talismans*
★ *To enhance and empower the aura, through bathing*
★ *For spiritual protection, to ward off evil*
★ *For cleansing spells*

The end of slavery in the nineteenth century, coinciding with the development of synthetic dyes, made true indigo rare. Although there are substitutes, none of them possess the magic power of true indigo.

True indigo water is merely a blend of indigo and water. The most accessible source may be *anil*, a West Indian and South American variation. Mexican anil is sometimes marketed in the form of small, vivid blue balls. Dissolve in water to create Indigo

Water or keep the ball whole for use as a protective amulet. Used this way, anil balls are a popular ingredient in Mexican Santeria mojo bags.

Laundry bluing or blue food coloring may substitute in any spell that calls for Indigo Water, with the understanding that the power is much reduced. However, *do not substitute* bluestone, also known as blue vitriol or Roman vitriol. Bluestone is copper sulfate, a naturally occurring substance which is truly a lovely shade of blue but, like those colorful Amazonian tree-frogs, is also very toxic. It has been used as a pesticide, now banned in many places, but was once easily obtainable, especially for rural, agricultural people. Because it is blue and was available, it's frequently cited in folk magic spells but is dangerous and should not be used.

Marie Laveau Water

This formula is attributed to Marie Laveau, the renowned Queen of New Orleans Voodoo. Born in 1792, Marie Laveau transformed Voodoo from a surreptitious and persecuted cult into an organized, respected (or feared), established tradition. Following her death, she has achieved unofficial saint status and continues to perform miracles from her grave at New Orleans's St. Louis Cemetery Number One.

This formula is sometimes marketed as Holy Water or as Blessing Water. It may substitute in any spell that calls for either one:

One cup rain water
One cup spring water
One cup rose water or hydrosol
One cup Holy Water
One cup lavender water, lavender hydrosol or twenty drops of essential oil of lavender

Marie Laveau Water is used for:

★ *Psychic enhancement*
★ *Protection*
★ *Aura cleansing*
★ *Cleansing spells*

Notre Dame Water

Although this is the name of a specific formula, blessed water from the Cathedral of Notre Dame may be substituted. The predominant ingredient in Notre Dame Water, without which it cannot be considered true Notre Dame formula water, is white roses.

The basic formula is:

Holy Water
White rose hydrosol
Orange hydrosol
Violet hydrosol

It may be necessary to substitute violet absolute for violet hydrosol, or to obtain your own violet fragrance via the infusion or enfleurage process. Violet is a notoriously difficult and expensive scent to extract. Most of what is available commercially is synthetic.

A simpler version of Notre Dame Water may be made by adding essential oil of white roses or white rose hydrosol to spring water.

Notre Dame Water is used for:

★ *Happy home spells, to promote peace, calm, and serenity*
★ *Cleansing spells*
★ *Spells to summon spirits*
★ *Uncrossing baths and spells*

Peace Water

This formula is designed to bring serenity to a troubled household. As peace is so elusive, it should come as no surprise that Peace Water is much more difficult to create than, say, War Water. It takes a skilled blender to concoct true Peace Water and it may be the one formula you are better off purchasing than making by hand. However, you need to understand the product in order to obtain or create the real thing.

True Peace Water is visibly identifiable. There should be three distinct layers: two light blue liquids with a clear layer in between. (Some versions only use two layers: one blue, one clear.)

The theory behind Peace Water stems from the biblical phrase regarding spreading oil over troubled waters. The natural propensity for oil and water to separate creates the layers. At its best, Peace Water is aesthetically a very beautiful product, with the light blue color evoking a sense of serenity. The mere visual presence of fine Peace Water is believed magically able to maintain a peaceful, tranquil atmosphere.

★ *Blue layers may be made with Indigo Water or with any of the blue components used to create Indigo Water*
★ *The clear layer may be made with Holy Water, Rose of Jericho Water, or Notre Dame Water*

★ *The tricky part is layering the oil and water so that the three layers remain distinct*

Peace Water is used in a variety of house blessing, cleansing, and healing spells. To use it, shake the bottle, so that the layers disperse. They should return to their positions once the bottle is at rest.

Rose of Jericho Water

Rose of Jericho is not a rose at all, but a Mexican desert plant with unusual properties. When its environment becomes too parched to support its existence, the plant hits the road to find a better home: it retracts its roots and allows the wind to carry it until it reaches a place where it may continue to grow. It is a choosy plant; it may not take root in the first place it alights.

The plant itself has evolved into a popular lucky charm, shared by many traditions from Mexican Santeria to Southern Conjure to mainstream Wicca. Its miraculous re-hydrating powers have made it a prized component of expensive anti-aging skin creams.

Water used to re-hydrate the plant simultaneously captures the essence of the plant. Water that has successfully resurrected a Rose of Jericho is magically transformed into Rose of Jericho Water. Use pure spring water if possible.

1. Place the rose in a saucer or dish with enough water to cover the bottom of the plant.
2. Wait for it to unfold. Don't be impatient; although some sources promise you that the transformation will occur overnight, realistically it may take three days or longer.
3. Change the water weekly, reserving the old water for magical use.

Rose of Jericho Water is used for:

★ *Cleansing spells*
★ *House blessing spells*
★ *Spell reversals and to repel malevolent magic*

Rose of Jericho Water may substitute in any spell that calls for Holy Water.

Tar Water

This might be the messiest of the formulas. Wear old clothes while concocting it, not your finest robe. Some old formulas suggest using creosote, however this has since been implicated as a possible carcinogen and cannot be recommended. Wood tar is required; you cannot substitute roofing or coal tar, which are petroleum products.

Basic formula:

1. Approximately one quart (1 liter) of wood tar is required, the sticky stuff scraped from a wood-burning fireplace chimney.
2. Put the tar in a bucket. (The bucket will be ruined; you will never be able to use it for any other purpose.)
3. Add about a gallon (4.5 liters) of water.
4. Stir the tar and water with a stick for about fifteen minutes. The stick will be ruined; use something disposable, literally a "stick" rather than your good wand.
5. Let the tar sit and settle for several hours.
6. Strain the water into a clean container.
7. Let the water settle again.
8. Strain it through cheesecloth or similar into a bottle.
9. Shake before using.

Tar Water is used for:

★ *Space and personal cleansings*
★ *Removal of negative thought-forms and psychic manifestations*

War Water, Iron Water or the Water of Mars

Once upon a time, this formula was a mainstay of folk healers, who used it to treat anemia. Although its medical uses are no longer popular, this remains a very important magical formula.

War Water is used:

★ *To gain protection. This is an extremely aggressive, forceful spiritual cleanser*
★ *To reverse a curse and send it back where it came from*
★ *To place a curse. War Water is a traditional and allegedly potent weapon during psychic warfare and witch wars*

Standard Protective War Water

1. Place iron nails in a mason jar. Cut iron nails are recommended because they rust very easily, but any iron nails may be used.

2. Add enough water to cover the nails. Leave this undisturbed until rust begins to form, typically within seven to ten days. Although the jar is usually kept shut, it should be opened periodically to encourage oxidation.
3. Once the rusting process begins, more water may be added. Keep the jar in a refrigerator or other cool area.
4. Strain the water and use as needed.

You may continue adding water to the original nails virtually indefinitely. Some people have a War Water starter lasting years, akin to a sour dough starter. However, should mold or bacteria ever form, discard *everything*, including the jar and start again from the beginning.

Standard Malevolent War Water

1. Collect water from a fierce thunderstorm in a jar.
2. Add rusty nails, sulfur, and some of your own urine.
3. Store this in a cold, dry place until you need it.

This version is used to either place or reverse a hex. The rusted nails from the Protective Formula may be used to create the Malevolent version.

Condition Oils, Formula Oils

Magical oils are among the oldest forms of enchantment, dating back to ancient Egypt, Mesopotamia, and Greece. However, their magical renaissance occurred among the New Orleans Voodoo, Hoodoo, and Conjure traditions of the late nineteenth and early twentieth centuries. Most of the standard formulas derive from that time, although many are based on much older roots. This period coincided with the development of the mail-order book trade; occultists are always voracious readers and the Hoodoo doctors were no exception. Many were exceptionally well versed in magical traditions from all over Earth. Hoodoo delights in word play: the genre of magic spell oils became known as *"condition oils"* as they will magically cure your *condition*.

Catchy, dramatic, evocative names became standardized as well. Although there are basic guidelines for making these oils, consider the formulas to be similar to recipes. *"Chicken soup"* or *"lasagna"* raise certain expectations; however every chef may prepare them slightly differently.

The standardization of these oils coincided with the mass marketing of occult products. Mass manufacture of condition oils meant that the people making and selling the product, some inspired by the realization that there might actually be some low-risk money to be made, might not have understood the product or in fact had contempt for the product and its users, their customers. Unscrupulous vendors began to market little more than colored water in bottles labeled with the names of famous condition oil formulas. This frequently remains the case. If your spell depends upon a condition formula, it is crucial for its success that you either purchase materials only from reputable manufacturers or that you mix the formula yourself.

Perfume formulas are marketed as perfume, cologne, dusting powder, soap, and other forms as well.

Likewise condition formulas may be available as oil, powder, incense, soap, floorwash, or other forms. The botanical formula remains constant; hence Commanding Oil is merely Commanding Powder added to oil. Any of the formulas may be converted to other forms as you please.

Although condition oils derive from New Orleans Voodoo and Hoodoo, they have become a mainstay of many other traditions including Palo, Santeria, and Wicca. New formulas consistently evolve to serve the needs of different practitioners and magical traditions.

All Saints Oil

This oil requires seven ingredients, similar to Seven African Powers Oil. The "saints" in this oil may be understood as the Seven African Powers, or as generic benevolent spirit powers, or however else you understand them. This oil evokes blessings of success.

Grind and powder cinnamon, tonka beans, patchouli, vetiver, lavender, gardenia, and mugwort. Cover with sweet almond and jojoba oils.

Attraction Oil

Grated lemon zest
Lovage
Vervain
Essential oil of lemon petitgrain,
melissa, may chang, or lemon
verbena
Rose attar

1. Grind the first three ingredients
together in a mortar and pestle.
2. Place them in a bottle together
with a lodestone chip.
3. Cover with sweet almond oil.
4. Add the essential oils, drop by
drop, until you achieve a scent
that pleases you.

Black Cat Oil

Essential oil of clary sage or dried
crumbled sage or clary sage
leaves
Essential oil of bay laurel or dried
crushed bay leaves
Essential oil of myrrh or solid
myrrh resin
A bit of steel wool
Fine iron shot

1. If you have a black cat, pick a hair
off the sofa and add it to the mix.
2. Blend with sweet almond oil, unless
using for hexes, in which case
blend with castor or mineral oil.

Black Cat Oil is used to break bad spells and hexes, but also to attract positive attention from the opposite sex. If protection is your major desire, blend the ingredients into castor oil and jojoba oil. If romance is your motivating factor, substitute sweet almond oil for the castor oil.

Cleopatra Oil

Essential oil of cypress
Essential oil of frankincense
Essential oil of myrrh
Essential oil of petitgrain or neroli
Apricot kernel oil, to blend into

Come to Me Lover Oil

Jasmine absolute
Rose attar
Neroli or essential oil of petitgrain
Gardenia absolute (or fragrance
oil)
Tuberose absolute

Blend the above into apricot kernel or sweet almond oil.

This is the most deluxe love-drawing oil. The ingredients are extremely expensive. It is not required that all of them be used, although the first three are fairly standard. The substitution of petitgrain for neroli will keep costs down.

Command and Compel Oil

Depending upon the manufacturer, this classic oil may be marketed as Commanding Oil, Compelling Oil, Commanding and Compelling Oil, Controlling Oil, or Conquering Oil.

It is not analogous with High John the Conqueror Oil, which is a completely different condition formula used for completely different purposes. What is marketed as All High Conquering Oil may be either High John the Conqueror or Command and Compel, providing there are any real ingredients in it at all.

The basic commanding formula consists of a blend of sweet flag (calamus) and licorice. They have been used together as such since the days of ancient Egypt. These two plants, blended together and reduced to a powder, may be added to oil to create a potent Commanding Oil.

Other plants also have commanding properties and may be added. Vetiver is a typical addition, as is essential oil of bergamot, which is a strong component of financial commanding spells. Before you add bergamot, however, decide how you wish to use this formula. Essential oil of bergamot is highly photosensitizing. It was once the primary ingredient in European fast-tanning products. If applied to the skin, you must avoid exposure to the sun as odd and long-lasting pigmentation may occur. Bergamot provides the distinctive fragrance of Earl Grey tea. It's very beautiful and tempting to apply to the body. Essential oils of bergamot are marketed with the photosensitizing component removed; these are known as bergaptene-free oils and are worth the trouble of finding.

Add commanding oils to a blend of castor oil and jojoba oil. Malevolent-intent spells would substitute a base of baby oil or mineral oil.

Crown of Success Oil

Essential oil of bay laurel or dried crushed bay leaves

Essential oil of frankincense or the powdered resin

Essential oil of sandalwood or the powder

Essential oil of vetiver or dried, powdered vetiver roots

Add the above to a blend of sunflower, olive, and/or jojoba oil

Essence of Bend Over or Bend Over Oil

This formula compels others to bend over and do your bidding. Create an extremely concentrated version of Command and Compel Oil.

Because there may be a sexual component to Essence of Bend Over, consider adding aphrodisiac botanicals to the basic blend, such as damiana, cubebs, or Grains of Paradise.

Eve Oil

1. Place dried apple blossoms and pomegranate seeds in a bottle and cover with blended sweet almond and jojoba oils.
2. Add one of the snake roots.

Fiery Wall of Protection

1. Blend powdered dragon's blood and sea salt together with a mortar and pestle.
2. Frankincense and myrrh are required. If you are using solid resins, grind them together with

the ingredients in Step 1. If you prefer to use essential oils, then add them last, following Step 3.
3. Add these to castor oil, which has protective capacities of its own but is a very thick oil. You may wish to add jojoba oil, as a preservative, but also so that the oil will flow nicely.

Some variations suggest adding ground ginger and/or cinnamon, too. Just be aware that these are skin irritants and may limit the uses of the oil. Without these ingredients, Fiery Wall can be added to the bath or worn as a protective perfume.

Flying Devil Oil

For the basic formula:

1. Blend red pepper flakes and/or cayenne pepper into an olive oil base.
2. When you shake the oil, you should see the red pepper fly around.

More complex versions also include some or all of the following: black pepper, dragon's blood powder, ground cinnamon, dried patchouli or the essential oil, and dried vetiver or the essential oil.

Follow Me Boy! Oil

Typically, although not always, marketed with that exclamation mark in its name so as to emphasize that this is a command, not a request. Follow Me Boy! is the most erotic of the commanding oils. It may be used by either men or women but the target of the command is invariably male as exemplified by the legend that this condition oil was once a staple of New Orleans prostitutes of either gender, reputedly guaranteed to generate business.

The basic formula:

Sweet fag/Calamus
Catnip
Damiana
Optional ingredients: Licorice, sweet flag's traditional partner, strengthens the commanding aspect. Other botanicals and fragrances may be added as desired to strengthen erotic impact, particularly vetiver, bergamot, sweet orange, tuberose, or any vividly red flowers.

1. Grind and powder the dried botanicals.
2. Cover with one or a combination of these oils: castor, sweet almond, and apricot kernel.

Castor emphasizes the commanding aspect, sweet almond and apricot kernel increase aphrodisiac appeal.

Has No Hanna Oil

Essential oil of jasmine
Essential oil of tangerine (mandarin orange)
Dried powdered oakmoss or the essential oil
Dried powdered vervain

High John the Conqueror Oil

High John the Conqueror can be a very elusive and mysterious botanical. It has very unique properties. There really is nothing that substitutes for it. If there is one condition oil that you should make for yourself, this is it, if only to be sure you are getting the proper ingredients.

High John the Conqueror provides luck and success in all areas of life. It is particularly beneficial for men in regards to romance, although many women swear by it too. High John is considered a completely benevolent botanical. It is used to achieve the highest success without mal intent toward others. Saint John's Wort and tormentil are frequently substituted for High John. Although they are both plants packed with magic powers and used in many spells, their powers are different and cannot be used to provide High John's unique effect.

High John the Conqueror is the root of a member of the morning glory family. It also goes by the name *jalap* and as such was once an important medical product in the United States, although it has fallen out of favor and perhaps for good reasons. Do not take High John internally: it is an extremely potent purgative and laxative. Reserve it for magical use.

It's the root that's used and it has a very characteristic appearance. Once you are familiar with it, it's difficult to be confused. High John is large, solid, and brown with a vaguely earthy aroma. Its shape ranges from perfectly circular to extremely phallic. This oil calls for High John chips, as do many other spells. Once a root is broken up, it is typically indistinguishable from any other. Grind your own High John so that you are not fooled.

1. Break up a High John root. Use a mortar and pestle if you're strong. This is a hard root; grinding may not be easy. Place it between a sheet of folded wax paper and smash it with a hammer, if necessary. Small chips are sufficient; the root doesn't have to be powdered.
2. Put the pieces in a dish and cover them with peanut, olive, sunflower, and/or jojoba oils.
3. Expose the dish to sunlight for seven days.
4. Strain out the root pieces or leave in the oil, as desired. Bottle the oil and use.

Home Protection Oil

Dried five-finger grass (cinquefoil)
Dried gardenia petals
Dried lavender blossoms or the essential oil
Dried purslane
Sandalwood powder or the essential oil

Blend the above into a jojoba oil base. Add a pinch of salt.

Jezebel Oil

1. Hold a Jezebel root in your left hand and charge it with your desires.

2. Place it in a small jar and cover it with jojoba and sunflower oil. (If you intend to use this oil for stern commanding, add castor oil.)
3. Add essential oils of myrrh, frankincense, bergamot, and amyris.

Love Drawing Oil

Essential oil of lavender or the dried, ground blossoms
Essential oil of jasmine or dried flowers
Rose attar or dried rose petals

1. If using dried botanicals, blend them and grind into a fine powder.
2. Cover them with sweet almond oil.
3. Essential oils should be added drop by drop to the sweet almond oil, until the desired intensity of fragrance is achieved.
4. Add an orrisroot to the bottle.

Lucky Lodestone Oil

Add crushed, powdered lodestone to Van Van Oil.

Maximon Oil

Essential oil of citronella
Essential oil of pink grapefruit
Essential oil of lemongrass
Essential oil of mandarin orange (tangerine)

Blend the essential oils into a base of jojoba oil.

Magnet or Lodestone Oil

Commercial preparations are sold under both of these names, however the term Magnet Oil is used throughout the text of this book to distinguish it from Lucky Lodestone Oil, which is a completely different formulation.

1. Place either seven or nine lodestones in a mason jar.
2. Sprinkle them with magnetic sand.
3. Cover the lodestones with a blend of sweet almond and jojoba oils.
4. Close the jar and let the lodestones rest for seven days, exposed to sunlight and moonbeams.
5. Pick up the jar and swirl the contents around once a day.
6. After seven days, the oil may be strained and used.
7. Transfer the oil to different bottles. Feed the lodestones with magnetic sand and use them to make more oil.

Protection Oil

- Ground cinnamon
- Galangal root
- Dried ground peppermint leaves
- Dried rue
- Dried ground vervain
- Dried ground vetiver or the essential oil

Blend and powder the above ingredients. Add them to a base of sunflower, olive, and/or jojoba oil.

Queen of Sheba Oil

Makeda, Queen of Sheba, visited King Solomon bearing gifts of precious resins and spices. She allegedly introduced the balm of Gilead or balsam tree, a source of fragrant, precious resin (although not the same as the balm of Gilead buds currently so popular in magic). The finest balsam resin in the ancient world was allegedly produced in Judea from trees introduced by the Queen of Sheba. These balsam groves were completely eradicated by the Romans during their conquest of Judea. Essential oil of amyris is the closest modern substitute.

If you'd like to wear this as perfume, keep the quantity of cinnamon oil to a bare minimum

to avoid skin irritation. The oil i made from essential oils o amyris, cinnamon bark, frankin cense, myrrh, rose, and spike nard, added to grapeseed oil.

Saint Martha the Dominator Oil

1. Grind spikenard root shavings, sweet flag, licorice root, and myrrh resin together.
2. Cover with olive oil.

Saint Martha the Dominator Oil i used for happy home spells, domination spells, and protection spells

San Cipriano Oil

There are two Saint Cyprians both former master magi whc converted to Christianity and were martyred. One was a Bishop of Carthage. One or both of them seems to have resumed his former profession after death. San Cipriano is the most influential figure in the magical traditions of the Iberian Peninsula. A prominent grimoire is attributed to him. San Cipriano is a miracle worker; the oil named in his honor allegedly casts miraculous spells.

Cinnamon powder
Low John the Conqueror
Orrisroot
Myrrh resin or the essential oil
Essential oil of cedarwood
Essential oil of cypress

1. Blend and grind all solid materials together to form a powder.
2. Cover them with olive, sunflower, and/or jojoba oils.
3. Add the essential oils as the last step, drop by drop, until you've achieved the desired intensity of fragrance.

Low John the Conqueror, also known as bethroot, was not long ago a very common magical plant and is a traditional component of San Cipriano Oil. It is now highly endangered and it is very likely that you will not be able to obtain it. Even if you can, it should be verified whether it was ethically gathered, for the success of your spells as well as for the sake of the plant. There really is no adequate substitute for it. However, leave it out if necessary and compensate by strengthening other areas of spell work, visualization for instance. Perhaps the best alternative is to attempt to grow your own supply of bethroot.

Seven African Powers Oil

Add the following to palm oil: real coconut extract, black pepper, mugwort, cinnamon, seaweed (dulse, agar-agar or other), real almond extract, and either mimosa or jasmine for a total of seven ingredients.

Uncrossing Oil

Essential oil of hyssop
Essential oil of angelica
Essential oil of frankincense
A pinch of sea salt
A pinch of black pepper
A pinch of cayenne pepper
A sprig of rue
A sliver of fresh garlic
A section of broken chain, e.g., from a key-chain or necklace

Add the ingredients to a bottle filled with blended castor oil and jojoba oil. The crucial ingredients are the hyssop and the chain. Add the other ingredients as desired. Essential oil of angelica has photosensitizing properties: if worn on the body, avoid exposure to the sun.

Van Van Oil

The epitome of condition oils, Van Van may be the single most versatile oil, drawing luck, love, and prosperity and repelling malevolent magic directed toward you. Many confuse the name with "vanilla." It may be added if you like, however true Van Van is a blend of five wild Asian grasses. Similar formulas may also be marketed as Hindu Grass Oil or Henry's Grass Oil.

The five grasses are lemongrass, citronella, palmarosa, gingergrass, and vetiver. All of them are available as essential oils, although gingergrass is rare. Van Van may be made from essential oils, dried botanicals, or a combination of the two. Add them to a base of jojoba, sunflower, and/or safflower oils. Patchouli, another Asian grass, may be added for some extra power.

For optimum power, all five grasses should be used, however any combination is acceptable. Lemongrass is the predominant ingredient, if only because its aroma is so potent. Many versions of Van Van contain only lemongrass.

Wall of Protection Oil

Fiery Wall of Protection Oil minus dragon's blood.

Incense and Powders

Loose incense consists of nothing more than the dried, powdered ingredients. "Powders" may be identical to incense, the words are sometimes used interchangeably, or you may blend them with arrowroot powder, cornstarch, or rice powder, to create a dusting powder.

Amber

Do not burn amber beads! The confusion lies between the solidified resin known as amber and ambergris, the fragrant substance derived from sperm whales, also often called "ambra." This "Amber" formula somewhat replicates the fragrance of ambergris. Blend ground powdered labdanum, benzoin, and vanilla bean.

Black Salt

Although there is an actual black salt used in Indian cuisine, magical black salt is concocted by blending salt with the scrapings from cast iron cookware. Black salt is mainly used in protection spells and to cast hexes.

Cascarilla Powder

This is powdered eggshell: the only ingredient is eggshell. Eggshells once had profound associations with European witches. Witches were believed able to transform an emptied eggshell into a vehicle for travel over water or through the air. To make sure they weren't helping the witches have fun, many insisted on crumbling emptied eggshells before disposing of them. To leave them whole was to invite the witches' use. Ironically, powdered eggshell is a magical ingredient in many spells, both benevolent and otherwise.

Cascarilla Powder can be either white or brown:

White Cascarilla Powder

1. Clean the eggshells and let them dry out.
2. Crumble the pieces and place them in a mortar and pestle.
3. Grind these into a fine powder.

Brown Cascarilla Powder

1. Clean the eggshells.
2. Break up the shells so that the pieces lie flat.
3. Toast these pieces in a low, slow oven until the shells brown.
4. Grind these to a fine powder.

Drawing Powder

This is confectioner's sugar.

Graveyard Dust

Graveyard dust may be self-explanatory: dirt from the graveyard. It may also be various botanicals or a combination of the two.

Valerian, patchouli, and mullein all bear the nickname "*graveyard dust.*" Grind and powder the botanicals and use them where graveyard dust or dirt is indicated. Alternatively, collect dirt from the cemetery.

Goofer Dust

"*Goofer*" derives from the Kikongo word "*kufwa,*" meaning "to die," and 99.5 percent of Goofer Dust's uses are malevolent. It is a usually a blend of graveyard dirt (real dirt, not botanicals) with other substances. Thousands of recipes exist, with practitioners boasting of the potency of their private blends.

Goofer Dust allegedly causes the target of the spell to become weak and confused. Powers of speech, concentration, and thought are allegedly affected; the target acts *"goofy."* Some claim Goofer Dust leaves victims crawling on all fours, barking like a dog. Particularly potent Goofer Dust, real *"killing powder,"* causes the victim to waste away, eventually dying if an antidote is not found.

The most common basic version is a blend of graveyard dust, salt, and sulfur (brimstone.) Other popular ingredients include gunpowder and church bell grease.

Goofer Dust's most famous associations are with New Orleans-styled Voodoo and Hoodoo, from whence it derives its name. Although it may not be called Goofer Dust elsewhere, this is not an isolated formula. In his autobiography, Dr. John, the brilliant New Orleans musician, recalls scraping grease from church bells for the dust. Across the Atlantic Ocean, far from African influence, Slavic witches traditionally climbed into church steeples on Saint George's Day to obtain grease from bell axles for similar purposes.

Henna Powder and Paste

Henna powder derives from the dried ground leaves of the henna plant. Henna paste is created from the powder. Although henna paste may be purchased, choose your vendor carefully: for optimum magic power and aesthetic beauty both powder and paste must be fresh, not aged. There are thousands of methods of preparing henna paste: technique and intuition combine. Here is a suggestion:

1. Henna powder should be green and fragrant.
2. Even though a reputable vendor will sift their henna, further sifting may be required and will certainly be beneficial. Sieves are ancient magical tools: while sifting, concentrate on your desires for the henna design, whether aesthetic or enchanted.
3. Boil approximately one half cup of loose black tea in roughly four cups of water until the

water has been reduced by about one half.

4. Add any additional ingredients: suggestions include rose petals, saffron, fenugreek, or cloves.

5. Simmer this brew for approximately an hour.

6. Strain and discard the solids, reserving only the liquid.

7. Strain a lemon or lime and add only the juice, not pulp or seeds, to the brew.

8. Warm the brew but do not allow it to boil.

9. Begin to add approximately one half cup of henna powder. Add it slowly, spoonful by spoonful, keeping an eye on the texture. The goal is to achieve something that is similar in consistency to cake batter.

10. Once the consistency has been achieved, add approximately one teaspoon of essential oil of eucalyptus.

11. Test the paste by dabbing a little on your skin and leaving it there for fifteen minutes. Although the henna is not yet full strength, a faint orange tinge should still develop.

12. Let the finished paste rest in a warm place, covered, for approximately six hours before using it to paint designs.

Kyphi

Kyphi was an Egyptian temple incense formula so important that its formula was engraved onto temple walls. Various formulas existed. Kyphi is an oil- and fat-free formula, based on wine and raisins with added fragrant botanicals. It was used in sacred ritual but also to relieve insomnia and provide deep sleep. Ingredients might include:

Cardamom pods
Cinnamon
Coriander seeds
Frankincense
Golden raisins
Honey
Juniper berries
Mastic resin
Myrrh
Red wine
Rosebuds
Sweet flag/calamus root

The scent traveled through the ancient world: the Egyptians were scandalized when the Greeks began to use kyphi as an aphrodisiac. The Egyptian method of creating kyphi was complex. An example follows. The name "kyphi" is frequently used by manufacturers of spiritual products to indicate any incense possessing an ancient Egyptian "ambience."

Egyptian Kyphi

1. Begin by blending equal parts dried ground acacia, henna, and juniper.
2. Soak the resulting powder in wine.
3. In a separate container soak golden raisins in wine.
4. Allow this soaking process to continue for seven days.
5. Take equal parts cardamom, sweet flag/calamus, cinnamon, peppermint, bay leaves, galangal, and orrisroot.
6. Grind each one separately then blend and grind again into a fine powder.
7. Add a tablespoon of honey and a tablespoon of myrrh resin to the spice mixture.
8. Drain the herbs and raisins soaking in wine and add them to the honey/myrrh/spice mixture.
9. Add sufficient wine to steep the combined materials, plus terebinth and raisins to form a thick paste.
10. Use this as is (simmer it to release the fragrance) or dry it, cut into squares, and burn as incense.

New Home Incense

Coriander seeds
Frankincense
Mastic pearls
Myrrh

Grind the above ingredients together and burn.

Magic Inks

Many spells involve a written component. Once upon a time, magicians chose their ink carefully depending upon the purpose of the spell, in the manner that someone today might choose a candle or condition oil. Some magicians still do. The most popular magical inks used in Western magic tend to be named after the blood of various creatures. They are marketed commercially and are readily available through occult sources. However, in many cases what is purchased is nothing more than plain ink with a label bearing a catchy title.

A long history exists of using animal names as a code for various plant substances. Among the reasons for this practice was the desire to maintain secret formulas. Unfortunately, when the formulas are obtained without understanding or even knowing of the existence of the code, all sorts of misunderstanding and tragedy may follow. While some complain that modern manufactured *"blood"* inks no longer contain the botanical formulas, others claim that the formulas actually demand blood; the only way to produce "true" dove's blood ink, for instance, being to slit the throat of a dove. This is untrue. Dove's blood ink is frequently used to write love spells. Doves are sacred to Aphrodite, Genius of Love. Do you think that, having done very bad things to her bird, she will look kindly on your petition? The only blood typically called for in magic spells may be your own, and even that requires no more than a few drops from a finger.

Formulas are frequently very similar. The red color typically derives from the resin dragon's blood, a powerful magical agent. Even if a formula doesn't specifically call for it, it is extremely likely that adding gum arabica or gum tragacanth to the mix will be necessary in order to make the ink thick enough to be functional. Typically one quarter to one half teaspoon is needed.

If mixing inks from scratch is forbidding, a simple yet magically charged method of creating the various "blood" inks is to add the appropriate essential oils and resins to plain red ink.

Dove's Blood Ink

Dragon's blood
Alcohol
Gum arabica
Scent with essential oils of bay laurel, cinnamon, and rose

For love spells.

Dragon's Blood Ink

Alcohol
Dragon's blood
Gum arabica
Optional: Essential oil of cinnamon

Tips for Magic Ink and Written Spells

★ *Wormwood allegedly possesses the magic power to provide protection for the written word from all sorts of dangers, spiritual and magical as well as the verminous kind with little teeth. Dioscorides recommended adding wormwood juice to ink, in order to keep mice away from papyrus. Add it to any of the above recipes, or to any other ink*

★ *The grimoire* Grimorium Verum, *allegedly published in Egypt in 1517, recommends that, regardless*

of what's actually in the inkwell, a magician's inkwell should be inscribed with the following, transliterated from the Hebrew:

YOD HE VAV HE
METATRON
YAD
KADOSH
ELOYM
SABAOTH

This serves to infuse divine power into the ink and to ward off evil influences.